Programming Arduino Projects with the PIC Microcontroller

A Line-by-Line Code Analysis and Complete Reference Guide for Embedded Programming in C

Hubert Henry Ward

Apress®

Programming Arduino Projects with the PIC Microcontroller: A Line-by-Line Code Analysis and Complete Reference Guide for Embedded Programming in C

Hubert Henry Ward
Leigh, UK

ISBN-13 (pbk): 978-1-4842-7232-9 ISBN-13 (electronic): 978-1-4842-7230-5
https://doi.org/10.1007/978-1-4842-7230-5

Managing Director, Apress Media LLC: Welmoed Spahr
Acquisitions Editor: Susan McDermott
Development Editor: James Markham
Coordinating Editor: Jessica Vakili

Distributed to the book trade worldwide by Springer Science+Business Media New York, 1 NY Plaza, New York, NY 10004. Phone 1-800-SPRINGER, fax (201) 348-4505, e-mail orders-ny@springer-sbm.com, or visit www.springeronline.com. Apress Media, LLC is a California LLC and the sole member (owner) is Springer Science + Business Media Finance Inc (SSBM Finance Inc). SSBM Finance Inc is a **Delaware** corporation.

For information on translations, please e-mail booktranslations@springernature.com; for reprint, paperback, or audio rights, please email bookpermissions@springernature.com.

Apress titles may be purchased in bulk for academic, corporate, or promotional use. eBook versions and licenses are also available for most titles. For more information, reference our Print and eBook Bulk Sales web page at http://www.apress.com/bulk-sales.

Any source code or other supplementary material referenced by the author in this book is available to readers on GitHub via the book's product page, located at www.apress.com/ 978-1-4842-7232-9. For more detailed information, please visit http://www.apress.com/source-code.

Printed on acid-free paper

Table of Contents

About the Author

Hubert Henry Ward has nearly 25 years of experience as a college lecturer delivering the BTEC, and now Pearson's, Higher National Certificate and Higher Diploma in Electrical & Electronic Engineering. Hubert has a 2.1 Honors Bachelor's Degree in Electrical & Electronic Engineering. Hubert has also worked as a consultant in embedded programming. His work has established his expertise in the assembler and C programming languages, within the MPLABX IDE from Microchip, as well as designing electronic circuits, and PCBs, using ECAD software. Hubert was also the UK technical expert in Mechatronics for three years, training the UK team and taking them to enter in the Skills Olympics in Seoul 2001, resulting in one of the best outcomes to date for the UK in Mechatronics.

About the Technical Reviewer

Massimo Nardone has more than 22 years of experiences in Security, Web/Mobile development, Cloud, and IT Architecture. His true IT passions are Security and Android.

He has been programming and teaching how to program with Android, Perl, PHP, Java, VB, Python, C/C++, and MySQL for more than 20 years.

He holds a Master of Science degree in Computing Science from the University of Salerno, Italy.

He has worked as a Project Manager, Software Engineer, Research Engineer, Chief Security Architect, Information Security Manager, PCI/SCADA Auditor, and Senior Lead IT Security/Cloud/SCADA Architect for many years.

About the Technical Reviewer

Massimo Nardone has more than 25 years of experience in [illegible]

[illegible]

Introduction

This book looks at using some useful aspects of the PIC microcontroller. It explains how to write programs in C so that you can use the PIC micro to control a variety of electronics devices and DC motors. After reading this book, you will be well on your way to becoming an embedded programmer using the C program language.

I have two main aims in writing this book. First and foremost, I have a real passion for writing programs in that I am enthralled by the way we can use simple '1's and '0's, really '5V' and '0V', to make a circuit do almost anything we want it to do. The extent of what we can get these microcontrollers to do is limited only by our imagination and experience. In my youth, we thought the flip phone used by Captain James T. Kirk in *Star Trek* was just a gimmick and we would never get there. Well, our mobile phones do a lot more than just video calls. All of what we do with our phones is done with just '1's and '0's. In writing this book, my primary goal is to hopefully inspire you guys into wanting to understand how we make the '1's and '0's work for us. That is why I will explain how all the instructions in my programs actually work and how they achieve the outcomes we want.

The second aim in writing this book is to transfer all those Arduino Sketches, which use a range of useful peripheral devices, and show you how to get them to work on a PIC microcontroller. In doing so, I hope to show you that the world of PIC controllers is not complicated and really anyone can work with them. It does not matter what experience you have with PICs, as I will assume you know nothing. This book will take the complete novice and not only allow them to run those Arduino Sketches on the PIC, but it will explain in detail every aspect of how the programs work. After reading this book, you will hopefully not only enjoy programming PIC micros in the 'C' programming language, but should be well prepared to take on a new career as an embedded programmer.

In addition to getting to know how to program in 'C', I will show you how to build a range of circuits so that you end up using the peripherals in a practical environment. I will show you how, if you so wish, you can make your own prototype boards to program your PICs and run the programs you write. We will learn about the electronic principles of the components we use to interface the PIC to a wide range of useful peripherals.

Goals of the Book

After reading through this book, you should be able to program the PIC to use all the following peripherals:

- The seven-segment display
- The eight-by-eight matrix display
- The joystick controller
- The HC-04 ultrasonic sensor
- The stepper motor
- THE SERVO MOTOR
- The DS1307 real-time clock module
- The DHT11 humidity and temperature sensor
- The DC motor and fan
- The membrane keypad module

You should also gain a good understanding of some of the basic and advanced programming techniques for PIC micros, such as the following:

- The configuration words
- The TRIS registers and PORTS

- The timer registers
- The ADC (analog-to-digital converter) module
- The CCPM (capture, compare, and pulse width modulation) module.
- The MSSP (master synchronous serial port) module using SPI (serial peripheral interface) and I^2C (inter-integrated circuit) communication protocols.
- The EUSART (enhanced universal synchronous/asynchronous, receive and transmit) module
- Interrupts

You will be able to use an industrial IDE to write your programs in C, compile and download your programs using a variety of tools, and use the simulator in MPLABX, the IDE, to debug your programs.

You should be able to download your programs to your PIC in a practical situation where you have the ability to design and build some useful projects.

You will have learned the basic principles of a range of electronic components such as resistors, capacitors, transistors and the Darlington array, diodes, and light-emitting diodes.

The Prerequisites

There are none really, but if you understand 'C' programming it would be useful. However, I will explain how each of the programs work as we go through them.

Also, if you understand the binary and hexadecimal number systems, it would be an advantage, but there is a section in the appendix that will help you with that and I will explain the important aspects as we need them.

However, to get the full use out of this book, you will need to have installed the following software:

- MPLABX, which is the IDE from Microchip. The version in the book is MPLABX version 5.25. However, any version later than 2.20 will be OK.
- A 'C' compiler for the eight-bit micro. I use XC8 (V2.10), but with some programs I use XC8 (V1.35) compiler software. However, you should be aware that some of the later compilers have some useful libraries missing. That is why I sometimes use version 1.35.

All these programs are freely available from the Microchip website.

Another useful piece of software would be a suitable ECAD (electronic computer-aided design) software that supports eight-bit micros. The ECAD software that I have used in the past is PROTEUS. However, this is not free and so I will show you how to use a suitable prototype board to run the programs in a practical situation.

If you want to go down the practical route, you will need to purchase a programming tool and you may need to buy a prototype board. However, I do have a chapter where I show you how to make your own prototype board using vero board.

The programming tools I use are either the ICD3 can; now Microchip has moved on to the ICD4 can, or the PICkit3 programmer, to download the programs from MPLABX to the PIC.

The off-the-shelf prototype board that I may use is the PICdem2 plus demo board.

This book has been written based around using MPLABX V5.25. However, the principles of how to create projects and write programs are transferable to earlier and later versions of MPLABX. There may be some slight differences in the detail; however, these shouldn't cause you too much of a problem.

I will base the book around the following two PICs:

- The PIC16f88: This is a very versatile eight-bit micro that comes in an 18-pin or 20-pin dual inline package.
- The PIC18F4525: This is a very versatile eight-bit micro that comes in a 40-pin dual inline package.

As long as the PIC you want to use has the same firmware modules, then the programs in the book can easily be used on other PIC micros with some minor modifications. However, you should always refer to the data sheet for the particular PIC you use, as some of the SFRs (special function registers) may differ. For example, the PIC18F4525 uses the ADCON0, ADCON1, and ADCON2 special function registers to control the ADC module, but the 16F88 uses the ANSEL, ADCON0, and ADCON1 registers. I will show you how to use the datasheets, as it is important that an engineer can obtain the relevant information from datasheets.

Throughout the book, I will be including some program listings. I will then go through an analysis of any new instructions that the listings introduce. With respect to the first listing, I will assume all the instructions are new to you the reader.

I hope you will enjoy reading and learning from my book and that it will ignite that spark in you that motivates you to move into a career as an embedded programmer. Good luck and happy reading.

CHAPTER 1

Introducing MPLABX

In this chapter we are going to learn about the MPLABX, an industrial integrated development environment (IDE) from Microchip. We will learn what an IDE is and how to create a project with MPLABX. We will also learn about the configuration bits for programmable interrupt controller (PIC) micros. Finally, we will learn about header files: why we use them and how to create one in MPLABX.

MPLABX: The IDE from Microchip

An IDE is actually a collection of the different programs needed to write program instructions in our chosen language, and then convert them to the actual machine code that the micro understands and also link together any bits of program we may want to use.

The programs we need in the IDE are as follows:

- A text editor to write the instructions for the program. Note that the simple text editor Notepad could be used, but the text editor in MPLABX is by far a more advanced text editor.

- A compiler to change the instructions into a format the micro can understand.

- A linker to combine any files the programmer wants to use.

H. H. Ward, *Programming Arduino Projects with the PIC Microcontroller*,
https://doi.org/10.1007/978-1-4842-7230-5_1

- A driver that will allow the programming tool we use to load the program into the micro.
- A variety of debug tools to allow the programmer to test the program live within the micro.

All these are in, or should be in, the IDE we choose to use. Microsoft has Visual Studio, Microchip has MPLABX, and Freescale uses CodeWarrior. The Arduino has its own IDE. There is also CODEBLOCK, which is an IDE for writing generic 'C' programs that will run on your PC. As this book is based on the PIC micro, we will concentrate on MPLABX. MPLABX has an improved text editor to give the text different color codes when we save the file as an .asm or .c for c program file, such as light blue for keywords, light gray for comments, and so on.

There are some other organization programs within MPLABX, such as those that support the ability to write to the configuration registers for the PIC. There is also the ability to debug your programs within the IDE. All this makes MPLABX a useful tool for programming PICs.

There is also a program called MCC (Microchip Code Configurator). This will actually produce a lot of the code you need to use various aspects of the PIC. However, I firmly believe that you should produce the code you use yourself so that you fully understand it. I will not cover the use of MCC. Also, Microchip has not written the MCC for all its PICs, and the 18F4525 is one it has missed so far. Really, when asked who the programmer is, you should be able to say that you are and not the MCC. When you take the time to study how to write your own code, you will find it is not as hard as you first thought. Also you will get a better self-reward if you write it all yourself.

The only aspect of the programs that I let Microchip do for me is to write the code configuration bits that set up the PIC. This is only because it is so simple to do this and it covers all the #pragma statements that we used to write ourselves.

Creating a Project in MPLABX

Once you have downloaded both the MPLABX software and the XC8 (V2.10) compiler software or XC8 (V1.35), when you open the software the opening screen will be as shown in Figure 1-1.

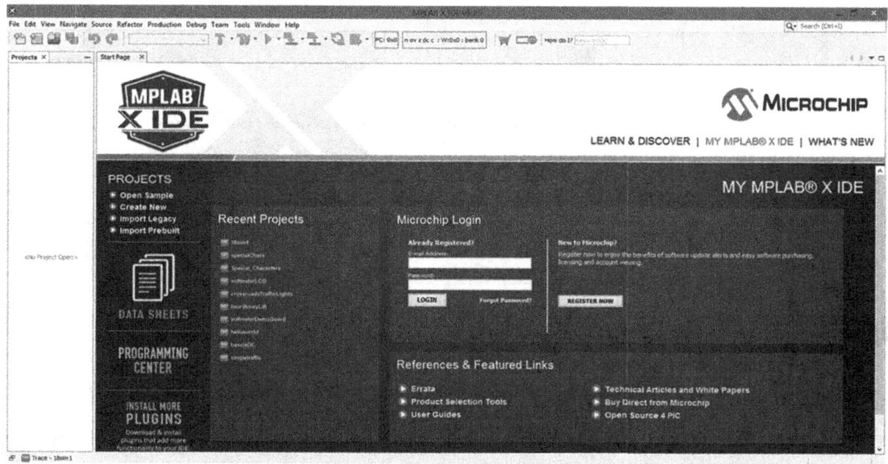

Figure 1-1. *The opening screen in MPLABX*

The project window on the left-hand side may not be shown. If you want it shown, then you should select the word "window" from the top menu bar. You should then click the mouse on the word "projects", with the orange boxes in front of it, and the window should appear. You may have to move the window about to get it in the position shown.

Now, assuming you are ready to create a project, you should either click the mouse on the word "file", in the main menu bar, and select new project, or click the mouse on the orange box, with the small green cross, on the second menu bar. This is the second symbol from the left-hand side of the second menu bar.

When you have selected the create project option, you should now see the window shown in Figure 1-2.

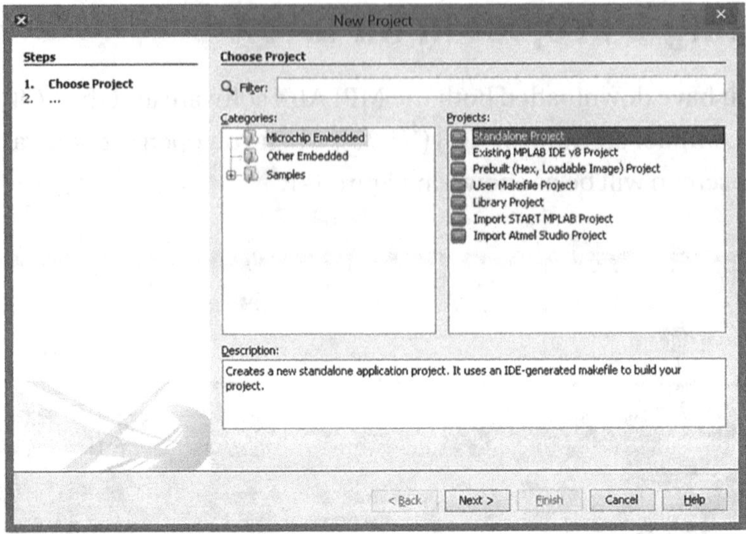

Figure 1-2. The new project window

Most of the projects we will create are Microchip Embedded and Standalone. Therefore, make sure these two options are highlighted and then click "Next". The select device window should now be visible as shown in Figure 1-3.

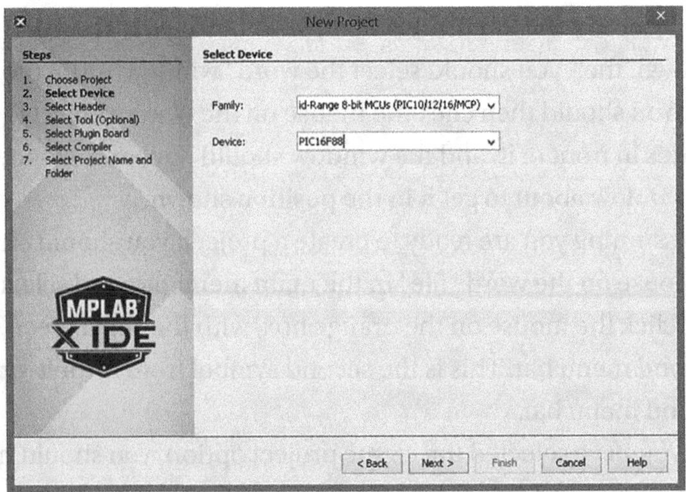

Figure 1-3. The select device window

In this window, we can choose which PIC we want to use. For our first project, we are going to use the PIC16F88 micro. You need to select the midrange eight-bit MCUs (PIC10, 12, 16/MCP) in the small box alongside Family, as shown in Figure 1-3. Then, in the device window, you need to select the PIC16F88. The result is shown in Figure 1-3. To make these options visible, you need to click the small downward-pointing arrows in the respective boxes. The different options should then become visible. If the device window is highlighted in blue, you could simply type in the PIC number you want (i.e., PIC16F88). Your selected device should appear in the window shown in Figure 1-3.

If you are using a different PIC then you should select it here.

Once you are happy with your selection, you need to click the next box in the window.

The next window to appear is the select tool window. This is shown in Figure 1-4. With this window, you can select the programming tool you want to use to download the program to your prototype board. There are a range of tools you can use. I mainly use the ICD3 CAN or the PICkit3 tool. We will select the PICkit3 as shown in Figure 1-4. If you are using a different tool to download your program, simply select it here. Do not worry if you don't see the serial number of your device, as shown in Figure 1-4. This would be because you have not yet connected it to your laptop.

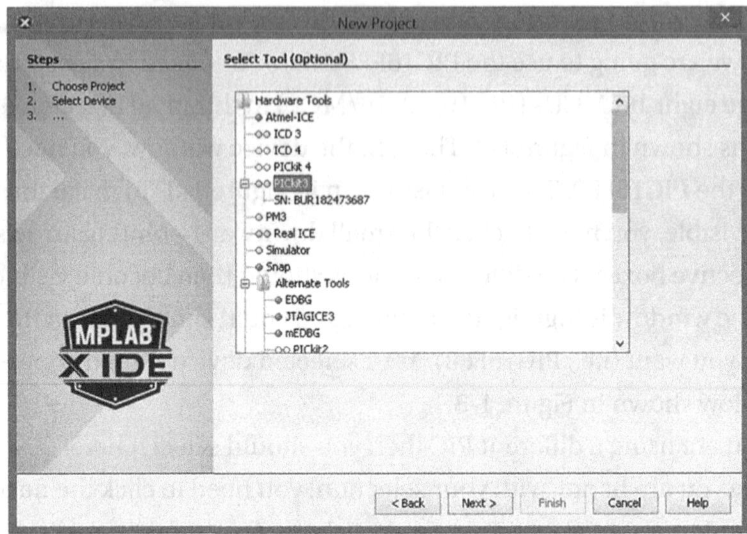

Figure 1-4. *The select tool window*

Having selected the tool you want, simply click "Next" to move on to the next window, where you can select the compiler software you want to use, assuming you have downloaded the appropriate compiler software.

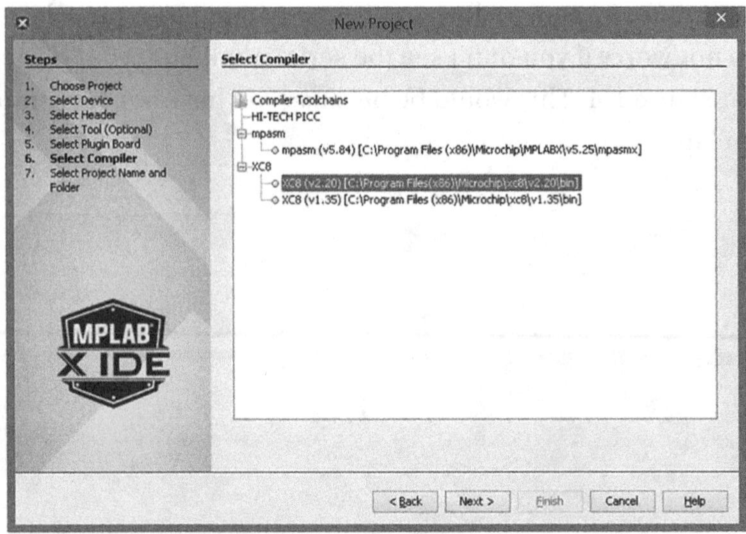

Figure 1-5. *The select compiler window*

You should select the XC8 (V2.20) compiler software, although with some later projects we will use V1.35, as shown in Figure 1-5. Then click "Next" to move to the select project name and folder window, as shown in Figure 1-6.

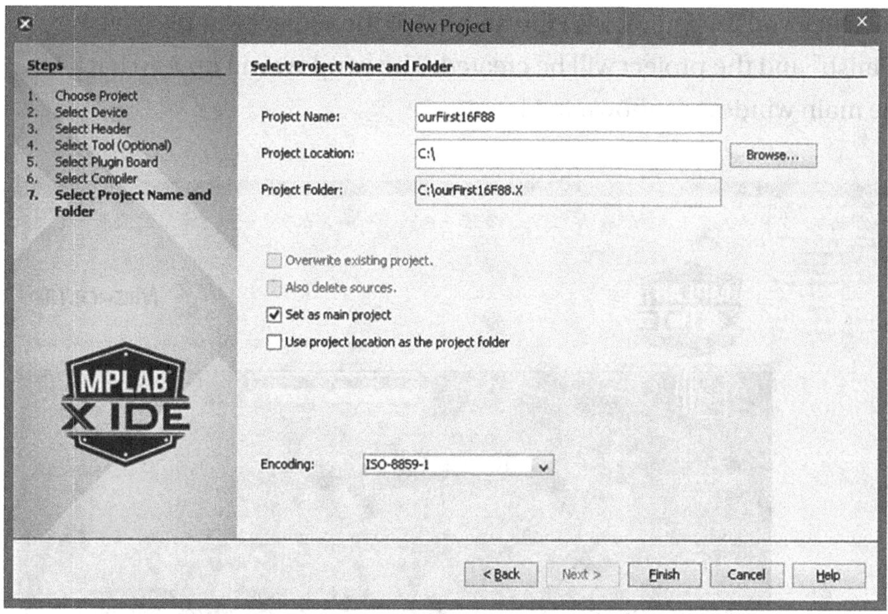

Figure 1-6. *The select project name and folder window*

In this window, you will specify the name of the project and where you want to save it. The software will create a new directory on your computer with the project name you create here. It is not recommended to use long-winded complicated path names to the new folder, so I normally save all my projects on the root directory of my laptop.

I have suggested a project name for this new project as ourFirst16F88. Note that I am using camel case, in which two words, or more, are combined together. The first letter of the first word is in lowercase and the first letters of any subsequent words are in uppercase. In this way, multiple words can be combined together to make one long word.

As you type the name for your project you should see that the folder is created on the root drive, or wherever you have specified it should be. The folder name will have a .X added to it.

It will be in this new folder that all the files associated with the project will be saved as well as some important subdirectories that are created.

Once you are happy with the naming of the project, simply click "Finish" and the project will be created. The window will now go back to the main window as shown in Figure 1-7.

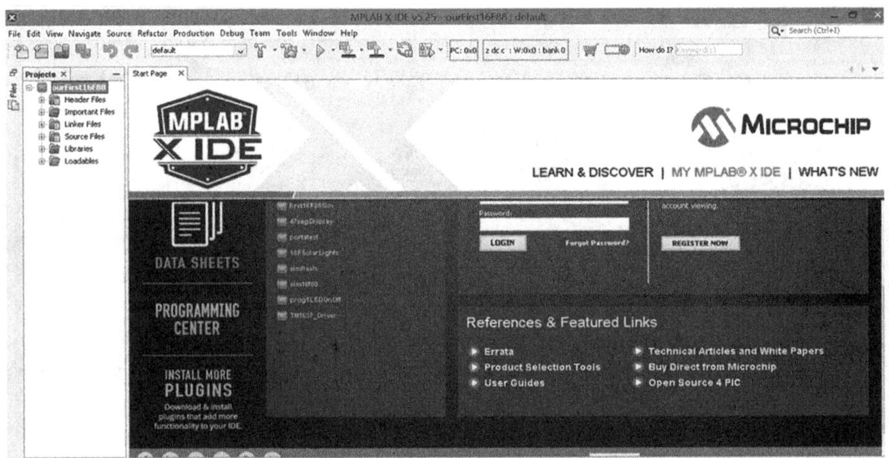

Figure 1-7. *The main window with the project created*

You should now see the project window at the left-hand side of your screen as shown in Figure 1-7. Note that you may need to move the window around to get it the same in Figure 1-7.

The Configuration Words

This section discusses one of the major differences between the PIC microcontrollers and the Arduino. It may seem rather cumbersome, but it reflects the versatility of PICs. It will also give me an opportunity to introduce you to header files and show you how we can create them.

With the Arduino, it is most likely that the configuration work has been done for you; this may make it seem that the Arduino is easier to use. However, I think it has removed the versatility of the device and restricts your understanding of the microcontroller. Certainly, MPLABX, the industrial IDE developed by Microchip, does not have any preconfigured setups for their PICs. This does give you the full range of their versatility, but it does mean you have an extra bit of studying to do before you can program the PICs. Thankfully, it is not a lot to study and Microchip has made it very easy for you to configure the PICs as you want.

The configuration words actually configure, or set up, certain aspects of the PIC and how we want to use them. The most important of these aspects is the source of the oscillator we will be using. The oscillator produces the clocking signal that synchronizes all the actions of the PIC. Microchip allows us to choose from a very wide range of sources from the simple RC (resistor capacitor) oscillator, for low frequencies that don't need to be very accurate, to the more accurate crystal oscillators with frequencies above 20Mhz. These are external devices that can be connected to the PIC. However, Microchip also gives us the choice of using oscillators that are internal (i.e., already set up inside the PIC). This can save the cost of buying an oscillator and save the use of two pins that would have to be used to connect an external oscillator to the PIC. When you use the Arduino, you don't have to worry about which oscillator source you are using because you have had that choice done for you.

There are other aspects of the PIC you need to configure, such as the WDT (watch dog timer) and the Low Voltage Programming (LVP); we will look at them now.

I have tried to explain the use of the configuration words; now let's see how we can configure them. As this is something you have to do for all your projects and for all the different PICs you might use, Microchip has tried to make it easier for you. I know when I first started writing programs for PICs it wasn't quite as easy as it is now.

To write the code for the configuration words, we use a special window in the MPLABX IDE. To open this window, click the word "window" on the main menu bar and then select "Target Memory Views" from the drop-down menu that appears. Then select "configuration bits" from the slide-out menu that appears. This process is shown in Figure 1-8.

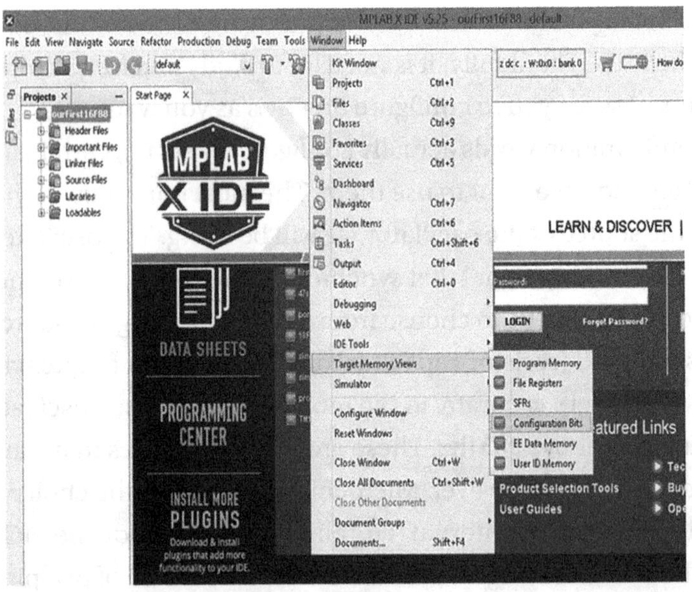

***Figure 1-8.** Opening up the configuration bits*

Once you have selected the configuration bits option, your main window will change to that shown in Figure 1-9.

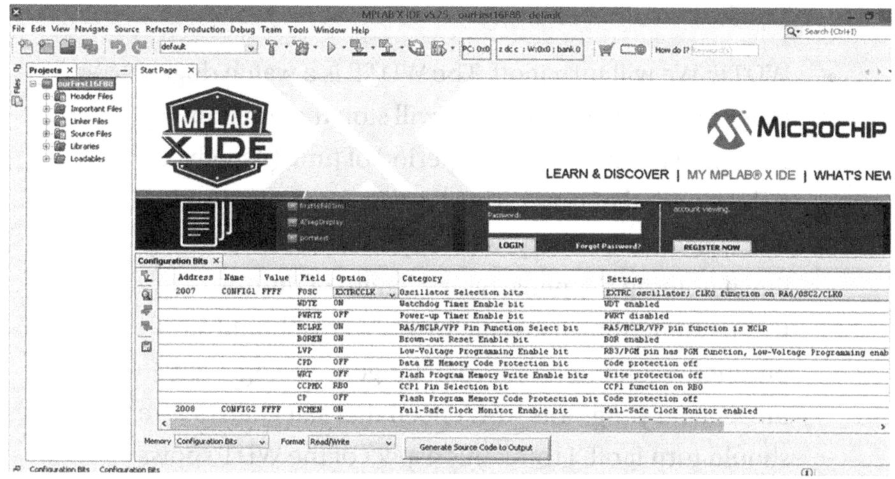

***Figure 1-9.** The configuration bits*

As this is the PIC16F88, there are not that many settings for us to consider. The first one listed is the main one we need to change. It is labeled FOSC (for frequency of oscillator). The default setting is usually the external RC oscillator. You should see under the "setting" label that it indicates that it is connected to RA6. This means that the pin RA6 (i.e., bit6 of PORTA) cannot be used for anything else, as it is used to take the signal from the external RC oscillator into the PIC.

I always prefer to use the internal oscillator block because it saves the cost of the external oscillator and it frees up pin RA6 and more, as we will see. To change this setting, we must click the mouse on the small arrow at the side of the phrase "EXTRCCLK" and select the option "INTOSCIO", which means the internal oscillator with input/output function on pins RA6 and RA7. You should see that the comments under the label "setting" have changed to show this and they are shown in blue.

We will make two other changes:

- WDTE: We will turn it off. The WDTE is a watch dog timer enable that, if enabled, will stop the program if nothing happens for a set period of time (usually a short period of time). This is really a safety factor that is used in industry, whereby on a production line if nothing happens for any length of time, it means something has gone wrong so we should stop production and find out what has gone wrong. Well, most of our programs won't need that safeguard so we should turn it off. I think this aspect of the WDT shows that the Arduino is not really meant for industry, as again this option has already been taken out of your hands.
- The third item to change is the LVP. We should turn it off so that bit3 of PORTB is left as a normal input output pin.
- Those are the changes that we need to make for this PIC, and these changes are shown in Figure 1-10.

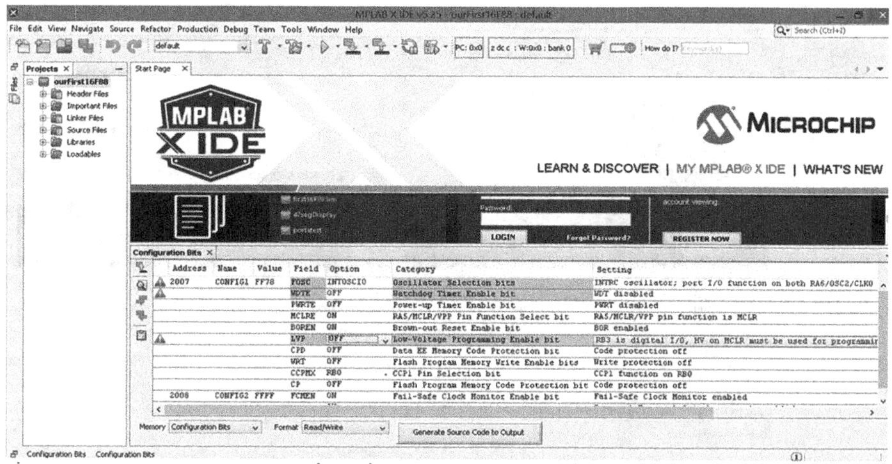

***Figure 1-10.** The changes to the configuration words*

All we need to do now is generate the source code and use it in our program. This process is a lot easier than it has been, because all we need to do now is click the tab "Generate Source Code to Output" and MPLABX will do it for us. This tab is at the bottom of the screen as shown in Figure 1-9 and Figure 1-10. Once you generate the code, it should appear as shown in Figure 1-11. You may have to minimize the configuration bits window to show the source code better.

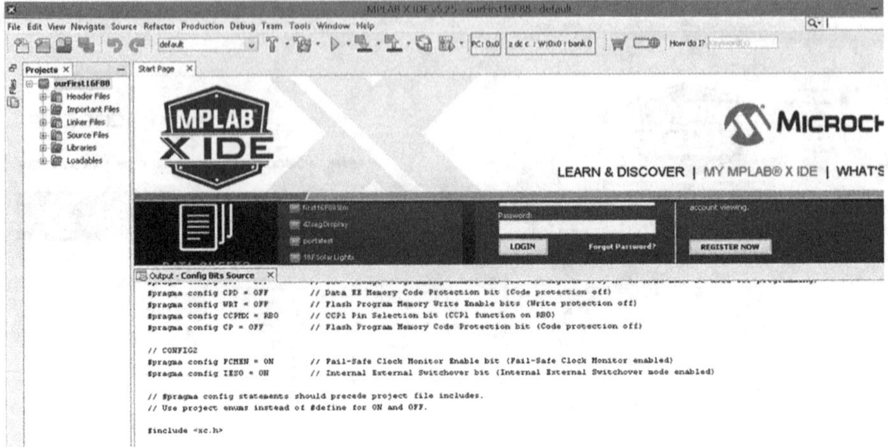

***Figure 1-11.** The config bits source*

What we are going to do is copy these instructions and paste them into a header file. We could paste them into the program listing that we will use for the first program. However, we will not start writing that program until we get to chapter 2. Also I want you to understand that when we write our other programs for the 16F88, we will use the same configuration words. There may be times when we want to use a different set of configuration words, but that won't happen in the programs in this book. Therefore, to remove the need to repeat the process of writing the same configuration words in all our other PIC16F88 projects, we will save these instructions to a header file: first a local header file and then a global header file.

Creating a Header File

The process of creating a header file is quite simple and yet very useful. First, in the main editing window, you need to right-click the mouse on the phrase "Header Files" in the project tree. Then select "New" and then the "xc8_header,h.." option from the fly-out menu that appears. This is shown in Figure 1-12.

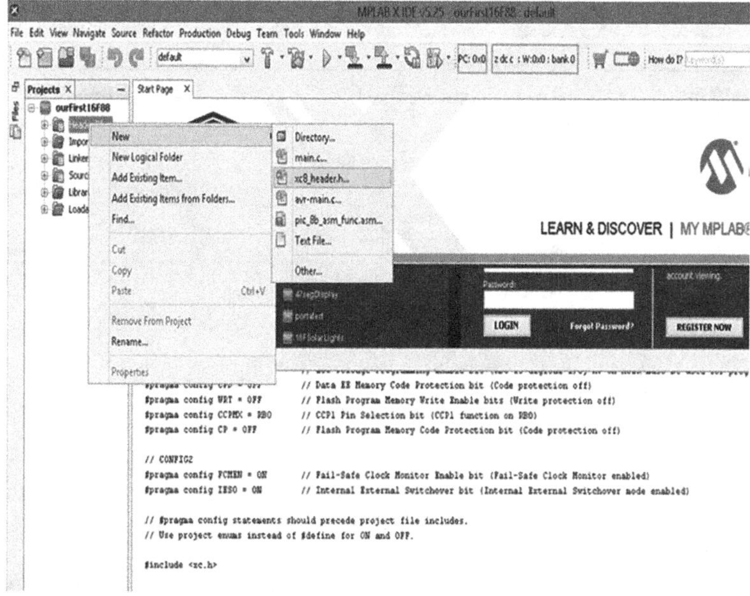

Figure 1-12. *Creating the new header file*

You will be asked to give the file a name. I have suggested "pic16F88ConfigSettings" as shown in Figure 1-13.

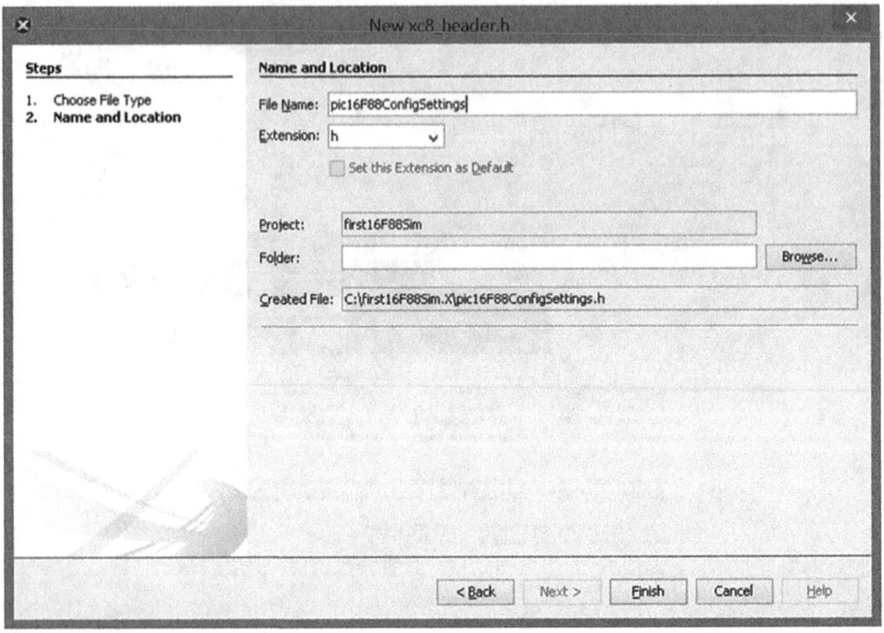

Figure 1-13. *Naming the new header file*

Once you are happy with the name of the file, click “Finish”, and the main editing window should change to show the new file open and ready for editing. This is shown in Figure 1-14.

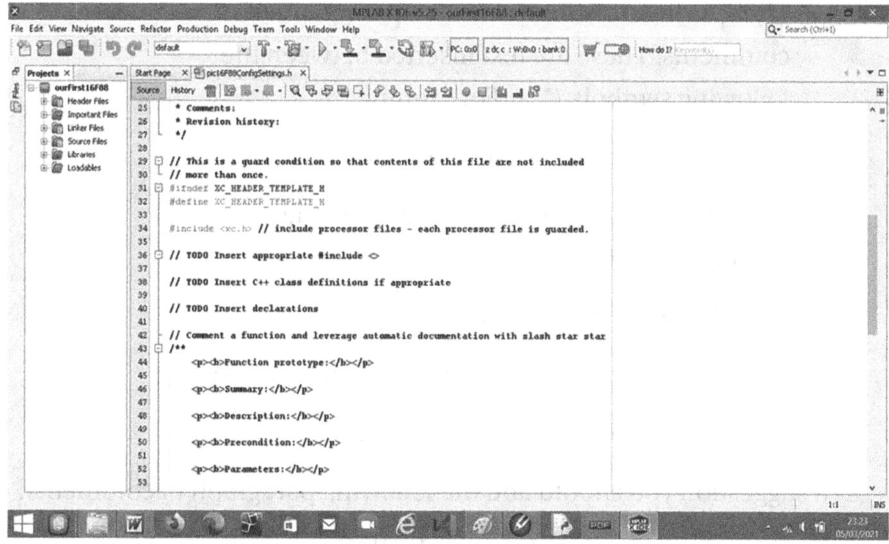

***Figure 1-14.** The header file in the main editing window*

You will see that Microchip automatically inserts an awful lot of text into the file. I have never used any of it and I simply delete it all. To ensure that your windows look exactly as I expect them to, I would like you to delete all that text; thank you.

Before we copy the instructions for the configuration words into this file, we should add some comments. It is good practice to include comments in all your programs. You know what you are doing now but in six months or less, you will wonder why you did what you have done; therefore, always add comments.

There are two types of comments in 'C' programs:

- Single-line comments, which start with two forward slashes as shown here //. Anything on the same line after the two forward slashes is ignored by the compiler, as they are simply comments. For example: //these words are just comments.

- Multiple lines of comments or a paragraph of comments. These are text inserted between the following symbols /* */. For example:
    - /* Your comments are written in here */
- Your comments should have the following content at least:
    - Who wrote it (i.e., you)
    - What PIC you wrote it for and when you wrote it
    - What you are trying to do with it

As a suggestion you should add the following paragraph of comments:

/*Configuration words for the PIC16F88

Using the internal oscillator block

Turning the WDT off and the LVP off.

Written by Mr. H. H. Ward dated 22/02/2021*/

These should go at the top of the empty file.

Obviously you should insert your name and the appropriate date.

Now we need to get back the configuration bits we created before. There should be a tab on the bottom left of the screen with the words "configuration bits". If you click the mouse on that tab, the window should appear in the editing screen. You now need to click the mouse on "Generate Source Code to Output" to create the source code. The source code may not automatically appear and you may have to click the mouse on an empty area of the header file to bring them into view. When you have them in view, I want you to copy everything EXCEPT the last phrase, which is #include <xc.h>; I want to discuss the importance of this include statement in chapter 2. Once you have copied the source code, you should paste it into the header file starting on the next line after your initial comments.

Your editing window should now look like that shown in Figure 1-15.

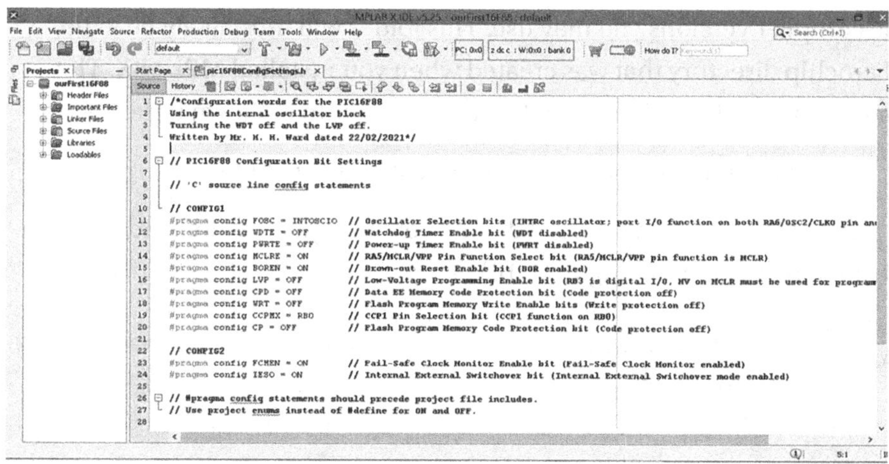

***Figure 1-15.** The source code pasted into the header file*

All we have to do now is save the file using the save option under the word "file" on the main menu bar.

So now we have created a "local header file". We will look at how we can use this and other header files in chapter 2. I want to explain why I am calling it a local header file and why we need to make it a "global header file". A local header file is one that can only be used in the current project you have created it in. It is used to split your project up into small sections so that a group of programmers may work on the different sections. However, it does not fit our purpose as it stands at present. We want to create a header file that we can use in all our projects that used the same configuration words. To do that, we must change this local header file into a global header file, which is one we can use in all our projects that use the same configuration words. At present, this header file is saved in the directory for this project, and therefore only this project will find the file. What we need to do is save a copy of this file in a place where all projects will find it. This will be the "include" folder of the XC8 compiler software we are using within MPLABX. If you are using more than one compiler version, then you must save a copy in the "include" folder for all the compiler versions you may use. This folder will most likely be in the Microchip directory that was created when you installed MPLABX. The path to the "include" folder I will copy this file into is shown here:

C:\Program Files (x86)\Microchip\xc8\v1.35\include

You will have to find the header file you have just created and the path to find it on my laptop (Figure 1-16).

Figure 1-16. *The first16F88Sim folder and header file*

You should remember that I said when you create a project in MPLABX, the software will create a folder on your system where it will store all the files for your project.

Once you have found the "include" folder of the compiler software you use, you can paste a copy of the header file you have just created into the folder. By creating a copy of the header file, you will get a global header file that will be available for all our future projects that use the same configuration settings. What happens in the other projects, where you have asked to have the header file included, is that the linker program will go to the include folder in the compiler software and find the header file you want to use.

We will look at this more closely when we write our first program in chapter 2.

Changing the Fonts and Colors

You will notice that I have changed the color of my comments to black and bold, size 14. This is to try and make them more visible than the default gray.

If you want to change the color, you can do so by selecting the word "options" from the drop-down menu that appears when you select the "tools" and the options choice from the main menu bar. You will get the window shown in Figure 1-17.

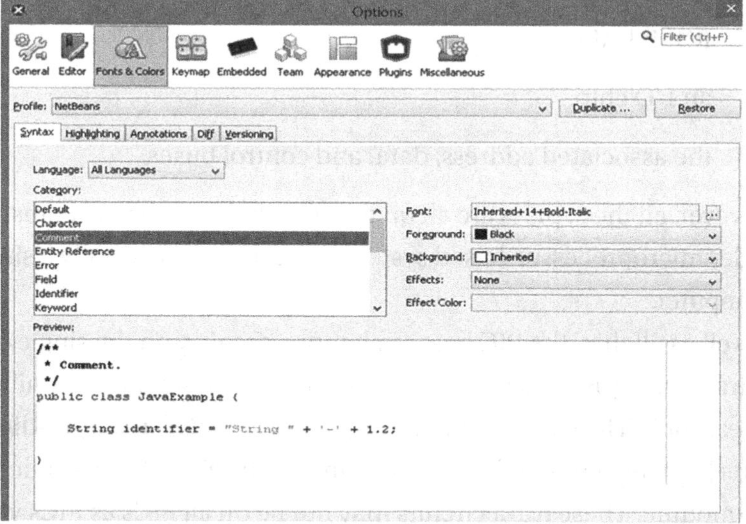

Figure 1-17. Changing the font and colors

You should click the tag for fonts and colors. Then select what you want to change. Once you are happy with your choice, click "OK". I have selected the fonts and colors and then changed the color of the comments to black, as shown in Figure 1-17.

The PIC Microcontroller

Just before we finish this first chapter, I think it might be useful to discuss what a PIC is. Some people say it stands for programmable industrial controllers, or programmable intelligent controller, or programmable interface controller. However, some say it is really just a trademark for the microcontrollers produced by Microchip. The term PIC is used by Microchip to cover an extremely wide range of microcontrollers produced by them. I will simply refer to the microcontroller as the PIC.

Each PIC will have all the components of a microprocessor-based system as shown in Figure 1-18, such as the following:

- a microprocessor
- ROM, RAM
- an I/O chip
- the associated address, data, and control buses.

However, all these parts are all on a single chip, not several chips, as with older microprocessor-based systems. This means it is really a single-chip computer.

As well as all that, the PIC has much more circuitry on the single chip. This extra circuitry is used to make it into a control system with a micro at the heart of it. The extra circuit may include an ADC (analog-to-digital converter), opamp circuits for compare and capture, a PWM module, and a UART module. These extra circuits may not be on all PICs as PICs vary in their makeup for different applications.

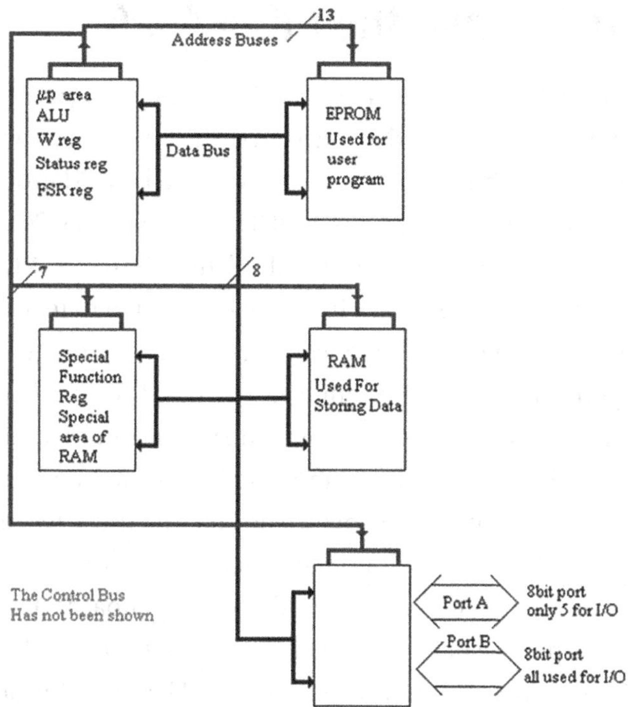

Figure 1-18. *The basic microprocessor system*

One more thing before we move on is that the PIC is a RISC chip as opposed to a CISC chip. RISC stands for reduced instruction set chip, whereas CISC stands for complex instruction set chip. Indeed, the instruction sets for PIC micros range from 35 to 75 core instructions. However, the 18F4525 has an extended instruction set at your disposal. The Intel processor, which is a CISC chip, uses hundreds of instructions, so the PIC is pretty efficient.

The PIC16F88 and the PIC8F4525

This book is based around using these two PICs. They are both eight-bit micros, which basically means they have an eight-bit data bus and so take data in chunks of eight bits, which is referred to as a byte. Microchip also produces PICs that are 16 bits, 24 bits, and 32 bits. Modern PCs use 64-bit processors now. However, you shouldn't think that these two PICs are old hat and that what you will learn in this book is out of date. First, these two PICs, especially the PIC18F4525, can perform a wide range of control functions, as you will find out. It is quite easy to build control boards with them on simple vero boards, as they come in 18-pin, 20-pin, and 40-pin dual inline (DIL) chips. I have used the 32-bit PICs from Microchip and they are 100-pin surface mount devices. The fact that these two eight-bit PICs come in DIL packages does make them easy to use and to make prototype boards with them. When I build my circuit boards, I use the 18 pin, 20-pin, or 40-pin IC sockets so that I don't have to solder the actual PICs to my circuits. Also, the 'C' language you will learn in this book is the same 'C' language you will use on the 32-bit PICs.

Figures 1-19 and 1-20 show the two PICs we are using. As you grow in confidence with using these PICs, it will be useful if you downloaded a copy of the data sheets for the PICs. These can be found on the Microchip web site. Indeed, as you develop your experience in electronics, you will need to keep a copy of the datasheet for any device you use. I must have hundreds of datasheets that I use in all my work.

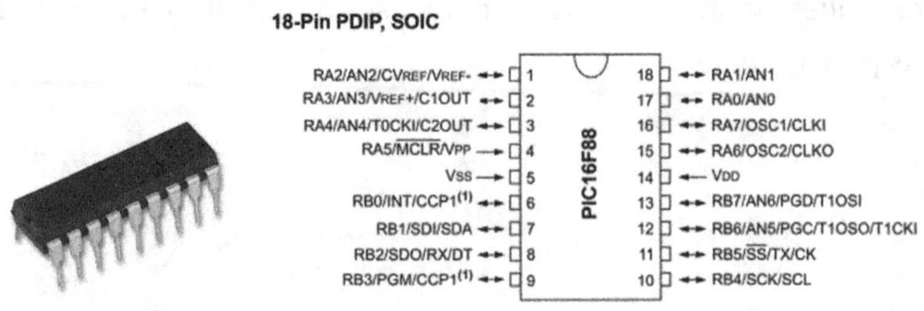

Figure 1-19. *The PIC16F88*

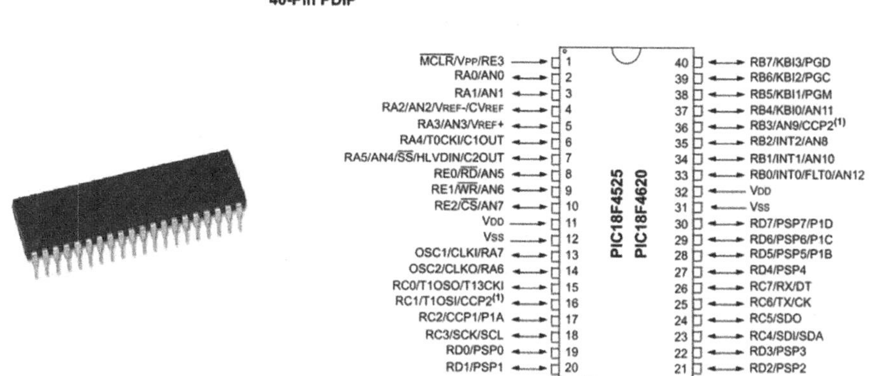

Figure 1-20. *The PIC18F4525*

Summary

In this chapter, we have learned what an IDE is and how to create a project within MPLABX, the IDE from Microchip. We have looked at the importance of header files, and the difference between local and global header files. We will go on to create our own header files for functions that we will use in exactly the same way in most of our programs as the book progresses. We have also looked at what a PIC is and the two PICs we will be using in this book.

In the next chapter, we will create our first program and learn how to use the header file we have just created, and other header files, in it. We will also start our analysis of 'C' programs as to how a 'C' program works and how the instructions of the 'C' program operate. I hope you will enjoy reading this book and learn a lot from it. Good luck and happy reading.

CHAPTER 2

Programming Basics

This chapter covers the following main topics:

- A standard approach to writing a program
- How to create a source file within a project
- How to use the header file into source file
- How to set up different types of oscillators
- How PIC communicates with the outside world using PORTS
- How to use TRIS registers to set the PORTS
- The main aspects of a 'C' program
- How to download a program to a development board

It also looks at how you might build your own development board and use ICSP (in-circuit serial programming). However, you should be fairly confident with building circuits on vero boards. After reading this chapter, you should be able to create a project and write a program that can be run on a development board.

H. H. Ward, *Programming Arduino Projects with the PIC Microcontroller*,
https://doi.org/10.1007/978-1-4842-7230-5_2

Good Programming Practice

You have an idea of what you want to do and you can't wait to start writing code. However, you cannot rush things; there is just too much to consider and too many things you can miss if you don't plan your work first. You need to consider which PIC you will use: there are so many different PICs, from the simplest 8-pin device to ones with 100 pins. You will most likely find a PIC that will do all you want and then stick with that one; however, you should really learn to be adaptive.

The very least you should do is to write down a plan of how you are going to solve the problem you are faced with. Will you need a lot of I/O pins (input/output pins)? Will you need an ADC (analog-to-digital converter)? This will depend upon whether or not you will need any analog inputs, or if you with just use digital inputs and outputs. Your written plan should answer all these questions, and more, then help you decide what PIC you will use.

Algorithms

This is really a posh word for your written plan. It is really simply putting your thoughts of how you are going to get the PIC to do what is asked of it down on paper. The algorithm should cover at least the following:

- You should explain the sequence of events you want to control.
- You should then identify all the input and output devices you will need.
- You should then create an allocation list for the I/O and identify any special inputs or outputs or controls you will need, such as analog inputs, PWM outputs, and any timers.

The algorithm should ideally break the process down to questions that have one of two possible answers (i.e., pure logical questions). This is why we use the binary number system to represent logic, as it is a number system that has only two digits: 0 and 1.

Flowcharts

Flowcharts are diagrams that show how any process flows through its constituent parts. They are very useful diagrams for designing computer programs. All flowcharts use four basic symbols; there are more but the four most common symbols are shown in Figure 2-1.

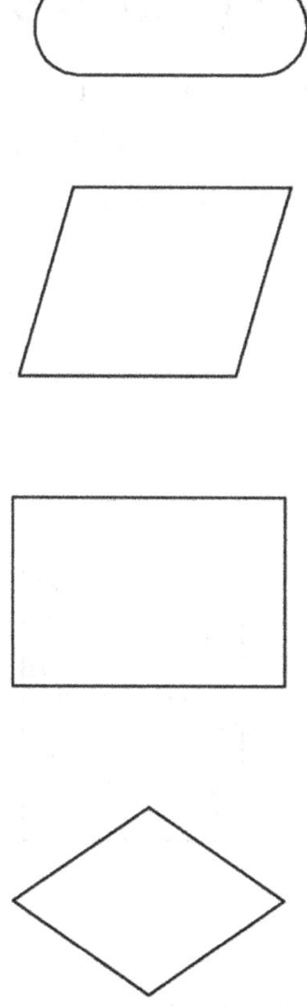

Figure 2-1. *The main flowchart symbols*

Program Listings

This is a list of the actual instructions written in your chosen language. It should be the last thing you do; but as you become more experienced, you will tend to do this after you have written your algorithm, leaving flowcharts only for the most intricate parts of your program. You can decide which approach is best for you.

If you have constructed your flowchart correctly, then each block in your flowchart will produce the correct lines of coding in your program listing.

Program 2.1: Turning On and Off an LED

In Program 2.1 we will learn about the inputs to the PIC to control an output of the PIC. We will use a start switch to turn an LED on and a stop switch to turn it off. The circuit for the project is shown in Figure 2-2.

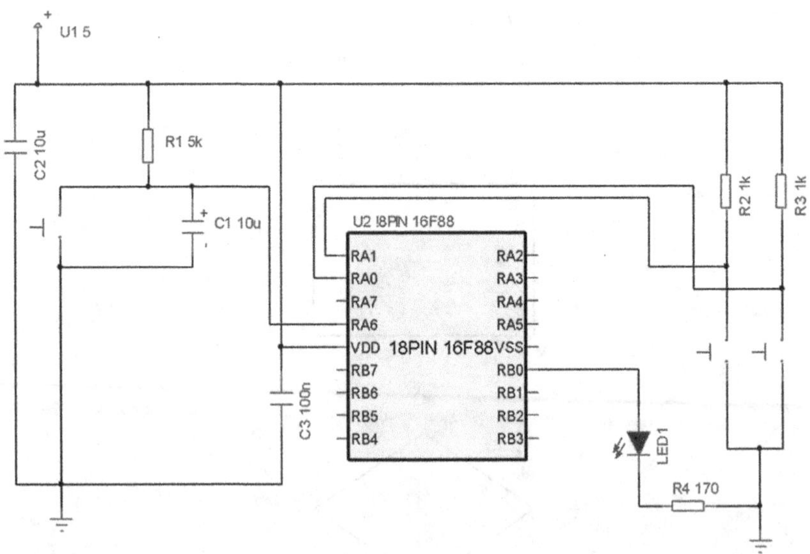

***Figure 2-2.** The minimal circuit diagram for Program 2.1*

Now we are ready to get down to the real part of this process, writing the code for the program. First we will start with the algorithm.

Algorithm for Program 2.1

The sequence of events is as follows.

1. The PIC will wait for the momentary switch, the start button, to be pressed (i.e., go to 0V, a logic '0'). Being a momentary switch, it will go back to 5V, a logic '1', automatically.
2. The PIC will then turn the LED on.
3. The PIC will then wait until the stop switch is pressed, in the same way as the start switch.
4. The PIC will then turn the LED off.
5. The program will loop back to the beginning where it waits for the start switch to be pressed.
6. The program will require two inputs: one for each switch and one output for the LED.
7. The start switch will be allocated to bit0 of PORTA and the stop switch will be allocated to bit1 of PORTA.
8. The LED will be allocated to bit0 of PORTB.
9. There will be no need for any analog inputs and so no ADC.
10. To save I/O, we will use the internal oscillator block of the PIC.

I have included the last two items in the algorithm to try and show you that a good algorithm can help you choose what PIC you need for your project. There are a lot of PICs to choose from and they have different capabilities. However, you will most likely settle down to using your favorite PIC as you gain more experience. In this book, we have already chosen the PICs we will use.

Flowchart for Program 2.1

The flowchart for Program 2.1 is shown in Figure 2-3. If the flowchart is complete enough, then every block in the flowchart should relate to a section of instructions in the program listing.

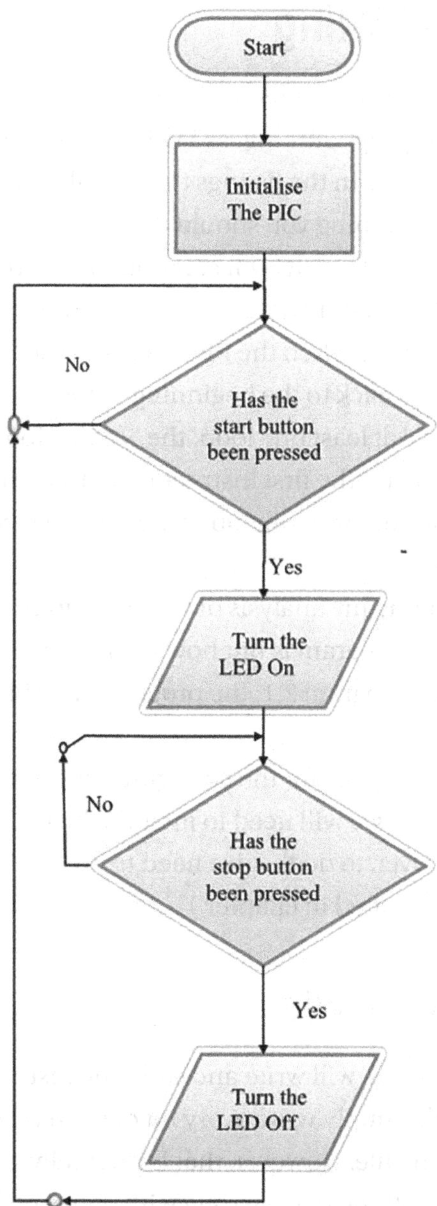

Figure 2-3. *The flowchart for Program 2.1*

The Program Listing

I will assume you have never written a C program before. It is not essential that you understand C programming, as I will carry out a line-by-line analysis of the instructions in the listings that should help explain how a C program works. The only thing you should appreciate is that a C program works in a series of loops. The PIC will carry out the instructions in those loops sequentially one at a time unless the programmer forces the PIC to move out of that sequence. When the PIC comes to the last instruction in the loop, the PIC will go back to the beginning of the loop and start again. A C program must have at least one loop: the "**main**" loop. The micro will go to this main loop to find the first instruction of the program. We will discuss the importance of this main loop when we go through the analysis of Listing 2-1.

I hope that by reading my analysis of these program listings, you will not only learn what a C program is but how the instructions work and do what we want them to. Program 2.1, the program we will look at, is quite simple.

We will use the header file for the configuration words that we created in chapter 1. This means we will need to include the header file into our source code file. However, to do that we need to create the source file from within the project we created in chapter 1.

Creating a Source File

The source file is where we will write and store the instructions for the program. We could simply write every bit of code we need for the program inside this one file. However, that is not really good practice, even though there is nothing really wrong with it except that it could mean you writing the same code over and over again. A better approach would be to use header files—which we will look at as we progress with the book—but header files you have written, not someone else. Indeed, when programming the Arduino, you will use a whole range of header files. However, with the Arduino, that is done to make your work in writing programs for the Arduino much less arduous, as these header files have already been written for you. In my opinion, it does far too much for you. I know when I have programmed the Arduino it is easy to get it to do what you want, but you are left not really understanding how it does it and you have not learned much if anything at all. I firmly believe that a good programmer should know exactly how all the code they write works. They should be able to write all the code they use themselves, even the header files they use, not rely on header files that someone else has written for you. It is my main aim that, after reading this book, you will become a programmer who understands all the code they write and use.

Program 2.1 is written for the PIC16F88. The first few programs will be written for that PIC. This means that we could be writing the same configuration words for the next few programs. However, instead of doing that, we are going to use the header file we created in chapter 1, as we will be using the same setting for these programs.

Assume we have the MPLABX software open with the project we created in a chapter 1 open. If it is not open (i.e., it is not in the project tree window), then you can select the word "file" from the main menu bar. Then select "Open Recent Project" and you should see the project title appear in the fly-out window. Once you have selected or opened the project, the software should look like that shown in Figure 2-4.

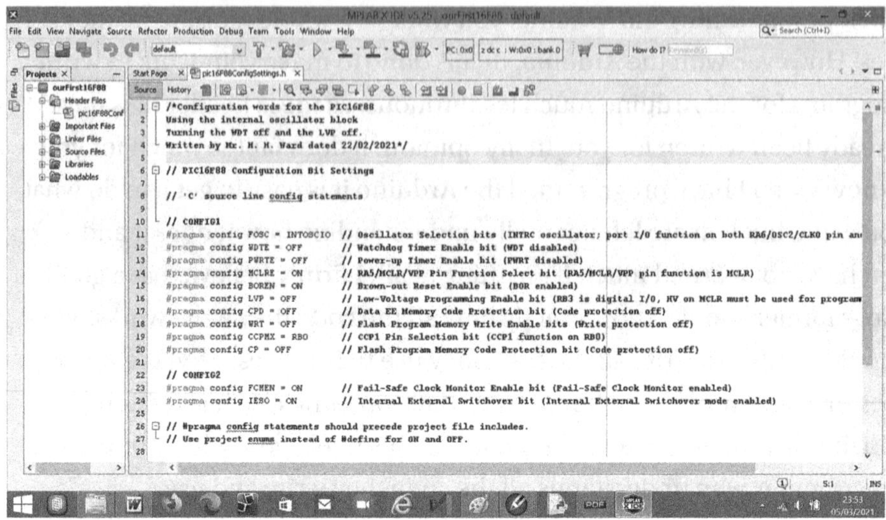

Figure 2-4. *The editing window with the project opened*

If the project tree is minimized in the project window (i.e., not shown), then you need to click the '+' sign in the small square next to the gray folder box alongside the project title "ourFirst16F88". This should open up the tree. If the project window is not visible, then you will have to click the word "window" on the main menu bar and select the orange project option for the drop-down menu that appears.

Once you have got the editing window open and the project tree on view, you need to right-click the mouse on the phrase "Source Files" then select "New" and then "main C" from the fly-out menus that appear. This is shown in Figure 2-5.

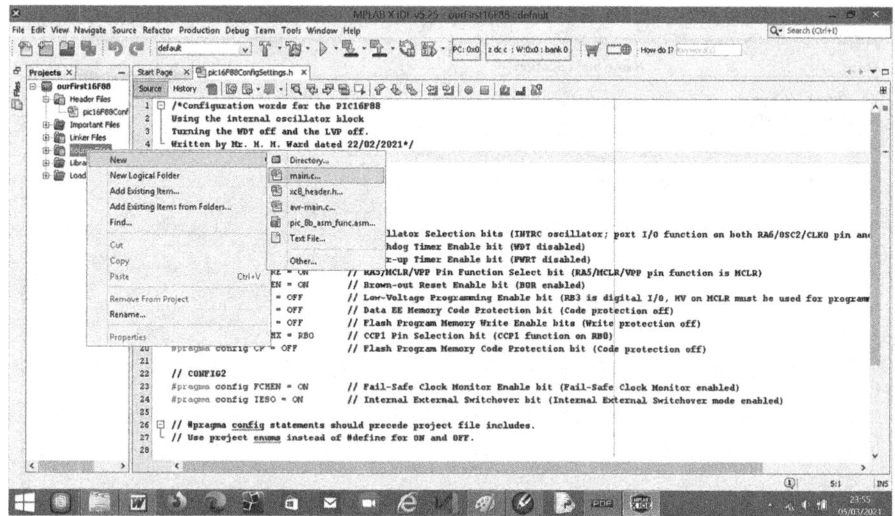

***Figure 2-5.** The new main c source file menu*

Having done that, you will be presented with the name and location window. I tend to give my source files the same name as the project but with the addition of "Prog". This is shown in Figure 2-6.

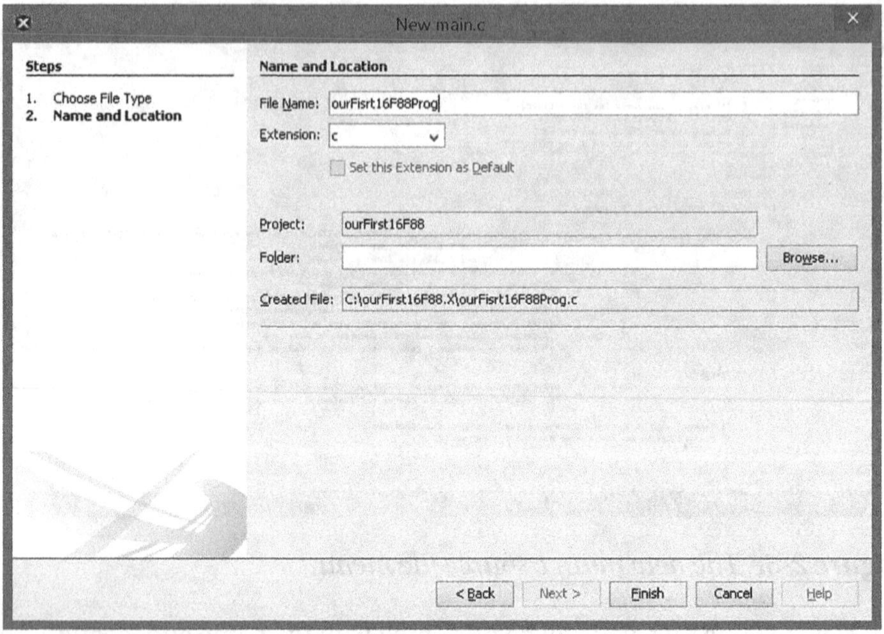

Figure 2-6. The name and location window

I always accept the default location, which is the folder that the software created when we created the project. There is no need to add the extension, as the software will give the file the required 'c' extension as shown in Figure 2-6.

Once you are happy with the name and location, simply click "Finish". The window will close and the main editing window will change to show the file we have just created open ready for you to add your instructions.

If you still have a tab with the start-up page evident in the editing window (it may not be the top tab), you can close the tab by clicking the mouse on the small square with the 'x' in it associated with that tab.

Microchip automatically inserts a paragraph of comments and the main loop, which must be in the C program, along with an include statement. I see no point in adding the word "void" inside the two normal brackets, and I like to have my opening and closing curly brackets on their own separate line. I will explain these changes when we start to look at the program listing. I would, however, like you to make the same changes so that our screens do look the same. This is shown in Figure 2-7.

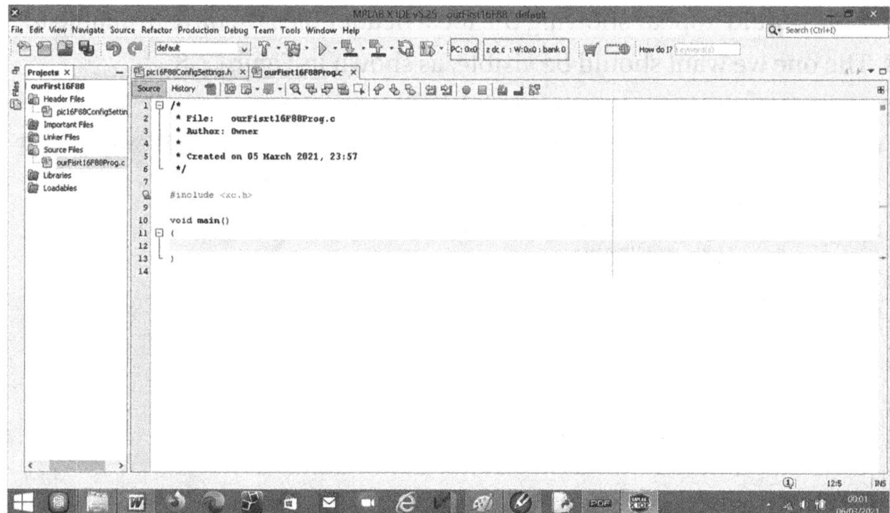

***Figure 2-7.** The source file opened in the editing window*

Adding the Header File

There are two ways of adding the header file we want, because it has been created in the project, which means it is local to the project. However, we should have copied it into the include directory of the compiler software, which means it is globally available to any project we want to use it in. Firstly, we will add it as a local header file. To do this, move the mouse to the beginning of line 8 (i.e., the next line after the paragraph of comments), and place the insertion point there. Now type in the hash key '#'. As you type this symbol, the "intellisense" of the compiler software takes over. This is a bit like predictive text on your mobile phone. The compiler tries to guess what it is you are going to type next. The software presents you with a drop-down menu that shows a list of possible directives, shown in green, that you may want to use. The one we want is "include", shown at the bottom of the list. You can simply click the mouse on that word or type "include", without the quotation marks, into the file. When you finish either inserting or typing the word "include", if you press the spacebar a small window should appear showing the local header files we have available to us. The one we want should be visible, as shown in Figure 2-8.

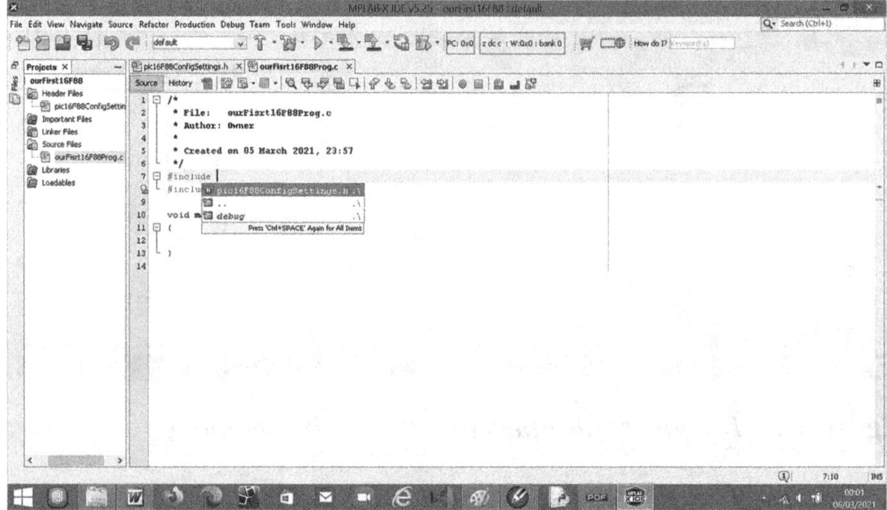

Figure 2-8. *The intellisense displaying the local header file*

If it is visible, then you can click the mouse on the file name and it should be inserted in the file. If it is not visible, then you may have to type the name in as shown here:

"pic16F88ConfigSettings.h".

Note that you will have to include the quotation marks and the .h. The quotation marks tells the compiler software it is a local header file. When you have typed it in correctly, the screen should look like that shown in Figure 2-9.

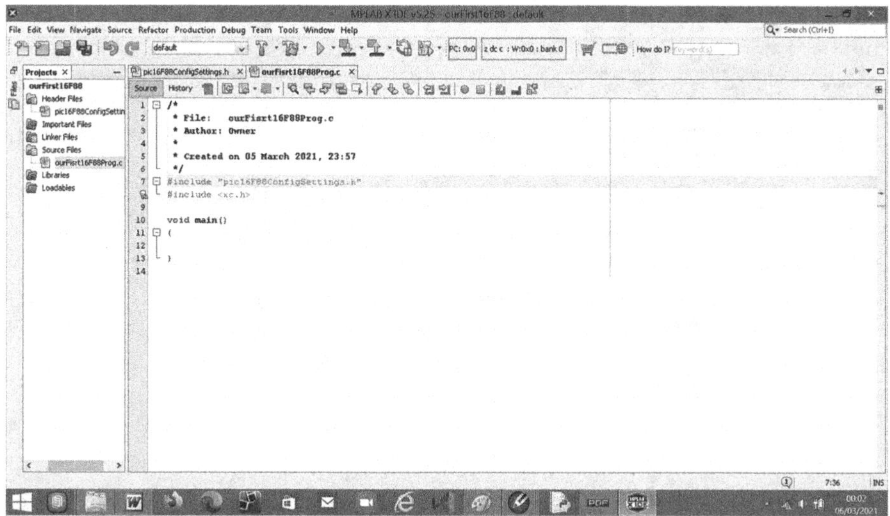

Figure 2-9. *The local header file included*

Note that the text uses different colors to show the different uses: keywords are in blue, key directives are in green, and so on. This is because this is more than a simple text editor.

However, as we want to use the same header file in all our projects that use the PIC16F88, and so, as we will always use the same settings, we need to use the global header file. So, I want you to delete the line we have just added completely. Then start by typing the '#' symbol again and selecting the directive "include" again. However, now when you press the spacebar, I want you to ignore the first pop-up menu and simply type the greater-than character "<" (without the quotation marks). As soon as you do, the intellisense takes over and adds the less-than symbol and pops up a different menu. What has happened is that the linker software has gone to the include directory in the compiler software and is now showing you a list of all the header files that are available to you there. This is shown in Figure 2-10.

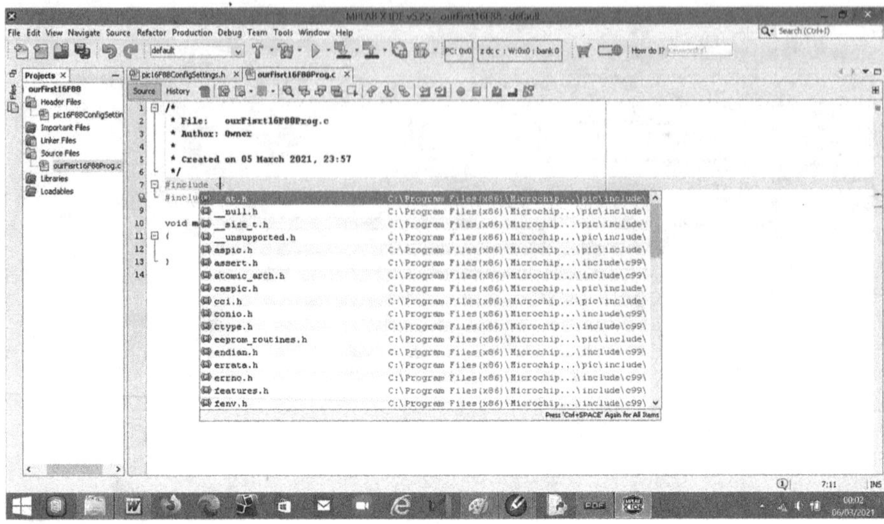

***Figure 2-10.** The list of global header files*

If you start typing in the name of the header file you want, namely pic16, you should see the list reduce until you can see the file name you want. You can then select it to insert it into your source file. This is shown in Figure 2-11.

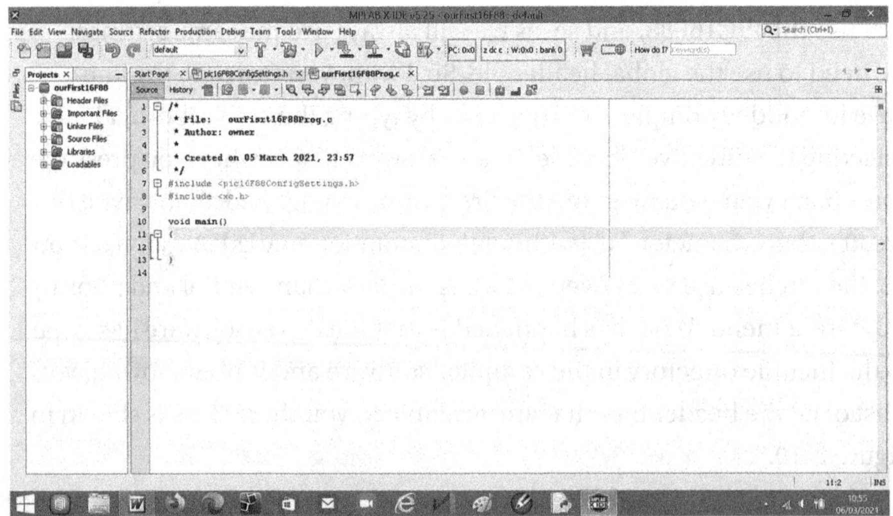

***Figure 2-11.** The global header file inserted into the source file*

Now, when we compile the program, the linker program will find that header file and the software will compile it along with our instructions just as if we had written them here in the source file. This is a very powerful use of header files that save us a lot of work. We will create a range of header files ourselves that we will use in our programs. Those of you who have used the Arduino will know that your sketches are full of header files. The difference with this approach is that we will know exactly what is in the header files and how they work, since we will have written them.

Well, what about the other header file, the <xc.h>, which is included automatically? What does that do? I will explain what it does when we start to analyze Program 2.1.

Before we look at that listing, we will insert some useful comments into our program. We have discussed the use of comments in chapter 1. I will replace the comments that were automatically inserted when we created the source file with the following.

```
/*

* File: ourFisrt16F88Prog.c

* Author: H. H. Ward

* A simple program to turn on and off a single LED

* Written for the PIC16F88

* Created on 05 March 2021, 23:57

*/
```

You should change them to suit yourself accordingly.

Program 2.1

To move on then, I would like you to type the rest of the program into the source file. The complete program is shown in Listing 2-1.

Listing 2-1. Program 2.1

```
/*
* File:   ourFisrt16F88Prog.c
Author: H. H. Ward
A simple program to turn on and off a single LED
Written for the PIC16F88
Created on 05 March 2021, 23:57
*/
#include <pic16F88ConfigSettings.h>
#include <xc.h>
#define startbutton PORTAbits.RA0
#define stopbutton  PORTAbits.RA1
#define LED1        PORTBbits.RB0
void main()
{
PORTA = 0;
PORTB = 0;
TRISA = 0XFF;
TRISB = 0;
OSCTUNE = 0;
OSCCON = 0b01111100;
ANSEL = 0;
while (1)
{
while (startbutton);
LED1 = 1;
while (stopbutton);
LED1 = 0;
}
}
```

Analysis of Listing 2-1

I feel that I should warn you that this first analysis will be a lot longer than a normal analysis. This is because I want to explain much more than I would normally do, as I am assuming you know nothing about C programs and C instructions. As we progress with our programs, the analysis will be much more succinct and focused on what the instructions are doing. I hope you will bear with me. Of course, if you do understand the instructions already, then you can skip some or all of the analysis, but you might learn something new if you go through it.

The line numbers in the listing are there just so that I can easily refer to the individual instructions.

Lines 1 to 7 are simply a paragraph of comments that I have inserted to do the following.

- Obtain ownership to the listing.
- Give a brief explanation of what the program is doing and what PIC it is written for.
- Give the listing a name and the date it was written.
- If there are any revisions then we can add the revision number and the date it was created. If you want to try any changes to a program, it is good practice to save them as a revision and keep the original separate just in case the changes are not an improvement and you want to go back to the old program.

There are two types of comments in C programs. These are

- **Single-line comments,** which are anything on the current line written after two forward slashes '//'.

  For example:

  //This is a single-line comment and the compiler will ignore everything written on this one line after the '//'.

- **Multiple lines of comments or a paragraph of comments,** which are everything written between the symbols /*.....*/.

  For example, lines 1 to 7 in Listing 2-1.

Line 8 #include <pic16F88ConfigSettings.h>

This tells the linker and compiler to add the instructions written in this header file when the software compiles the program.

Line 9 #include <xc.h>

This is the first time we have seen this instruction. Every time we come across a new instruction, I will explain how the instruction works and what it is trying to achieve. After that initial explanation, when we come across the same instruction again, I will refer you back to the first analysis and restrict my explanation to any new aspect of the instruction. I hope this is OK as I don't really want to keep repeating myself in these analyses.

I hope you have an appreciation of why we use header files and how to include them into our source files. I want to explain what this "xc.h" header file does. In every program, you are going to use a range of SFRs (special function registers). Note that a register is a collection of cells, or bits, that are used to store the logic '1's and logic '0's that all micros use. These SFRs are given names to help identify them. They are the same as the memory locations that we will create, except that the data in SFRs are used to control the various actions of the PIC; for example, OSCCON is a CONtrol register that controls the internal OSCillator. The memory locations that we set up, not these SFRs, are where we will store the data of the different variables we will create to represent different aspects of our programs.

Now to the xc.h header file that we are asking the compiler to include in our program. The concept is that all these SFRs that we will use have their own address numbers, just like we have addresses for our homes, where the PIC can be told to go to when it wants to write to or read from these SFRs. So what? Well, the issue is that these addresses are really binary numbers such as 0b00000000 for the first SRF or 0b11111111 for the last SRF. If we used this type of address for them it would be very difficult to know which SFR we were referring to. We could make it slightly easier if we used hexadecimal numbers (i.e., 0X00 or 0XFF) which represent the same numbers. Note that the "0b" in front of the number tells the software that this is a binary number and the "0X" tells the software that it is a hexadecimal number. There is a section in the appendix that explains how these number systems work.

However, it would be better if we could give these SFRs a name instead of using a number. As an example, we will be using the SFR "PORTA". The phrase PORTA helps us to identify that the SFR is a PORT and that it is PORTA and not PORTB. If we simply used the address number, we would be writing 0b00000101 in binary, or 0X05 in hexadecimal, as this is the actual address of the SFR for PORTA. I know I would prefer to use the reference PORTA. However, the compiler software really only wants to use the number 0X05 or 0b00000101, as that is where the compiler will write the data to or from. As humans, we would like to use the naming for all the SFRs we will use in our PIC programs. We could do that by using equate instructions or #define instructions, where we tell the compiler that wherever we use the reference PORTA we mean the number 0X05 and that would work. But it is a lot of writing for us, as there are a lot of SFRs that we could use. Well thankfully, Microchip has done that for us and saved them in the header file xc.h. All we have to do is tell the compiler that we want to include that file in our program. What happens then, when our program file is compiled, is that the linker software inside the IDE will look through the header file we want to include and find the equates for the phrases or labels we want to use in our programs. That is why we need to have this include instruction in all our programs. It means we can use all the labels for all the SFRs that are in the data sheet for our particular PIC, or any PIC in this xc series.

One important aspect of these labels inside that header file is that they are all written in capital letters. If we wrote porta instead of PORTA, then the program would not compile because the linker program would not be able to find the label porta. Try it and see what happens.

Another test you might want to try is place two forward slashes // in front of the #include <xc/h> line. You will see that the program won't compile correctly, as the compiler will simply ignore the line //#include <xc.h> because it thinks it is just a line of comments. I do use this aspect of commenting out some instructions when I want to debug some of my programs.

Line 10 #define startbutton PORTAbits.RA0

This is another key directive, and the intellisense tries to suggest what we want in the same way as it did with lines 8 and 9. This time we are using the 'c' equivalent of the equate instruction. What we are doing here is telling the compiler software that wherever we use the phrase, in this case, "startbutton," we mean the reference stated here, in this case PORTAbits. RA0. This is identifying one of the eight bits that are in the register PORTA. The register is termed PORTA because it is one of the eight-bit registers that are used by the PIC to connect to the outside world (just like the UK would use the port of Liverpool to connect to the other countries of the world). Also, just as the port of Liverpool would take goods into the UK and send goods out of the UK, then the PORTS of the PIC can take data into and out of the PIC. We will see later how we can make this work.

What we are doing here is simply telling the PIC that we are connecting the start switch to bit0 of PORTA. This will be an input, and in line 17 we will tell the PIC to make this bit and input later. Now, whenever the compiler sees the phrase "startbutton", it will know we mean bit0 of PORTA.

Line 11 #define stopbutton PORTAbits.RA1

This does the same as the previous instruction but now for the stop switch, which is connected to bit1 of PORTA. Again, this bit will be set as an input later.

Line 12 #define LED1 PORTBbits.RB0

This does the same but for the phrase LED1. This time it is allocated to bit0 of PORTB and it will be set as an output later.

We don't need to use these #define statements, as we could simply refer to the switches and outputs by using the bit references (i.e., PORTBbits.RB0 = 1). However, it is both neater and more efficient to use these #defines: neater because we see what the bit is used for in the listing, and more efficient as it makes it simpler if we want to change the I/O bits later. We need only change the I/O here in the one line instead of searching the whole program for the I/O reference and changing them in the listing.

Line 13 void main ()

To appreciate this instruction, you need to know something about how a C program is executed. All C programs are written inside loops, and every C program must have at least one loop. This is that one loop that all C programs must have. That is why it is called the "**main**" loop. The main loop can have small loops inside it, and this one does. The PIC will carry out the instructions written inside the loop sequentially one at a time. When it gets to the last instruction in the main loop, or any loop, it will go back to the first instruction of the loop and start all over again. There is no real halt or stop instruction in a C program. We may insert a stop-type instruction but it is not normal practice.

The main loop can make the PIC jump out of its normal sequential operation and go through other loops written outside this main loop. These other loops are what I call subroutines, although there are others who may refer to them as "functions" or "methods"; to me, an old programmer, they are really subroutines and I will call them that. The main program must "call" these subroutines, at which point the PIC breaks away from the main loop to carry out the instructions of these subroutines. It will return back to the main loop, when it has finished, to the point where the main program called the subroutine. I am making this point at this time because all loops, including the main loop, have keywords at the beginning, which appear in blue text in the IDE, followed by the name, which appears in black bold text in the IDE, for the loop. After the name for the loop, the intellisense automatically adds the opening and closing normal brackets and inserts the cursor insertion point between these normal brackets. The opening and closing normal brackets are inserted there because a loop, especially a subroutine, may require a value, in the form of a variable, to be passed up to it when it is called from within the program. Also, the loop or subroutine may need to pass a value, in the form of a variable, back to wherever it was called from. The keyword "void" written in front of the main loop here, as in line 13, means that this loop will not be passing a value back to wherever it was called from. Being the main loop, it cannot pass anything back to itself. If the loop were going to pass a value back, then we would have to declare it now using a keyword that describes the type of variable it would be passing back. For example, if we declared a subroutine using the following

int delay (unsigned char t)

Then this would mean that this subroutine would be passing a variable of the type int, or integer, back to wherever it was called from. Also, because we have written the term (unsigned char t) inside the normal brackets, this subroutine will expect a value of type unsigned char, to be passed up to it whenever it is called upon.

In line 13, we are just confirming that this loop will not be passing any values back and it will not require any value to be passed up to it; after all, it is the "main loop". Remember, when we created the source file, Microchip automatically inserted the word "void" between the two normal brackets. I personally think this is overkill, as the main loop is not called to like a subroutine, so it will never ask for a value to be passed to it. If I am wrong on this point, then please let me know, but I have always written my programs this way with no problems.

The other important factor about this main loop is that this is where the PIC must go to when it starts the program, as this is where the very first instruction of the program can be found.

Line 14 {

This is the other type of bracket we use in C programs. It is an opening curly bracket, and it will have a corresponding closing curly bracket. In this program, the closing curly bracket is on line 29. The importance of these curly brackets is that all the instructions for the loop are written between these opening and closing curly brackets.

Note that as you type this opening curly bracket the intellisense takes over and writes the closing curly bracket and places the cursor insertion point between the two curly brackets ready for us to type the instructions for that loop.

Line 15 PORTA = 0;

This is really there for safety. What it does is load PORTA with the decimal value of zero. Note that the default radix in the MPLABX editor is decimal. In eight-bit binary, zero is 0b00000000, and so this instruction sets all eight bits in PORTA to a logic '0,' which is 0V. This is just a simple safety step to ensure nothing connected to PORTA can be inadvertently turned on.

Line 16 PORTB =0;

This does exactly the same but this time with PORTB.

I feel I should point out that both these lines end with the semicolon symbol ';.' This is because the semicolon symbol ';' denotes the end of the current instruction. I also want to explain that with lines 10, 11, and 12 there are no semicolons. That is because these lines are not instructions for the PIC. They are directives to the compiler software. There is also no semicolon on line 13. This is because we are creating a loop and the instructions for that loop will be written between the two curly brackets.

Also with these two instructions, on lines 15 and 16, we are expressing the values that should be loaded into the registers PORTA and PORTB in decimal format. Decimal format is the default radix, or number system, that is used in the IDE. If we want to use any other radix, we have to identify it before we state the number. The other two number systems we will use are binary and hexadecimal. They are written as follows.

- PORTB = 0b00000000; the '0b' means binary, where we state the value for all eight bits.
- PORTB = 0X00; the '0X' means hexadecimal, where we use one digit to represent four binary bits. the high nibble and the low nibble.

Note that both formats will do the same as the following: PORTB = 0; (i.e., load all 8 bits in PORTB to a logic '0').

Line 17 TRISA = 0XFF;

This instruction is loading all eight bits in the SFR TRISA with logic '1's. Note that 0X means we are using the hexadecimal format, and 0XFF is the same as 0b11111111 in binary or the same as 255 in decimal. For those who are not too confident with binary and hexadecimal numbers, there is a section in the appendix that explains how they relate to each other.

So, you should be asking: Why are we loading all the bits in the TRISA register with logic '1's? The TRISA register is a special SFR that is linked to the PORTA register. Indeed, each of the PORTS in a PIC has its own TRIS register linked to it. This is because all the PORTS are used to take data into the PIC or take data out of the PIC. However, the PIC has no idea which way we, as programmers, want to use the PORTS. We, as programmers, need to tell the PIC how we want to use the PORTS and their bits. The PORTS are identified as PORT A, B, C, and so on. Each PORT will have a number of individual bits that can be set to take data into the PIC (i.e., be inputs), or to send data out of the PIC (i.e., be outputs). An 8-bit PIC, such as the 16f88 and the 18F4525, has up to 8 bits on each PORT, whereas the 32-bit PICS have up to 16 bits per PORT. The PIC does not know which type you want the bits to be, either input or output.

To enable you to tell the PIC which way you want to use the bits of the PORTS, we have the SFRs, called TRIS. Each TRIS has the same number of bits as the PORT it is associated with. The particular bit of each TRIS maps onto the same bit in the corresponding PORT, as shown in Figure 2-12.

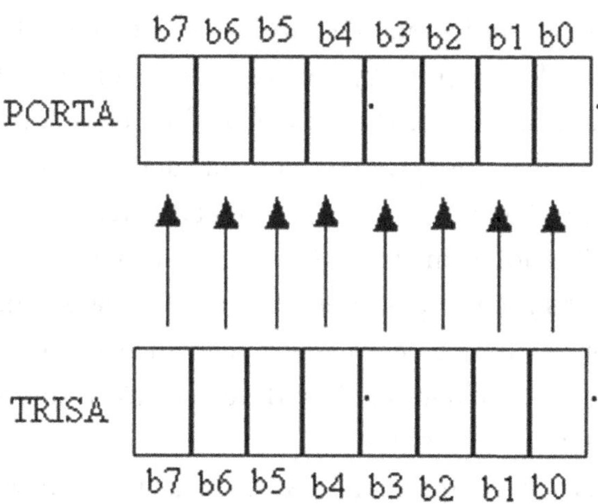

***Figure 2-12.** The mapping of the TRIS onto the PORT*

In this way, the bits of the TRIS can control the corresponding bits of the PORT as to whether or not the bit in the PORT is an input or output. If the bit in the TRIS is a logic '1', then the corresponding bit in the PORT would be an input. If the bit in the TRIS is a logic '0', then the bit in the PORT would be an output.

Knowing this, we should be able to understand that the instruction TRISA = 0XFF; is really setting all the bits in PORTA as inputs.

Line 18 TRISB = 0;

This is setting all the bits in the register TRISB to logic '0'. In this way then, it is setting all the bits in PORTB as outputs.

Line 19 OSCTUNE = 0;

This sets all the bits in another SFR, the OSCTUNE, to logic '0'. This is a control register that controls the fine-tuning of the internal oscillator block. As we don't really need any fine-tuning, we can simply set all the bits to a logic '0'. This is what this instruction does.

Line 20 OSCCON = 0b01111100

When we set the configuration words, we set the internal oscillator block as the source for the primary oscillator. However, we did not set the frequency of the oscillator. There are eight different frequencies we could use, which makes the PIC a very versatile device. It is the OSCCON (OSCillator CONtrol) register that we use to set the frequency of the oscillator block. The following tables have been taken from the data sheet for the PIC16f88. As you move deeper into your work as an embedded programmer, you will have to learn how to read and use data sheets. Every device we use has its own data sheet, and we need to be able to read them to understand how we can use them.

Table 2-1 lists all eight bits of the OSCCON register and what they are used for.

Table 2-1. *The Bits of the OSCON0 Register*

Bit 7	Bit 6	Bit 5	Bit 4	Bit 3	Bit 2	Bit 1	Bit 0
Not used	IRCF2	IRCF1	IRCF0	OSTS	IOFS	SCS1	SCS0
	See Table 2-3			Logic 1 device is running from the primary system clock Logic 0 device is running from the T1OSC or INTRC	Logic 1 internal oscillator is stable Logic 0 internal oscillator not stable	See Table 2-4	

Table 2-2. *Bits 6, 5, and 4 of the OSCON0 Register Setting the Oscillator Frequency*

Bit 6 ICRF2	Bit 5 ICRF1	Bit 4 ICRFO	Oscillator Frequency
0	0	0	31.25kHz
0	0	1	125kHz
0	1	0	250kHz
0	1	1	500kHz
1	0	0	1Mhz
1	0	1	2MHz
1	1	0	4MHz
1	1	1	8MHz

Table 2-3. *The Usage of Bit 1 and Bit0 of OSCCON0 Register to Select Source of Oscillator Frequency Signal*

Bit 1 SCS1	Bit 0 SCS0	Oscillator Source
0	0	Oscillator mode as defined in configuration words
0	1	T1OSC used for system clock
1	0	Internal RC oscillator used for system clock
1	1	Reserved

By studying these tables, we can understand how the eight bits in the OSCCON register will set the frequency of the oscillator block.

- **Bit7** is set to logic '0' as this is not used.
- **Bit6, Bit5, and Bit4** are all set to logic '1,' which sets the frequency to 8MHz. See Table 2-2.
- **Bit3** is set to a logic '1,' which means we are using the primary oscillator as the source for the system clock. However, you should remember that we have set the internal oscillator block as the source for the primary oscillator. This was done with the configuration words. This means that the system clock will use the 8Mhz oscillator as its source. See Table 2-1.
- **Bit2** is a logic '1.' This makes the oscillator output stable. See Table 2-1.
- **Bit1 and Bit0** are both at a logic '0.' This confirms that the oscillator is defined in the configuration words. See Table 2-3.

I hope this shows you how the logic '1's and '0's in these control registers actually do control how the PIC works. We will look at a lot more of these control registers as we progress. Those of you who have used the Arduino have not come across this aspect of setting the oscillator. This is because it has already been done for you and you are not given a real choice.

Line 21 ANSEL = 0;

This simply sets all the bits in this SFR to logic '0.' This is another control register, and it controls whether or not the bits on PORTA, when they are set to inputs, are used as analog or digital inputs. Table 2-4 shows the eight bits in the ANSEL register.

Table 2-4. *The Bits of the ANSEL Register*

Bit7	Bit6	Bit5	Bit4	Bit3	Bit2	Bit1	Bit0
Not used	ANS6	ANS5	ANS4	ANS3	ANS2	ANS1	ANS0

There are seven inputs on PORTA that could be used for either analog or digital inputs. A logic '0' in the bit in the ANSEL means that the corresponding bit in PORTA is set as a digital input. A logic '1' means they would be set as an analog input. When we use analog inputs, the signal at the input is converted to a digital number that represents the value at the input. To do this, the PIC uses an ADC, which converts the analog voltage at the input to a digital number. We will discuss how the ADC works when we write a program that uses analog inputs.

Note that there are not seven ADC circuits in the PIC, as this would take up too much space. There is only one ADC and it is switched onto whichever input is being used to input the analog signal. This is a form of multiplexing.

Therefore, knowing what we know now, we can appreciate that this instruction; ANSEL = 0; is simply setting all the inputs on PORTA to digital.

Line 22 while (1)

This is the first of our test type instructions in C. This is a very special type of test instruction. The "while" type test instruction is saying "while the result of the test is true do what I tell you to do". The test will be described inside the normal brackets that follow the while statement. However, this while instruction is a very special test as it is simply the number '1' inside the normal brackets.

To appreciate what this is doing, we will look at a simpler while test. The example is as follows:

```
while (PORTAbits.RA0 == 0)
{
    PORTBbits.RB0 = 1;
    PORTBbist.RB1 = 1;
}
```

This test is asking whether the logic on bit0 of PORTA is a logic 0. If the result of the test is true (i.e., the logic on bit0 of PORTA is '0'), then the PIC must do the instructions written between the two curly brackets (i.e., it will make the logic on bit0 and bit1 of PORTB both logic '1's). This will actually put 5V out on the two bits of PORTB and so turn on whatever is connected to them.

First, there is a difference in that the test inside the brackets uses two '= =' signs. That is because it is asking whether the logic has become equal to 0. When we use just one '=' equal sign, however, we are forcing the logic on that bit to go to the logic we state in the instruction.

Next, it should be fairly easy to see that there is a test written between the normal brackets of the while instruction. Of course, the logic on bit0 of PORTA will either be a '1' or a '0' and so the result of the test will be true, in this case, when bit0 of PORTA is a logic '0'. It will be false if the logic on the bit was actually a logic '1'. In this way, it is easy to appreciate that this instruction is of the type "while the test is true do what I say". However, when we look at the instruction on line 22;

while (1)

It is not so easy to see that it is of the same type of test. Well, it is of the same type and to appreciate that it fits the format, we have to understand how the "while the test is true do what I say" works. With this type of test, as with all tests we will use, the PIC will create a flag or bit where it will store the result of the test. If the test is true, then this bit will be set to a logic '1'. If the result of the test is false, then the PIC will store a logic '0' in the result bit. With our instruction "while (1)", the result bit will be automatically set to a logic '1'. It does not test anything but the result bit will always be a logic '1'. This means that the PIC will always carry out the instructions that it must do if the test was true. That is why this instruction is sometimes referred to as the "forever loop". The PIC will continuously carry out the instructions associated with the while (1) test. The instructions that the PIC will always carryout will be written between the two curly brackets that follow; in this case, between lines 23 and 28.

I know this is a very wordy description of this simple but powerful instruction, but I do think you need to appreciate how it works.

What we are trying to achieve, and do achieve, is to make sure the PIC does not carry out the instructions on lines 15 to 21 again. Remember we said that when the PIC gets to the end of the loop, it will go back to the beginning of the loop and start again. That would mean that if we didn't have this inner "forever loop", the PIC would again set up the TRISA, TRISB, and other control registers again. There is no need for the PIC to carry out those instruction again, so the use of the "forever loop" in this way prevents that waste.

I hope this explanation does show you how this instruction works and why we have used it here. Please take the time to read through it again; when you start to fully understand how instructions work you can really learn how to use them.

Line 23 {

This is the opening curly bracket of what you should do in this forever loop. The closing bracket is on line 28.

Line 24 while (startswitch);

Here we are again with another "while the test is true do what I say"; most programs will use them. The test is stated in a special way. It is saying while (startbutton') which is the same as saying 'while (startbutton ==1). I interpret the two '==' equal signs as meaning becomes equal to and so we are saying 'while (startbutton becomes equal to 1).

So that is the test; it is testing to see if startbutton is at a logic '1.' To understand what we mean by 'startbutton,' you should remember that on line 10 we defined the phrase startbutton to mean PORTAbits.RA0. So, we are really testing 'while (PORTAbits RA0 becomes equal to 1). I hope you now understand the test, but what do we do if the test is true and contrarily if the test is untrue? We have to write the instructions that the PIC must do when the test is true between the closing normal bracket and the end of the instruction. You now need to remember that when we looked at lines 14 and 15, we discussed the use of the semicolon, ';.' This is used to signify the end of the current instruction. It has to be used with every instruction, as all instructions have an end. There is a semicolon with this instruction. It is placed immediately after the closing normal bracket. But that means there are no instructions written there, between the closing normal bracket and the semicolon, that tell the PIC what to do if the test is true. That is because we want the PIC to do nothing if the test is true. No, I am not being crazy. You have to appreciate that the startbutton, or bit0 of PORTA, is connected to a switch that we use to start the process, hence the name startbutton. The switch will either be switched to ground (i.e., 0V), or VCC (i.e., 5V). In this way, the logic will be either logic '0' (i.e., 0V, or logic '1' +5V). The way we have wired both the start switch and the stop switch is that if they are not pressed, the voltage at the input will be 5V (i.e., logic '1'). If we press the switch to start the process, then the voltage will go momentarily to 0V (i.e., a logic '0').

This means that while the logic on bit0 of PORTA is a logic '1' then the start button has not been pressed and so the PIC must do nothing. When the switch is pressed and the logic goes to a logic '0', then the test will be untrue and the PIC can move onto the next instruction in the program.

So, this instruction is simply getting the PIC to wait until the start switch is pressed. I know I could have just written this last statement, but I believe it is important you fully understand the mechanics of every instruction you use.

Line 25 LED1 = 1;

This will force bit0 of PORTB to a logic '1', note the use of just one '=' sign. This will set the voltage at that bit to +5V. Then, because the LED is connected to this bit, the LED will turn on. You should appreciate that in line 12 we defined the phrase LED1 to mean bit0 of PORTB.

Line 26 while (stopbutton);

Just as with line 24, this makes the PIC wait for the logic, this time, on bit1 of PORTA, to go to a logic '0' before it will carry on with the rest of the program. In this way, we are making the PIC wait until someone presses the stop switch.

Line 27 LED1 = 0;

This simply sets the logic on bit0 of PORTB to a logic '0' (i.e., 0V). This then turns the LED1 off.

Line 28 }

This is the closing curly bracket of the forever loop.

Line 29 }

This is the closing curly bracket of the main loop.

If you now compare the program listing to the flowchart shown in Figure 2-3, I hope you can see how the instructions relate to the symbols in the flowchart. Lines 8 to 21 relate to the initialize block. Line 24 is the first decision box. Line 25 is the first process block. Line 26 is the second decision block. Line 27 is the second process block. It is useful to construct a good flowchart.

Running Program 2.1

In the past, I have gone through simulating some programs from within MPLABX. This is possible, but really the monitoring tools within MPLABX are more suitable for debugging a program. Therefore, I will restrict my use of these tools to show you how we can debug a program and confirm some aspects of C instructions. This will be done later in the book in chapter 14.

That still leaves us with the problem of running our programs. Really, you will need a prototype board that is versatile enough to allow you to run a variety of programs. You can buy some ready-made development boards, and they range from as little as £15:00 to around £70:00 or more. There is such a large range of development boards that it is pretty difficult to know which one to choose. Before you buy a board, you should think about what you need to use within your programs. Does the prototype board have them already on board, or can you simply connect the peripherals you want to use to the board? Here are some of the main peripherals you will be using in this book:

- A set of switches which can switch either 5V or 0V to the inputs of the PIC. The switches will use a series resistor, usually about 1kΩ, to limit the current through the switch. I think you will need about four switches. Some boards supply switches but they will have already been allocated to inputs on the PIC; see Figure 2-17.
- A set of LEDs that can be connected to outputs of the PIC. Again, these LEDs will have a series resistor to limit the current through the LED to around 20mA. A 220Ω resistor should be fine for this. I think you can manage with at least four but six LEDs or eight may be better. Again, the off-the-shelf boards will have these LEDs already allocated to outputs; see Figure 2-17.
- A LCD, liquid crystal display, usually one that has two lines of 16 characters. These can be used in either four-bit mode or eight-bit mode. Again, an off-the-shelf board that has one of these will already have it allocated to a PORT and their outputs.

These are the main peripherals that an off-the-shelf prototype board should have. Some boards may have more peripherals such as a temperature sensor or a 32.85kHz crystal for an RTCC (real-time clock circuit), but these would increase the cost. In the front matter of the book, we looked at the peripherals that we are going to use in this book. All those can be bought as separate components and so can the switches, LEDs, and LCDs listed previously.

I have used, and I am still using, the PICdem2 plus development board from Microchip; see Figure 2-21. It cost around £60:00 when I bought it, and it's a pretty good board. However, Microchip no longer supplies this board, so it might be difficult for you to get hold of it.

However, spending that sort of money may be off-putting, especially as you don't really need anything too fancy. All you want is a board you can put your PIC in and remove it. You also need to get easy access to the inputs and outputs and be able to program your PIC without too much trouble. I have made two boards of my own that do just that. One is for the PIC16F88, or really any eight-bit PIC that can fit an 18-pin dual in-line socket. The other is for my PIC18F4525 or any 40-pin dual in-line PIC. Both these boards can use the PicKit3 programming tool which uses ICSP. If you intend to use different PICs, you should check that the ICSP pins are allocated to the same pins. The three main pins for ICSP are as follows:

- The MCLR (Master Clear), which for the PIC16F88 is connected to pin4 of the PIC and for the PIC18f4525 is connected to pin1.
- The PGD (Programming Data), which for the PIC16F88 is connected to pin13 and for the PIC18F4525 is connected to pin40.
- The PGC (Programming Clock), which for the PIC16F88 is connected to pin12 and for the PIC18F4525 is connected to pin39.

I have built my two boards on vero board, and I am including the circuit diagrams, the vero board planning diagrams, and the parts list. These homemade boards give me total flexibility over the inputs and outputs that I can connect any of the peripherals to. It also reduces the cost. Assuming you are fairly good at soldering (I am no expert myself), you should be able to build your own boards and get them running quite easily. However, you need to be very careful when you build them. I have some advice that you might want to read through in the appendix concerning building these boards. I can give no guarantee that what you make will work except that I have used both my boards successfully with all the programs in this book. I also build my own interface boards for the peripherals. I will include all the circuit diagrams, vero board plans, and parts lists for all those boards as well. If you are not used to soldering, then I suggest you try building some of the peripheral boards first. The switch board and LED board as detailed in this chapter are quite easy to do. Therefore, perhaps you should start with those boards first. Also, the board for the four seven-segment displays that is detailed in chapter 3 is fairly simple, and so that is also a good one to gain more experience with. If you take your time in building the boards, then you should be able to save yourself a lot of money and gain some useful understanding of electronics and experience with soldering techniques.

If you really want to try simulating the programs, then PROTEUS is a good ECAD (electronic computer-aided design) package. PROTEUS is an excellent ECAD software that I used when I was lecturing, but it must have the ability to simulate eight-bit micros and it is not free; however, it is one of the best ones I have used.

The PIC16F88 Development Board

As Program 2.1 we are writing is for the 16F88 PIC, we will look at the development board I have built. I will add a section at the end on how to use the PICdem2 plus board from Microchip.

The complete vero board I have built for the PIC16F88 development board is shown in Figure 2-13.

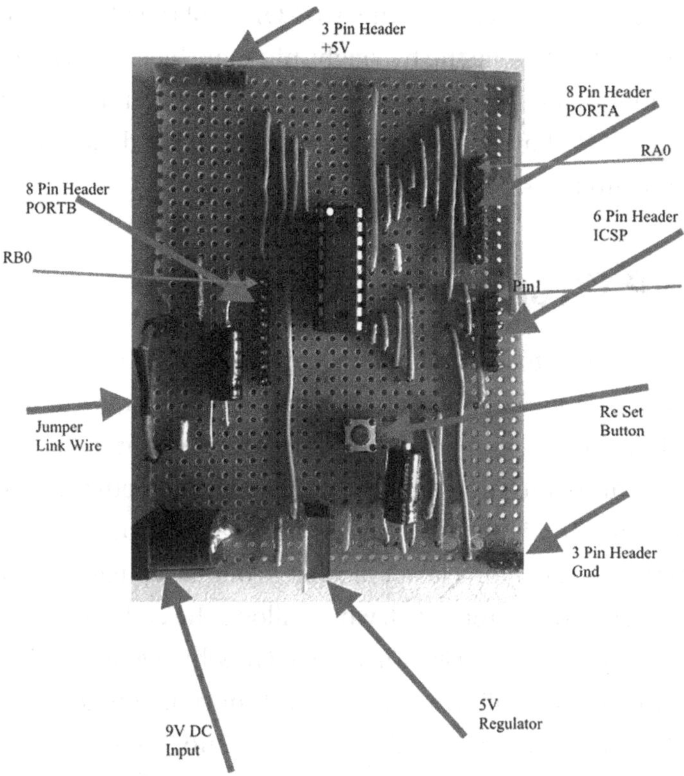

Figure 2-13. *The PIC16F88 development board*

The white dot is there to show which pin is pin1 on the PIC. If you try to build this board yourself, you need to ensure that both ground pins on the DC input jack are soldered together. This is to give a solid ground reference to the board. Figure 2-13 suggests a 9V DC input but 12V can be used as an alternative. However, you should read the data sheet for the 5V regulator to determine the maximum DC input voltage. The 5V regulator I have used is the MC7805, which has a maximum input voltage of 35V.

This board gives full access to the two PORTS of the PIC, and so access to all the I/O on the PIC, via the two eight-pin male headers. There is a six-pin male header that is used to connect the PICkit3 or 4 for programming the PIC using ICSP. I have also added two three-pin headers to give access to the ground and the +5V.

The ICSP Circuit

You don't really need to understand how this aspect of the circuit of the ICSP circuit works, but it's not too difficult to understand and all knowledge is useful. So, you can skip this part if you want to.

The ICSP part of the circuit may be a little overprotective, as there are two diodes in the circuit. Refer to the circuit diagram shown in Figure 2-15. The diode D1 is to allow for a faster discharge of the capacitor C1. This happens when the +5V is removed, which allows the cathode of D1 to go to 0V. As the anode of D1 is connected to C1, which will have been charged up to +5V, D1 is allowed to close and short out the resistor R1, thus allowing C1 to discharge quicker than if D1 were not there.

When the programming tool starts to program the PIC, it delivers a high voltage of around 13V to the MCLR pin of the PIC. This is to put the PIC into the programming mode. The diode D2 is there to prevent this high voltage from forcing a current to flow into the 5V regulator.

I have added the two jumpers to allow a link wire to be connected once the PIC has been programmed. This actually shorts out D2. The reason why I have done this is because with D2 in circuit, there is no path to the +5V via R1; see the circuit diagram in Figure 2-15. This means that the MCLR pin is what is termed "floating", which means it can go to an unknown voltage. This is not a problem when the PITkit3 is connected, as that will set the voltage on the MCLR pin. However, when the PITkit3 is removed, the MCLR pin will float. Also, when you close the reset pin, it will not connect the MCLR to 0V, which is what is required to reset the PIC. Therefore, once the PITkit3 has been removed you must connect the link to short out the diode D2. This connects the MCLR pin to the bottom of R1. As no current is, at present, flowing through R1, then the voltage at the MCLR pin will go to 5V, as no voltage is dropped across R1. This is required when NOT resetting the PIC. Now when the reset switch is pressed, a ground is connected to the MCLR pin, which resets the PIC. The resistor R1 is there to limit the current flowing through the switch to around 1mA and so prevent the switch from burning out. You must remove this link when you are trying to program the PIC.

I know you don't need to understand this to program the PIC, but as you will be connecting the PIC to electrical circuits, you should really develop your understanding of electronics.

The vero board plan for this development board is shown in Figure 2-14.

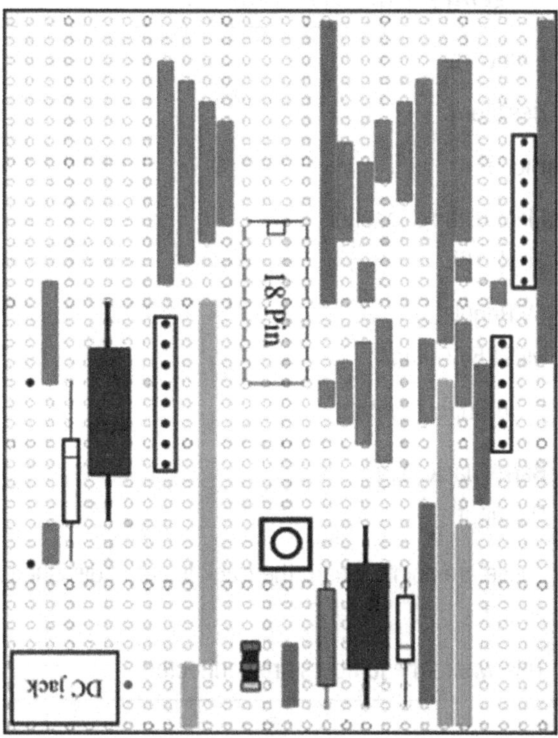

Figure 2-14. *The vero board plan for the PIC16F88 development board*

If you are happy with soldering components to a vero board, then building your own board could save you money. You must be aware that you build it at your own risk. However, as the voltage is less than 50V, as long as you are careful the risks are small, but I cannot give you any guarantee the board will work except that I am using both my homebuilt development boards and peripheral boards for all the programs in this book and they work fine.

I do have some advice when building your boards in the appendix and you might find it useful to read this. Therefore, if you are going to try and build your own boards, please read this first.

The legend for the vero board plan is shown in Table 2-5.

Table 2-5. *The Legend for the Vero Board Plan*

Symbol	Description
	Link Wire
	Resistor
	Diode
	Electrolytic Capacitor 10µF 16V
	5V Regulator MC785V 500mA
	Push Button Switch
DC jack	Barrel Jack Plug DC Input
	These are points where the track is cut to disconnect parts of the circuit
	This where the jumpers are connected.

Track cutting is done with a small handheld drill bit, and it is used to break the continuity of the copper track on the vero board. This is done to isolate different parts of the circuit from one another.

The circuit diagram for this project is shown in Figure 2-15. It is only the basic minimum circuit for the project, and the mains input and 5V regulator are not shown. The "U2 5" is the 5V supply to the PIC and the rest of the circuit. So, this is really made up of the mains input and the 5V regulator. In the vero board plan, the mains input is from an AC adapter that gives out a 9V DC output. This is connected to the board via a 4mm jack plug that plugs into the DC jack plug on the vero board.

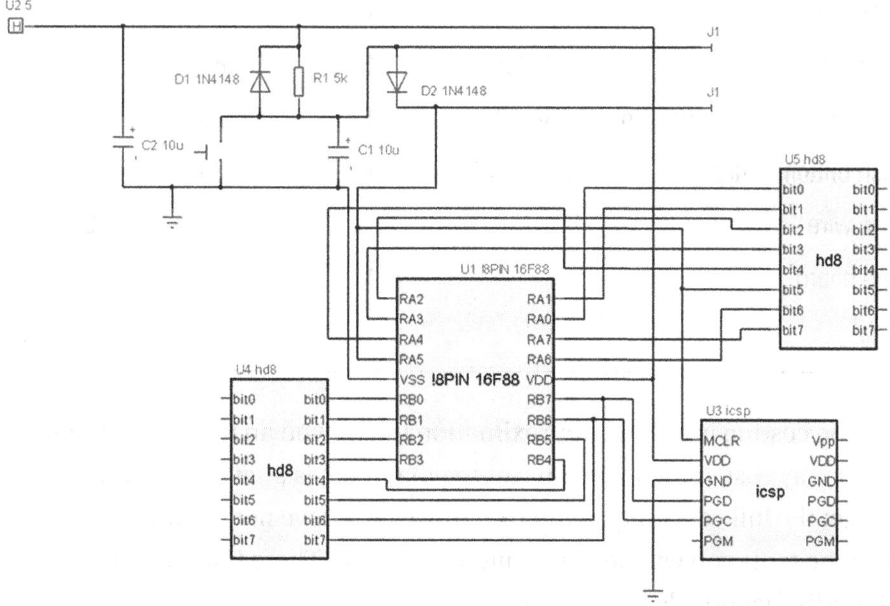

Figure 2-15. *The circuit diagram for the PIC16F88 development board*

I am suggesting that building your own development board could possibly save you money. Therefore, it would be a good idea to give you a parts list with costing for the board. This is shown in Table 2-6.

Table 2-6. *The Parts List and Costing for the PIC16F88 Development Board*

Item	Part Number	Quantity	Unit cost1	Total
18-Pin DIL Socket	4818 3000CP	1	0.4	0.4
PIC16F88		1	3.25	3.25
10µF 16V Cap Electrolytic	ECA1CAD100X	2	0.16	0.32
Diode	1n1414	2	0.1	0.2
5kΩ resistor		1	0.04	0.04
5V regulator	L7905CV	1	0.6	0.6
40pin strip male header pins	83-15402	1	0.25	0.25
Push button switch	B3F 1020	1	0.28	0.28
Misc wire			0.2	0.2
Vero board		1	0.4	0.4
Total				5.94

The costing is only an approximation to give you an idea of what the board may cost, but I hope you can see that there is a saving to make and you get the full versatility of the I/O. However, I have not included the cost of all the tools you will need to build your board. There is a section in the appendix that details this aspect.

In all further programs, I will be programming the PICs on my homemade development boards. You will have to adapt the I/O and possible polarities to match your own board. Really, this book is about understanding the 'C' programming instructions and how they work. After reading this book, you should have an understanding of what you are doing and be able to adapt the programs accordingly. I am only discussing my development boards, as you will have to use a board to test your programs. When dealing with the Arduino, you have to buy a development board to start with, and a lot of your choices are made for you.

Testing Program 2.1

To test Program 2.1, we will use the switch board and the LED board. If you are using an off-the-shelf development board you may have to change the allocation of the I/O accordingly. The switch board is shown in Figure 2-16.

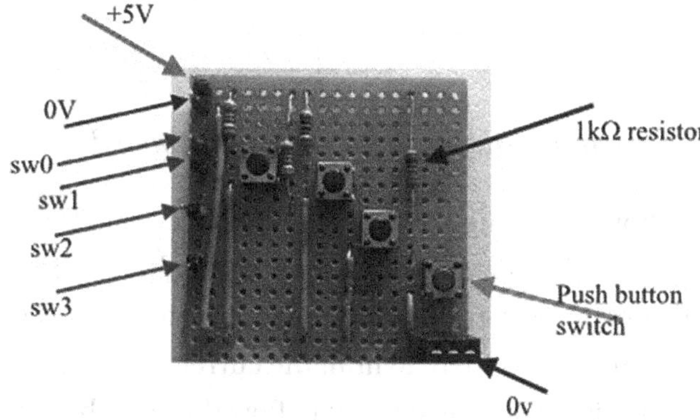

***Figure 2-16.** The four-switch interface board*

The circuit diagram for this switch board is shown in Figure 2-17.

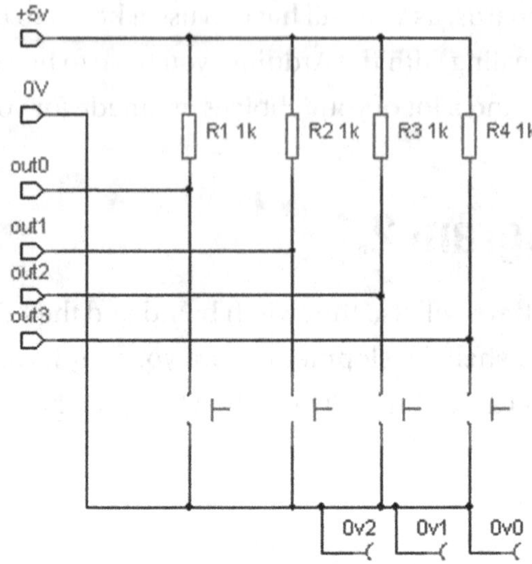

***Figure 2-17.** The circuit diagram for the switch board*

The circuit shows that when the switches are left open, the voltage at the output of the board, which becomes an input to the PIC, is 5V, as no current flows through the 1k resistors. When the switch closes, the output goes to 0V. The 1k resistor is there to limit the current flowing through the switch to 5mA. This is a very safe current to flow through the switch and so it will not burn out, which it would do if too much current were allowed to flow through it.

The four-LED board is shown in Figure 2-18.

***Figure 2-18.** The four-LED interface board*

The circuit diagram for this LED board is shown in Figure 2-19.

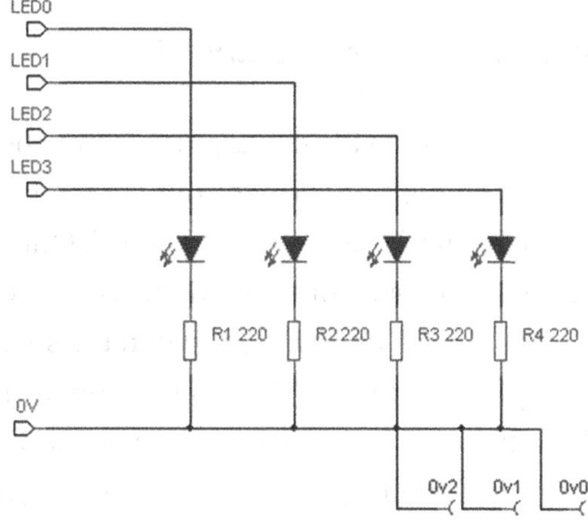

***Figure 2-19.** The circuit diagram for the four-LED board*

To turn the LED on, we need to supply 5V to the anode of the LED. This is done by setting the output of the PIC to a logic '1.' Note that the 220Ω resistor is there to limit the current flowing through the LED to around 18mA. This is enough to get enough brightness on the LED without being too much and risking burning out the LED.

In Program 2.1, the two switches, sw0 and sw1, are connected to bit0 and bit1 of the u5 hd8 connector shown in Figure 2-15. The LED0 pin was connected to bit0 of the u4 hd8 connector shown in Figure 2-20.

Figure 2-20. *Complete setup for Program 2.1*

Finally, Figure 2-21 shows the PICdem2 plus off-the-shelf prototype board from Microchip. It shows how we can connect the PICkit3 programming tool and the available I/O on the board. One concern you need to be aware of is that the push button switches connect 0V to the input when the switch is closed, or operated. When the switch is left open, or not operated, the input goes to +5V. The switches on my homemade board operate in the same way. If the switches on your prototype board work the other way around, then you would have to change the while (startbutton); to while (!startbutton);. You would have to change the stopbutton in the same way.

Figure 2-21. *The PICdem2 plus development board from Microchip*

As the I/O on the PICdem2 plus board is different from what I have used with my own board, I had to make the following changes to the program:

```
#define startbutton PORTAbits.RA4
#define stopbutton  PORTBbits.RB0
#define LED1        PORTBbits.RB1
void main()
{
PORTA = 0;
PORTB = 0;
TRISA = 0XFF;
TRISB = 0B00000001;
```

Note that the use of the #define directives made these changes easier. Also, I have to set bit0 of TRISB to a logic '1.' This is to make bit0 of PORTB an input, as the stopbutton has now been connected to it.

Downloading Our Program

We are now ready to initially test the syntax of our program to make sure it is correct, then download the program to our development board.

To test the syntax of our program, we can simply click the mouse on the blue hammer symbol in the main menu bar. This will test the syntax of your listing and show the results in the output window, as shown in Figure 2-22.

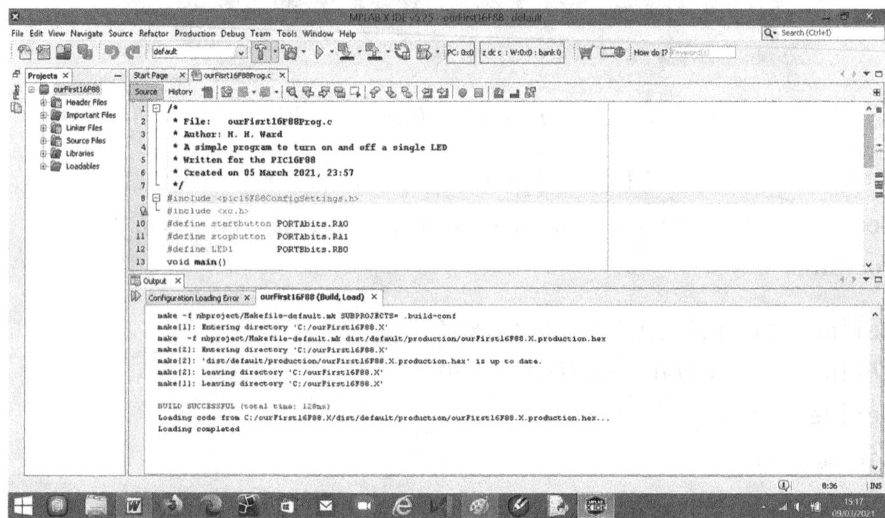

Figure 2-22. *Using the build icon to test the syntax of the source file*

If there are any errors, then they will be listed in the output window written in blue text. If you scroll to find the first error and click the mouse on the blue text, then the software should take you to that error in your source file. Note that the error may not be on that particular line; it could be on the preceding line, so check both lines carefully. However, assuming you have written exactly what is in Listing 2-1, then there should be no errors.

Note also that you may get warnings written in blue. These are not as serious as errors. Also, you may still get some red warning signals in the source file. If the text in the output window states that the build was successful, then there should be no problems running the program. This means we can go on to download the program.

To download the program, you need to connect your programming tool to your laptop and your development board. I will be using the PICkit3 programming tool. So, connect the USB end of the PICkit3 to the laptop and the six-pin female socket end to the six-pin male header on your development board. You must make sure that pin1, marked by the small white arrow on the PICkit3, goes onto the correct pin1 on your six-pin header on your development board. See Figure 2-13 to find pin1 on my development board.

Now that you have connected the PICkit3, simply click the green downward-facing arrow in the main menu bar. The software will again check the syntax of your source file, and then it will connect to your programming tool. If this is the first time you have connected the PICkit3 tool to your PIC, a pop-up window should appear as shown in Figure 2-23. It is just asking you to confirm that you are using a 5V PIC; some PICs only use 3.3V for their supply.

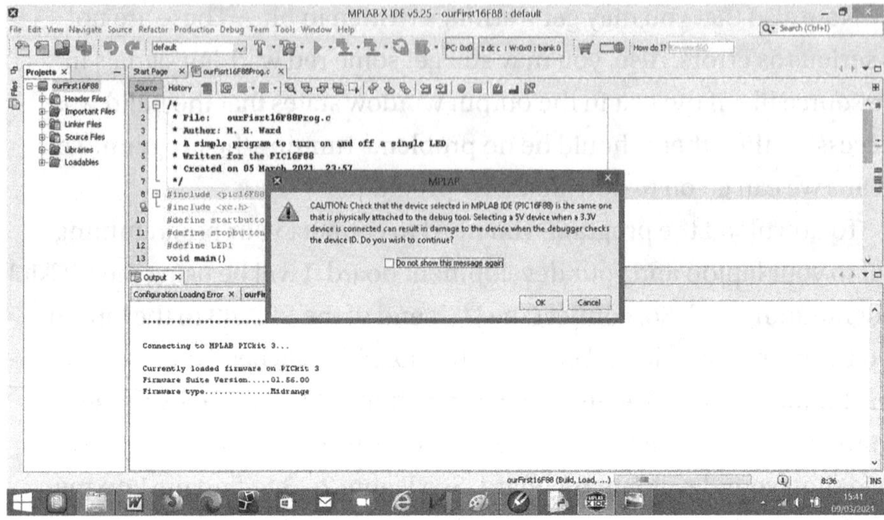

Figure 2-23. *The caution pop-up window*

Simply click "OK" and the software will continue the download. Finally, the output window will display the verification message, as shown in Figure 2-24, and your source file will have been downloaded to your PIC.

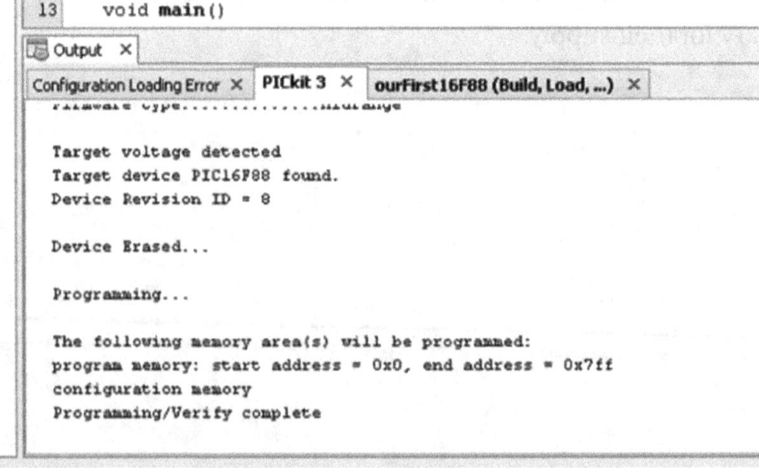

Figure 2-24. *The verification window*

Figure 2-25 shows the PICkit3 connected to my laptop and development board. Note the orientation of the PICkit3 tool to ensure pin1 is connected correctly on my development board. Also, I have removed the small link wire that is used to short out D2. You must remove this link wire before you download your program.

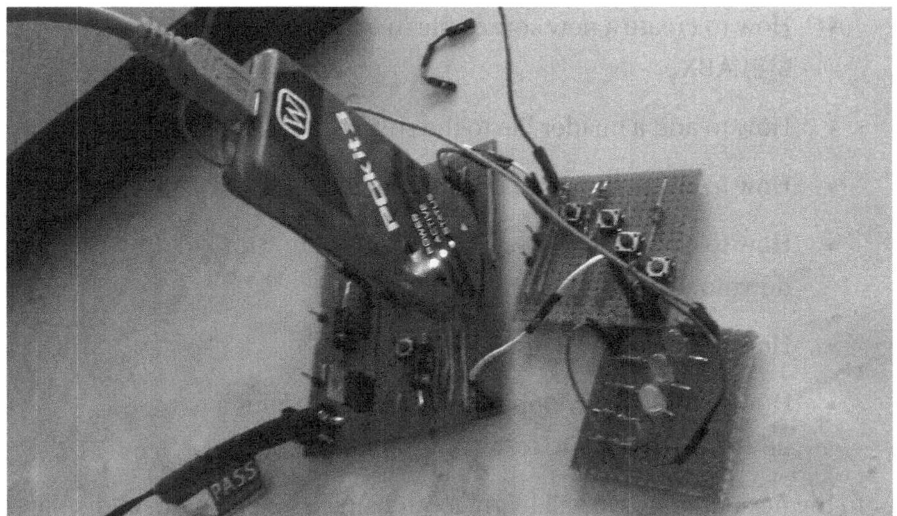

***Figure 2-25.** Connecting The PICkit3 programming tool*

You should now be able to test Program 2.1 by momentarily pressing the start button to turn the LED on. Then, press the stop button to turn the LED off. Assuming it works as it should, you should give yourself a pat on the back. If you have a partner, like my wife, they will not be overwhelmed, but you know you have achieved an awful lot and you have also learned how it all works. You are now ready to go on to bigger and better things.

Summary

In this chapter we have studied the following:

- Algorithm
- How to use a flowchart
- How to create a new source file in a project within MPLABX
- How to add a header file to the source file
- How to check the syntax of the source file
- How to choose and connect a programming tool to download a program
- How to download a program
- How to build a development board and useful peripheral boards to test a program

In the next chapter, we will learn about using a seven-segment display. We will then go on to run a peripheral using four seven-segment displays. We will learn about how we can use the timers within the PIC to create a variable delay and so control the timing of operations of our PIC. We will then move on to write a program to control a small, but useful, stepper motor.

CHAPTER 3

The Seven-Segment Display and the Stepper Motor

In this chapter, we will look at seven-segment displays and learn what they are and how they work. We will write a program to control the display on a single seven-segment display and then move on to a program to control a collection of four seven-segment displays. We will learn about the timers in a PIC and how to use them to create a variable delay. We will then move on to look at a simple stepper motor and write a program to drive it clockwise and anticlockwise. After reading this chapter, you will know how to use a delay and how to control and use a seven-segment display and drive a 5V DC stepper motor.

Program 3.1: Controlling a Seven-Segment Display

Turning an LED (light-emitting diode) on or off is not very exciting, but for a first program it is a good place to start. With the next program, we are going to look at something that might be a bit more useful. It could be used to make electronic dice.

H. H. Ward, *Programming Arduino Projects with the PIC Microcontroller*,
https://doi.org/10.1007/978-1-4842-7230-5_3

Seven-Segment Displays

This is a device that can be used to display numbers. A typical seven-segment display is shown in Figure 3-1.

Figure 3-1. *A typical seven-segment display*

There are actually seven LEDs; hence the name for the device. Some displays may have eight LEDs, with the extra LED being used for a decimal place, or dot. The LEDs can be switched on in different arrangements to display the numbers 0 to 9 and if required the letters A, B, C, D, E, and F as in the hexadecimal number system.

They come in a range of colors: red, green, blue, yellow, and white. They can also come in extra-bright LEDs. The display can be either common anode or common cathode.

Common Anode Seven-Segment Display

With this type of seven-segment display, the anodes of all seven LEDs are connected together, hence they are common. The anodes are usually connected to a +5V supply. To turn each LED on, the cathode of each LED must be connected, independently, to ground or 0V. However, to limit the current that flows through the LEDs, and so prevent them from burning out, a resistor is inserted between the cathode and ground. This arrangement is shown in Figure 3-2.

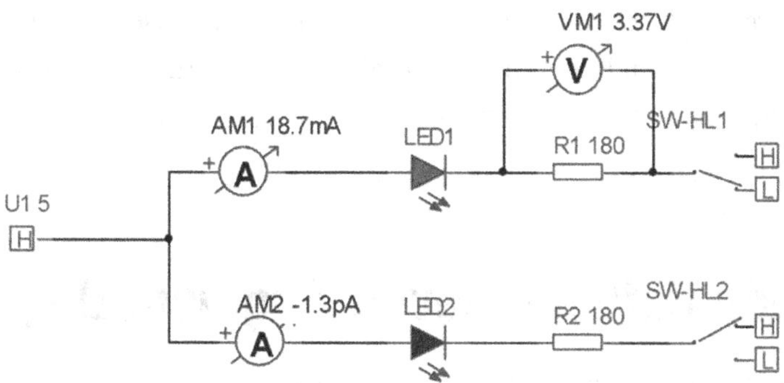

Figure 3-2. *The basic circuit to turn on an LED in common anode*

In Figure 3-2, the LED1 is shown illuminated. This is because the cathode is switched to 'L,' a low voltage, which is ground or 0V. The full 5V supply is divided between the LED and the resistor. Another reason we need a resistor is to drop the extra 3.37V. The voltmeter is shown measuring 3.37V across the resistor R1. The remaining 1.63V must be dropped across the LED. The value of the resistor is chosen to limit the current flowing through the LED to its maximum. From the data sheet, this is around 25mA. However, a typical value of 20mA is good enough. Using this typical value, an expression for resistance (R) can be derived from Ohm's law as follows:

$$I = \frac{V}{R}$$

$$\therefore R = \frac{V}{I}$$

$$\therefore R = \frac{3.37}{20E^{-3}} = 168.5\Omega$$

If we use the standard E12 series of resistors, then there is no 168.5Ω resistor, so we must use a 180Ω, which is the next-higher value. Note that you should always go higher so as to limit the current more not less.

In Figure 3-2, LED2 is not illuminated. This is because it is turned off, as the cathode is switched to a 'H' or high voltage, in this case 5V. For any diode (including an LED) to be turned on, the cathode must be at a lower voltage than the anode.

Common Cathode Seven-Segment Display

This type of arrangement is shown in Figure 3-3.

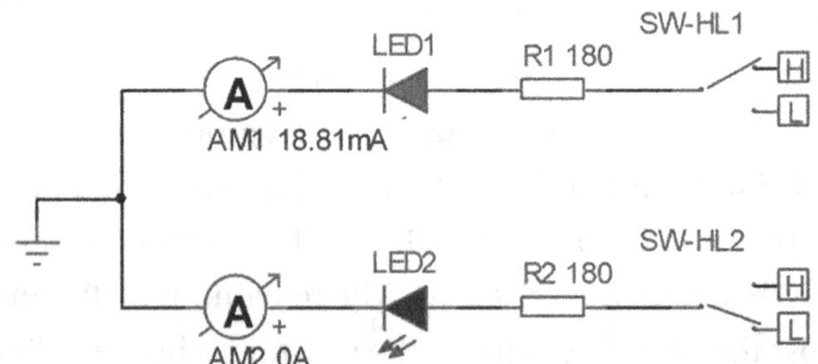

Figure 3-3. *The common cathode arrangement*

With this arrangement, the cathodes of all the LEDs (only two are shown in Figure 3-3) are connected to ground or 0V. To turn an LED on, its anode must be connected to, in this case, 5V. This is controlled by two switches, as shown in Figure 3-3. The two resistors are inserted between the anodes and the 5V to limit the current flowing through the LEDs.

Arrangement for a Common Anode Seven-Segment Display

Figure 3-4 shows how the seven LEDs are arranged on the display, and Table 3-1 shows which cathode of the LEDs needs to be connected to the ground via the resistor to display the appropriate number.

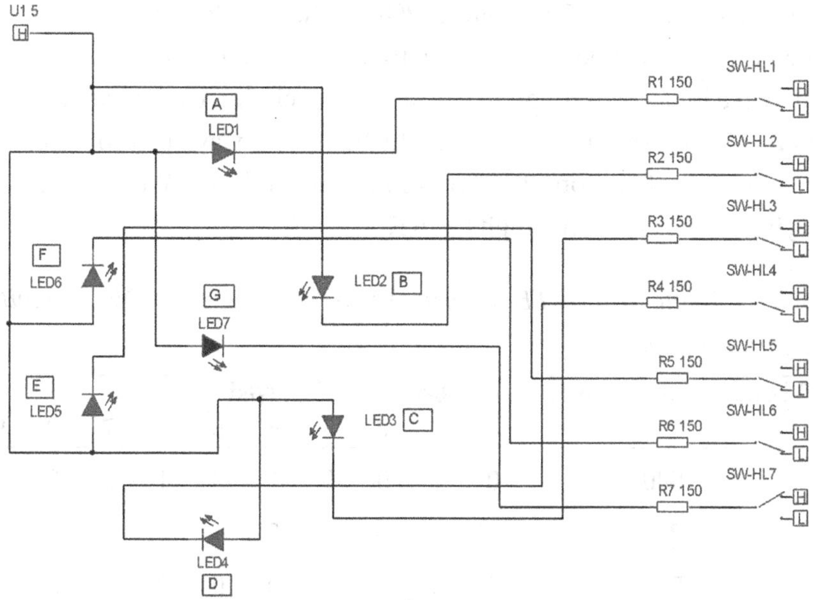

Figure 3-4. *The circuit of a common anode seven-segment display*

Figure 3-4 is an attempt to show you the circuitry of the common anode display. The seven LEDs are laid out to form a ring going from LED 'A' to LED 'F' in six LEDs. Then there is the seventh LED, LED 'G,' which lies central to the display. Figure 3-4 shows the six outer LEDs turned on by closing their respective switches to connect their respective cathodes to ground, or 0V, via the series resistor. This means those six LEDs are switched on and current flows through them. It is hoped that you can see that this forms the number zero.

Controlling the Display with the PIC

You can buy seven-segment displays that have their own driver which will change a four-bit value, which can produce numerals from 0 to 9 and also letters A, B, C, D, E, and F, to turn on and off the seven LEDs in the display. We won't use that type of display as we will be using the PIC to control the display. We will connect R1 to bit0 of PORTB, R2 to bit2 of PORTB, and so on with R7 connected to bit6. Then to turn on the respective LED, we would load a logic '0' or 0V on to the bit. To switch the respective LED off, we would load a logic '1' or +5V on to the bit. In this way, the numbers 0 to 9 can be controlled from PORTB as shown in Table 3-1. We won't be displaying the hexadecimal digits A to F.

Table 3-1. *Logic at PORTB to Drive the Seven-Segment Display with a Common Anode*

LED ID Letter	Bit of PORTB	Number to Be Displayed									
		0	1	2	3	4	5	6	7	8	9
A	Bit0	0	1	0	0	1	0	1	0	0	0
B	Bit1	0	0	0	0	0	1	1	0	0	0
C	Bit2	0	0	1	0	0	0	0	0	0	0
D	Bit3	0	1	0	0	1	0	0	1	0	1
E	Bit4	0	1	0	1	1	1	0	1	0	1
F	Bit5	0	1	1	1	0	0	0	1	0	0
G	Bit6	1	1	0	0	0	0	0	1	0	0
DOT	Bit7	0	0	0	0	0	0	0	0	0	0

Note that it does not matter what logic is set to bit7, as it is connected to the dot on the display. I have just left it at a logic '0', which would turn the dot on. If the display has a decimal point, then bit7 would turn it on or off. The table shows how the PIC can control the display.

Seven-Segment Display Program

All good programs start with an algorithm. The algorithm is basically a description in your own words of how you are going to get the PIC to carry out the requirements of the program. This program is simply to get a seven-segment display to count down from 9 to 0. The count will decrement once every second. The display will then go back to 9 and the countdown will start again.

Just to show you the difference between common anode and common cathode, this program will use a common cathode seven-segment display. This means that we won't be using the logic shown in Table 3-1.

Algorithm for Program 3.1

There is no defined format of how you construct the algorithm; I just like to create a bullet list as follows.

- We will make it a variable delay. The program will simply decrement the number displayed on the display every second from 9 to 0. Then repeat the sequence.
- The delay subroutine will require a global variable 'n' and a local variable 't'.
- To initiate the start of the count, the program will wait for a start button to be momentarily pressed to logic '0'. The program will start the count with the display set at 9.
- There will be a stop button that will halt the count at the current value on the display.

- We will need two digital inputs for the two switches. We will use bit0 of PORTA for the start button and bit1 of PORTA for the stop button.
- There is no need for any analog inputs; therefore we don't need to turn the ADC on. Note that we will need to make all inputs digital inputs.
- As the seven-segment display requires eight outputs, we will connect the display to PORTB, which will be set to all outputs.
- We will use the internal oscillator block for the source of the clock, as this saves I/O and the cost of a crystal.
- We will be using the 8MHz internal crystal and TMR0 set to count at 7182.5Hz.
- There is no need for anything else, so really a basic PIC will do the job. However, this book is based on the PIC16F88 and the PIC18F4525. We will use the PIC16f88 for this program. I have added the last item in the list to try and show you that you can use the algorithm to decide which PIC you should use for your project. This could save money; you must remember that in industry your project could go into production and if you can save 10 cents by choosing a more basic PIC, then you should.

Note The stop button should be pressed for a long time because the PIC will respond to the stop button only while it is carrying out the instruction on lines 48, 51, and so on. This is where it carries out the instruction if(!stopbutton) goto start; the PIC only asks the question for a split second. It then will carry out the 1-second delay. We need to keep the stop button pressed, as the PIC could be stuck in this 1-second delay subroutine, or somewhere else in the instructions, and so it could miss the action of us pressing the stop button. This is a very important problem you need to be aware of. We will see later how we can overcome this problem with the use of interrupts.

Flowchart for Program 3.1

As previously mentioned, it is always a good idea to construct a flowchart for your programs. However, as this book is really aimed at explaining how the C code works, so this will be the last flowchart in the book. The flowchart for this program is shown in Figure 3-5.

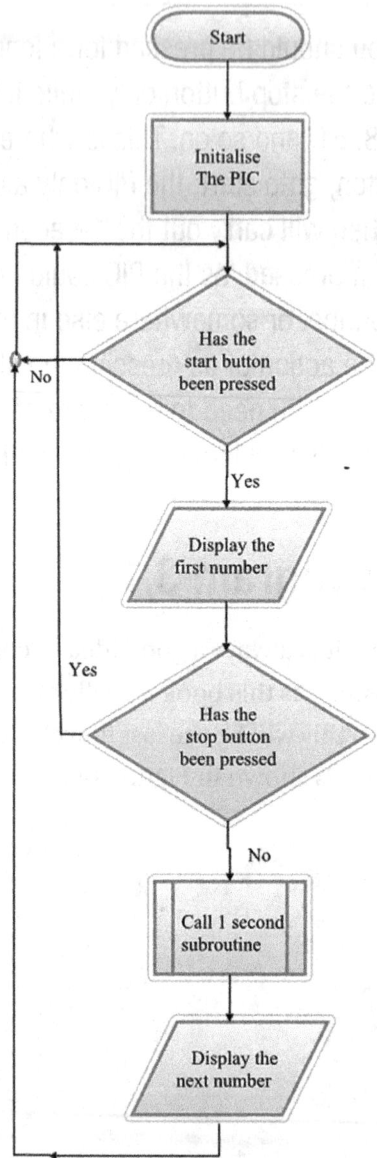

Figure 3-5. *The flowchart for the seven-segment display*

This is a very much reduced flowchart, as the symbols after the first decision box would have to be repeated some nine times. This would be too cumbersome, and I only want to give you an idea of what the flowchart would be.

Program Listing for the Common Cathode Seven-Segment Display

You should create a new project following the procedure described in chapter 1. I suggest you call the project 16f88SevenSeg. However, you can name it what you want. Once you have created the project, you should create a new main c source file as described in chapter 2. I suggest you name the source file 16f88SevenSegProg with the default extension '.c'.

I think you should create a new project for every program we write, as practice makes perfect, or at least a better understanding of the process. However, in all the future programs I will not add this section, as I will assume you have created a new project.

The complete code for the single common cathode seven-segment display is shown in Listing 3-1.

Listing 3-1. Single Seven-Segment Display Program

```
/*
* File:   16f88SevenSegProg.c
Author: H. H. Ward
A program that makes a seven-segment display count down from 9 to 0 in one second intervals
Common Cathode
Created on 10 February 2021, 00:20
*/
//declare any include files
```

```
#include <xc.h>
#include <pic16F88ConfigSettings.h>
//declare any global variables
unsigned char n;
// declare any definitions
#define zero    0b10111111
#define one     0b10000110
#define two     0b11011011
#define three   0b11001111
#define four    0b11100110
#define five    0b11101101
#define six     0b11111100
#define seven   0b10000111
#define eight   0b11111111
#define nine    0b11100111
#define startButton PORTAbits.RA0
#define stopButton PORTAbits.RA1
//declare any subroutines
void delay (unsigned char t)
{
for (n = 0; n < t; n++)
{
TMR0 = 0;
while (TMR0 < 255);
}
}
void main ()
{
PORTA = 0;
PORTB = 0;
TRISA = 0XFF;
```

```
TRISB = 0;
OSCTUNE = 0;
OSCCON = 0b01111100;
ANSEL = 0;
OPTION_REG = 0b10000111;
start: while (startButton);
while (1)
{
if (!stopButton) goto start;
PORTB = nine;
delay (30);
if (!stopButton) goto start;
PORTB = eight;
delay (30);
if (!stopButton) goto start;
PORTB = seven;
delay (30);
if (!stopButton) goto start;
PORTB = six;
delay (30);
if (!stopButton) goto start;
PORTB = five;
delay (30);
if (!stopButton) goto start;
PORTB = four;
delay (30);
if (!stopButton) goto start;
PORTB = three;
delay (30);
if (!stopButton) goto start;
PORTB = two;
```

```
71. delay (30);
72. if (!stopButton) goto start;
73. PORTB = one;
74. delay (30);
75. if (!stopButton) goto start;
76. PORTB = zero;
77. delay (30);
78. }
79. }
```

Analysis of Listing 3-1

Lines 1 to 7 are just the basic comments about the program.

Line 8 //declare any include files

Here I am just using comments to break up the program listing up into logical sections. The first section is where we tell the compiler program that we want to include some header files. Therefore, when the compiler program starts to compile our program instructions, it also finds the instructions in these header files and compiles them as well. Note that it is the linker program that finds all these other files we want to include in our project. In making this statement, I am trying to make you aware that the IDE, MPLABX, is a collection of a lot of programs that we use to write our projects.

Line 9 #include <xc.h>

This is a very important header file that has been created by Microchip. Is termed open source as it is freely available to us. It helps us identify the SFRs (special function registers) that we want to use in our programs and allows us to reference them using a set of labels. These labels are the actual name of the SRFs as stated in the datasheet for the appropriate PIC. It has to be included in all our projects if we want to use all the labels, as opposed to memory addresses, to reference the SFRs.

Line 10 #include <pic16F88ConfigSettings.h>

This is where we tell the compiler to include the first header file we created to set the primary source of the clock to the internal oscillator block and turn the WDT (watch dog timer) off and LVP.

Line 11 //declare any global variables

This simply splits the listing up for a section for global variables. Global variables are simply memory locations that we organize with a suitable name to refer to them. These can be used to store values that we will use in the program. As they are global, they can be used by any section of the program.

The other type of variables are local variables. The difference is that local variables can only be used in the subroutine where they were created.

Line 12 unsigned char n;

This creates a variable that is an eight-bit memory location, with the name 'n'. It is of type unsigned char. The "char" word means it is only eight bits long. The word "unsigned" means that bit7 is not used to tell us the "sign" of the variable (i.e., whether it is positive; bit7 would be a logic '0' or a negative, bit7 would be a logic '1' number). With an unsigned char, bit7 is used to represent part of the number. This means we can store a value from 0 to 255 in this variable 'n'. If we want to use bit7 to represent the sign of the number, which is termed "signed number representation", then we would simply write "char" instead of "unsigned char". The variable 'n' would then store a value from -127 to 127. This is an important difference; the difference between "char" and 'unsigned char".

Note that the same applies to "int" and "unsigned int". However, an int uses 16 bits (note that "int" stands for integer).

Line 13 // declare any definitions

In this section, we are telling the compiler that wherever it sees the symbolic name written after the keyword #define, we actually mean what is written after that symbolic name. You should make the symbolic name as sensible as possible in terms of what it is going to represent. The actual meaning of the symbolic name can be almost anything, such as:

- an instruction (e.g., PORTB = 0)
- a reference to a bit such as PORTAbits.RA0
- a simply numeric value such as 0b00001111

Line 14 #define zero 0b10111111

With this definition, we are telling the compiler that wherever it sees the symbolic name "zero", it should read it as the binary number 0b10111111. When this value is loaded into PORTB, which is connected to the seven-segment display, all seven LEDs, except the last one named 'G' in Figure 3-4, are lit. Note that the display is a common cathode and so sending out a logic '1' to all the anodes except the 'G' anode forces the anodes high, or 5V, and so turns those LEDs on. The fact that the 'G' cathode is connected to a logic '0' or 0V outputted from the PIC means that the 'G' LED is turned off.

This means that the seven-segment display will actually display the number 0. This is why the symbolic name is "zero".

The next lines down to 23 do exactly the same except that they define the binary number to make the display show the numbers 1, 2, 3, 4, 5, 6, 7, 8, and 9. Figure 3-4 should help you understand this.

Line 24 #define startButton PORTAbits.RA0

This is the same type of instruction, except that it tells the compiler software that wherever it sees the symbolic name startButton, it knows that we mean the reference PORTAbits.RA0 (i.e., bit0 of PORTA).

Line 25 #define stopButton PORTAbits.RA1

This tells the compiler that wherever it sees the label stopButton, we mean the reference PORTAbits.RA1 (i.e., bit1 of PORTA).

Note that with all these definitions, there is no semicolon ";" at the end. That is because these are not instructions for the PIC but are commands to the compiler software.

Line 26 //declare any subroutines

Here we are splitting the program up and creating a section of subroutines. Subroutines are small sections of a program that are written outside the **main** program loop.

You should use a subroutine if your program uses a section of instructions in EXACTLY the same way more than once in your program. With the subroutine, you would only write the instructions once instead of writing them many times; note that even twice is deemed to be many times. This concept would save your program memory, and believe you me, memory is the villain with all programmers.

To run a subroutine, the main section of the program has to call the subroutine. The micro would then jump out of its normal sequential operation and go through the instructions of the subroutine. When it completes the subroutine, the micro jumps back to the main program at the point where it called the subroutine.

Line 27 void delay (unsigned char t)

This actually creates the subroutine. It starts off with the keyword "void", which is blue in the 'c' editor. This word means that the subroutine will not be passing any values back to the main loop.

The next word, "delay", is the name for the subroutine; note that it will be in black and bold in the editor. You should give the subroutine a suitable name to reflect its purpose.

Next, we insert a set of normal brackets. Inside these normal brackets we can, if we want to, instruct the main program that we want the main program to pass a value up to the subroutine when the main program calls it. We use the statement inside the bracket to define what type of data we want the main program to send up to it. The statement "unsigned char t" means this subroutine wants an eight-bit unsigned number to be sent up to it when it is called from the main program, or from other subroutines, as with nested subroutines. The subroutine will then copy the value that has been passed up to it into the variable 't'. Note that in this instance the variable 't' is a local variable that can only be used in this subroutine.

I feel I should point out that a subroutine can use any global variable we have previously defined. Indeed, this subroutine is using the variable 'n,' which because it is a global variable, the subroutine can use.

If the subroutine did not want the main program to pass a variable up to it when called, then you would leave the space between the two normal brackets empty.

Line 28 {

This is the opening curly bracket that defines the start of the loop within which all the instructions of the subroutine are written. Note that there must now be a closing curly bracket for this loop. Indeed, as you type the first opening curly bracket, the intellisense takes over and puts in the closing curly bracket and inserts the cursor between the two curly brackets indented one space.

Line 29 for (n = 0; n < t; n++)

This is a very powerful "for do loop" type instruction. It is really four instructions in one.

First, it loads the variable 'n' with the value 0, using n = 0;. Note that 'n' is a global variable (i.e., one that can be used in any part of the program) that was declared in line 12.

It then compares the value of n, which is now 0, with the value that the main program passed up and the subroutine assigned to the local variable 't,' using n < t;. For this analysis, we will assume the value of 't' is 2.

The comparison asks this question: is n less than t? In this case, it will be, as n has just been loaded with '0.' Therefore, the result of the test is said to be true and so the micro will carry out the instructions that are inside the following loop or set of curly brackets. When the micro has carried out all the instructions inside the loop, it will automatically increase the value of n by one, using the n++ shown in the normal bracket.

Now the micro carries out the comparison again, n < t;. Well, n is still less than t, as n is now 1 and t is 2, so the micro must carry out the instructions in the loop a second time. Again, at the end of the loop the micro will increment the value of n.

Now the micro again carries out the comparison, but this time n is equal to t as both have the value of 2. Therefore, the comparison is not true, as n is not less than t. So, the micro does not carry out the instructions in the loop. It simply breaks away from the "for do loop" and carries on with the rest of the program.

The semicolons ';' after n = 0; and n < t; need to be there, as these are single-line instructions. The n++ is not a single-line instruction. It is the last instruction in a series of multiple-line instructions stated inside the curly brackets.

Line 30 {

This is the opening curly bracket of the "for do loop". We need the curly brackets because there is more than just one instruction inside the "for do loop".

Line 31 TMR0 = 0;

This is the first instruction in the "for do loop". It loads the SFR TMR0 with the value 0. This is the register that is associated with timer0. Timer0 is a counting piece of firmware that simply increments its own register, TMR0, at a frequency we set using the control register for timer0, which is the OPTION_REG register. Note that we will set timer0, using the instruction on line 44, to increment at a frequency of 7812.5Hz. This means it will increment every 128μs. Note that we also set the timer0 to be an eight-bit register, which means the maximum value it can count up to is 255.

Line 32 while (TMR0 < 255);

This is another very powerful 'c' instruction. The principle on which it works is as follows:

while (the test I specify inside this bracket is true) do what I tell you to do here;.

I have written the instruction again in the previous manner to try and help explain how it works. The while sets up a test. The test is written inside the normal brackets; in line 32 the test is as follows:

(is the value in the TMR0 less than 255, i.e. TMR0 < 255).

If the value is less than 255, the test is true and so the micro must carry out the instructions I specify here outside the normal bracket and before the semicolon ";".

To fully understand this particular instruction, we must appreciate that the semicolon ';' signifies the end of the current instruction. You can see that there are no instructions between the closing normal bracket and the semicolon. That is because we want the micro to do **nothing** while the test is true. This is because we are simply creating a delay that lasts until the micro increments the value of the TMR0 register to 255. Note that the PIC automatically increments the TMR0 register. When the TMR0 reaches 255, the test will become untrue as TMR0 is no longer less than 255. Therefore, as the test is untrue, the micro can break away from doing nothing and carry on with the rest of the program.

The while (TMR0 < 255); simply creates a 255 × 128μs delay, which is approximately a 32.77ms delay. I say approximately, as to be accurate you need to add the time it takes to carry out the instructions. How timer0 is set up to count at one every 128μs will be explained later in this analysis when we look at the OPTION_REG.

I hope this has helped you to understand how this "while (test is true) do what I say here;" type of instruction works. The doing section may be just a single-line instruction as with line 45. However, it could be a number of instructions. If that is the case, then the set of instructions will be written inside a set of opening and closing curly brackets.

Line 33 }

This is simply the closing curly bracket for the "for do loop" started on line 30.

Line 34 }

This is the closing bracket for the delay subroutine. This then creates a variable delay with a minimum delay of around 32ms. This is because lines 31 and 32 create the minimum delay of 32ms. However, as these two lines are within the "for do loop" of lines 29 to 33, then, as the number of times this for do loop is executed is controlled by the value in the variable 't', the number of times the PIC executes this "for do loop" is controlled by the number we pass up to the subroutine, which is loaded into the local variable 't'. In this way, then we can make this delay last for just one 32ms wait or any number of 32ms waits, up to a maximum of 255 32ms waits. This is because the variable 't' is an eight-bit number and an eight-bit number can go from 0 to 2^8 or 0 to 255.

Lines 35 to 43 have been discussed in Listing 2-1.

Line 44 OPTION_REG = 0b10000111;

This simply loads the OPTION_REG with the binary value 0b10000111. The OPTION_REG is an SFR that controls the operation of timer0. The individual bits perform the following operations:

- **Bit7** $\overline{RBPU}$
- This is used to either enable or disable the pull up resistors on PORTB (i.e., **R**esistor **B** **P**ull **U**p). The bar "-" written above the term means it is active low. This in turn means that if bit7 is low (i.e., a logic '0'), then the pull up resistors are enabled. If bit7 is high (i.e., a logic '1'), then the pull up resistors are not enabled. These pull up resistors can be used if you need to ensure that an input actually goes to +5V when its input is not switched to ground. This could be useful with some communication requirements.
- **Bit6 INTEDG**
- If an interrupt is being used, this bit is used to choose which edge the interrupt will be triggered on. A logic '1' means it will be a positive edge, and a logic '0' means it will be a negative edge.

- **Bit5 TOSC**
- This bit is used to select which oscillator will be used to synchronize when timer0 increments the value in the TMR0 register. When this bit is a logic '1', timer0 uses the external oscillator. If the bit is a logic '0', then timer0 will use the internal oscillator block.
- **Bit4 TOSE**
- When synchronizing a change in state as with the count value in TMR0, it is always more accurate to synchronize to either the rising or falling edge of the oscillator signal. This bit decides which edge we use. A logic '1' means we use the falling edge (i.e., from high down to low). A logic '0' means we use the rising edge (i.e., from low to high).
- **Bit3 PSA Prescaler Assignment Bit**
- The PIC offers the use of a prescaler, which can be used to divide down the oscillator frequency we use for the timer. However, you as a programmer can decide to assign the prescaler to either timer0 or the WDT. A logic '1' in this bit assigns the prescaler to the WDT. A logic '0' assigns it to timer0.
- **Bit2,1 and 0 PS<> Prescaler Rate Select Bits**
- These three bits allow you to determine by how much you divide the oscillator frequency before assigning it to either timer0 or the WDT. The rates are set out in Table 3-2. Note that we have eight options (i.e., 2^3) available to us.

Table 3-2. The Timer0 Divide Rates

Bit2	Bit1	Bit0	Divide Rate For Timer0	Divide Rate For WDT
0	0	0	2	1
0	0	1	4	2
0	1	0	8	4
0	1	1	16	8
1	0	0	32	16
1	0	1	64	32
1	1	0	128	64
1	1	1	256	128

The instruction on line 44 loads the OPTION_REG with the binary number 0b10000111. Therefore, using the preceding information regarding the OPTION_REG, we can see that it sets up the following:

- Bit7 = 1 therefore disables the pull up resistors.
- Bit6 = 0 this selects the falling edge.
- Bit5 = 0 timer0 uses the internal oscillator block.
- Bit4 = 0 increments the count on the rising edge of the oscillator signal.
- Bit3 = 0 assigns the prescaler to timer0.
- Bit2, Bit1, and Bit0 are all logic '1.' This assigns the maximum divide rate to the timer0 frequency signal. This sets the frequency at which timer0 increments the value stored in its TMR0 register to 7812.5Hz. This value is calculated as follows:

- The clock frequency that synchronizes all operations of the PIC runs at a quarter of the oscillator. We have set the oscillator frequency to 8Mhz in line 42, OSCCON = 0b01111100; therefore the clock runs at 8/4 (i.e., 2MHz).
- We divide this 2MHz clock frequency by 256 before applying it to timer0. Therefore, timer0 counts at 2Mz/256 = 7812.5Hz. This means that it will take 1/7812.5 seconds (i.e., 128μs) to increment the TMR0 register by 1.

This should help explain how the instruction on line 44 sets timer0 to count at a rate of 7812.5 counts in one second.

Line 45 start: while (startButton);

There is a very similar instruction in Listing 2-1. The only difference here is that there is the word "start" followed by the colon ":". This is how we create a label that is going to be used as a point in the program we may want to jump to from a "goto" part of an instruction somewhere else in the program. Indeed, this label can be jumped back to from lines 48, 51, 54, 57, 60, 63, 66, 69, 72, and 75 in the program.

Line 46 while {1)

This is the opening forever loop as discussed in Listing 2-1.

Line 47 {

This is the opening curly bracket for the forever loop.

Line 48 if (!stopButton) goto start;

This introduces the "if (this test is true) then do what I tell you to do" type of instruction. The instruction is in the form of a test and if the test is true then we must do what we are told to do "else" we do something else.

In line 48, the test is "is the logic on the stop button a logic '0'"); note that we are using the '!' NOT label to indicate that we are testing for a logic '0'. If the test is true, then the micro must carry out the instruction or instructions that are written here. This is a simple one-line instruction that tells the micro to go to the label start. Note that we define the label start on line 45 before.

What this instruction is doing is asking if someone has pressed the stop button. If they have, then the micro must go back to the start label where we get it to wait until someone presses the start button. If no one has pressed the stop button, then the micro simply carries on with the rest of the program. This is the "else" part of this type of instruction. However, as we are not getting the PIC to do anything different from simply carrying on with the program, we don't need to describe it with an "else" statement. There will be times when we need to use the "else" statement, and we will analyze it then.

This shows up the difference between the while and the if type instruction. The while traps the micro in that instruction while the test is true, whereas the if only asks is my test true. If it is true, do what I tell you to do; if it's not true, then simply carry on with the rest of the program, as the micro is not trapped.

Line 49 PORTB = nine;

This line forces the data stored in the PORTB register to take on the value indicated by the phrase "nine". Note that we have defined the phrase "nine" to mean the binary number 0b11100111 in line 23. This then means the seven-segment display shows the numeral 9.

Line 50 delay (30);

This calls the subroutine delay and passes up the value 30 to the subroutine. The subroutine then loads the local variable 't' with the number 30. This makes the "for do loop" in that subroutine to be carried out 30 times. Each time there is a delay of around 32ms; therefore, the total delay is 30 × 32ms = 0.99s, an approximately 1-second delay.

Line 51 if (!stopButton) goto start;

This works in the same way as the instruction on line 48.

Line 52 PORTB = eight;

This overwrites the data in PORTB with the data to display the numeral 8 on the seven-segment display.

This procedure continues in lines 53 to 77 and so displays the numbers 9 down to 0 with a 1-second delay between each change of number.

Line 78 }

This is the closing curly bracket for the forever loop started on line 47.

Line 79 }

This is the closing curly bracket of the **main** loop started on line 35.

I hope the preceding analysis does help explain how the instructions work.

Figure 3-6 shows a board with just one of four seven-segment displays being used to display a value between 9 and 0. The display is being controlled using the program in Listing 3-1.

Figure 3-6. *The single seven-segment display countdown*

Figure 3-7 shows the same seven-segment display board being connected to my PIC16F88 development board.

Figure 3-7. *Connecting the seven-segment display and button board to the PIC16F88 development board*

This program is used to control just one single seven-segment display. Figure 3-6 shows a board with four seven-segment displays. Each of them are the common cathode type. Refer to the data sheet sc56-11gwa for the details of the seven-segment display. This means we must connect a ground to pins 3 and 8 of each seven-segment display we want to use. That is because the cathodes are connected to pins 3 and 8. The anodes of each of the LEDs in the seven-segment display are connected to a bit of PORTB. In this way, the logic on PORTB can control what is displayed on the seven-segment display.

Program 3.2: 3461BS Common Anode Four Seven-Segment Display Module

In this next program, we are going to control four seven-segment displays. The module we will use is the 3461BS module shown in Figure 3-8. As stated in this section's heading, this is a common anode device and we need to use the logic as shown in Table 3-1 to control the number displayed on the seven-segment display.

Figure 3-8. *Four seven-segment display*

The complete code for this project is shown in Listing 3-2.

Listing 3-2. Four Seven-Segment Display Program

```
/*
* File:   pic16F88Four7SegDisplayProg.c
Author: H. H. Ward
This control 4 7segment displays
This is for the common Anode type seven-segment display
Created on 06 March 2021, 15:45
*/
```

```
//List any include files you want to use
#include <pic16F88ConfigSettings.h>
#include <xc.h>
// declare any definitions
#define zero    0b11000000
#define one     0b11111001
#define two     0b10100100
#define three   0b10110000
#define four    0b10011001
#define five    0b10010010
#define six     0b10000011
#define seven   0b11111000
#define eight   0b10000000
#define nine    0b10011000
//declare any global variables
unsigned char n;
//some subroutines
void delay (unsigned char t)
{
for (n = 0; n < t; n++)
{
a.   TMR0 = 0;
b.   while (TMR0 < 3);
}
}
//the main program
void main ()
{
PORTA = 0;
PORTB = 0;
TRISA = 0X0;
```

```
TRISB = 0;
OPTION_REG = 0b00000111;
OSCTUNE = 0;
OSCCON = 0b01111100;
ANSEL = 0;
while (1)
{
    PORTA = 0b00000001;
    PORTB = one;
    delay (3);
    PORTA = 0b00000010;
    PORTB = two;
    delay (3);
    PORTA = 0b000000100;
    PORTB = three;
    delay (3);
    PORTA = 0b000001000;
    PORTB = four;
    delay (3);
}
}
```

Figure 3-9 shows the program running with the displays connected to a simple vero board I have built. Note that I am using PORTA to control which seven-segment display is turned on and PORTB to control what value is sent to the seven-segment displays.

***Figure 3-9.** The four seven-segment display board*

The board also has a 4116-220LF chip. If you compare this board with that shown in Figure 3-6, you will see that the series resistors that are connected to the pins of the displays are not shown on this board. That is because there are 8 220Ω resistors in the 4116 chip. This does make the board neater and smaller, but it comes at a cost. You could use a network of resistors or just use individual resistors, as in Figure 3-6, which is the cheapest option. The choice is up to you.

The pin allocation for PORTA is shown in Table 3-3.

***Table 3-3.** The Allocation for the 3416BS and PORTA*

3416BS Pin	12	9	8	6
PORTA bit	0	1	2	3

The pin allocation for PORTB is shown in Table 3-4.

Table 3-4. *The Allocation for the 3416BS and PORTB*

3416BS Pin	1	2	3	4	5	7	10	**11**
PORTB bit	4	3	7	2	6	1	5	0

Figure 3-10 shows how the LEDs are connected inside the 3416BS module. The eight anodes of each of the seven-segment displays are connected together and are brought out on one of the four individual pins: 12, 9, 8, or 6. These are controlled from PORTA of the PIC.

The eight cathodes are connected individually to the output pins 11, 7, 4, 2, 1, 10, 5, and 3. These are controlled by PORTB on the PIC. Note that the four seven-segment displays have their cathodes connected in parallel, as shown in Figure 3-10. This means that whatever data is sent to one seven-segment display, the other three get the same data. However, only one display has its anode connected to +5V at a time. In this way, only one display is active and will show the current number even though the data goes to all four displays. Knowing that once lit, it will take time for the LEDs to turn off, and so go out, then if we can change the data sent to all displays and at the same time change which display is turned on quick enough, then we can display four different numbers on the module. This is confirmed in Figure 3-9, where the module displays the numbers 1, 2, 3, and 4. That is the principle of how we can control the four seven-segment display module.

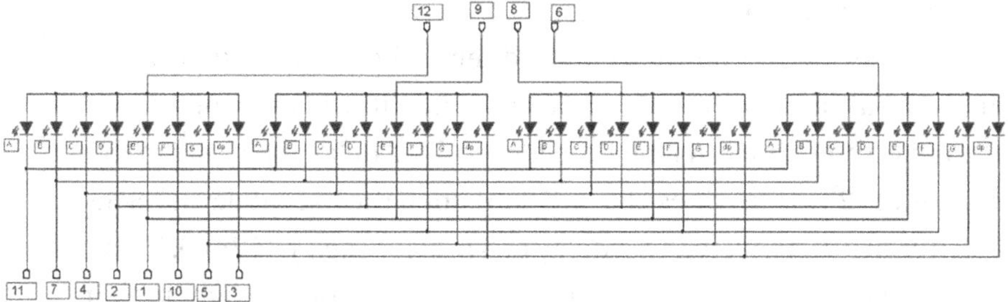

***Figure 3-10.** The connections of the LEDs in the 3461BS module*

Analysis of Listing 3-2

We will look at the new instructions and discuss how they work here.

Lines 1 to 7 are the normal comments. Lines 8, 9, and 10 are the usual includes. Lines 11 to 43 have been discussed in Listing 3-1.

Line 43 a PORTA = 0b00000001;

This is just loading PORTA with the binary data 0b00000001. This means that only bit0 is sending +5V (i.e., a logic '1') out on its pin. This means that only one of the four sets of eight anodes is ready to be turned on, the set connected to pin12 on the 3461BS module; see Figure 3-10. If each of the cathodes are now connected to 0V (i.e., logic '0'), then the LED will turn on. Note that there must be a resistor, with a typical value of 220Ω, in series with the cathodes to limit the current through each LED.

Therefore, this instruction is getting only the first of the four seven-segment displays ready to display the current number.

Line 43b PORTB = one;

This is loading PORTB with the binary value of 0b11111001. This means that only the cathodes for B and C (i.e., pins 7 and 4), of the seven-segment display, will go to 0V (i.e., a logic '0'). All the rest will go to +5V. This means that only those two LEDs will turn on and so the first seven-segment display will show the number "1".

Line 43c delay(3);

This calls the subroutine delay and sends the value "3" to be loaded into the local variable "t". This means that the PIC will carry out the fixed delay three times. As the time for the fixed delay is also set to three intervals of 128μs (see lines 28a and 28b), then the fixed delay is 384μs. Then this instruction creates a delay of 3 × 384μs (i.e., 1.152ms). This is long enough for the LEDs in the seven-segment display to light up but quick enough for the displays to change state without the seven segments actually turning off at each change.

Line 43d PORTA = 0b00000010;

This turns the first seven-segment display off and turns the second one on.

Line 43e PORTB = Two;

This sends the data to the displays to display the number 2. However, as only the second seven-segment display is turned on, then only this seven-segment display shows the number 2. Note that the first seven-segment display will still be showing the number 1, as it takes time for that display to extinguish.

Line 43f delay (3);

This calls the delay subroutine again to create the 1.152ms delay.

Lines 43g to 43l perform the same function but display the other two different values on the other two seven-segment displays.

As there are no real new instructions we have not come across before, I hope this quick analysis helps you to understand how the program works. In the next program, we will control a stepper motor.

The Stepper Motor

The stepper motor is a DC motor that has a number of coils encased in the stator part of the motor. To make the rotor rotate, each of the coils in the stator are turned on sequentially and so the rotor rotates in steps as it is attracted by the magnetic fields set up in the stator coils. The PIC program basically has to turn on these coils in a certain sequence to make the motor turn. In this way, the motor can turn through one revolution or just a few degrees of a revolution or through many revolutions.

The stepper motor we will use in this example is very small motor, but it can be used for many applications. The actual motor is a 5V four-phase five-wire stepper motor, and it is shown in Figure 3-11.

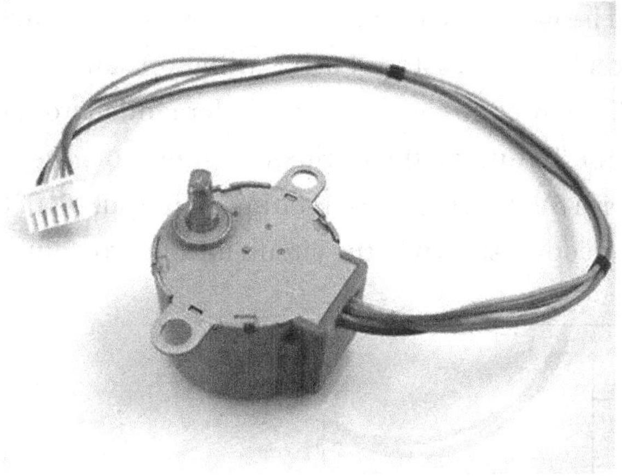

Figure 3-11. *The 5V four-phase stepper motor (28BYJ-48)*

There are five wires that can be connected to a driver circuit:

- Red connected to the +5V supply
- Orange connected to coil 1
- Yellow connected to coil 2
- Pink connected to coil 3
- Blue connected to coil 4

The red lead supplies the 5V to all the coils and needs to be able to supply enough current to the motor, and so it may need to be a different supply than the supply to the PIC. However, you should ensure all the 0V, or ground, of the supplies are connected together.

So, to energize the coils, the ground has to be connected to each coil to allow current to flow through them. If this is done in the correct sequence, then the motor will turn in individual steps in either clockwise or anticlockwise direction. The simplest way to switch the ground on to each coil would be to use the ULN2004 driver I.C. This has an array of seven Darlington NPN transistors. Each Darlington can sink up to 500mA and so they will easily cope with the current demanded from the coils of the stepper motor. To turn on the Darlington transistors, we need to supply the transistor with 5V. This is done by setting an output bit of the PIC to a logic '1'. This concept is shown in the circuit for the program in Figure 3-12.

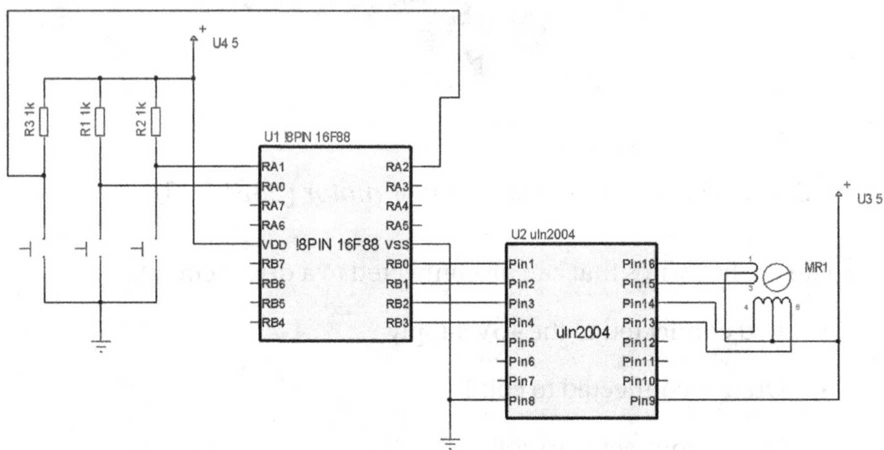

Figure 3-12. *The circuit diagram for the stepper motor program*

The sequence to make the motor move in a clockwise direction is stated in Table 3-5.

Table 3-5. *The Sequence to Rotate the Motor Clockwise*

Coil Number	Coil Color
then coils 4 and 1	blue and orange
then coil 4	blue
then coils 3 and 4	pink and blue
then coil 3	pink
then coils 3 and 2	yellow and pink
then coil 2	yellow
then coils 1 and 2	Orange and yellow
then coil 1	orange

Note that clockwise is seen looking into the motor from the end of the shaft. The sequence provides in Table 3-6 shows how to make the motor rotate in an anticlockwise direction.

Table 3-6. *The Sequence for Rotating the Motor Anticlockwise*

Coil Number	Coil Color
coil 1	orange
then coils 1 and 2	orange and yellow
then coil 2	yellow
then coils 2 and 3	yellow and pink
then coil 3	pink
then coils 3 and 4	pink and blue
then coil 4	Blue
then coils 4 and 1	blue and orange

There should be a delay between changing from one step to the next step in the sequence. This delay must be long enough for the current in the coil to build up and so create the magnetic field that steps the motor around. However, the time constant of the coils is very short and so this delay can be short.

This stepper motor goes through 4,096 of these individual steps, to make one complete revolution. Therefore, each single step turns the stepper motor rotor through 0.08789 of a degree. As there are eight single steps in each sequence of steps, as shown in Tables 3-5 and 3-6, each sequence moves the motor through 0.70312 degrees. Therefore, it takes 360/0.70312 (i.e., 512) sequences of steps to move the motor through 360 degrees or one complete revolution.

Using this information, we can determine how many steps or sequences are required to make the motor turn by any number of degrees. The complete code for the stepper motor is shown in Listing 3-3.

Listing 3-3. The Listing for the Stepper Motor Program

```
/*
* File:   pic16f88StepperProg.c
Author: H. H. Ward
A program to control a stepper motor
Created on 13 March 2021, 15:10
*/
//Some include files
#include <xc.h>
#include <pic16F88ConfigSettings.h>
// Some definitions
# define orange    PORTBbits.RB3
# define yellow    PORTBbits.RB2
# define pink      PORTBbits.RB1
# define blue      PORTBbits.RB0
```

```
//Global variables
unsigned char n, speed, clkcount;
unsigned int ck;
//some subroutines
void delay (unsigned char t)
{
while (clkcount < t)
{
TMRO = 0;
while (TMRO < 255);
clkcount ++;
}
}
void main()
{
PORTA = 0;
PORTB = 0;
TRISA = OXFF;
TRISB = 0;
OSCTUNE = 0;
OSCCON = 0b01111100;
ANSEL = 0;
OPTION_REG = 0b10000111;
speed = 50;
while (1)
{
if (!PORTAbits.RA0) speed = 75;
if (!PORTAbits.RA1) speed = 40;
if (!PORTAbits.RA2) speed = 20;
ck = 0;
clockwise:    while (ck < 400)
```

```
{
orange = 1;
yellow = 0;
pink = 0;
blue = 1;
TMR0 = 0;
while (TMR0 < speed);
orange = 0;
yellow = 0;
pink = 0;
blue = 1;
TMR0 = 0;
while (TMR0 < speed);
orange = 0;
yellow = 0;
pink = 1;
blue = 1;
TMR0 = 0;
while (TMR0 < speed);
orange = 0;
yellow = 0;
pink = 1;
blue = 0;
TMR0 = 0;
while (TMR0 < speed);
orange = 0;
yellow = 1;
pink = 1;
blue = 0;
TMR0 = 0;
while (TMR0 < speed);
```

```
orange = 0;
yellow = 1;
pink = 0;
blue = 0;
TMR0 = 0;
while (TMR0 < speed);
orange = 1;
yellow = 1;
pink = 0;
blue = 0;
TMR0 = 0;
while (TMR0 < speed);
orange = 1;
yellow = 0;
pink = 0;
blue = 0;
TMR0 = 0;
while (TMR0 < speed);
ck ++;
goto clockwise;
}
ck = 0;
anticlockwise:   while (ck < 500)
{
TMR0 = 0;
while (TMR0 < speed);
orange = 1;
yellow = 0;
pink = 0;
blue = 0;
TMR0 = 0;
```

```
while (TMR0 < speed);
orange = 1;
yellow = 1;
pink = 0;
blue = 0;
TMR0 = 0;
while (TMR0 < speed);
orange = 0;
yellow = 1;
pink = 0;
blue = 0;
TMR0 = 0;
while (TMR0 < speed);
orange = 0;
yellow = 1;
pink = 1;
blue = 0;
TMR0 = 0;
while (TMR0 < speed);
orange = 0;
yellow = 0;
pink = 1;
blue = 0;
TMR0 = 0;
while (TMR0 < speed);
orange = 0;
yellow = 0;
pink = 1;
blue = 1;
TMR0 = 0;
while (TMR0 < speed);
```

```
orange = 0;
yellow = 0;
pink = 0;
blue = 1;
TMRO = 0;
while (TMRO < speed);
orange = 1;
yellow = 0;
blue = 1;
TMRO = 0;
while (TMRO < speed);
ck ++;
goto anticlockwise;
}
clkcount = 0;
delay (16);
}
}
```

Analysis of Listing 3-3

There are no real new instructions to look at, so really, we need to discuss the principle and look at how the main instructions comply with the principle. As stated earlier, we need to turn on the coils in such a way as to set up a magnetic field that will attract the rotor to the coils of the stators in the motor. When a current is forced to flow through a coil, a magnetic field will be created around it. As one end of each coil is connected to +5V, then we only need to connect the other end to ground or 0V. Using the Darlington array chip, ULN2004 (see Figure 3-12) we can switch a ground onto the coils by setting an output of the PIC to a logic '1.' If we do this while keeping some of the other coils turned off, then the motor will rotate one step.

This is done initially in lines 47 to 50.

```
47   orange = 1;
48   yellow = 0;
49   pink = 0;
50   blue = 1;
```

This completes the first step in a clockwise direction; see Table 3-5.

Now we need to move to the next step. The speed of the motor is controlled by the time period between turning on and off the coils of the motor and so stepping through these steps. The quicker we turn these coils on and off, the faster the motor rotates. However, we need to appreciate that it will take a finite time for the current to build up in the coil and create enough of a magnetic field to make the rotor move the one step. There has to be a minimum delay between turning the coils on and off. Without the technical data of the inductance and resistance of the coils, it is difficult to determine this minimum time, but it should be on the order of around 100μs. With the way we have set up timer0, the minimum time for one count is 128μs; therefore we don't really need to be too concerned about this time period but it does exist and it may explain why you can't get the motor to rotate as fast as you think it would. Some trial and error may help you investigate this aspect.

We must create this delay between each step in the cycle of eight steps. That is what we are doing with lines 51 and 52:

Line 51 TMR0 = 0;

Line 52 while (TMR0 < speed);

In line 51, we are resetting the value in the timer0 register to zero, so that we can start counting timer0 clock cycles from the beginning.

In line 52, we are using the while (the test I describe here is true) do what I tell you to do now.

The test is asking if the value in the timer0 register is less than the value stored in the variable "speed". If the test is true, then do nothing.

In this way, we are doing nothing until the value in the timer0 register is equal to the value stored in "speed". This is our delay. Initially, the value in the variable "speed" is set to 50 (see line 38). This means that the delay is equal to 50 × 128μs = 6.4ms between each step.

This means we can control the speed of the motor by the value stored in this variable "speed". That is why we can change the value in this variable by closing one of the three switches connected to PORTA; see lines 41, 42, and 43, where if one of the buttons is closed, we change the value in "speed". The only problem with this approach is that you have to keep the button pressed until the motor has completed its full sequence of both clockwise and anticlockwise rotation. We will look at a way of improving this later in the book in chapter 11.

We have looked at how we use the variable "speed" to control the speed of the motor. Now we will look at what we are using the variables clkcount and ck. These are set up in lines 16 and 17.

```
16   unsigned char n, speed, clkcount;
17   unsigned int ck;
```

Note that clkcount is set up as an unsigned char. This is because the maximum value we will store in it is 255. Indeed, the normal value is less than 255, whereas the value we will store in ck will normally be greater than 255. To store a value greater than 255, we need to use a variable of type int or integer. Also, because we will never give ck a negative value, we will use an unsigned int or integer.

An int use 16 bits, which takes up two 8-bit registers cascaded together. A char only uses eight bits. Therefore, if you don't need more than eight bits for a variable, you should use a char and not an int as it saves memory.

I should also explain why we are using unsigned char and unsigned int. This is to do with how we recognize positive and negative numbers. We cannot simply write a minus sign in front of the variable, as the micro does not have any paper to write on, or eyes to see it. All we can use are the logic '1's and logic '0's of the bits in a register or memory location.

They are really 5V or 0V, but we use '1' and '0' as it is easier. The way we recognize a negative number is to use the msb (most significant bit) to indicate the "sign" of the number. If the msb, bit 7 in a char or bit 15 in an int (remember we count from 0 to 7 or 0 to 15), is a logic '1', then the number is negative. If the msb is a logic '0', then the number is positive. This is called "signed number representation". However, if we are using signed number representation, then we cannot use the msb as part of the number. That is why a signed char, normally referred to as a char, can only hold up to +127. But it can also go down to -127. Therefore, I hope it is pretty obvious that the unsigned char and unsigned int do not use "signed number representation" and so they can hold only positive numbers which go up to 255 in an 8-bit and 65535 in a 16-bit number.

I have digressed a bit here, but as I have introduced the two types of variables, I thought it would be a good time to explain the concept of signed number representation.

We are using the variable clkcount to control the delay in the subroutine delay; see lines 19 to 27. Note that we call this delay at the end of the forever loop; see lines 153 and 154.

The variable ck is used to control how many times we go through the eight steps in both the clockwise and anticlockwise sequences; see lines 45 and 99.

Line 45 clockwise: while (ck < 400)

Here we are telling the PIC to carry out all the instructions that are enclosed in the curly brackets on lines 46 and 97, while the value in the variable ck is less than 400. These instructions make the motor rotate in a clockwise direction. Note that the variable "ck" must be able to go to 400 here. That is why we have used an unsigned int.

Line 95 ck++;

This simply increments the value stored in ck by one so that it will eventually reach 400.

Line 96 goto clockwise;

With this instruction, we are telling the PIC to go to the label "clockwise" which is on line 45. The PIC will continue carrying out this goto instruction as long as the value in ck is less than 400. When the value in ck reaches 400, then the PIC will move on to lines 97, 98, and 99.

On line 99, the PIC does the same but in an anticlockwise direction. Also, it will repeat the anticlockwise direction 500 times with the instruction while (ck < 500).

In this way, the program makes the stepper motor rotate clockwise through 400 steps and anticlockwise through 500 steps. Note that both directions are less than one full revolution, as it takes 512 steps to make the stepper motor rotate through 360 degrees.

Note that with lines 153 and 154, we are resetting the value in clkcount to 0 and getting the PIC to wait some 2ms before we start the process again. We as humans should not be able to perceive this delay, but it is there to give enough time to allow the magnetism in the coils to diminish.

I hope you have now gotten a good idea of how we can control this little stepper motor. Figure 3-13 shows the motor mounted on a plaque with a cogwheel attached to the rotor. We can now add a variety of cogs and ratchets to produce a range of motions that we can make use of. You should have some fun making things move with this motor.

Figure 3-13. *The stepper motor connected to the PIC16F88 development board*

This figure shows the stepper motor connected to my PIC16F88 development board. The ULN2004 driver chip is on the green PCB with the four LEDs indicating when the coils are turned on. There is an extra 5V supply for the motor and my small board with four switches on for the inputs for the program.

Summary

In this chapter, we have looked at how we can use the PIC to control a single seven-segment display and a group of four seven-segment displays. We have learned what a seven-segment display is and the difference between common anode and common cathode.

We have also studied how a stepper motor works and how we can control the movement of a stepper motor with the PIC.

In the next chapter, we are going to learn how an LCD (liquid crystal display) works and how to control it with a PIC. We will then learn how we can use the ADC (analog-to-digital converter) on a PIC to measure the movement of a small joystick attached to a PIC.

I hope you have enjoyed reading this chapter and found it both useful and challenging.

CHAPTER 4

The Joystick and the Stepper Motor

In this chapter, we will look at a simple joystick module and a small stepper motor. The joystick program will use two analog inputs to the PIC and output the results to the LCD showing the position of the joystick in the x and y axes. This means we will investigate the use of the ADC and how to control an LCD display.

The second part of this chapter will investigate the control of a stepper motor. It will also combine the output of the joystick in controlling the position of a stepper motor in relation to one of the axes of the joystick.

We will also cover the use of arrays in C programming. After reading this chapter, you will understand how the ADC inside the PIC works. You will also understand how we use the ASCII character set with the LCD as well as using a stepper motor. I hope you will find this chapter useful.

Using the Joystick

With this program, we will use the PIC18F4525. This is because the memory of the PIC16F88 is rather limited. It has 4,096 bytes or 4k bytes of memory whereas the PIC18F4525 has 49,152 bytes or 48k bytes of memory. You could run some of the remaining programs written in the book with the PIC16F88, but you may have to consider the memory usage.

H. H. Ward, *Programming Arduino Projects with the PIC Microcontroller*,
https://doi.org/10.1007/978-1-4842-7230-5_4

You could reduce the load on the memory by using the licensed version of the compiler software, as they say it is 40% more efficient than the free version we are using. However, the licensed version is not free. The PIC16F88 has an advantage in its size, but if, like me, you are not too concerned about the size of the PIC, then the PIC18F4525 is likely to become your favorite PIC, as it has for me. It has enough memory for me and a lot of features such as ADC, SPI, I^{2}C, UARTs, and CCP. It comes in a 40-pin dual inline package that makes it easy to make prototype boards on a vero board. I have also made my own prototype board similar to the one for the PIC16F88. I will include the circuit diagram, vero board plan, and parts list for that board. Please note that you should only attempt to build your own board if you are confident at building your own circuits. I cannot guarantee that the board you build will work, as there are many problems you can come across. I can only say that the board I have built works fine for all the programs in this book.

The Principal Operation of the Joystick

The main principle of how the joystick works is that there are two variable resistors that are connected across the supply (i.e., from VCC to ground). The output of these two variable resistors can be altered by moving the joystick control knob from one end of its travel to the other end. The voltage will then vary from its maximum, VCC, to its minimum ground. The output of one of these variable resistors is allocated to the x axis and the other is allocated to the y axis. In this way, the joystick simply gives out two variable voltages than we can interpret as movement in the two axes, x and y.

In reality, the two outputs of the joystick can take up any voltage from VCC to ground. If we use a VCC of +5V then the outputs can be any value between 5 and 0V (e.g., 5V or 4V or 4.11245V; any voltage imaginable).

That is what an analog signal is. However, PICs are not analog devices; they cannot see any value imaginable. Indeed, they can only see numbers, which are normally whole numbers unless we use something called "floats". But even floats are really whole numbers that allow the PICs to use numbers with a higher definition. Even we humans are not analog; we split many parameters into discrete steps. How often have we said the time is "a quarter to" when it is really 44 minutes and 50 seconds or even fractions of seconds. So even though there are real analog signals, we are used to seeing them in discrete steps. That is how the PIC will see these analog inputs (i.e., in discrete steps).

How then does the PIC turn these two analog signals into something it can use? It uses an ADC (analog-to-digital converter). We won't go into the electronics of how the ADC works, but we do need to know how the PIC uses the ADC. There is one ADC circuit in the PIC, and it is a ten-bit ADC. The ADC will attempt to mimic the analog input but using discrete steps. So as the analog input changes, the ADC will wait for the input to reach the next discrete step the ADC can take up before it changes. These discrete steps of the ADC are termed the "resolution" of the ADC. If the range of voltage is the normal 0 to 5V, then knowing the ADC uses ten bits, the resolution of the ADC can be calculated using Equation 4-1:

$$resolution = \frac{range}{2^n}$$

where 'n' is the number of bits of the ADC

Equation 4-1: Resolution of an ADC

The resolution of the ADC is determined with Equation 4-2:

$$\therefore resolution = \frac{range}{2^n} = \frac{5}{2^{10}} = \frac{5}{1024} = 4.883mV$$

Equation 4-2: Resolution of ten-bit ADC

What this means is that the ADC will see 0V and then the next higher voltage will be 4.883mV and the next would be 9.766mV and so on. Therefore, the PIC cannot really see every possible voltage from 0 to 5V. However, the result will be close enough for us humans.

The PIC has up to 13 analog inputs available to it, even though it has only one ADC circuit. We as programmers must learn how to use them. There are three control registers that are used with the ADC: ADCON0, ADCON1, and ADCON2 (i.e., ADCONtrol registers 0, 1, and 2).

To help explain how these three control registers are used, we will look at each register individually. The following tables will look at the usage of the bits in each control register.

The ADCON0 Control Register

The main purpose of this control register is to allow the programmer to choose which analog input, or channel, is connected to the ADC. Note that this is a form of multiplexing where many inputs feed into one device one at a time. The choice is controlled by the data in bits 5, 4, 3, and 2 of the ADCON0 register; see Table 4-1. Note that bits 7 and 6 are not used so they are set to logic '0'.

Table 4-1. The ADCON0 Register (See Data Sheet)

Bit 7	Bit 6	Bit 5	Bit 4	Bit 3	Bit 2	Bit 1	Bit 0
Not Used	Not Used	CHS3	CHS2	CHS1	CHS0	GO/DONE	ADON
Bit 7		Not Used read as 0					
Bit 6		Not Used read as 0					
Bit 5 to Bit 2		Bit 5	Bit 4	Bit 3	Bit 2	ADC Channel Selected	
		0	0	0	0	Channel 0 AN0	
		0	0	0	1	Channel 1 AN1	
		0	0	1	0	Channel 2 AN2	
		0	0	1	1	Channel 3 AN3	
		0	1	0	0	Channel 4 AN4	
		0	1	0	1	Channel 5 AN5	
		0	1	1	0	Channel 6 AN6	
		0	1	1	1	Channel 7 AN7	
		1	0	0	0	Channel 8 AN8	
		1	0	0	1	Channel 9 AN9	
		1	0	1	0	Channel 10 AN10	
		1	0	1	1	Channel 11 AN11	
		1	1	0	0	Channel 12 AN12	
		1	1	0	1	Not Used	
		1	1	1	0	Not Used	
		1	1	1	1	Not Used	

(*continued*)

Table 4-1. (*continued*)

Bit 7	Bit 6	Bit 5	Bit 4	Bit 3	Bit 2	Bit 1	Bit 0
Bit 1		1 Start a conversion, and A conversion is now taking place 0 A conversion has finished					
Bit 0		1 Enable the ADC 0 Disable the ADC					

Bit 0 is the bit that actually turns the ADC on or not. A logic '1' means the ADC is enabled, whereas a logic '0' means it is disabled.

The last remaining bit still to be discussed (i.e., bit 1) is used to start the ADC conversion and tell the programmer when the conversion is finished or done. The programmer must set this bit to a logic '1' to start the ADC conversion. Then when the conversion is finished, the microprocessor sets this bit back to a logic '0' automatically. This is a signal to tell the programmer the ADC conversion has finished.

The ADCON1 Register

This register mostly controls whether the 13 inputs are to be used as analog or digital. It is the first four bits (b0, b1, b2, and b3) that do this. Table 4-2 clearly shows how this is achieved.

Table 4-2. *The ADCON1 Register (See Data Sheet)*

Bit 7	Bit 6	Bit 5	Bit 4	Bit 3	Bit 2	Bit 1	Bit 0
Not Used	Not Used	VCFG1	VCFG0	PCFG3	PCFG2	PCFG1	PCFG0
Bit 7		Not Used read as 0					
Bit 6		Not Used read as 0					
Bit 5		1 negative reference from AN2 0 negative reference from VSS					
Bit 4		1 positive reference from AN3 0 positive reference from VDD					

B3	B2	B1	B0	AN 112	AN 111	AN 10	AN 9	AN 8	AN 7	AN 6	AN 5	AN 4	AN 3	AN 2	AN 1	AN 0
0	0	0	0	A	A	A	A	A	A	A	A	A	A	A	A	A
0	0	0	1	A	A	A	A	A	A	A	A	A	A	A	A	A
0	0	1	0	A	A	A	A	A	A	A	A	A	A	A	A	A
0	0	1	1	D	A	A	A	A	A	A	A	A	A	A	A	A
0	1	0	0	D	D	A	A	A	A	A	A	A	A	A	A	A
0	1	0	1	D	D	D	A	A	A	A	A	A	A	A	A	A
0	1	1	0	D	D	D	D	A	A	A	A	A	A	A	A	A
0	1	1	1	D	D	D	D	D	A	A	A	A	A	A	A	A
1	0	0	0	D	D	D	D	D	D	A	A	A	A	A	A	A
1	0	0	1	D	D	D	D	D	D	D	A	A	A	A	A	A
1	0	1	0	D	D	D	D	D	D	D	D	A	A	A	A	A
1	0	1	1	D	D	D	D	D	D	D	D	D	A	A	A	A
1	1	0	0	D	D	D	D	D	D	D	D	D	D	A	A	A
1	1	0	1	D	D	D	D	D	D	D	D	D	D	D	A	A
1	1	1	0	D	D	D	D	D	D	D	D	D	D	D	D	A
1	1	1	1	D	D	D	D	D	D	D	D	D	D	D	D	D

The ADC needs a reference voltage to help determine the level of the analog input. Bit 4 controls where the PIC gets the positive reference. The default, and so normal setting, is to use the supply to the PIC (i.e., VCC or VDD).

Bit 5 controls where the PIC gets the negative reference. The default, and so normal setting, is to use the supply to the PIC (i.e., VSS or ground).

Bits 6 and 7 are not used.

The ADCON2 Register

Bit 7, ADFM or ADC format, of the ADCON2 control register is used to set what format the result of the ADC is stored in. This is because the ADC returns a ten-bit binary number as the result of a conversion. However, the PIC18F4525 is an eight-bit PIC, which means it only has eight-bit registers. This means that the PIC uses two registers to store the result.

Table 4-3. *The ADCON2 Register (See Data Sheet)*

Bit 7	Bit 6	Bit 5	Bit 4	Bit 3	Bit 2	Bit 1	Bit 0
ADFM	**Not Used**	**ACQT2**	**ACQT1**	**ACQT0**	**ADCS2**	**ADCS1**	**ADCS0**
BIT 7		1 right justify 2 bits in ADRESH (b1 b0) 8 bits in ADRESL 0 left justify 8 bits in ADRESH 2 bits in ADRESL (b7 b6)					
BIT 6		Not used					

(*continued*)

Table 4-3. (*continued*)

Bit 7	Bit 6	Bit 5	Bit 4	Bit 3	Bit 2	Bit 1	Bit 0
Bit 5 - Bit 3		BIT 5	BIT 4	BIT 3	**Selected TADs**		
		0	0	0	0 TAD		
		0	0	1	2 TAD		
		0	1	0	4 TAD		
		0	1	1	6 TAD		
		1	0	0	8 TAD		
		1	0	1	12 TAD		
		1	1	0	16 TAD		
		1	1	1	20 TAD		
BIT 2 – BIT 0		BIT 2	BIT 1	BIT 0	**AD Clock Select Bits**		
		0	0	0	FOsc/2		
		0	0	1	FOsc/8		
		0	1	0	FOsc/32		
		0	1	1	FRC (RC Clock)		
		1	0	0	FOsc/4		
		1	0	1	FOsc/16		
		1	1	0	FOsc/64		
		1	1	1	FRC (RC Clock)		

The two registers are ADRESH (Analog to Digital RESult High byte) and ADRESL (Analog to Digital RESult Low byte). Eight bits of the result can be stored in one register and the other two bits are stored in the other register. The diagram shown in Figure 4-1 helps to explain what is meant by right and left justification. The top diagram where the ADFM or B7 is a logic '0' is termed left justification. Right justification is shown in the bottom diagram. I normally choose left justification.

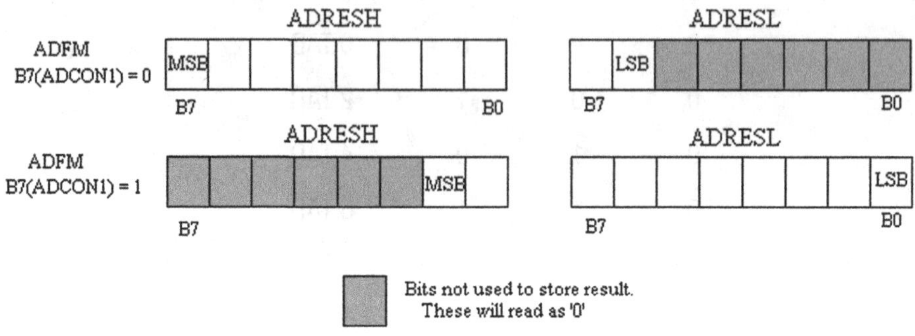

Figure 4-1. *The storing of the ten-bit result of the ADC conversion*

Bits 5, 4, and 3 of the ADCON2 register are used to select the "TAD", the conversion time per bit. Bits 2, 1, and 0 select the clock signal that times the TAD. The following is my attempt to explain what happens when you turn the ADC on and try to get an ADC conversion result.

When you start a conversion the following actions happen:

- The PIC will connect the ADC to the particular input, termed ADC channel, that is measuring the physical analog input.
- Then, once the ADC is connected to the input, it will use the voltage at that input to charge up a capacitor in what is termed a sample and hold circuit.
    - It will take a finite time for the capacitor to charge up to the voltage at that input; this total time to change the channel and charge up the capacitor is termed the acquisition time (i.e., the TACQ).

    - This charge-up time will depend upon the value of the capacitor in the sample and hold circuit and the resistance at the input. This will change depending upon the particular PIC you are using. For the 18F4525, the capacitor has a value of 25pF; see section 19 in the data sheet.
    - Using this value, and various other parameters, an approximate acquisition time for the capacitor to charge up is 2.4µs; see section 19 in the data sheet.
- The ADC will then create a binary number that represents the analog input. This will take a finite time per bit set as the TAD time.

You must get the PIC to wait this 2.4µs, with the PIC18F4525, before the ADC starts its conversion; if it doesn't wait that time the result could be inaccurate.

Microchip offers two ways of creating this delay. You could manually create a delay routine that you run every time before you start an ADC conversion. To use this method, bits 5, 4, and 3 of the ADCON2 register must be set to logic '0.' However, you as the programmer must make sure that you use this delay before starting a conversion and that it is long enough. Note that to start a conversion, you simply have to set bit 1 of the ADCON0 register, the GO/DONE bit, to a logic '1.'

Microchip offers an approach that creates this delay automatically every time you start a conversion. To use this method, you need to know the period 'T' of the frequency of the timing waveform controlling the ADC conversion process. Microchip offers a variety of options for choosing the frequency of the timing waveform. This is because Microchip offers the user a wide variety of oscillator sources for the PIC. Therefore, bits 2, 1, and 0 offer the choice of using the RC oscillator as the timing source for the

ADC or dividing the oscillator frequency by 2, 4, 8, 16, 32, or 64. The idea is to create, in this case, a 2.4μs delay. We then have to wait for the ADC to complete the conversion.

To appreciate what we are trying to create, it would be useful to consider the timing waveform shown in Figure 4-2.

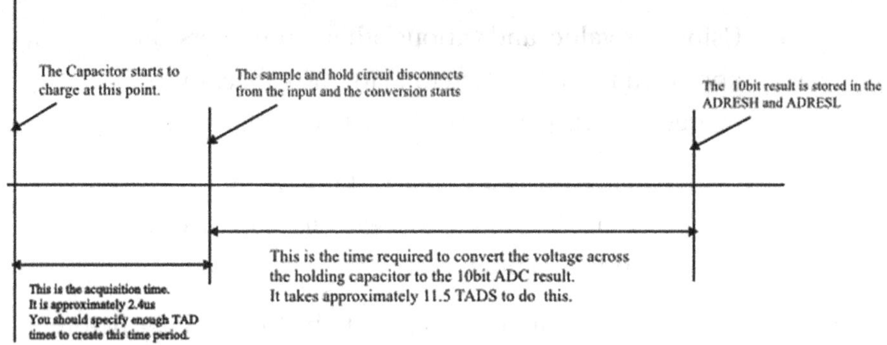

***Figure 4-2.** The timing for the ADC operation of the PIC*

Figure 4-2 depicts what happens when the PIC goes through an ADC conversion. The ADC is connected to the relevant analog input. The voltage at that input is acquired. This means that the input is switched onto the sample and hold circuit inside the PIC and the capacitor in that circuit is charged up to the voltage at the input.

This charge-up time is termed the acquisition time, and the PIC must wait long enough for the capacitor to fully charge up.

The time that the PIC will wait is set by the chosen number of TAD periods that you, as the programmer, select. You must select enough TAD periods for the capacitor to fully charge up. This then means you must know how long each TAD period is. This is again chosen by you, the programmer.

Note that the TAD time is equal to the periodic time 'T' of the chosen frequency you select using bits 0, 1, and 2 of the ADCON2 register. These bits are named ADCS0, ADCS1, and ADCS2. With these bits, you can choose the frequency at which the ADC system runs and so the TAD time for the system. Table 4-3 shows the possible selections you can choose.

This then means that it is the combination of the number of TADs used to create the acquisition time and the actual TAD period you have chosen that controls how long the PIC waits while the capacitor is allowed to charge up. The one overriding consideration is that the TAD and the minimum number of TADs, which is 2TAD, must create a time that is equal to or greater than the acquisition time. This means that if the TAD time that you choose worked out to be 500ns and the acquisition time was 2.4µs, then the system could possibly throw up an error, as the minimum 2TAD time would be 2 × 500ns = 1µs; not long enough. Of course, you would not choose the 2TAD; you would choose the 6TAD, as 6TAD would make the PIC wait 3µs, which is greater than the 2.4µs acquisition time for the PIC18F4525. However, you must be aware of the problem.

The process then moves onto the conversion and this takes 11.5 TAD periods, as shown in Figure 4-2.

This is rather a lot to appreciate and so to help you understand the process I will go through some examples.

Example 1: Creating the Required Acquisition Time

In this example, we will be using the 8Mhz oscillator.

- Choosing a divide by 8 makes the frequency of the ADC operation 1Mhz.
- This in turn means that the period, known as TAD, is 1µs (i.e., $1/1E^{6} = 1E^{-6} = 1\mu s$).
- Therefore, to create the required acquisition time of 2.4µS, we would need a 2.4 TAD time for the delay (i.e., $2.4E^{-6}/1E^{-6} = 2.4$).

- Using bits 5, 4, and 3 of the ADCON2 register, we have options to use 2, 4, 6, 8, 12, 16, and 20 TAD time periods.
- To obtain the required 2.4μs, you should select the 4 TAD option; the closest to 2.4μs will still be greater than 2.4μs. Note that 2.4μs is the minimum not the maximum time the PIC should allow for the acquisition time; however, you should make this delay time the shortest you can.
- To select this option, we need to write the following:
    - b5 = 0
    - b4 = 1
    - b3 = 0 4TAD
    - b2 = 0
    - b1 = 0
    - b0 = 1 divide by 8.
- This means that the whole operation will take 15.5 TAD periods and so take 15.5μs.

Example 2: TAD Time

In this example, we will be using the 20Mhz oscillator.

- Choosing a divide by 4 makes the frequency of the ADC operation 5Mhz.
- This in turn means that the period, known as TAD, is 200ns.

- Therefore, to create the required acquisition time of 2.4µS, we would need a 12 TAD time for the delay (i.e., $2.4E^{-6}/2E^{-9} = 12$).
- Using bits 5, 4, and 3 of the ADCON2 register, we have options of use 2, 4, 6, 8, 12, 16, and 20 TAD time periods.
- To obtain the required 2.4µs, you should select the 16 TAD option. Note that 12 TAD would equal the 2.4µs. However, this 2.4µs is the minimum not the maximum and it is safer to make the acquisition time slightly longer than is required. If it is too short, the result may not be accurate enough.
- To select this option we need to write
  - b5 = 1
  - b4 = 1
  - b3 = 0 16TAD
  - b2 = 1
  - b1 = 0
  - b0 = 0 divide by 4.
- This means that the whole operation will take 27.5 TAD periods and so take 5.5µs.

These two examples are to help you appreciate the importance of this acquisition time and how to use it to determine the TAD time. It also helps explain why the PIC offers so many options, as you can choose so many different oscillator options. Those of you who program the Arduino might think that the Arduino performs the ADC in a much simpler fashion. However, I believe it works in the same way as the PIC, but you are not given any options and it is all done for you.

Changing the ADC Input Channels

There is the possibility that you, as the programmer, will ask the ADC to switch to a different channel. Indeed, we will need to do this in the program for the joystick, as we are using two analog inputs. It is the data in the ADCON0 register that determines which channel the ADC is connected to; see Table 4-1.

Left or Right Justification

Figure 4-1 showed us what is meant by "justification". It is basically how we split the ten-bit result of the ADC into an eight-bit number and a two-bit number. I always use left justification, B7 = logic '0'. This is because it means that the two least significant bits are stored in ADRESL (see Figure 4-1). For all but the most accurate uses, the programmer can ignore these two bits, as they only represent voltages from 0 to 20mV approximately, at 5mV/bit. Indeed, if you ignore these two bits, it really means that you are using an eight-bit ADC instead of a ten-bit. The resolution then reduces to around 19mV per bit. This eight-bit result will be saved in the ADRESH. The remaining two bits will be stored in bit 7 and bit 6 of the ADRESL.

To select the appropriate channel or input to the ADC, we need only change the appropriate bits in the ADCON0 register. We will look at this in the next program.

The Joystick Program

The next thing to do is program the joystick and analyze Listing 4-1. There is a section of the program listing that is there to set up the LCD. We will be using the LCD to display the current x and y positions of the joystick. However, we will use the same LCD in a number of other programs that we will write. Therefore, we will create a header file that we can use for the LCD to save writing the same instructions again in the other programs.

Listing 4-1. The Joystick

```
/*
* File:   joyStickProg.c
Author: H. H. Ward
Created on 05 January 2021, 23:05
*/
#include <xc.h>
#include <conFigInternalOscNoWDTNoLVP.h>
#include <stdio.h>
//some definitions
      #define firstbyte      0b00110011
      #define secondbyte     0b00110011
      #define fourBitOp     0b00110010
      #define twoLines       0b00101100
      #define incPosition    0b00000110
      #define cursorNoBlink  0b00001100
      #define clearScreen     0b00000001
      #define returnHome      0b00000010
      #define lineTwo         0b11000000
      #define doBlink         0b00001111
      #define shiftLeft       0b00010000
      #define shiftRight      0b00010100
      #define shdisright      0b00011100
      #define lcdPort         PORTB
      #define eBit            PORTBbits.RB5
      #define RSpin           PORTBbits.RB4
      //some variables
```

```
unsigned char n, lcdData, lcdTempData, rsLine, dataIn;
char str[80];
unsigned char lcdInitialise [8] =
{
firstbyte,
secondbyte,
fourBitOp,
twoLines,
incPosition,
cursorNoBlink,
clearScreen,
returnHome,
};
//some subroutines
void sendData ()
{
lcdTempData = (lcdTempData << 4 | lcdTempData >>4);
lcdData = lcdTempData & 0x0F;
lcdData = lcdData | rsLine;
lcdPort = lcdData;
eBit = 1;
eBit = 0;
TMR0 = 0; while (TMR0 < 20);
}
void lcdOut ()
{
lcdTempData = lcdData;
sendData ();
sendData ();
}
```

```
void setUpTheLCD ()
{
TMR0 = 0;
while (TMR0 <255);
n = 0;
rsLine = 0X00;
while (n < 8)
{
lcdData = lcdInitialise [n];
lcdOut ();
n ++;
}
rsLine = 0x10;
}
void line2 ()
{
rsLine = 0X00;
lcdData = lineTwo;
lcdOut ();
rsLine = 0x10;
}
void clearTheScreen ()
{
rsLine = 0X00;
lcdData = clearScreen;
lcdOut ();
rsLine = 0x10;
}
void sendcursorhome ()
{
rsLine = 0X00;
lcdData = returnHome;
```

```
lcdOut ();
rsLine = 0x10;
}
void shiftcurleft ( unsigned char l)
{
for (n = 0; n < l; n ++)
{
rsLine = 0X00;
lcdData = shiftLeft;
lcdOut ();
rsLine = 0x10;
}
}
void shiftcurright (unsigned char r)
{
for (n = 0; n < r; n ++)
{
rsLine = 0X00;
lcdData = shdisright;
lcdOut ();
rsLine = 0x10;
}
}
void writeString (const char *words)
{
while (*words)
{
lcdData = *words;
lcdOut ();
*words ++;
}
}
```

```
//some variables
unsigned char Xvalue, Yvalue;
//some subroutines
void readX ()
{
ADCON0 = 0b00000001;
ADCON0bits.GODONE = 1;
while (ADCON0bits.GODONE);
Xvalue = ADRESH;
}
void readY ()
{
ADCON0 = 0b000000101;
ADCON0bits.GODONE = 1;
while (ADCON0bits.GODONE);
Yvalue = ADRESH;
}
void displayreading(float dp)
{
sprintf(str, "%.1f", dp);
writeString(str);
}
void main ()
{
PORTA = 0;
PORTB = 0;
PORTC = 0;
PORTD = 0;
TRISA = 0b00000011;
TRISB = 0x00;
TRISC = 0b00000000;
```

```
        TRISD = 0x00;
        ADCON0 = 0b00000001;
        ADCON1 = 0b00001101;
        ADCON2 = 0b00010001;
        OSCCON = 0b01110000;
        OSCTUNE = 0b10000000;
        T0CON = 0b11000111;
        setUpTheLCD ();
        writeString ("Coded Joystick");
        getreading: line2 ();
        lcdData = 0X58;
        lcdOut ();
        lcdData = 0X3D;
        lcdOut ();
        readX();
        displayreading(Xvalue);
        lcdData = 0X59;
        lcdOut ();
        lcdData = 0X3D;
        lcdOut ();
        readY();
        displayreading(Yvalue);
        goto getreading;
        }
```

The circuit for this project is shown in Figure 4-3. Jump ahead to Figure 4-6 to see the program working.

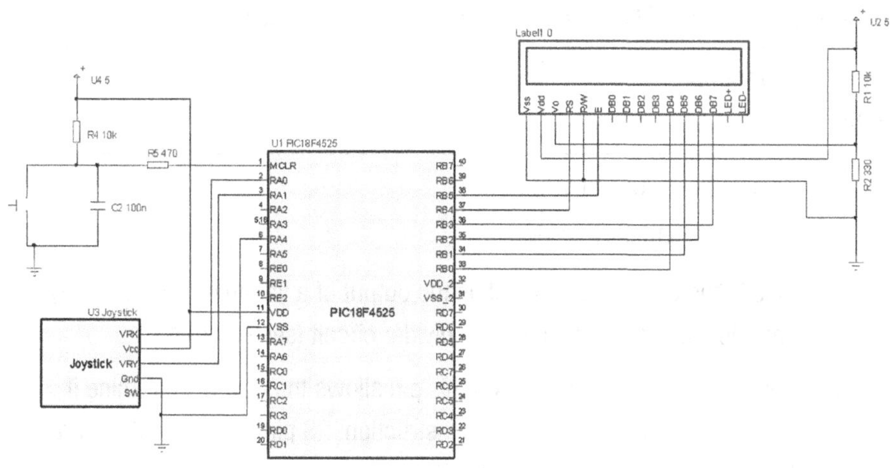

***Figure 4-3.** The basic circuit for the joystick project*

The instructions we will use to create the header file for the LCD are from line 10 to line 121 inclusive. We will do that after we have analyzed the listing. However, before we go into the analysis, I think we should look at how the LCD works.

The LCD

The LCD we will use is based on the LCD 1602 module, which can display two lines of text each with 16 characters. It is also the common module used with the Arduino. Like most LCDs, it uses either the Samsung KS0066U or the Hitachi HD44780 driver, which converts your binary digits into the required signals. Figure 4-4 shows the LCD and Table 4-4 gives a listing of the pin numbers.

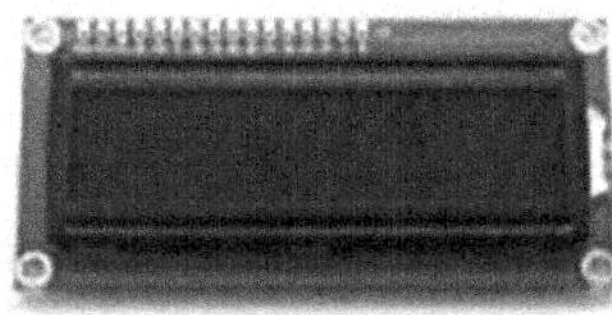

***Figure 4-4.** The LCD 1602 module*

Table 4-4. *The Pin Usage for the LCD 1602 Module*

Pin Number	Pin Usage
1	This is the ground or VSS Pin
2	This is the +5V or VDD Pin
3	This is the contrast pin, which is the output of a variable resistor. Really I set this pin to 0.3V via a voltage divider circuit (see Figure 4-3)
4	This is the RS pin. The logic on this pin allows the LCD to determine if the information being sent is an instruction: RS pin is a logic '0' or data to be displayed, RS pin is a logic '1'
5	This is the R/W pin. I simply connect this to ground for the 'W' or write operation
6	This is the 'E' pin. This is sent high then low to tell the LCD new information has been sent
7	This is data pin D0
8	This is data pin D1
9	This is data pin D2
10	This is data pin D3
11	This is data pin D4
12	This is data pin D5
13	This is data pin D6
14	This is data pin D7
15	This is the anode of the LED
16	This is the cathode of the LED

It can be set up to use eight data lines or just four data lines. We will use it with just four data lines and so save on the usage of I/O. I do have a header file I created that uses eight data lines, and I will include that in the appendix with a brief description of the differences. Note that both header files are set to PORTB as the PORT to which the LCD is connected. If you want to use a different PORT, you must change that in the header file and create a new header file.

We can communicate with the LCD in either instruction mode or data mode.

Instruction or Command Mode

This is used to first initialize the LCD (i.e., decide if we will operate it in eight-bit or four-bit data and other operational aspects). We then use the instruction mode to move the cursor positions. For example:

- Send the cursor to line 2.
- Shift cursor to right or left a number of characters.
- Move the cursor one bit to right after each character or not.
- Send the cursor to the home position.
- Clear the screen.
- Blink or not blink the cursor.

Data Mode

The LCD is programmed to recognize characters using ASCII code for each character. Basically, the LCD has memory locations, which are nonvolatile; the memory keeps the data even when the power is removed. In these memory locations, the pixel information to draw any one of the ASCII characters is stored. The address of each of these memory locations with pixel maps for a character corresponds to the same address found in the ASCII character standard table, shown in appendix, for that particular character. For example, the address in the LCD's memory, where it stores the pixel map for the number 3, is 0X33 or 0b00110011. If you look at the ASCII character set, you will see that 0X33 is the ASCII for the number 3. Also to display the character "a", you would send the information 0b01100001 to open up that location in the LCD's memory, and find the pixel map for the letter "a". The number 0b01100001 is the ASCII for the letter "a". This is to make it a more logical action to display any character on the LCD.

In another program that uses the LCD, we will look at creating our own characters to display on the LCD. We will need this level of understanding to be able to create our own characters.

Bytes and Nibbles

You should be able to appreciate that the information is sent to the LCD in the form of an eight-bit binary number, as each address in the LCD's memory is an eight-bit number. This includes the instructions for the LCD as well as the characters to be displayed. However, I have already said we will be operating the LCD in four-bit mode, which means we will be sending this information in just four bits at a time. Of course, eight-bit mode would be easier and faster but it would take up four more I/O pins. How can we use just four bits? This is because eight bits, which is usually termed "a byte", can be split up into two pieces of four bits, termed "a nibble". These are called the "high nibble" for bits 7, 6, 5, and 4 and the "low nibble" for bits 3, 2, 1, and 0. This means that we will be sending the information in two nibbles. The sequence is to send the high nibble first and then send the low nibble.

We will connect the LCD to PORTB, but really any port would do except perhaps PORTA, as this is used for the analog inputs.

Data 4 on the LCD goes to b0 on PORTB of the PIC.

Data 5 on the LCD goes to b1 on PORTB of the PIC.

Data 6 on the LCD goes to b2 on PORTB of the PIC.

Data 7 on the LCD goes to b3 on PORTB of the PIC.

Data pins D0 to D3 are not connected, as we will set the LCD to four-bit operation.

The Control Pins of the LCD

There are four control pins on the LCD:

- RS pin, which goes to bit 4 of PORTB.
- E pin, which goes to bit 5 of PORTB.
- R/W pin, which goes to ground as the write operation is active low.
- VEE or V0 pin, which controls the contrast of the display. This is connected to the output of a variable resistor or set to 0.3V with a simple voltage divider circuit (see Figure 4-3).

The RS pin on the LCD is used to allow the LCD to distinguish between instructions to the LCD or data to be displayed on the LCD. The RS pin goes to logic '0' for instructions, and the RS pin goes to logic '1' for data to be displayed. We must make this happen with the instructions we write in our program.

The 'E' pin is used to tell the driver inside the LCD that some new information has been sent to the LCD and it should deal with it. This is done by simply sending this pin high then back to low, with no delay, every time information is sent to the LCD.

The R/W pin is simply connected to 0V as the W, or Write, function is active low. This means that to write to the LCD, we need to set this pin to 0V. The 'R' I assume means Read but I have never used this function.

A variable voltage can be connected to the VEE pin of the LCD to control the contrast of the LCD. However, I find that using two resistors to divide the voltage down to around 300mV works fine.

The full pin connection is shown in Figure 4-5.

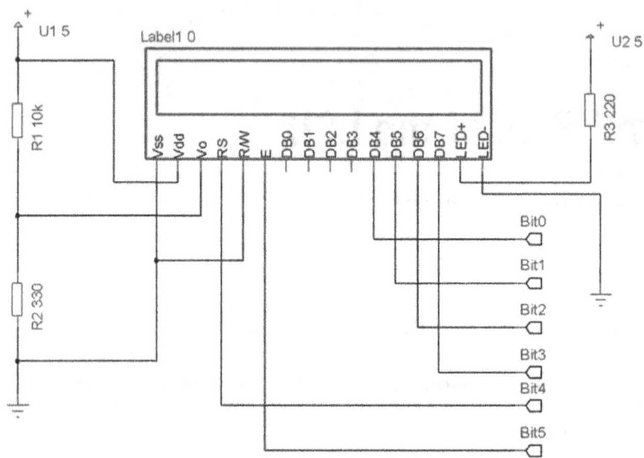

***Figure 4-5.** Connecting the LCD*

Analysis of Listing 4-1

Lines 1 to 6 have been looked at previously.

Line 7 #include #include <conFigInternalOscNoWDTNoLVP.h>

This includes a header file to write the configuration words for the PIC18F4525. This uses the same process as described in chapter 1 for the 16F88. The actual header file is listed in the appendix. You will need to ensure you have created this header file and saved in the include directory of your XC8 compiler. This would make it a global header file. We will use this header file in all the remaining programs.

Line 8 #include stdio.h

This is a header file that is open source; that is, it is made free for anyone to use. It allows us to use the "sprintf" function, which is used in the subroutine display reading on lines 139 to 143 in the listing. This allows us to send a value to the LCD without having to split it into hundreds, tens, units, and decimals. I have created my own header file that splits a value into hundreds, tens, units, and decimals but I want to introduce you to this "sprintf" function in this program. We will look at my header file in a later project. To use the "sprintf" function, you need to include this header file: stdio.h.

Line 9 //some definitions

I like to use comments to split my listings up into identifiable sections. That is what I am doing here.

Line 10 #define firstbyte 0b00110011

We have used definitions before in chapter 3. With lines 10 to 22, I am simply defining some useful phrases to represent the binary number for all the different instructions we may want to use to control the LCD. Indeed we will use eight of these instructions to set up the LCD before we start to use it. The information for these instructions has been derived from the LCD instruction set shown in the appendix.

Line 23 #define lcdPort PORTB

This simply tells the compiler that wherever we use the phrase lcdPort we mean PORTB. This is because we are connecting the LCD to PORTB. If we wanted to change the actual PORT we connected the LCD to, we would simply have to edit the actual PORT reference here in this line instead of finding every reference we made to the lcdPort in the program.

Line 24 #define eBit PORTBbits.RB5

Line 25 #define RSpin PORTBbits.RB4

These two instructions allocate the e pin and RS pin of the LCD to the two bits on PORTB. If we wanted to change the PORT the LCD was connected to, we would also have to change these references here.

Line 26 //some variables

This is just splitting the listing up.

Line 27 unsigned char n, lcdData, lcdTempData, rsLine, dataIn;

This gets the compiler to set aside five eight-bit memory locations for us to store some values. We give some of them meaningful names and others just letters by which we can refer to them.

Line 28 char str [80];

This is a very special instruction in that it gets the compiler to organize an array. We can have just one-dimensional arrays or multidimensional arrays. Here we are creating a one-dimensional array. We will consider the use of a two-dimensional array in another chapter. However, to help explain what this instruction is doing, I think I need to explain what an array is. This is the first of two arrays used in this program. This first array is used with the "sprintf" function used on line 140.

One-Dimensional Array

This is a method by which you can create a single list of variables, and store them in locations one after the other. Then use them sequentially one at a time or randomly. It is very important to appreciate that the memory locations are set up one after the other in order. The array can store a variable using all the common data types (unsigned char, integer, float, etc.). To create an array you simply declare it using the data type you want to use, then give it a sensible name followed by the '[6]' square brackets. Inside the square bracket, you state how many memory locations you want to place in your array. When the compiler program compiles the program, it will place the start of the array in a memory location and then create the total number of memory locations immediately after the start location, one after the other. There are two arrays used in the preceding LCD program, and line 28 is where the first one is created: char str[80]. This creates an array, named 'str', of 80 memory locations long in which data type char;, eight bits long. However, bit7 is used to indicate the sign, positive or negative, of the number stored in the loaction.

At line 29, I have declared the second array. It is of data type unsigned char and it has eight locations. This is where we will store the eight instructions to set up the LCD in the order that we want them to be used. Note that by declaring the array as follows; unsigned char lcdInitialise

[8] = , we have stated, by using the '=' sign, that we will define what should be stored in those eight memory locations at the same time as declaring the array. That is why there is no ';' semicolon at the end of this line; the instruction does not end here. In line 28, there is a semicolon, as that instruction has ended at the end of that line. That instruction is simply asking the compiler to create the array of 80 memory locations; we will load data in those locations later. With the array set up on line 29, we are defining the end of the instruction on line 39 with the closing curly bracket and the semicolon. The whole sequence of text in lines 29 to 39 is a program instruction. Try removing the ';' semicolon on line 39 and see what happens.

There is a comma after each statement of what is stored in this array. This is because this is a list, not a set of instructions; therefore, we don't use the semicolon.

Accessing Data in the Array

You can access the data in an array in two ways, one using a pointer, which is explained in the next section of the book, or one by calling the array in a similar way to calling a subroutine, but the array is not a subroutine. An example of assessing the data in the array without a pointer is as follows:
lcdInfo = lcdInitialise [4];

This will pull up the contents of location 4 in the array and place a copy of it in the variable lcdInfo. Note that the number of the first location in the array is always '0', so location [4] is the fifth item in the array.

Using Pointers

Pointers can be used to point to locations inside an array. To create a pointer, it is best to create an array then create the pointer with the same name and type as the array. This is best explained by going through some example instructions as shown in the following.

unsigned char dataArrayStore [6];

This creates an array of six locations one after the other, each being eight-bit memory locations, and gives it the name dataArrayStore.

unsigned char *dataArrayPointer;

This creates a memory location that can be loaded with a particular address of a location in the dataArrayStore array. The '*' signifies that this is a pointer.

The array and pointer have now been created. Note that you can use any name you want for the array and pointer; I tend to make them similar so that I know which pointer belongs to which array.

The next step is to load the pointer with the address of the first memory location in the array. This is done with the following instruction:

dataArrayPointer = dataArrayStore;

This will load the dataArrayPointer with the address of where the first memory location of the dataArrayStore array is in memory. This means that the dataArrayPointer is now pointing to the first location in the dataArrayStore array.

Now we can load some variables with the contents of the array using the following instructions.

Data0 = *dataArrayPointer;

This loads the variable Data0 with the contents of the memory location that dataArrayPointer is pointing to. In this case, it is pointing to the first location in the dataArrayStore array.

dataArrayPointer++;

This increments the contents of the dataArrayPointer, which means it now points to the next location in the dataArrayStore array.

Data1 = *dataArrayPointer;

This loads Data1 with the contents of the next memory location in the dataArrayStore array.

dataArrayPointer++;

This increments the contents of the dataArrayPointer, which means it now points to the next location in the dataArrayStore array.

I hope this text helps you to understand what arrays are and how we can use them. In this program, we are not using any pointers, as we don't need them.

Line 29 unsigned char [8] =

This tells the compiler to create an array with eight memory locations of eight unsigned chars. We will also be telling the compiler what data it should load into these eight locations when it creates this array.

Line 30 {

This is the opening curly bracket that encloses the data we want the compiler to store in the eight locations in the array.

Line 31 to 38 simply list the data we want to store in the array. The list uses the phrases we defined earlier in lines 10 to 22.

Line 31 firstbyte,

This is a byte that must be sent first to the LCD as an instruction to format the LCD. It is repeated on line 32, as some LCDs need this to be sent twice but some only need it sent once. To save writing two different header files, I simply send it twice. The LCD does not care if you repeat the same instruction so long as you send it once.

Line 33 fourBitOp,

This sets the LCD to four-bit mode not eight bit. This does mean we must send the information, instructions as well as data, in two sets of nibbles, which means more programming, but it saves on I/O.

Lines 34 to 38 are the other five instructions that we need to set up the LCD for operation in four-bit mode. I hope the phrases I have used to describe the instructions do explain what the instruction is for.

Line 39 };

This is the closing curly bracket of the array. Note the semicolon at the end of the line.

Line 40 // some subroutines

We are now going to list the subroutines that are used with sending information to the LCD. It will become apparent that some of these subroutines will call other subroutines in the list here. This is termed nested subroutines. However, you must ensure that when you are using nested subroutines, you list the subroutines that the other will call before them in the program listing. The compiler compiles the program in the order it is listed. Therefore, if an instruction is going to use a label that is declared in another part of the listing, the compiler will try to find it in what it has already compiled. If it has not been compiled yet, the compiler will throw up an error.

To help you appreciate what I am trying to tell you here, comment out the definition of the line #define secondbyte, on line 11, and write the line on the line below line 39 (i.e., insert it after the closing curly bracket of the array). Now when you try the compile the program by clicking the blue hammer on the main menu bar in MPLABX, it should throw up an error saying it cannot find the identifier "secondbyte". Note that you can comment out a line by writing the two forward slashes "//" in front of it. Make sure you return the program back to what it was (i.e., to the correct program).

It is sometimes useful in debugging your programs to comment out lines of instructions in this way.

Line 41 void sendData ()

This creates a subroutine that the setUpTheLCD subroutine, written on lines 57 to 70, will call later. It is a subroutine that will, as the name suggests, send the data, be it an instruction or data to be displayed, to the LCD.

Line 42 {

The opening curly bracket that envelopes the instructions for the sendData subroutine.

Line 43 lcdTempData = (lcdTempData << 4 | lcdTempData >>4);

This is a complex instruction that takes the data that is in the LcdTemData variable and swaps the nibbles around. The data that was the high nibble in bits 7, 6, 5, and 4 becomes the data in the low nibble in bits 3, 2, 1, and 0. Also what was in the low nibble becomes the data in the high nibble.

For example,

if the data in LcdTemData was

0b11010010

then after this instruction the data would be

0b00101101.

This is done because we must send the high nibble of the information to the LCD first, then send the low nibble.

Note that the variable lcdTempData will have been loaded with the information we want to send to the LCD in another part of the program. Indeed, it is done in the next subroutine, which then calls this subroutine.

Line 44 lcdData = lcdTempData & 0x0F;

This loads the variable lcdData with a copy of what is in the variable lcdTempData. However, before the copy is made, the contents of lcdTempData are bit ANDED with the data 0X0F. Note that 0X0F is 0b00001111 in binary, and so this instruction does a bit AND with the two pieces of data (i.e., what is in lcdTempData and 0X0F). As an example of what this will do, we will use the concept that the content in lcdTempData is 0b00101101 after the swapping example for line 43. This means that the bit AND will be performed as shown in Table 4-5.

Table 4-5. *The Swapping of the Nibbles in lcdTempData*

	High Nibble				**Low Nibble**			
	Bit 7	Bit 6	Bit 5	Bit 4	Bit 3	Bit 2	Bit 1	Bit 0
lcdTempData	0	0	1	0	1	1	0	1
0X0F	0	0	0	0	1	1	1	1
Result	**0**	**0**	**0**	**0**	**1**	**1**	**0**	**1**

To appreciate what is happening here, it might be useful to show the truth table for a two-bit logical AND operation.

This is shown in Table 4-6.

Table 4-6. *The Two-Input AND Truth Table*

B	A	F
0	0	0
0	1	0
1	0	0
1	1	1

This shows that the result 'F' is only a logic '1' when input 'A' AND input 'B' are each a logic '1'.

Therefore, when we perform a bit AND operation with any eight bits and 0b00001111; the result will always be the same as the low nibble of the first eight bits and the high nibble will always be logic '0's. This is termed bit masking, where we mask out the bits we are not interested in by ANDING them with a logic '0'. With this instruction on line 44, we only want the data in lcdData to be a copy of the low nibble of what is in lcdTempData. That is because we are only sending the low nibble of lcdData to the LCD.

Line 45 lcdData = lcdData | rsLine;

This is another rather complex instruction. This may be another wordy explanation of how it works. However, please bear with me as I do think it is important that you understand how these instructions work; you may then be able to modify and use them for your own uses.

The main part of the instruction is the symbol "|", which in C programming stands for the logical OR operation. This will perform a logical OR operation on each of the bits in the two eight-bit variables, lcdData and rsLine. Both these variables are global variables that have been set up in line 27. The truth table for a two-bit logical OR operation is shown in Table 4-7.

Table 4-7. *The Two-Input OR Truth Table*

B	A	F
0	0	0
0	1	1
1	0	1
1	1	1

This shows that the output 'F' will be a logic '1' when A OR B is a logic '1.' However, it shows that the output 'F' will also be a logic '1' when both A AND B are a logic '1.' That is not a true OR function, and that is why this function is sometimes called, correctly, the "Inclusive OR," as it includes the AND function.

The real OR function will produce a logic '1' only when A OR B is a logic '1' and exclude the AND function. That logic operation is called the "EXOR" (i.e., the EXclusive OR, as it excludes the AND function).

However, I digress; we really want to know what this instruction is doing. To understand that we need to remember that there is a "RS" pin on the LCD. It is the logic on the RS pin which allows the LCD to determine if the information being sent to it is an instruction or data to be displayed. If the information is an instruction, then the logic on this pin must be set to a logic '0.' If the information is data to be displayed, then the logic on the RS pin must be set to a logic '1.' It is this instruction that makes this happen.

Using the example data we have used for the previous instructions, we should know that at this point in the program the data in lcdData will be 0b00001101 (see Table 4-5). If we assume that this will be data to be sent to be displayed on the LCD, then we would have already loaded the variable rsLine with the data 0b00010000. You should note that bit 4 of the rsLine is a logic '1.'

If we now perform the logical bit OR operation on both variables, the result will be as shown in Table 4-8.

Table 4-8. *The Logical OR Operation with lcdData and rsLine with Data to Be Displayed*

	High Nibble				**Low Nibble**			
	Bit 7	Bit 6	Bit 5	Bit 4	Bit 3	Bit 2	Bit 1	Bit 0
lcdData	0	0	0	0	1	1	0	1
rsLine	0	0	0	1	0	0	0	0
lcdData Result	**0**	**0**	**0**	**1**	**1**	**1**	**0**	**1**

This means that bit 4 of the variable lcdData will go to a logic '1'. Therefore, when PORTB, which is connected to the LCD, is loaded with the data in the variable lcdData, then bit 4 will be a logic '1'. As bit 4 of PORTB is connected to the RS pin on the LCD, then the LCD will know that this information is part of the data to be displayed on the LCD.

However, if we were sending an instruction to the LCD, we would have previously loaded the variable rsLine with the data 0b00000000 (i.e., bit 4 is a logic '0'). If we now perform the logical OR operation, we would get the result shown in Table 4-9.

Table 4-9. *The Logical OR Operation with lcdData and rsLine with an Instruction to the LCD*

	High Nibble				Low Nibble			
	Bit 7	Bit 6	Bit 5	Bit 4	Bit 3	Bit 2	Bit 1	Bit 0
lcdData	0	0	0	0	1	1	0	1
rsLine	0	0	0	0	0	0	0	0
lcdData Result	**0**	**0**	**0**	**0**	**1**	**1**	**0**	**1**

In this way, the logic on bit 4, which is the RS pin of the LCD, will be set to a logic '0'. This means the LCD will know that the four bits being sent to it are part of an instruction.

I hope this goes some way to explaining what this instruction is trying to do and how it achieves it.

Line 46 lcdPort = lcdData;

This simply copies the information in lcdData to the lcdPort. Note that this has been defined on line 23 as PORTB, which is connected to the LCD. Therefore, this sends the information directly to the LCD.

Line 47 ebit = 1;

Line 48 ebit = 0;

These two instructions force the logic on bit 5 of PORTB (i.e., the "e" pin of the LCD), high then low with no delay. This is done to tell the LCD that some new information has been sent to it and that it should deal with it.

Line 49 TMR0 = 0; while (TMR0 < 20);

This is actually two instructions written on the same line in the text editor in MPLABX. The two instructions are separated by the semicolon ";", which denotes the end of each separate instruction. It is down to user preference to do this or not. I prefer to have all instructions written on their own lines. I have just done this here to show you it is OK to do this.

The first instruction, TMR0 = 0; simply loads the variable TMR0 with the value 0 or 0b00000000. This is an SFR (special function register), used by timer0 to keep track of the value it has counted up to at present. Here we are setting it back to zero so that it starts counting again from zero.

The next instruction, while (TMR0 <20); simply gets the PIC to do nothing while the value in TMR0 is less than 20. This simply creates a 20 × 128μs delay (i.e., a 2.56ms delay). This delay is required to ensure the LCD has time to react to any information sent to it. There are different times required for different instructions (see LCD instruction set in the appendix), but it is simpler to have one delay that is long enough for all instructions.

Lime 50}

This is the closing bracket of the sendData subroutine.

Line 51 void lcdOut ()

This creates the subroutine lcdOut. This calls the subroutine sendData.

Line 53 lcdTempData = lcdData;

This just puts a copy of the data in the variable lcdData into the variable lcdTempData. The variable lcdTempData is used in the subroutine sendData.

Note that I have omitted line 52, which is simply the opening curly bracket of the subroutine. I will omit these curly brackets from now on, as I am sure you know that they have to be included and what they are used for.

Line 54 sendData ();

This calls the subroutine sendData the first time to send just the high nibble of lcdTempData to the LCD.

Line 55 sendData ();

This calls the subroutine sendData a second time, but this time it will send the low nibble on lcdTempData to the LCD.

Line 57 void setUpTheLcd ()

This creates the subroutine to set up the LCD.

Line 59 TMR0 = 0;

Line 60 while (TMR0 < 255);

These two instructions create a 256 × 128µs delay, which is approximately 33ms. This delay must be run before we send any information, data, or instruction to the LCD. This is to allow the circuitry of the LCD to settle down and be ready to receive instructions or data.

Line 61 n =0;

This simply loads the global variable created on line 27, with the value 0. This is to get it ready for the instruction on lines 63 and 65.

Line 62 rsLine = 0X00;

This loads the variable rsLine with zero. This is because the information we are going to send to the LCD will be instructions not data to be displayed.

Line 63 while (n < 8)

This sets up a loop that the PIC will carry out as long as the result of the test is true. The test simply asks if the value in the variable 'n' is less than 8. While the test is true, the PIC must carry out the instructions within the curly brackets on lines 64 and 68.

Line 65 lcdData = lcdInitialise [n];

This gets the PIC to place a copy of what is in the array location indicated by the value in the variable 'n'. The array used is the lcdInitialise array as stated in the instruction.

As the value in the variable 'n' is 0, at this point in the program, then the variable lcdData will be loaded with a copy of what is in the first location of the array. That will be the data for the instruction firstbyte.

Line 66 lcdOut ( );

This simply calls the subroutine lcdOut, which will send the information in lcdData to the LCD.

Line 67 n ++;

This simply increments the value in the variable 'n' by 1. This gets the variable ready for the test in line 63 and then the instruction in line 65 as long as n is less than 8.

Note that after this instruction, the PIC carries out the test on line 63. When n finally becomes equal to 8, the PIC will stop going through the instructions between the curly brackets and go to line 69 in the program listing.

Line 69 rsLine = 0X10;

This ensures bit 4 of the rsLine variable is set to a logic '1'. This is done to get the variable rsLine ready for the instruction on line 45, where it is "OR ed" with the variable lcdTempData. Bit 4 is set to a logic '1' because most information to be sent to the LCD will be data to be displayed.

Line 71 void line2 ()

This creates a subroutine that will send the cursor to the beginning of the second line on the LCD.

Line 73 rsLine = 0X00;

This ensures that bit 4 of the rsLine variable is a logic '0'. This is done because the next information to be sent to the LCD will be an instruction.

Line 74 lcdData = lineTwo;

This loads the variable lcdData with the instruction "lineTwo" ready for the next instruction. This phrase "lineTwo" has been defined in line 18 to mean the number 0b11000000. This is the code to send the cursor to the beginning of the second line on the LCD.

Line 75 lcdOut ();

This calls the subroutine to send the instruction to the LCD.

Line 76 rsLine = 0X00;

This ensures bit 4 of rsLine is set back to a logic '0'.

Lines 78 to 84 do the same but with the instruction "clearScreen".

Lines 85 to 91 do the same but with the instruction "returnHome".

Line 92 void shiftcurleft (unsigned char l)

This sets up a subroutine that is used to shift the cursor a number of places to the left (i.e., back toward the start of the line it's on). This subroutine expects a value to be sent up to it when it is called. This value will be loaded into the local variable 'l' for left. Note that this variable can only be used in this subroutine, as it is local to it. There is the possibility that you could create a global variable, or even another local variable with the same name (i.e., 'l'). However, you should avoid doing this as it will cause you confusion, not the PIC but you, so don't do it.

Line 94 for (n = 0; n < l; n ++)

This sets up a normal for (test is true) do what I say loop that will get the PIC to carry out the instructions from line 95 to 100 a set number of times controlled by the value in the variable 'l.'

This subroutine will move the cursor a set number of places to the left controlled by the value in the variable 'l.'

Lines 102 to 111 do the same as in the preceding but this time shift the cursor to the right (i.e., further toward the end of the line).

These two subroutines can be used when you only want to change a certain number of characters on the LCD screen.

Line 112 void writeString (const char *words)

This sets up a subroutine that will send a string of characters to the LCD. This is rather a complex instruction that is using a local pointer *words. This pointer is used to select the character that is to be sent to the LCD. To appreciate how this subroutine works we need to look at the following instructions.

Line 114 while (*words)

This creates a loop that the PIC will carry out while the test is true. The problem is understanding what the test is. The test, written inside the normal brackets, is simply the pointer *words. This is actually testing to see what character the pointer *words is pointing to. This is linked to the instruction that calls this subroutine. The first instance of the call is on line 160 writeString ("Coded Joystick"). This is sending the ASCII for the characters written inside the normal brackets between the quotation marks to the subroutine writeString. The ASCII for these characters will be loaded sequentially into an array which was set up automatically with the writeString type instruction. However, what also happens automatically by the compiler program, but is hidden from you, is that the ASCII for the important "null" character is added to this array.

Now the test in the while (*words) is actually saying that while the pointer *words is **NOT** pointing to the "null" character, the PIC must carry out the instructions between lines 115 and 119. This important "null" character is inserted into the array to tell the PIC that it has come to the end of the characters that need to be sent to the LCD. The null character is not sent to the LCD. When the pointer *words is pointing to this null character, the test while (*words) will become untrue and the PIC jumps out of the loop.

Line 116 lcdData = *words;

This loads the variable lcdData with the contents of the array, created with the writeString instruction, at the memory location that the pointer *words is pointing to. The pointer *words would have automatically been set to point to the first location in the array when this subroutine was called as in line 160.

Line 117 lcdOut ();

This calls the subroutine to send the character to the LCD.

Line 118 *words ++;

This simply increments the contents of the pointer *words. The PIC then goes back to line 114, where it tests to see if the pointer is still not pointing to the null character. If it isn't, then the PIC carries out the instructions between line 115 and 119 again.

Lines 119 and 120 are the closing curly brackets.

I know this analysis of these instructions for the writeString subroutine is quite wordy, but it is a complex set of instructions. However, it is a very powerful set of instructions, and I think it is important you understand how they work. You may need to read through them again but it is worth it.

Note that the instructions between lines 9 and 120 can be used to create a header file for the LCD. I have done that and named the header file "4bitLCDPortb.h". I suggest you do the same. The procedure for creating a header file has been described in chapter 2. Remember to store a copy of your header file in the include folder of the xc8 compiler software. This will make the header file a global header file.

Lines 121 to 123 are procedures we have covered before.

Line 124 void readX ()

This is creating a subroutine to read the value for the x axis from the joystick.

Line 126 ADCON0 = 0b00000001;

This turns the ADC on (i.e., bit 1 is set to a logic '1') and selects channel 0 to be connected to the ADC (i.e., bits 5, 4, 3, and 2 are set to a logic '0').

Line 127 ADCON0bits.GODONE = 1;

This starts the ADC conversion after the capacitor in the sample and hold circuit has acquired the input voltage. The PIC will automatically reset this bit back to a logic '0' when all ten bits have been converted.

Line 128 while (ADCONbits.GODONE);

This gets the PIC to do nothing while the GODONE bit is at a logic '1'. This makes the PIC wait until the conversion has completed.

Line 129 Xvalue = ADRESH;

This loads the variable Xvalue with the most significant eight bits of the result of the ADC conversion. We are not using the two least significant bits. The value in the ADRESH register goes from 0 to 255. This actually will create a small problem in that the x axis should really go from 0 to 360. We will overcome this problem with the next program.

Lines 131 to 137 do the same but for the Yvalue, which is for the y axis of the joystick. Note that the ADC is changed to connect to channel 1 with the instruction ADCON0 = 0b00000101 (i.e., bits 5, 4, 3, and 2 are set to 0001; see Table 4-1).

Line 138 void displayreading (float, dp)

This creates a subroutine that will eventually display the reading of the joystick on the LCD. This expects a float value to be sent up to it which will be copied into the local variable dp. The float is a value that includes decimal values.

Line 140 sprintf (str, "%.1f", dp);

This is a function that is in the stdio.h header file. It will fill the array "str" with the data that has been loaded into the float variable "dp" when the subroutine displayreading was called. The term "%.1f" sets the value to contain one number after the decimal point.

Line 141 writeString (str);

This will send the data in the array str with the float value that was put into it in the last instruction.

Lines 143 to 152 have been used in chapters 2 and 3.

Line 153 ADCON0 = 0b00000001;

This turns the ADC on and selects channel 0.

Line 154 ADCON1 = 0b00001101;

This makes all the inputs digital except AN0 and AN1, which are set to analog. This is done with the bits 3, 2, 1, and 0 (see Table 4-2).

Line 155 ADCON2 = 0b00010001;

This sets the ADC to left justification using 4TAD at a frequency of 1Mhz. This process has been looked at earlier in this chapter (see Table 4-3).

Lines 156, 157, and 158 have been analyzed previously.

Line 159 setUpTheLCD ();

This calls the subroutine to set up the LCD.

Line 160 writeString ("Coded Joystick");

This calls the subroutine writeString and sends the ASCII for the characters between the two quotation marks to the subroutine. Note that this also automatically sends the ASCII for the "null" character to signify the end of the string of characters.

Line 161 getreading: line2 ();

This is creating the label "getreading". This label is used in the instruction on line 174, where the PIC is forced to "goto" this label.

This instruction part calls the subroutine line2 () to send the cursor to the beginning of the second line on the LCD.

Line 162 lcdData 0X58;

This loads the variable lcdData with the value 0X58 in hexadecimal. This is the ASCII for the character "X".

Line 163 lcdOut();

This calls the subroutine “lcdOut” to send this ASCII value in lcdData to the LCD screen.

Line 164 lcdData = 0X3D;

This loads the variable lcdData with the value 0X3D. This is the ASCII for the equal sign “=”.

Line 165 lcdOut ();

This calls the subroutine “lcdOut” to send the value to the LCD screen.

Line 166 readX ();

This calls the subroutine readX to get the current value for the X axis from the joystick.

Line 167 displayreading (Xvalue);

This calls the subroutine displayreading and sends the value in the variable Xvalue to that subroutine. This will then display the value on the LCD.

Lines 168 to 173 do the same process but now for the y axis reading from the joystick.

Line 174 goto getreading;

This makes the PIC jump back to the label “getreading”, which is on line 161. The PIC then repeats lines 161 to 174 forever until the PIC is switched off.

I hope this analysis does help you to understand how this program actually works.

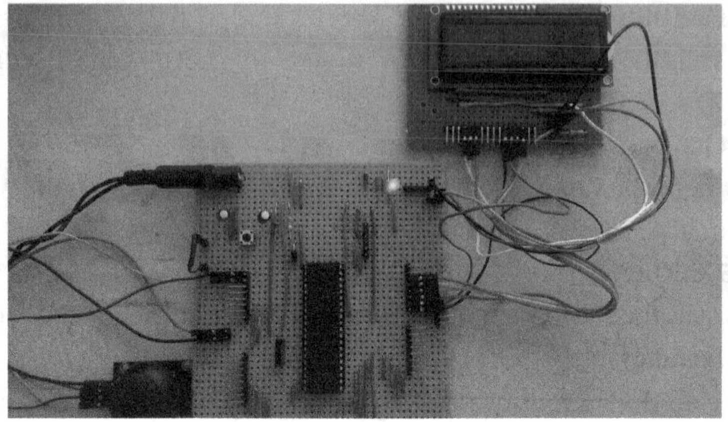

Figure 4-6. *The joystick program working with the homemade prototype board*

Figure 4-6 shows the program working. The joystick is on the bottom left-hand corner. The two inputs are connected to bit 0 and bit 1 of PORTA. The LCD is shown in the top right corner and it is connected to PORTB.

Joystick and Stepper Motor

Listing 4-2 is an attempt to show you how you can make use of the joystick program to control the rotation of a small stepper motor. The program only controls the motor in one axis, the y axis, but the principle can be extended to two or more axis using two or more motors.

Listing 4-2. The Joystick and Stepper Motor Program

```
/*Program to control a Stepping Motor
with a joystick
Written By Mr Hubert Ward for the PIC18F4525
Dated 16/01/2021
Configuration PIC18F4525
```

```
OSC set to INTIO67
WDT set to OFF
LVP set to OFF*/
#include <xc.h>
     #include <conFigInternalOscNoWDTNoLVP.h>
     #include <4bitLCDPortb.h>
     #include <stdio.h>
     #include <math.h>
     // Some definitions
     # define orange    PORTDbits.RD3
     # define yellow    PORTDbits.RD2
     # define pink      PORTDbits.RD1
     # define blue      PORTDbits.RD0
     # define startButton    PORTAbits.RA2
     //Global variables
     unsigned char n, speed, clkcount;
     unsigned int ck, rest = 256, dist;
     unsigned int Xvalue, Yvalue, first180;
     //some subroutines
     void readX ()
     {
     ADCON0 = 0b00000001;
     ADCON0bits.GODONE = 1;
     while (ADCON0bits.GODONE);
     Xvalue = ADRESH;
     }
     void readY ()
     {
     ADCON0 = 0b000000101;
     ADCON0bits.GODONE = 1;
     while (ADCON0bits.GODONE);
```

```
Yvalue = ADRESH;
}
void displayreading(float dp)
{
sprintf(str, "%.1f", dp);
writeString(str);
}
void delay (unsigned char t)
{
while (clkcount < t)
{
TMR0 = 0;
while (TMR0 < 250);
clkcount ++;
}
}
void set180 ()
{
while (startButton)
{
orange = 1;
yellow = 0;
pink = 0;
blue = 1;
TMR0 = 0;
while (TMR0 < speed);
orange = 0;
yellow = 0;
pink = 0;
blue = 1;
TMR0 = 0;
```

```
        while (TMR0 < speed);
        orange = 0;
        yellow = 0;
        pink = 1;
        blue = 1;
        TMR0 = 0;
        while (TMR0 < speed);
        orange = 0;
        yellow = 0;
        pink = 1;
        blue = 0;
        TMR0 = 0;
        while (TMR0 < speed);
        orange = 0;
        yellow = 1;
        pink = 1;
        blue = 0;
        TMR0 = 0;
        while (TMR0 < speed);
        orange = 0;
        yellow = 1;
        pink = 0;
        blue = 0;
        TMR0 = 0;
        while (TMR0 < speed);
        orange = 1;
        yellow = 1;
        pink = 0;
        blue = 0;
        TMR0 = 0;
        while (TMR0 < speed);
```

```
        orange = 1;
        yellow = 0;
        pink = 0;
        blue = 0;
        TMR0 = 0;
        while (TMR0 < speed);
        }
        }
        void main()
        {
        PORTA = 0;
        PORTB = 0;
        PORTC = 0;
        PORTD = 0;
        TRISA = 0b00000111;
        TRISB = 0x00;
        TRISC = 0b00000000;
        TRISD = 0x00;
        ADCON0 = 0b00000001;
        ADCON1 = 0b00001101;
        ADCON2 = 0b00111001;
        OSCCON = 0b01110000;
        OSCTUNE = 0b10000000;
        T0CON = 0b11000111;
        T1CON = 0b00010001;
        setUpTheLCD ();
        clearTheScreen ();
        PORTC = 0;
        writeString ("Coded Joystick");
        getreading: line2 ();
        speed = 50;
```

```
ck = 0;
set180 ();
while (1)
{
read:  delay (16);
line2 ();
lcdData = 0X59;
lcdOut ();
lcdData = 0X3D;
lcdOut ();
readY();
displayreading(Yvalue*1.40625);
if (round (2*Yvalue) > rest) goto clockwise;
if (round (2*Yvalue) < rest) goto anticlockwise;
if (round  (2*Yvalue) == rest) goto read;
clockwise:    while (rest != round (2*Yvalue))
{
orange = 1;
yellow = 0;
pink = 0;
blue = 1;
TMR0 = 0;
while (TMR0 < speed);
orange = 0;
yellow = 0;
pink = 0;
blue = 1;
TMR0 = 0;
while (TMR0 < speed);
orange = 0;
yellow = 0;
```

```
pink = 1;
blue = 1;
TMR0 = 0;
while (TMR0 < speed);
orange = 0;
yellow = 0;
pink = 1;
blue = 0;
TMR0 = 0;
while (TMR0 < speed);
orange = 0;
yellow = 1;
pink = 1;
blue = 0;
TMR0 = 0;
while (TMR0 < speed);
orange = 0;
yellow = 1;
pink = 0;
blue = 0;
TMR0 = 0;
while (TMR0 < speed);
orange = 1;
yellow = 1;
pink = 0;
blue = 0;
TMR0 = 0;
while (TMR0 < speed);
orange = 1;
yellow = 0;
pink = 0;
```

```
blue = 0;
TMR0 = 0;
while (TMR0 < speed);
rest ++;
}
orange = 0;
yellow = 0;
pink = 0;
blue = 0;
TMR0 = 0;
while (TMR0 < speed);
goto read;
anticlockwise:   while (rest != round (2*Yvalue))
{
TMR0 = 0;
while (TMR0 < speed);
orange = 1;
yellow = 0;
pink = 0;
blue = 0;
TMR0 = 0;
while (TMR0 < speed);
orange = 1;
yellow = 1;
pink = 0;
blue = 0;
TMR0 = 0;
while (TMR0 < speed);
orange = 0;
yellow = 1;
pink = 0;
```

```
        blue = 0;
        TMR0 = 0;
        while (TMR0 < speed);
        orange = 0;
        yellow = 1;
        pink = 1;
        blue = 0;
        TMR0 = 0;
        while (TMR0 < speed);
        orange = 0;
        yellow = 0;
        pink = 1;
        blue = 0;
        TMR0 = 0;
        while (TMR0 < speed);
        orange = 0;
        yellow = 0;
        pink = 1;
        blue = 1;
        TMR0 = 0;
        while (TMR0 < speed);
        orange = 0;
        yellow = 0;
        pink = 0;
        blue = 1;
        TMR0 = 0;
        while (TMR0 < speed);
        orange = 1;
        yellow = 0;
        blue = 1;
        TMR0 = 0;
```

```
        while (TMR0 < speed);
        rest --;
        }
        orange = 0;
        yellow = 0;
        pink = 0;
        blue = 0;
        TMR0 = 0;
        while (TMR0 < speed);
        goto read;
        }
        }
```

Figure 4-7 shows the circuit diagram for this project, and Figure 4-8 shows the small stepper motor that was used.

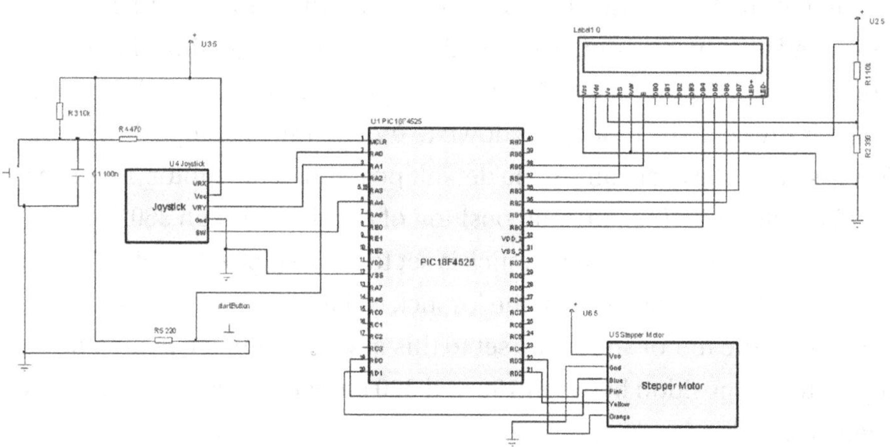

Figure 4-7. *The circuit diagram for joystick and stepper motor program*

Figure 4-8. *The 5V four-phase stepper motor*

This is the stepper motor used in the program. It can be connected to a small driver circuit as shown in Figure 4-9. This uses a ULN2004 Darlington array chip.

Analysis of Listing 4-2

The first thing the program does is allow the motor to rotate until it is signaled to stop. The signal to stop the motor is the pressing of the momentary stop button, which is connected to bit 2 of PORTA. When this switch is pressed, the input goes down to 0V and the PIC stops the motor. This is so that the user can set the default position of the motor. This can then be called 180° (i.e., the mid position of rotating through 360°).

This is done because the joystick is set to the mid position of its travel. Therefore, the starting point of the joystick is that it is set to a position of 180° and so the motor should be set to this mid position. It can then be moved to any position between 180 and 360 degrees as well as from 180 to 0 degrees.

The program then moves on to the loop whereby it gets the current position of the joystick and then moves the stepper motor to that position.

Lines 1 to 52 have no real new instructions; they have been used in all the programs so far. However, we should look at the following instruction:

Line 13 #include <math.h>

This is a freely available header file that includes the instructions for some mathematical operations. This is required for the "round" function we use in the program. This will round up a value that has decimal values to an integer value.

Lines 53 to 106 simply create a subroutine that gets the stepper motor to constantly rotate until the user presses the stop button. This is to allow the user to define the 180° mid travel position of the motor. These instructions have been analyzed in chapter 3 (see analysis of Listing 3-3).

Lines 107 to 130 have been analyzed with Listing 3-3.

Line 131 set180 ();

This calls the set180 subroutine, which is used to set the default position of the motor. This subroutine is written between lines 53 and 106. The instructions have been analyzed in Listing 3-3 already.

Lines 132 to 139 have been analyzed in Listing 4-1.

Line 140 readY();

This calls the subroutine to get the current value of the y axis from the joystick.

Line 141 displayreading(Yvalue*1.40625);

This calls the subroutine displayreading. It will send the data in the variable Yvalue to be used in the subroutine. However, before the data is sent, it is multiplied by 1.40625. This is required to convert the data in Yvalue to a value related to the 0 to 360 degrees of rotation. The value of 1.40625 is calculated as 360/256 = 1.40625. This is because the maximum value that the Yvalue could take, without this multiplication, is 255 when it should go to 360. This solves the issue identified in the previous program listing.

Line 142 if (round (2*Yvalue) > rest) goto clockwise;

This is a test to see if the reading from the y axis is greater than what is stored in the variable "rest". If the result of the test is true, then the PIC is forced to go to the instruction at the label "clockwise". In line 22, the variable "rest" was created and loaded with the value 256. The value of

256 is related to the number of sequences the stepper motor would have turned by to get to the mid position of 180°. Note that in chapter 3 we stated that the stepper motor would go through 512 sequences of the eight steps to move through 360°. This means that with this test we are asking whether the position of the joystick is at a position that is greater than the 180° of rotation. If the reading is greater, then we must move the motor in a clockwise direction to align with the position of the joystick. In the test we are multiplying the value in the Yvalue variable by 2 because the joystick is being operated in eight-bit resolution. Remember that we are only using the ADRESH register, which uses the eight most significant bits of the ten-bit ADC result. As we are only using eight bits, then the value in the variable Yvalue can only go from 0 to 255, not 0 to 512. Therefore, we must multiply the value in Yvalue by 2 before we compare it with the variable "rest". This is done by writing 2*Yvalue in the instruction. We are using the "round" operation that is in the header file math.h. This would round the value up if we needed it to. This is not really required as we are multiplying by 2. However, if we were dividing by 2, we would need this round function and so I am adding this just to show you how it can be used.

Line 143 if (round (2*Yvalue) < rest) goto anticlockwise;

This does the same as the previous instruction; however, it is testing to see if the joystick position is at a position less than 180°. If it is, then we must move the motor anticlockwise to align the motor with the joystick.

Line 144 if (round (2*Yvalue) == rest) goto read;

This test is to see if the joystick position is at the midpoint of 180°. If it is, then we simply get the PIC to go back to the label "read" that is on line 134. Here, after a small delay of 16 × 128μs (i.e., approximately 2ms), we get the PIC to get the position of the joystick again. Note the use of the two '==' equal signs. This is because we are asking the question of whether the 2*Yvalue has become equal to the value in the variable "rest".

Line 145 clockwise: while (rest != round (2*Yvalue))

This is where the PIC will go to if the test in line 142 is true, using the label clockwise. The instruction part is while (rest != round (2*Yvalue)).

This test will be true as long as the value in rest is NOT equal to 2*Yvalue. While the test is true, the PIC must carry out the instructions between lines 146 and 196, which get the PIC to turn the motor clockwise.

Line 195 rest++;

This increments the value in rest. This means there will be a time when the test on line 145 will become untrue, as rest will equal 2*Yvalue. The PIC would then stop turning the motor clockwise, as the motor has moved to the new position.

Line 197 to 202 simply stop the motor by turning off the supply to all the coils in stepper motor.

Line 203 goto read;

This forces the PIC to go to the label 'read' on line 134. This is where the PIC waits approximately half a second. Then, on lines 135 to 139, it gets the LCD ready to display the reading from the joystick. Then, on line 140, it calls the subroutine to get the current position of the y axis reading from the joystick.

Line 204 anticlockwise: while (rest != round (2*Yvalue))

This is where the PIC goes to if the instruction on line 143 is true using the label anticlockwise. The PIC will carry out the instructions between lines 205 and 256, while the value in rest is NOT equal to the round(2*Yvalue), which gets the PIC to turn the motor anticlockwise. Note that on line 255 we decrement the value in rest. This will continue until the value in rest has been reduced to be equal to the round(2*Yvalue).

Lines 257 to 262 stop the stepper motor by turning off all the coils and waiting for the current to die down.

Then on line 263 we force the PIC to go back to the label read on line 134 and the process starts again.

I hope this analysis has explained how the program works.

Figure 4-10 shows the program working. I have just stopped the motor at the reference point for 180° of rotation. The LCD display does show the current position of the joystick, but it is hard to see the display.

Homemade Prototype Board for the PIC18F4525

I have included some information about the prototype board I have built for the rest of the programs I have written for the PIC18F4525. The vero board plan is shown in Figure 4-9.

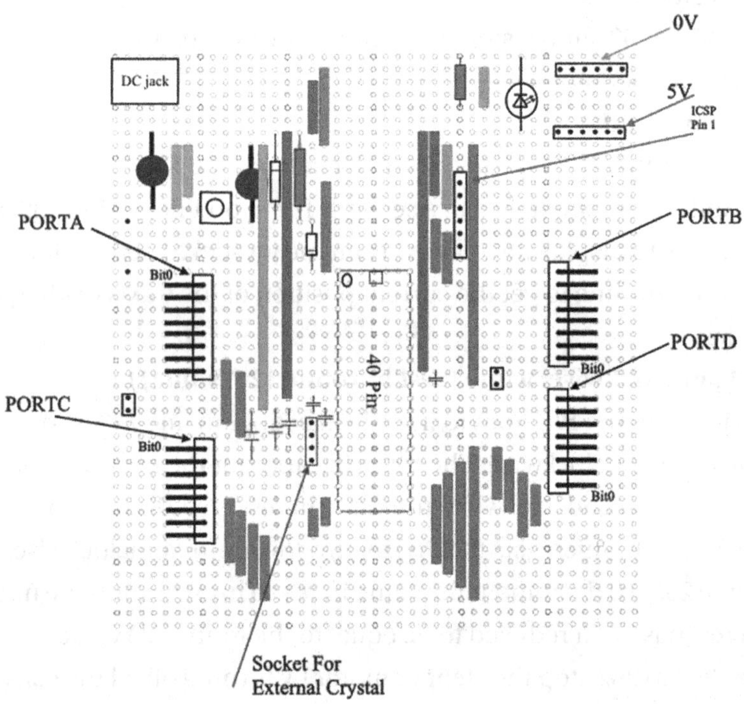

Figure 4-9. *The vero board plan for the PIC18f4525 prototype board*

This vero board plan is designed specifically for the PIC18F4525. However, if the pin out connections are the same, then it could be used for other 40-pin PICs, but you must make sure the pin outs are the same. Also, I feel I must reiterate that you do need to have some good experience with building your own circuit boards before you attempt to build this board.

You could try building some of the easier boards I have described in this book first before you attempt to build this prototype board. I cannot guarantee that your build will be successful; it is really up to your patience, as you will need a lot of it, along with experience. All I can say is that I have used this board and my PIC16F88 board for all the programs in this book, as you will see. If you are confident at building circuit boards, then it can be exciting and you can save some money. I do have some practical hints with regards to building a circuit on vero board in the appendix. You might find it useful to read that section first before you build any of the circuit boards in this book; there are some photos that might be of help to you.

With this circuit board I have used a 5V supply that can source a total of 1 amp. This avoids having to use a 5V regulator and gives us up to 1 amp of current. This 1 amp means we can use the same supply to run the 5V stepper motor, which does require quite a bit of current.

The legend for the diagram of the vero board plan is shown in Table 4-10.

Table 4-10. *The Legend for the PIC18F4525 Board*

Symbol	Description
	Link wire
	Resistor
	Diode
	Electrolytic capacitor 10μF 16V
	Push button switch
DC jack	Barrel jack plug DC input
	These are points where the track is cut to disconnect parts of the circuit
	This where the jumpers are connected

The parts list and costing for the board are shown in Table 4-11.

Table 4-11. *The Parts List and Costing for the PIC18F4525 Board*

Item	Part Number	Quantity	Unit cost	total
40-pin DIL socket	4818 3000CP	1	0.4	0.4
PIC18F4525		1	3.25	3.25
10μF 16V cap electrolytic	ECA1CAD100X	2	0.16	0.32
Diode	1n1414	2	0.1	0.2
5kΩ resistor		1	0.04	0.04
40-pin strip male header pins	83-15402	1	0.25	0.25
Push button switch	B3F 1020	1	0.28	0.28
Misc wire			0.2	0.2
Vero board		1	0.4	0.4
Total				5.94

The costing is only approximate, and so costs may vary. However, you should also consider the cost of buying the tools you will need to build the board. This is detailed in the appendix.

Figure 4-10. *Joystick and stepper motor working with my prototype board*

Summary

In this chapter, we have learned how to use the 1602 LED module and the joystick module. To use the joystick, we had to study how the PIC uses the ADC to take analog inputs. To use the LCD, we had to study how the LCD works and how we can control it. We then linked the joystick to the stepper motor and learned how we could control the position of the stepper motor with the joystick.

In the next chapter, we will look at how a small servo motor works and how we can control the position of the servo motor with the joystick.

CHAPTER 5

DC Motors

In this chapter, we will look at how the PIC can be used to vary the speed of a DC (direct current) motor. This will involve creating a square wave output and varying the mark, or on, time of the waveform. This is termed PWM (pulse width modulation). We will learn how we can use the output of a variable resistor to vary the speed of the DC motor.

We will then move on to the servo motor. We will learn how it works and how we can use the PIC to vary the position of the servo. This will initially use the output of a variable resistor, but it will then move on to using the joystick we looked at in the last chapter.

After reading this chapter, you will be able to create a square wave output on the PIC of any frequency. You will understand how the PIC implements PWM and how we can use the PIC to control the position of a servo motor.

The Speed of the Simple DC Motor

The speed of the DC motor depends upon the current that is forced to, or allowed to, flow through the coils in the motor. However, we can vary this current in one of two ways. We could keep the DC voltage applied to the motor constant and simply vary the resistance of the motor circuit. This would mean adding a variable resistor in series with the motor. Indeed, this was how we varied the speed in the early days of DC motors.

H. H. Ward, *Programming Arduino Projects with the PIC Microcontroller*,
https://doi.org/10.1007/978-1-4842-7230-5_5

The problem with that approach was that we would simply be wasting some power across the added resistance we inserted in the circuit. This was very wasteful.

The other approach would be to keep the resistance constant, at just the resistance of the coils, termed the armature resistance of the motor, and vary the voltage applied to the motor. This idea of varying the voltage applied to the motor is termed PWM, and it is by far the most efficient way of varying the speed of the simple DC motor.

PWM

To appreciate what PWM is, and what pulse width we are modulating, it would be useful to look at a typical DC square wave. This is shown in Figure 5-1.

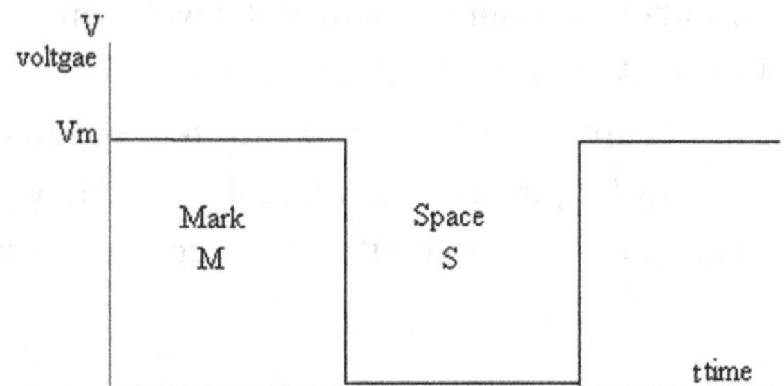

Figure 5-1. *A typical square wave*

The wave form shown in Figure 5-1 is DC, as the voltage never changes polarity. In this case, it is always positive. The up time, or on time, named "mark time", is the same as the down time, or off time, named "space time". This means that the square wave in Figure 5-1 has a 50/50 duty cycle. The duty cycle is the ratio of the mark time to the periodic time of the square wave. The mark time *M*, or up time, is the pulse that is referred to in PWM. The width is the length of time that the mark, or pulse, extends for. With PWM, we vary the length of time that the mark extends for. Note that as the total time (i.e., the mark time plus the space time), known as the periodic time *T*, does not vary; as we increase the mark time we must decrease the space time, and vice versa.

A DC motor would respond to the average of the square wave voltage. For any DC square wave, the average voltage can be calculated using Equation 5-1:

$$Vavge = \frac{VmM}{T} \; or = \frac{VmM}{M+S} \qquad \text{(Equation 5-1)}$$

Note "*Vavge*" is the average voltage, "*Vm*" is the voltage maximum, "*M*" is the mark time, "*T*" is the periodic time for the wave form (i.e., the time to complete one full cycle), and "*S*" is the space time.

Note that $\frac{M}{M+S}$ is termed the duty cycle. When the mark time is equal to the space time, then the duty cycle is termed 50/50 and the average voltage is $\frac{Vm}{2}$.

I hope the preceding paragraphs explain the importance of creating a square wave and the concept of PWM.

Creating a Square Wave with the PWM Mode

We can use the PWM mode of the CCP (Capture Compare and PWM) module of the PIC to create a square wave output on one of the two CCP outputs of the PIC. This module is a mixture of hardware, in that the actual circuitry is inside the PIC, and the firmware, preprogrammed operations that are in the PIC.

To create the square wave, we as programmers create the timings for periodic time *T* and the mark time *M* of the square wave. This is done using the timer2 inside the PIC, which just counts clock pulses. The procedure for doing this is as follows:

We use the control register 'CCPXCON' to configure the PIC into PWM mode (see Tables 5-1 and 5-2). The 18F4525 has two CCP modules and it uses the 'X', which should be replaced with '1' or '2' to set which module we are using. Table 5-1 shows the use of the bits in the CCPXCON control register. Note that there will be two such control registers, and the 'X' is replaced with 1 and 2.

Table 5-1. *The Bits of the CCPXCON Register*

Bit 7	Bit 6	Bit 5	Bit 4	Bit 3	Bit 2	Bit 1	Bit 0
-	-	DCxB1	DCxB0	CCPxM3	CCPxM2	CCPxM1	CCPxM0

Bits 7 and 6	These are not used and should be read as 0
Bits 5 and 4	These are used to store the two LSB (least significant bits) of the 10-bit number for the duty cycle
Bits 3, 2, 1, and 0	These are used to set the use of the CCP module according to the setting shown in Table 5-2

Table 5-2 shows how bits 3, 2, 1, and 0 set up the CCP into its respective modes of operation.

Table 5-2. The Four Bits That Configure the CCP Modules

Bit 3	Bit 2	Bit 1	Bit 0	Setting
0	0	0	0	CCP disabled
0	0	0	1	Reserved
0	0	1	0	Compare mode, toggle output on match
0	0	1	1	Reserved
0	1	0	0	Capture mode every falling edge
0	1	0	1	Capture mode every rising edge
0	1	1	0	Capture mode every 4th rising edge
0	1	1	1	Capture mode every 16th rising edge
1	0	0	0	Compare mode, initialize CCPx pin low
1	0	0	1	Compare mode, initialize CCPx pin high
1	0	1	0	Compare mode generate software interrupt
1	0	1	1	Compare mode trigger special event
1	1	0	0	PWM mode P1A,P1C active high P1B P1D active high
1	1	0	1	PWM mode P1A,P1C active high P1B P1D active low
1	1	1	0	PWM mode P1A,P1C active low P1B P1D active high
1	1	1	1	PWM mode P1A,P1C active low P1B P1D active low

The following is an explanation of the bits in the CCPXCON register.

- Bits 7 and 6 of the CCP1CON register are not used; therefore, leave them at logic '0'.
- Bits 5 and 4 are where we store the two LSB of the binary number that is used to control the width of the mark pulse. We will look at that later in the chapter.

- It is the four LSB (b3, b2, b1, and b0) of both CCPXCON registers that control what mode the CCP module is in. As we are trying to create a square wave with PWM, we want to set this module to PWM mode. This is done by setting these four bits as follows:
    - b3 = 1.
    - b2 = 1.
    - b1 = x.
    - b0 = x.
- The 'x' means it does not matter what logic level they are.

Bits 1 and 0 are really only used when we are creating two square waves and using both CCP1 and CCP2 outputs. These two bits can be used to control the phase relationship between the two square waves.

We need to know on what pin the two square waves will be outputted by the PIC. The two outputs are CCP1 and CCP2. CCP1 is fixed on PORTC bit 2 (i.e., PORTCbits.RC2). The CCP2 output can be sent out on PORTBbits.RB3, or PORTCbits.RC1. It is the CONFIG word 'CCP2MUX' that is used to set which bit the CCP2 output is on. The default setting is PORTCbits.RC1. I normally leave it at this so that I can use my configuration header file in all my projects.

The process around creating a square wave is based around letting timer2 count up until a time equal to the periodic time *T* of the desired square wave has been reached. Timer2, like all timers, simply counts clock pulses, and so a count of one will equal a specific time according to the clock frequency that timer2 counts at. Therefore, we need to know the number of pulses the timer has to count to reach the periodic time of the frequency of the square wave. This number is loaded into a special function register called PR2. When the value in timer2 matches the value in this PR2 register, then the square wave starts a new cycle.

Microchip has given us an equation (shown as Equation 15-1 in section 15.4 of the datasheet) which we can use to determine the specific value to load into PR2. I have rearranged this equation to produce an equation for PR2 value, which is what we want to work out. We simply want to know what value we need to load into the PR2 to set the frequency of the square wave. This is given in Equation 5-2:

$$\mathrm{PR2} = \frac{\mathrm{OscFreq}}{\mathrm{Frequency} \times 4 \times \mathrm{TMR2Preset}} - 1 \qquad \text{(Equation 5-2)}$$

Creating a 1kHz Square Wave

To help explain the process, we will go through an example to create a 1kHz square wave with an 8Mhz internal oscillator and TMR2Preset value of 16. I will explain what the timer preset value does later.

Putting all the values into Equation 5-2, we get Equation 5-3:

$$PR2 = \frac{8E^6}{1000 \times 4 \times 16} - 1 = 124 \qquad \text{(Equation 5-3)}$$

This means that to get a square wave with a frequency of 1kHz using an 8MHz oscillator, we simply have to load the PR2 with the value of 124, which is 0b01111100 or 0X7C, and then set the mark-to-space ratio.

Timer2 counts clock pulses, and the clock runs at a quarter of the frequency of the oscillator; note that this is why there is a number 4 in Equation 5-2. This means that, with an oscillator frequency of 8Mhz, the clock runs at 2Mhz. We can, if we wanted to, slow the timer2 even more by dividing this 2Mhz frequency further. This further divide is controlled by the timer2 preset value. There are three possible values this preset can be set to: 1, 4, and 16. We are using the value 16 for this timer preset, hence the 16 in Equation 5-3. This means that timer2 is counting at a rate of 2Mhz divided by 16, hence at a frequency of 125kHz. The periodic time for this frequency is $T = \frac{1}{f} = \frac{1}{125E^3} = 8E^{-6}$; therefore = 8μs. This means it takes 8μs for timer2 to count one tick and that it will take 125 × 8μs for timer2 to count from 0 to 124. It also means it will take 1ms for the timer to count from 0 to 124. This is the periodic time for the 1kHz square wave we are trying to produce. Remember I stated earlier that we want to know the number the timer2 must count up to create a time equal to the periodic time of the frequency of the square wave we are creating; this is what we have done.

The Mark Time or Duty Cycle

We now have a 1kHz square wave outputted on bit 2 of PORTC, the CCP1 output. However, we have not considered the mark time. There must be a mark time and a space time, or a duty cycle, for the square wave. We can't ignore this aspect of the square wave because the registers involved will have data in them already but it will most likely be an unusable value. We need to make sure the value in the registers used to control the mark-to-space ratio is the one we want.

We will start by creating a 50/50 duty cycle, which means the mark and space time are both equal to $\frac{T}{2} = \frac{1ms}{2} = 0.5ms = 500E^{-6}$.

Again, Microchip gives us an equation we can use to help with this. This is not the easiest expression to use, and so I have rearranged the expression to give us an expression to calculate the number we need; it is shown in Equation 5-4.

$$Number = \frac{MarkTime \times OscFreq}{TMR2\text{Preset}} \quad \text{(Equation 5-4)}$$

This is taken from Equation 15-2 in section 15.4 of the datasheet for the PIC18F4525.

Knowing that for a 50/50 duty cycle, the mark time must be $500E^{-6}$ for our 1kHz square wave, we can calculate the number according to Equation 5-5:

$$Number = \frac{MarkTime \times OscFreq}{TMR2\text{Preset}}$$
$$\therefore Number = \frac{500E^{-6} \times 8E^{6}}{16} \qquad \text{(Equation 5-5)}$$
$$\therefore Number = 250$$

So we have calculated two numbers that when used properly will give us a 1kHz square wave with a 50/50 duty cycle. There are two issues to consider when it comes to creating and storing these numbers.

The TMR2 Preset Value

There are three possible values for the TMR2 preset: 1, 4, and 16. Why did I choose 16? Well, if I had chosen 4, the PR2 number would have worked out at 449, and if I had chosen 1, the PR2 number would be 1999. The problem with that is that this PIC is an eight-bit PIC and unless we can change them, as we can with some SFRs, all registers are eight bits. An eight-bit register can only hold a value up to 255. So that is why a preset value of 16 was chosen: to reduce the value to below 255. We have the other possible values for the TMR 2 preset, because we could want different frequencies for the square wave and we could use different oscillator settings.

Storing a Ten-Bit Number

As the registers are only eight bits long, how can we store the number for the duty cycle if we wanted a high duty cycle? As an example, if we wanted a mark time of 900µs, which is a 90% duty cycle, the number we would have calculated would be 450. How can this be stored in an eight-bit register? The answer is it can't, and so we store the result in a similar way we store the ten-bit results of the ADC conversion. We actually make a ten-bit binary number of the result by adding logic '0's to the MSB end of the result if needed. We can then store the most significant eight bits of this extended ten-bit number in a special register called CCPRXL; note that there are two, one for each CCP module, so the 'X' will be either 1 or 2.

The two LSB go into b5 and b4 of the CCPXCON registers; again 'X' is 1 or 2. The number we calculated using Equation 5-5 was 250 or 0b0011111010. Note that I have added two logic '0's at the MSB end of the result. This means that b5 and b4 of the CCPXCON registers are set to logic '1' and logic '0', respectively. The remaining eight-bit number, 0b00111110, is loaded into the appropriate CCPRXL registers. We will use CCPR1L, as we will be using the CCP1 output and so the CCP1CON register to create the square wave. This will then make a 1kHz square wave appear on the CCP1 of the PIC with a 50/50 duty cycle, assuming you have set the CCP1 pin to output.

The code for this program is shown Listing 5-1.

Listing 5-1. The Program Listing for the 1kHz Square Wave

```
/*
* File:   basic1KhzWaveProg.c
Author: Mr H. H. Ward
*
Created on 16 April 2021, 16:37
*/
```

```
7.  #include <xc.h>
8.  #include <conFigInternalOscNoWDTNoLVP.h>
9.  void main ()
10. {
11. PORTA = 0;
12. PORTB = 0;
13. PORTC = 0;
14. PORTD = 0;
15. TRISA = 0xFF;
16. TRISB = 0;
17. TRISC = 0;
18. TRISD = 0;
19. ADCON0 = 0X01;
20. ADCON1 = 0X0E;
21. ADCON2 = 0b00100001;
22. OSCTUNE = 0;
23. OSCCON = 0b01110100;
24. T0CON = 0b11000111;
25. T2CON = 0x06;
26. PR2 = 124;
27. CCP1CON = 0b00101100;
28. CCPR1L = 0X37;
29. while (1);
30. }
```

Analysis of Listing 5-1

The new instructions for the program are analyzed here.

Lines 18, 19, and 20 set up the ADC to turn the ADC on to connect it to channel 0 (i.e., ADCON 0 = 0b00000001). Then, we make all inputs digital except PORTA bit 0 (i.e., ADCON1 = 0X0E) and finally select 4TAD with a timing frequency of 1MHz (i.e., ADCON2 = 0b00100001).

Line 25 T2CON = 0X06;

This instruction simply loads the control register T2CON with the following eight-bit number: 0b00000110.

To understand what this instruction is doing, it would be useful to look at the usage of the T2CON register. This is shown in Table 5-3.

Table 5-3. *The T2CON Register for Controlling Timer2*

Bit 7	Bit 6	Bit 5	Bit 4	Bit 3	Bit 2	Bit 1	Bit 0
-	T2OUTPS3	T2OUTPS2	T2OUTPS1	T2OUPS0	TMR2ON	T2CKPS1	T2CKPS0

Bit 7		Not used		
Bit 6 Bit 5 Bit 4 Bit 3		These are used to enable Postscales for timer2 0000 = 1:1 0001 = 1:2 " " " 1111 = 1:16		
Bit 2	TIMR2ON	Logic 0 means off; Logic 1 means on		
Bit 1 - 0	TMR2 preset	00 = 1	01 = 4	1x = 16

The following is an explanation of what loading the T2CON register with 0b00000110 does.

This sets bit 2 to a logic '1,' which simply turns the timer2 on.

This instruction also sets bit 1 to a logic '1' and bit 0 to a logic '0.' This sets the timer2 preset to a value of 16.

Note also that bits 6, 5, 4, and 3 are set to logic '0', which sets the Post Scalar to 0000.

Note that bit 7 is not used, so it is set to a logic '0'.

In essence then, this instruction turns timer2 on and sets the Preset value to 16.

Line 26 PR2 = 124;

This loads the PR2 register with the number 124, which is the value we calculated using Equation 5-5 to achieve a frequency of 1kHz. Note that we are using the default radix, which is the decimal number system.

Line 27 CCP1CON = 0b00101100;

This simply loads the CCP1CON, the control register for the CCP1 module with the value 0b00101100. A description of the usage of this control register is given in Tables 5-2 and 5-3. The particular use of the bits is given here.

Bits 7 and 6 of the CCP1CON register are not used; therefore, leave them at logic '0'.

Bits 5 and 4 are set to logic '1' and logic '0', respectively, as this is what the two LSB of the binary conversion of 250 are as calculated before.

The remaining four bits, 3, 2, 1, and 0, are set to 1100 to put the CCP module into the PWM mode of operation.

In essence then, loading the CCP1CON register with 0b00101100 sets the CCP module to PWM mode.

Line 28 CCPR1L = 0X37;

This loads the CCPR1L eight-bit register with the MSB bits of the 250 value calculated earlier.

In essence, it is the value in the CCPR1L register that sets the width of the up or mark time of the square wave.

Line 29 while (1);

This is using the while (test is true) type instruction. If the result of the test is true, we must do what the instruction tells us to do. With the test being the simple (1), then the test result is always true, as a logic '1' means true. This means that the micro must always do what the instruction tells it to do.

As there is nothing between the (1) and the semicolon ";", which signifies the end of the instruction, then this while (1) test means the micro will do nothing forever. In this way, we are halting the micro at this point in the program.

This will now simply create a 1kHz square wave outputted by the PIC on the CCP1 output. The oscilloscope shows a square wave with mark time and space time equal to each other. The oscilloscope confirms that the program creates a 1kHz square wave with a 50/50 duty cycle.

The Variable-Speed DC Motor Program

Now that we have learned how to create a square wave output, we are going to put it to some use in varying the speed of a simple DC motor. The circuit for this program (Listing 5-2) is shown in Figure 5-2. In that circuit, the 12V supply to the motor is constantly connected, but the ground is connected by the TIP122 NPN transistor. This is being used as a switch that switches the ground onto the motor when the transistor is turned on. Therefore, as we use a square wave output from the PIC, the ground is being switched on and off at the frequency set by the PIC. The transistor is switched on during the mark time of the square wave and turned off during the space time. This means we can vary the time the transistor is switched on and so the time the ground is switched on to the motor. This then allows us to vary the current flowing through the motor and so the speed of the motor. The longer the mark time, the faster the motor rotates and vice versa.

As the mark time of the square wave depends upon the value stored in the CCPR1L register, the principle of the program is to change the value in this register as we vary the input to the PIC from the variable resistor connected to bit 0 of PORTA. This is explained in the analysis of the program listing.

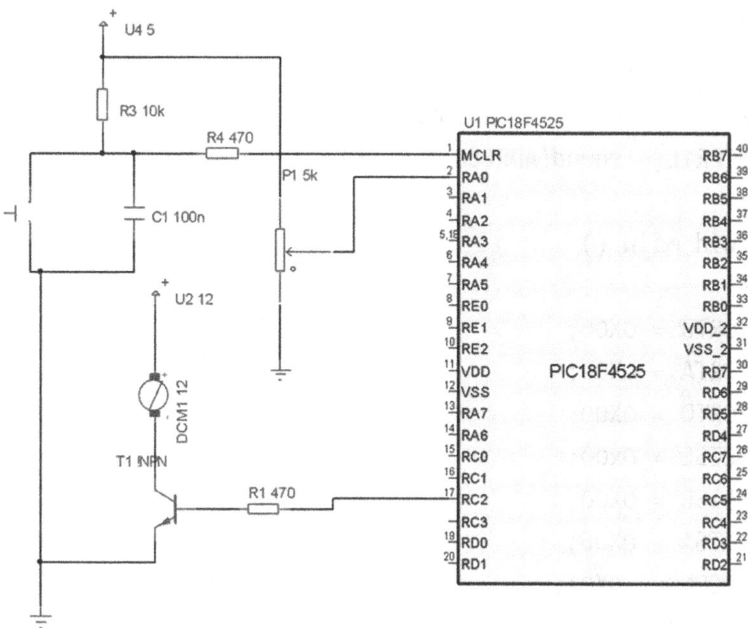

Figure 5-2. *The circuit for the variable-speed DC motor*

Listing 5-2. The Variable-Speed DC Motor Listing

```
/*A LCD Routine in C
Written by H H Ward 14/10/13 for pic18f4525
Base frequency is 1kHz
This uses a variable resistor connected to A0 to set the
CCPR1L value and so control the mark
time of the square wave. This varies the average voltage
across the motor.
```

```
Note the TIP122 Darlington transistor is used to drive
the motor*/
#include <xc.h>
#include <conFigInternalOscNoWDTNoLVP.h>
#include <math.h>
void changeSpeed ()
{
ADCON0bits.GODONE = 1;
while (ADCON0bits.GODONE);
CCPR1L = round(ADRESH * 0.48);
}
void main ()
{
PORTB = 0X00;
PORTA = 0X00;
PORTD = 0X00;
TRISC = 0x00;
TRISB = 0X00;
TRISA = 0X0F;
ADCON0 = 0X01;
ADCON1 = 0X0E;
ADCON2 = 0b00100001;
T0CON = 0b11000111;
T2CON = 0x06;
PR2 = 124;
CCP1CON = 0b00101100;
CCPR1L = 0X37;
OSCCON = 0X74;
OSCTUNE =0X00;
while (1)
{
```

```
36.   changeSpeed ();
37.   }
38.   }
```

Analysis of Listing 5-2

There are no real new instructions, as they have all been analyzed in Listing 5-1 and chapter 3. The only instruction that I hope needs some explanation is this one:

Line 14 CCPR1L = round (ADRESH * 0.48);

It is the value in the CCPR1L register that controls the pulse width of the PWM output on CCP1. This instruction will simply load the CCPR1L with the result of the ADC conversion of the input from the variable resistor on bit 0 of PORTA. We are using the "round" function from the math.h header file to round the result up or down to a whole number, as the CCPR1L cannot store decimal values. The value from the ADRESH is being multiplied by 0.48, as the maximum value we could get from the analog-to-digital conversion would be 255. This is greater than the 124 that is stored in the PR2 register. If we allowed the CCPR1L to store a value that is equal to or greater than the value in the PR2 register, then the square wave output would collapse, as any value greater than the PR2 would create a pulse width that is greater than the period of the square wave.

I hope this is the only instruction in Listing 5-2 that needs further analysis.

A Two-Directional DC Motor Program

There will be times when we need to have a DC motor that will rotate in both a clockwise and an anticlockwise direction. The direction in which the DC motor rotates is set by the direction in which the current flows through the motor. This in turn is controlled by the polarity of the voltage applied across the DC motor. Therefore, to change the direction of rotation of the DC motor, we simply need to change the polarity of the supply to the motor. The simplest way to do this is to place the motor in what is termed an "H" drive circuit. The concept of the "H" drive circuit is shown in Figure 5-3.

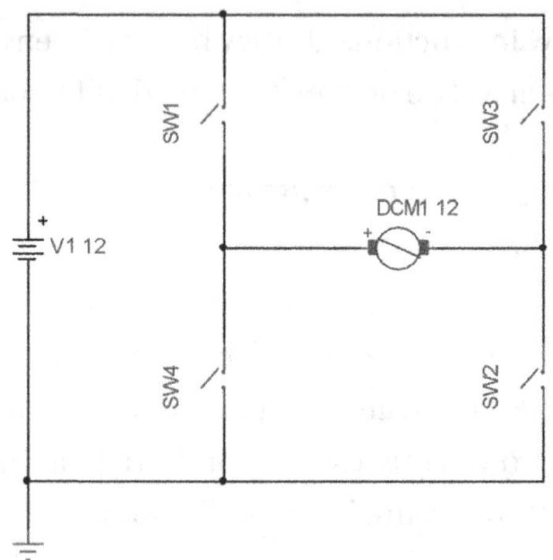

***Figure 5-3.** The H drive circuit for the DC motor*

The principle is that to turn the motor in a clockwise direction, we close switches 1 and 2 together. This forces the current to flow from left to right.

Then if we open switches 1 and 2 at the same time as we close switches 3 and 4, the current will flow from right to left and the motor will rotate in an anticlockwise direction.

The circuit is called the "H" drive, as it looks like an H. However, when we build the circuit as shown in Figure 5-4, the motor is simply pulled out of the middle of the H. It is still wired up in the H format.

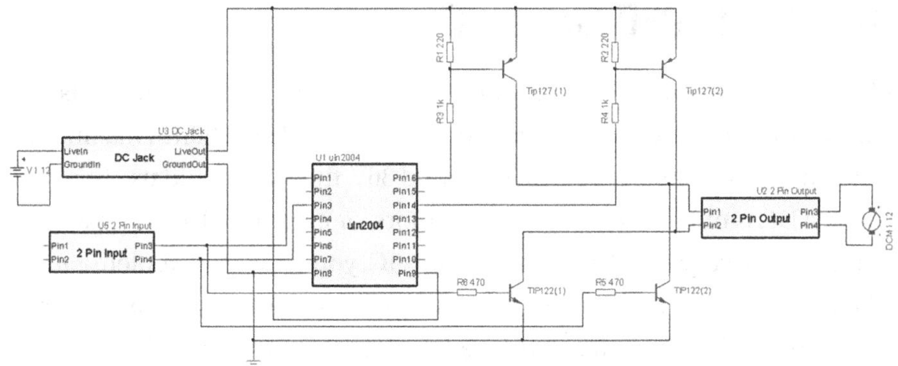

***Figure 5-4.** The practical circuit for the H drive circuit*

The circuit uses Darlington transistors TIP127 for the two NPN transistors and TIP122 for the two PNP transistors. The transistors TIP122(1) and TIP127(1) turn on together, and TIP122(2) and TIP127(2) come on together.

The Darlington array outputs on pins 18 and 16 of the ULN2004 turn on the ground to the resistor divider circuits of R1 and R3 and F2 and R4. This allows current to flow through the resistor divider circuits and so turns on the respective TIP122 PNP transistor.

The Darington array inputs on pins 1 and 3 come from the PIC. In this way, the PIC can control when the PNP transistors are turned on.

The NPN transistors are connected to the input of the ULN2004, and so when we turn on one of the PNPs we turn on the correct NPN at the same time.

We are using the TIP122 and TIP 127, as we need a PNP transistor; also, the TIPs are Darlington transistors that can supply up to 5 amps of current. The Darlington array, ULN2004, only supplies 500mA per output.

With this arrangement, it is not a simple process by which we can vary the speed of the motor, but it can be done. Therefore, this circuit only allows us to change the direction of rotation of the motors.

Using the L293D Driver IC

As long as the maximum current your motor will draw from the supply is around 600mA or up to 1.2A nonrepetitive, so I would say 600mA maximum, and the maximum supply voltage is around 36V, then you could use this IC to drive a DC motor or indeed two DC motors, or even four. However, we will use it to drive two DC motors. With this IC, you can easily implement a variable-speed drive for your DC motors. This makes the IC very useful for most users of DC motors. It can be used to place the motor in the H drive circuit and so give you the ability to change the direction of the motor as well as vary the speed. Figure 5-5 shows the basic circuit inside the IC. The basic idea is that the PWM signal, used to vary the speed of the two DC motors, is applied to pins 2 and 10; these are shown as U4 and U8 in Figure 5-5.

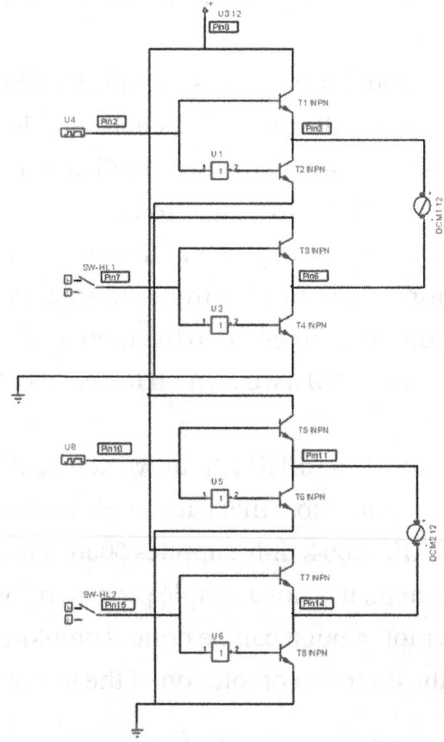

***Figure 5-5.** The basic internal circuit of the L239D driver IC*

The pin out of the L239D driver IC is shown in Figure 5-6.

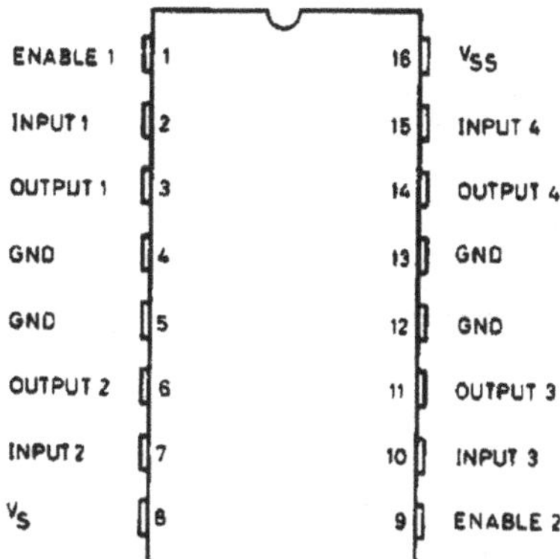

Figure 5-6. *The pin out of the L293D driver IC*

The driver IC can be used to control up to four DC motors. It has internal diode protection to prevent high voltage spikes at switch-off of the motors. The circuit shown in Figure 5-5 shows how to use the driver to control the speed and direction of rotation of two DC motors. The PIC will be used to supply the two PWM waveforms, shown as U4 and U8. The PIC will also supply the logic on pins 7 and 15, shown as two high/low switches, SW-HL1 and SW-HL2, in Figure 5-5. Both the enable inputs on pins 1 and 9 are permanently connected to the +5V so that both sets of outputs are permanently enabled. However, these could be connected to the output of a PIC, so that the enabling can be controlled by the PIC. Note that enable 1 controls outputs 1 and 2, whereas enable 2 controls outputs 3 and 4.

I will use the circuit shown in Figure 5-7 to try and explain how the driver works as an H drive to give both speed variation and directional control over the motor.

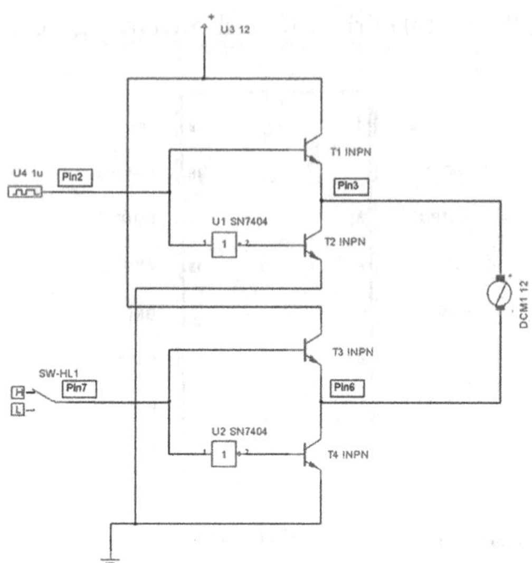

Figure 5-7. *The circuit for one H bridge driver*

If we assume that the logic on the SW-HL1 switch, which would be on pin7 of the IC, was at a logic '1' (i.e., high), as shown in Figure 5-7, then transistor T3 would be switched on. Also, because of the inverter (i.e., NOT gate) between pin7 and the base of T4, T4 would be turned off. This would mean that the +12V, which is connected internally to the collectors of the transistors T1 and T3, will be switched onto the negative end of the motor on pin6 of the IC via T3.

The PWM signal on pin2 will be supplying 12V on to the positive end of the motor at pin3 when the PWM signal goes high (i.e., during the mark time of the PWM signal). This is via the transistor T1, which will be turned on when the PWM signal goes high. Note that when the signal is high, the inverter, or NOT gate, between pin2 and the base of T2 will ensure that T2 is turned off. Now when the PWM signal goes low, T1 is turned off, which will remove the +12V on pin3. At the same time, T2 will be turned on, which means the ground will be connected to pin3 and so the positive end of the motor. Note that when the PWM signal is high (i.e., during the mark time), ideally no current will flow through the motor, as there will be +12V on both ends of the motor. However, when the PWM signal goes low (i.e., during the space time), then current will flow through the motor but up through the motor from the negative end to the positive end, as there will be +12V on pin6 bit 0V, or ground, on pin3. This would mean the motor would turn anticlockwise.

If we look at Figure 5-8, when pin7 goes high, the 12V from pin12 goes to the negative end of the motor on pin6. The PWM input from pin2 will be applied to the positive end of the motor on pin3. However, the voltage at pin3 will respond to the average of the PWM signal. If the PWM signal has a maximum mark time, then the average will be very close to 12V. This will mean the voltage difference across the motor will be almost 0V and so no current will flow through the motor and thus it will not rotate. Now if the PWM signal had a minimum mark time, then the average voltage at pin3 would be almost 0V. This would mean there is a maximum voltage difference across the motor, and the current flowing up through the motor from the negative terminal to the positive terminal would be at a maximum. Therefore, the motor would rotate anticlockwise at a maximum speed.

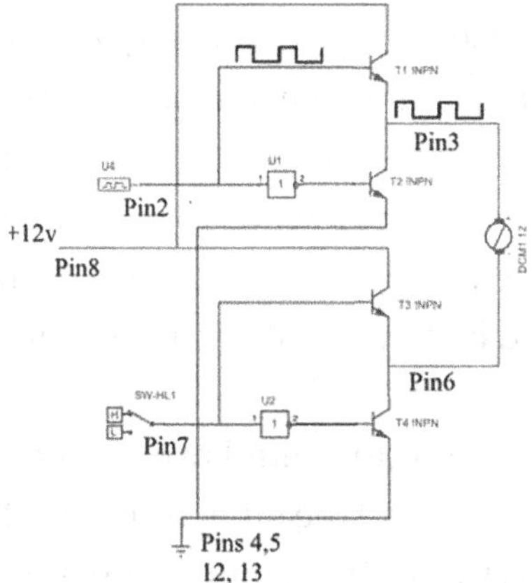

Figure 5-8. *Anticlockwise rotation when pin7 goes high*

If we now change the logic on pin7 (i.e., send it low to a logic ‘0’), then T3 turns off and T4 turns on. This puts a 0V or ground on pin6. The transistors T1 and T2 will still turn on and off as before and so put the average voltage on pin3 as before. However, this time the current will flow down from the positive end of the motor to the negative end, and so the motor will turn clockwise. This situation is shown in Figure 5-9.

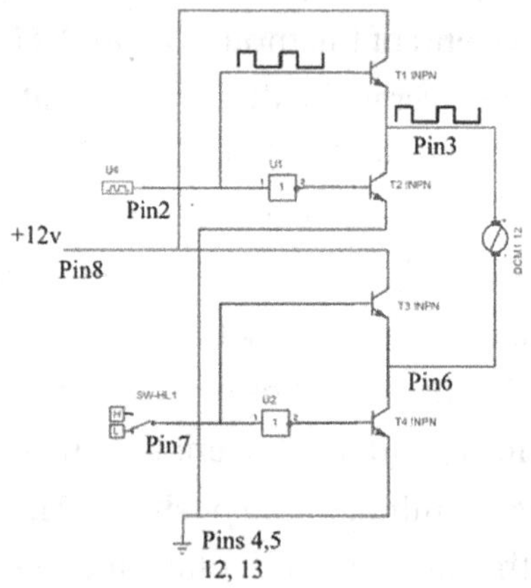

Figure 5-9. *Clockwise rotation when pin7 goes low*

In this way, you can see that we can achieve both directional control and speed variation of the motor. The one issue that you will find out is that during clockwise rotation, increasing the mark time of the PWM will increase the speed of the motor. However, during anticlockwise rotation, increasing the mark time will slow down the motor. This is not really a problem, but you should be aware of the issue and account for it in your programming.

When we use this driver IC to control two DC motors, one of the PWM signals will come from CCP1 and the other from CCP2; that is one reason why the PIC18F4525 has two PWM outputs. With this arrangement, we can use the PIC to control the speed and direction of a two-wheel drive buggy. That is what the next program will look at.

Controlling a Two-Wheel Drive System

Listing 5-3 will look at controlling the direction and varying the speed of two DC motors. The program will use the L293D motor driver IC.

The circuit for this project is shown in Figure 5-10.

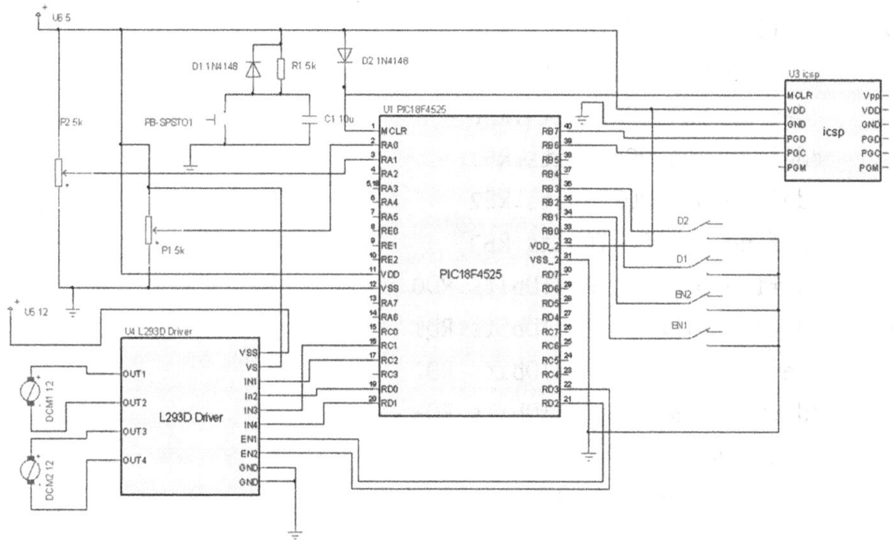

Figure 5-10. *The circuit diagram for the two-motor control project*

Listing 5-3. Controlling Two DC Motors

```
/*A Motor Routine in C
Written by H H Ward 14/04/2021 for pic18f4525
Base frequency is 1kHz
This uses two variable resistors connected to A0 and A1 to
set the CCPR1L and CCPR2L values and so control the mark
time of the square wave. This varies the average voltage
across the motors.
```

```
It uses the L293D driver IC to drive the motor*/
//some include files
#include <xc.h>
#include <conFigInternalOscNoWDTNoLVP.h>
#include <math.h>
//some definitions
#define SP1 PORTAbits.RA0
#define SP2 PORTAbits.RA1
#define EN1 PORTBbits.RB0
#define EN2 PORTBbits.RB1
#define D1  PORTBbits.RB2
#define D2  PORTBbits.RB3
#define DIN2    PORTDbits.RD0
#define DIN4    PORTDbits.RD1
#define DEN1    PORTDbits.RD2
#define DEN2    PORTDbits.RD3
//some subroutines
void changeSpeed ()
{
ADCON0bits.GODONE = 1;
while (ADCON0bits.GODONE);
CCPR1L = round(ADRESH * 0.48);
ADCON0 = 0b00000101;
ADCON0bits.GODONE = 1;
while (ADCON0bits.GODONE);
CCPR2L = round(ADRESH * 0.48);
ADCON0 = 0X01;
}
void setmotors ()
{
if (EN1 == 1) DEN1 = 1;
```

```
else DEN1 = 0;
if (EN2 == 1) DEN2 = 1;
else DEN2 = 0;
if (D1 == 1) DIN2 = 1;
else DIN2 = 0;
if (D2 == 1) DIN4 = 1;
else DIN4 = 0;
}
void main ()
{
PORTB = 0X00;
PORTA = 0X00;
PORTD = 0X00;
TRISC = 0x00;
TRISB = 0XFF;
TRISA = 0X0F;
TRISD = 0X00;
ADCON0 = 0X01;
ADCON1 = 0b00001101;
ADCON2 = 0b00100001;
T0CON = 0b11000111;
T2CON = 0x06;
PR2 = 124;
CCP1CON = 0b00101100;
CCPR1L = 0X37;
CCP2CON = 0b00101100;
CCPR2L = 0X37;
OSCCON = 0X74;
OSCTUNE =0X00;
while (1)
{
```

```
68.    setmotors ();
69.    changeSpeed ();
70.    }
71.    }
```

Analysis of Listing 5-3

I am hoping there is not much that I need to analyze, as we have used most of the instructions already. The first instruction I will look at is

Line 28 ADCON0 = 0b00000101;

This is turning the ADC on and then telling the PIC to connect the second channel, AN1, to the ADC. This gets the PIC ready to read the input from P2 in Figure 5-10, which is the variable voltage that varies the speed of the second motor.

Lines 28 to 31 get the PIC to read the voltage at AN1, convert it to a digital number, and then store the most significant eight bits into the CCPR2L register, which controls the pulse width of the CCP2 output. It is the square wave on this CCP2 output that varies the speed of the second DC motor.

Line 32 ADCON0 = 0X01;

This gets the PIC to connect the ADC to channel 0, AN0. Note that I am expressing the value in hexadecimal format, 0X01 = 0b00000001 in binary. See the appendix for an explanation of the various number systems we use.

Line 34 void setMotors ()

This creates a subroutine that is used for initializing the motors. The instructions for the subroutine are between lines 35 and 44.

Line 36 if (EN1 == 1) DEN1 = 1;

This sets up an "if this then do that else do something else" type of test. The test is asking, has the logic on the input EN1 become equal to a logic '1'? Note that I interpret the double '==' sign as meaning "becomes equal to", whereas the single '=' forces the logic to go to what is stated there, logic

'1' or logic '0' as in PORTBbit0 = 1;. You should remember we have defined the term 'EN1' to mean PORTBbits.RB0 (see line 14).

If the test is true (i.e., the logic on the EN1 input is a logic '1'), then the PIC will carry out the one-line instruction part, DEN1 = 1;, on this same line. As it is a one-line instruction the PIC must carry out, if the test is true, we don't need to enclose it within the curly brackets.

Also, if the result of the test is true, then the PIC will skip the next instruction on line 37.

If the result of the test is untrue (i.e., the logic on the EN1 input is a logic '0'), then the PIC will carry out the instruction on line 37 where it sets the logic on the DEN1 output to a logic '0'.

In this way, the PIC can accept a control signal from the user to either enable or disable the motor connected between outputs 1 and 2.

Lines 38 and 39 do the same operation to enable or disable the motor connected between outputs 3 and 4.

Lines 40 to 43 do the same operation, which allows a user to control the direction of rotation for the two motors. If the inputs go to a logic '1', then the corresponding outputs go to a logic '1' and the motors rotate anticlockwise. If the inputs go to a logic '0', then the motors rotate in a clockwise direction.

The program is using four switches to add some user control over when either or both the motors are turned on. Two switches, EN1 and EN2, control the two motors, with EN1 controlling outputs 1 and 2. EN2 controls outputs 3 and 4. The other two switches, D1 and D2, control the direction of the motors, with D1 controlling the motor connected to outputs 1 and 2. D2 controls the motor on outputs 3 and 4. Note that a logic '1' will make the motors rotate anticlockwise, whereas a logic '0' makes them rotate clockwise.

Figure 5-14 (at the end of this chapter) shows the two motor programs working. A still photo is not very good for showing the program working; it is really included to just show you that I have used my homemade prototype board as I said I would for all the programs in this book.

Controlling a Servo Motor

This will be the second time I have looked at controlling a servo motor. The reason I am looking at it again is because I have deepened my understanding of how we can control a servo motor. A servo motor is a motor that will rotate through a limited number of degrees; it does not normally rotate through a complete 360° or one revolution. Normally a servo motor rotates through 180°; there are some that do more and some that do less. With the normal 180°, it is normal to say they rotate from -90 through 0 to +90 degrees.

The method by which we can control how much the servo motor moves is to send a controlling signal that is made up of a 50Hz square wave in which the width of the mark time controls how far the motor rotates between this -90 to +90. There is no real difference here from my first analysis of how the servo motor works. The difference is that before I worked on the understanding that the mark time was allowed to vary from 1ms to 2ms only, and this would produce the movement of the motor from -90 to +90. However, when I worked to this principle, my servo motor only moved through 90°. I put this down to the range of my actual servo motor or maybe a faulty servo motor. However, in principle the programs I wrote did work, and really my books are more about C programming than creating specific projects.

In preparing this, my third book on programming PIC micros in C, I have revisited my analysis of the servo motor. I started to ask questions: Why have a mark time that started at 1ms? Why not start at 0ms, or as close to it as possible? The data sheet I used for the SG90 is Chinese, and even though it does show a 50Hz square wave with a 1ms to 2ms mark time (see Figure 5-11), I did think that it may not translate from Chinese to English correctly. Also I considered the possibility that the reason my servo motor only moved through 90°, half of what it should, was because I was only varying the mark time through half of its permitted time period.

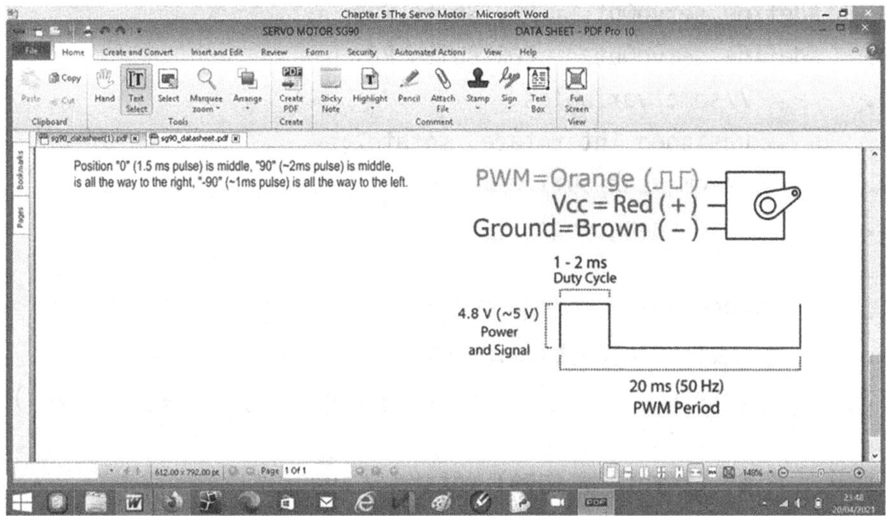

Figure 5-11. *The SG90 datasheet extract*

Therefore, I started to change my previous program to try and vary the mark time from less than 1ms to 2ms. I soon found that by starting off with a smaller mark time I could achieve a greater range of movement with the servo motor. This is indeed what happened. I have now come to the conclusion that the 1ms to 2ms variation in the mark time would only produce 50% movement of the servo motor, and that is why my first programs only produced a 90° movement of the motor and not the expected 180°. I have now come up with an improved program (Listing 5-4).

Listing 5-4. The Servo Motor Listing

```
/*A Program to control two servo motors
The 50Hz pulse train created with TMR0 16bit
Written by Mr H. H. Ward
For PIC 18f4525 dated 17/04/20*/
#include <xc.h>
#include <math.h>
#include <conFigInternalOscNoWDTNoLVP.h>
```

```
#define servoOut     PORTBbits.RB0
#define servoOut2    PORTBbits.RB1
     //some variables
     unsigned int rotate, rotate2;
     //some subroutines
     void changeAngle ()
     {
     ADCON0bits.GODONE = 1;
     while (ADCON0bits.GODONE);
     rotate = 240 +(round (((ADRESH << 2) + (ADRESL >>6))
     * 1.718));
     if (rotate > 1999) rotate = 1999;
     ADCON0 = 0b00000101;
     ADCON0bits.GODONE = 1;
     while (ADCON0bits.GODONE);
     rotate2 = 240 +(round (((ADRESH << 2) +
     (ADRESL >>6)) * 1.718));
     if (rotate2 > 1999) rotate2 = 1999;
     ADCON0 = 0X01;
     }
     void  main ()
     {
     PORTA = 0;
     PORTB = 0;
     PORTC = 0;
     PORTD = 0;
     TRISA = 0xFF;
     TRISB = 0;
     TRISC = 0;
     TRISD = 0;
     ADCON0 = 0X01;
```

```
37.         ADCON1 = 0X0E;
38.         ADCON2 = 0B00100001;
39.         OSCTUNE = 0;
40.         OSCCON = 0b01110100;
41.         T0CON = 0b10000000;
42.         rotate = 240;
43.         while (1)
44.         {
45.         begin:     TMR0 = 0;
46.         servoOut = 1;
47.         servoOut2 = 1;
48.         while(TMR0 < 2000)
49.         {
50.         if (TMR0 >= rotate)     servoOut = 0;
51.         if (TMR0 >= rotate2)    servoOut2 = 0;
52.         }
53.         while(TMR0 < 18500)   changeAngle ();
54.         while (TMR0 < 20000);
55.         goto begin;
56.         }
57.         }
```

This program controls two servo motors, and it uses the joystick from chapter 4 to produce the signal that will vary the mark time of the 50Hz square wave.

The 50Hz square wave is produced by setting the logic on bit 0 and bit 1 of PORTB, defined as servoOut for the first servo motor and servoOut2 for the second motor, on lines 8 and 9, to a logic '1' and then going through a 20ms period controlled by a count from timer0. During that period, the outputs on bit 0 and bit 1 go to a logic '0', at a signal from the program; then, at the end of the 20ms count, they are set back to a logic '1' and timer0 starts counting from 0 again. In this way, we can create the 50Hz square wave with a mark time that starts at time 0 and ends at a count equal to the time of our choice. Note that the maximum count must equate to 2ms. However, this program allows the logic on the two servo pins to go back to a logic ‘0’, and so end the mark time, at a minimum time equal to 0.24ms, or 240µs. This then produced a movement of approximately -20 to +90 degrees, much more than I produced with my previous program. I have tried to reduce the minimum mark time further, but I found that there was the possibility of the square wave collapsing and the servo motor just starting to rotate continuously. So this new servo program is, at present, the best I have come up with, and it does produce a very smooth movement of both servo motors controlled by the joystick. I am not saying this is the best program, and I may come back later with a better one, but I hope you will find it does work and you will learn a lot from it.

Analysis of Listing 5-4

I hope lines 1 to 10 don’t need any analysis, as we have used the instructions in previous programs.

Line 11 unsigned int rotate, rotate2;

This creates two 16-bit (i.e., int, or integer), data type, memory locations with the labels “rotate” and “rotate2”. These will be used to hold the values of the data that controls how wide the mark time is for the two 50Hz square waves. Note that it will use two 8-bit memory locations cascaded together for each variable, as this PIC is an 8-bit PIC (i.e., it does not have 16-bit memory locations).

Lines 13 to 25 create the subroutine that reads the voltage at the two analog inputs on bit 0 and bit 1 of PORTA. The subroutine converts these analog signals to digital numbers. We have looked at these instructions before in chapter 4 but I will present the following:

Line 17 rotate = 240 +(round (((ADRESH << 2) + (ADRESL >>6)) * 1.718));

With this instruction, we are loading the variable rotate with the number that will set the mark time of the square wave. I have stated that we are controlling the timing of the square wave with the counter timer0. Timer0 has been set to count at 1Mhz; see line 41. It has also been set up as a 16-bit register, as bit 6 is a logic '0'; see line 41. This means that a count of 1 equals 1μs. This further means that when timer0 has counted to 20,000 then 20ms will have passed and we can restart the square wave cycle again. However, this also means that the value of 240 that we load into the variable rotate creates a time period of 0.24ms. This is the setting for the minimum mark time of the square wave output on the servoOut pin. What this instruction does now is add to this minimum value of 240 the result of the ADC from the analog input from bit 0 of PORTA (i.e., the x axis of the joystick). The voltage at the input can vary from 0V to 5V, which means the result of the ADC can vary from 0 to 1023. The maximum of 1023 is because the ADC has a ten-bit resolution, which means it has a range of value set by Equation 5-6:

$$\begin{aligned} \max &= 2^n \\ \therefore \max &= 2^{10} = 1024 \end{aligned} \qquad \text{(Equation 5-6)}$$

If we did nothing to modify the value from the ADC, then the number in the variable rotate could go from 0 to 240+1024, which would be 0 to 1264. However, we need it to go from 0 to 2000 or really 240 to 2000. This means that the addition of the ADC result must add 2000 - 240 (i.e., 1760). This is why we multiply the result of the ADC by 1.718 as 1024 × 1.718 = 1754.232. We use the mathematical function of "round" to round the value up, as we can only store integers in the variable rotate because it is of the data type int.

However, we must remember that the ten-bit result of the ADC is stored in two parts. The two LSB are stored in bit 7 and bit 6 of the ADRESL register and the other eight bits are stored in the ADRESH register. This is because I have used left justification of the ADC result (see line 38).

The problem with this is that bits 7 and 6 of the ADRESL must become bits 1 and 0 of the rotate variable. This means these two bits must be shifted six places to the right. This is done with the **(ADRESL >>6)** part of the instruction. The other issue is that the eight bits in the ADRESH must become bits 9, 8, 7, 6, 5, 4, 3, and 2 of the rotate variable. This means they must be shifted two places to the left. This is achieved with the **((ADRESH << 2)** part of the instruction.

I hope this rather wordy analysis of this complex instruction does help you to understand how it works.

Line 18 if(rotate > 1999) rotate = 1999;

This is just making sure that the value in the variable rotate does not get any larger than 1999, as we don't want the mark time to extend past 2ms, which might happen if the value in rotate exceeded 2000.

Line 19 ADCON0 = 0b00000101;

This is done to change the channel that is connected to the ADC to channel 1. This is where the y axis of the joystick is connected to the PIC. Note that in line 36, we initially set the channel to channel 0.

Lines 20 to 23 repeat the ADC process but now store the result in the variable "rotate2", which controls the mark time for the second servo motor.

Line 24 ADCON0 = 0X01;

This simply reconnects the ADC to channel 0. Note that the logic '1' in bit 0 keeps the ADC turned on.

Lines 26 to 41 have been looked at in previous analysis, so I hope I don't need to do any more here.

Line 41 T0CON = 0b10000000;

This loads the control register for timer0 with the data 0b10000000. Bit 7 is set to a logic '1', and this simply turns timer0 on. Bit 6 is a logic '0', and this makes timer0 operate as a 16-bit register so that it can store a value from 0 to 65535 (i.e., 2^{16} = 65526). The fact that bits 2, 1, and 0 are at logic '0' means that timer0 will divide the clock frequency by 2 to create its counting frequency. Knowing that the clock runs at a quarter of the oscillator frequency, this then sets the frequency at which timer0 counts to:

8MHz / 4 = 2MHz

2MHz / 2 = 1Mhz

Therefore, timer0 counts at a frequency of 1MHz and so a count of 1 = 1μs. A count of 2000 = 2ms and a count of 20000 = 20ms.

Line 42 rotate = 240;

This loads the variable rotate with the value of 240, which sets the mark time initially to 0.24ms. This is the initial setting of the time that the square wave goes back to 0V, which is the end of the mark time. This momentarily moves the servo to the starting position.

Line 43 while (1)

This sets up the forever loop. This is done to make sure the PIC only carries out the previous instructions once.

Line 45 begin: TMR0 = 0;

The word "begin" with the colon ":" gets the compiler to create a label that the program can be forced to jump back to at some other part of the program. The rest of the instruction simply resets timer0 to 0 so that we start counting from 0.

Line 46 servoOut = 1;

This forces the logic on the servoOut pin to a logic '1'. This is the start of the mark time.

Line 47 servoOut2 = 1;

This forces the logic on the servoOut2 pin to a logic '1'. This is the start of the mark time for the second servo motor.

Line 48 while (TMR0 < 2000)

This uses a while (the test is true) do what I say type instruction. The test it creates is to see if the value in the timer0 register, TMR0, is less than 2000. This will be true if the time since starting the mark is less than 2ms. If the test is true, then the PIC will carry out the instructions described between the confines of the following opening and curly bracket.

Line 50 if (TMR0 >= rotate)servoOut = 0;

This is the first instruction within the curly brackets that the PIC must carry out while the value in TMR0 is less than 2000. It creates an "if (this test is true) do what I say if its not true then simply carry on". The test is asking if the value in the TMR0 register is equal to or greater than the value stored in the variable rotate. If the test is true, then the PIC must set the logic on the servoOut pin to logic '0'. This would end the mark time of the square wave applied to the first servo motor. If the test is not true, then the PIC should just carry on with the rest of the program.

Line 51 if (TMR0 >= rotate2)servoOut2 = 0;

This does the same as line 50 but with the variable rotate2 and so controls the mark time of the square wave applied to the second servo motor.

In this way, we are allowing the value in the variables "rotate" and "rotate2" to control the timing of the mark times for the two servo motors. However, this is allowed so long as the timing has not reached the maximum of the 2ms, as this is the maximum mark time allowed. The PIC is trapped in this instruction on line 48 with the "while (TMR0 < 2000)", which traps the PIC in this instruction until 2ms after starting the mark time has passed.

Line 53 while (TMR0 < 18500) changeAngle ();

This another while (test is true) do what I say loop that traps the micro and forces it to carry out this instruction until the value in timer0 gets to 18500, which equates to 18.5ms. While the PIC is trapped in this loop, the PIC will continually go to the subroutine changeAngle, where it will get the current readings of the x and y axes of the joystick.

We do not trap the PIC here until the full 20ms has passed, as we want to avoid the situation whereby the PIC is stuck in the subroutine changeAngle when the 20ms period for the 50Hz square wave has passed. Therefore, we leave a 1.5ms leeway time period to avoid that problem.

Line 54 while (TMR0 <20000);

This simply makes the PIC wait until the full 20ms time period has passed.

Line 55 goto begin;

This instruction simply forces the PIC to go back to line 45, as this is where the label "begin" is. This is being used to make the PIC cycle through the instructions again continuously.

Figures 5-12 and 5-13 show the program working with my homemade prototype board. A video would be better, but I hope you can see that I am using the joystick to alter the positions of the two servo motors.

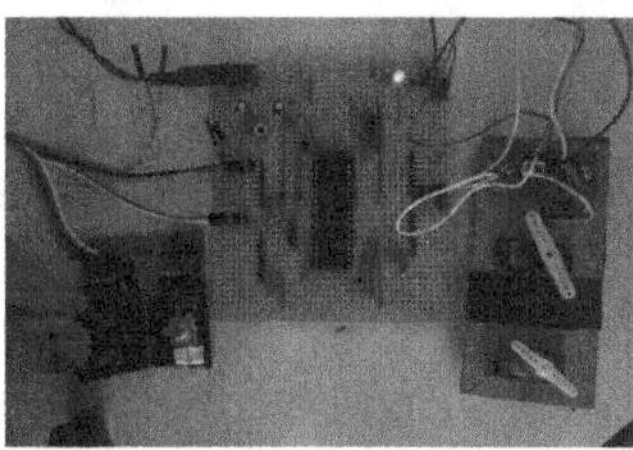

Figure 5-12. *The two-servo motor program working*

Figure 5-13. *The two-servo motor program working*

I am not saying this is the best program for the servo motors, as I am not getting the full 180° movement of the servo motor. However, the book is really about learning how C programs work. I will continue to look at improving the servo motor program, but as it stands it does do a very good job: the movement is smooth and covers around 150°. I hope you will use it to learn more about programming PICs in C; perhaps you will come up with a better program. If you do, then what more could a tutor want?

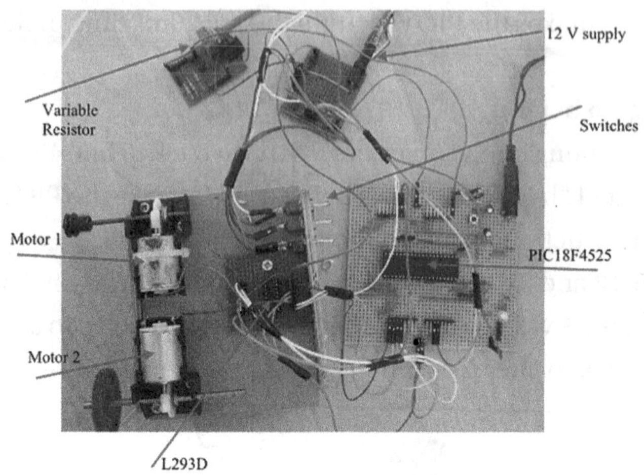

Figure 5-14. *The two-motor variable speed and rotation program*

This figure only really shows that I have used my homemade prototype board for the two motors being controlled with the L293D motor drive IC. A video would be better, but that's not practical in a book.

Summary

In this chapter, we have looked at how we can get the PIC to create a square wave output using the PWM module of the PIC. We will look at an alternative method later in the book, when we look at using interrupts. We have learned how to use the PWM module to create a varying voltage signal that can be applied to vary the speed of a DC motor.

We then went on to learn how a servo motor operates and how to create 50Hz square waves using a simple timer output. We then went on to use the joystick program of the previous chapter and apply it to vary the rotation of two servo motors.

Both these programs went through using the ADC to apply two analog inputs to the PIC. As always, I hope you have found this chapter useful.

In the next chapter, we will look at the HC-SR04 ultrasonic sensor and the HC-011 humidity and temperature sensor.

CHAPTER 6

Ultrasonic Distance, and Humidity and Temperature Sensors

In this chapter, we will look at using an ultrasonic sensor. This will be used for measuring the distance between the sensor and an object in front of it.

We will also look at using the DHT11 humidity and temperature sensor. This sensor could be used to form part of a weather station or just used to monitor the humidity and temperature in a room.

After reading this chapter, you will be able to put these two sensors to use and understand how they work.

Using the Ultrasonic Sensor

Figure 6-1 shows the actual sensor we will use. It is quite inexpensive at around £2.50 and can be used to measure distance from 2 to 400cm with a resolution of 3mm. This makes it a favorite among the would-be engineers.

H. H. Ward, *Programming Arduino Projects with the PIC Microcontroller*,
https://doi.org/10.1007/978-1-4842-7230-5_6

Figure 6-1. *The HC-SR04 ultrasonic sensor*

The main principle is that this will emit a sound wave that will travel out from the sensor. If the sound wave hits an object within range, then the wave will be reflected back and picked up by the receiver in the sensor. Therefore the device has a transmitter and a receiver.

The Basic Principle of Operation

The transmitter can be made to transmit eight pulses at a frequency of 40kHz. The frequency of 40kHz is way outside the range of frequencies that we humans can hear. Our audio range, depending upon age, is from 20Hz to 20kHz.

To start the transmission, we must set the Trig input pin to a logic '1' for a minimum of 10μs. After this 10μs pulse has been received, at the Trig input of the sensor, the sensor transmits eight cycles of the 40kHz square wave. At the end of this burst of transmission, the echo pin goes high. This echo pin will stay high until the sensor receives the eight pulses that were transmitted back at the receiver of the sensor. When this happens, the echo pin will return back to a logic '0'.

This means that there will be a pulse from low to high and back to low at the echo pin. The width of this pulse, or the time the pulse is high, will depend upon the distance from the sensor to the object that reflected the transmission. It is then a simple matter of converting this time period to a distance. To do this, you need to appreciate that the pulses that are transmitted are pulses of sound and so they will travel at the speed of sound. The speed of sound is 343m per second or 0.343 mm in 1μs or 0.0343 cm in 1μs. However, the total time period of the echo pulse would be the time for the eight-pulse train to reach the object and be reflected back. This means that we need to divide the time period by 2 before we multiply the value by 0.0343 for the distance in cm or 0.343 for the distance in mm. This assumes that we are measuring the time of the pulse in microseconds.

As an example, if the time period of the echo pulse was say 250μs then the distance in mm would be calculated as follows:

distance = (250/2) × 0.343 = 42.875 mm or 4.2875 cm.

There is a maximum time period for the echo pulse of 38ms. After that time, the echo pin will return to a logic '0'. Therefore, if the time period of the echo pulse reaches this maximum time of 38ms, then the closest object to the sensor is out of range for the sensor.

Figure 6-2 shows the timing diagram for the Trig input, the transmitted wave, and the echo output.

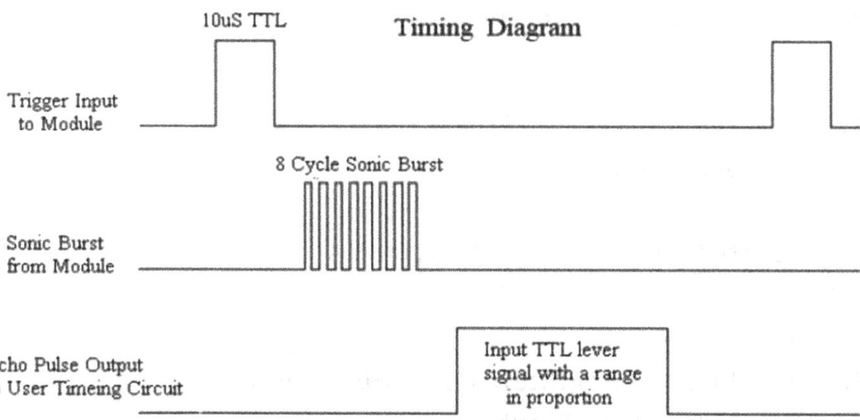

Figure 6-2. *The timing diagram for the sensor*

The Principal Operation of the Program

The program is quite simple in that it needs to send the Trig pin of the sensor to a logic '1' for 10μs. It then it has to measure the width of the echo pulse that will be seen on the echo pin of the sensor. We can use timer0 to start a count when the echo pin goes high and stop the count when it goes low. The value of the count multiplied by the time period of the frequency at which the timer is counting will enable us to determine the time period that the echo pulse is at a logic '1'. Therefore, we need to determine what frequency we must get timer0 to count at. The simplest frequency would be 1Mhz, as this results in a time period of 1μs. So, one tick (i.e., one count of timer0) means that 1μs has passed. This means that to calculate the distance, we simply need to multiply the value in timer0, after dividing it by 2, by 0.0343 for cm. This is what we will do.

At this setting, for the frequency of timer0, the maximum value that timer0 could reach would be the 38ms divided by the 1μs periodic time for timer0. This means the maximum value that timer0 could reach would be 38,000. This means we need to set timer0 to a 16-bit register as the 8 bit could only count to a maximum of 255.

The complete program is shown in Listing 6-1.

Listing 6-1. The Listing for the Ultrasonic Program

```
/*
* File:   ultrasonicProg.c
Author: H.H.Ward
*
Created on 09 January 2021, 16:05
*/
#include <xc.h>
#include <conFigInternalOscNoWDTNoLVP.h>
#include <4bitLCDPortb.h>
#include <stdio.h>
```

```
//some definitions
#define trigout PORTDbits.RD0
#define echoin PORTDbits.RD1
//some variables
unsigned char n, m;
float  distance;
//some subroutines
void delay (unsigned char t)
{
for (n = 0; n < t; n++)
{
TMR0 = 0;
while (TMR0 < 255);
}
}
void delayus (unsigned char v)
{
T0CON = 0b11000000;
TMR0 = 0;
while (TMR0 < v);
T0CON = 0b11000111;
}
void displayreading(float dp)
{
sprintf(str, "%.1f", dp);
writeString(str);
}
void main ()
{
PORTA = 0;
PORTB = 0;
PORTC = 0;
```

```
PORTD = 0;
TRISA = 0b00000001;
TRISB = 0x00;
TRISC = 0b00000000;
TRISD = 0b00000010;
ADCON0 = 0b00000000;
ADCON1 = 0b00001111;
ADCON2 = 0b00111001;
OSCCON = 0b01110100;
OSCTUNE = 0b10000000;
T0CON = 0b11000111;
T3CON = 0b10010001;
CCP1CON = 0b00000000;
setUpTheLCD ();
clearTheScreen ();
PORTC = 0;
writeString ("Coded Ultrasonic");
while (1)
{
trigout = 0;
delayus (4);
trigout = 1;
delayus (10);
trigout = 0;
while (echoin == 0);
TMR3 = 0;
while (echoin == 1);
distance = ((TMR3*0.0343)/2);
line2 ();
writeString ("Gap = ");
displayreading (distance);
writeString ("cm");
```

```
75.   if (distance < 10) PORTCbits.RC0 = 1;
76.   else PORTCbits.RC0 = 0;
77.   }
78.   }
```

Analysis of Listing 6-1

There are no real new instructions that have not been looked at before. I will just discuss some of the important instructions here.

Line 54 T3CON = 0b10010001;

The eight bits in this control register have their usage as described in Table 6-1.

Table 6-1. *The Usage of Timer 3 Control Register T3CON*

Bit Number & Name	Usage		
Bit 7 RD16	This is used to set the number of bits in the register for the count. Logic '1' makes it a 16-bit register Logic '0' makes it an 8-bit register		
Bit 6 linked with bit 3	The data in these two bits determine which is the capture/ compare source for which CCP output		
T3CCP2:T3CCP1	Bit 6	Bit 3	Usage
	1	x	Timer3 is source for both CCP modules
	0	1	Timer3 is source for CCP2 Timer1 is source for CCP1
	0	0	Timer1 is source for both CCP modules

(*continued*)

Table 6-1. (*continued*)

Bit Number & Name	Usage		
Bit 5 linked with bit 4 T3CKPS1: T3CKPS0	Timer3 Input Clock Prescale Select bits		
	Bit 5	Bit 4	Usage
	0	0	1:1 Prescale
	0	1	1:2 Prescale
	1	0	1:4 Prescale
	1	1	1:8 Prescale
Bit 2 T3SYNC	Timer3 External Clock Input Synchronization Control Bit Logic '1' means do not synchronize Logic '0' means do synchronize		
Bit 1 TMR3CS	Timer3 Clock Source Select Bit Logic '1' means source is external clock input from timer 1 or T13CK1 Logic '0' means Internal Clock (osc/4)		
Bit 0 TMR3ON	Timer3 On bit Logic '1' means timer3 enabled Logic '0' means timer3 disabled		

If we now refer the data loaded into the T3CON register with this instruction, we can see that it is doing the following:

Bit 7 = logic '1'; therefore TMR3 is a 16-bit register.

Bit 6 and bit 3 are both logic '0'; therefore timer1 is the source for both CCP modules. However, we are not using them in this program. This will be done in another chapter 13.

Bit 5 and bit 4 are logic '0' and logic '1' respectively, which selects a 1:2 prescale which divides the clock by 2.

Bit 2 is a logic '0', which means we don't synchronize to an external source.

Bit 1 is a logic '0', which means use the internal oscillator as the clock source for timer3.

Bit 0 is a logic '1', which turns timer3 on.

We are making timer3 a 16-bit register as it needs to count up to a value greater than 255.

It is sourced from the internal oscillator which is running at 8MHz (see line 51). This means it runs at 2Mhz (i.e., 8Mhz/4) but we are applying a further division by 2, so timer3 counts at a rate of 1MHz, which is one count every 1µs.

I hope you can see how the actual bits in these control registers can be used to achieve what we want.

Timer3 is set to run at a frequency of 1MHz, so that we can count the number of microseconds the echo pulse remains high. We use timer3 as timer0 is used with the LCD header file and that has been set to run at 7812.5Hz (see line 53).

However, to investigate changing the settings of a timer, in this case timer0, while the program is working, timer0 has been used to create two time delays. The normal delay in lines 18 to 25 produces the normal variable delay based on the 13ms definition. There is a second delay subroutine in lines 26 to 32 based on microseconds, **void delayus (unsigned char v);**. The first thing we do in this subroutine is to load the T0CON register with 0b11000000 in line 28. It is the last three bits which change the divide rate from the maximum to the lowest divide rate of 2. This means that timer0 will divide the 2Mhz clock down to 1MHz. This means one tick, or count, will take 1µs. We then set the timer register to 0 (see line 29) and make the PIC wait until timer0 has counted up to a value set by the variable 'v' (line 30). When we call this subroutine from the main program in lines 63 and 65, we send a value up to the subroutine that will be loaded into this local variable 'v'. Thus, we can select a different delay length every time we call the subroutine, but the units will be in microseconds. One thing you should be aware of with this delay is that because of the shortness of the delay, the actual instructions in the subroutine will make the physical delay longer than what you want. If you need to be very accurate, you should take into account the time the PIC will take to carry out each instruction and how many times it will carry them out. However, as the 10μs is the minimum time for this trigger signal, this will not be an issue. Note that the first 4μs delay, in line 63, when the trig output is low, is just to make sure the sensor has not been triggered already.

The final instruction of this second delay subroutine, on line 31, simply reloads the T0CON register with 0b11000111, which sets the divide rate back to the maximum to get timer0 counting at 7812.5Hz again. Therefore, we can set timer0 to work in a default setting as with line 53 but then change it to a different setting and then back to the default setting with the instructions in this second delay subroutine. This is quite a useful approach to programming.

As an alternative to that approach, we could have used the following instructions:

```
TMR3 = 0;
while (TMR3 < 4);
```

for the 4μs delay and

```
TMR3 = 0;
while (TMR3 < 10);
```

for the 10μs delay.

This would require us turning timer3 on at the beginning, but it would save time by not having to jump out of the main program to run a subroutine. I must admit the 4μs and 10μs pulses are much more accurate with this second method, but I wanted to show you that you can alter the settings in these SFRs within your program.

One issue I have avoided is that I have used the letter 't' for the local variable in the 13ms delay and the letter 'v' in the second delay. As both these variables are local, I could have used the letter 't' in both delays.

The PIC would not get confused, but you as a programmer may get confused. Therefore, always use different letters or names for all your variables.

Figure 6-3 shows the ultrasonic program working with the homemade prototype board.

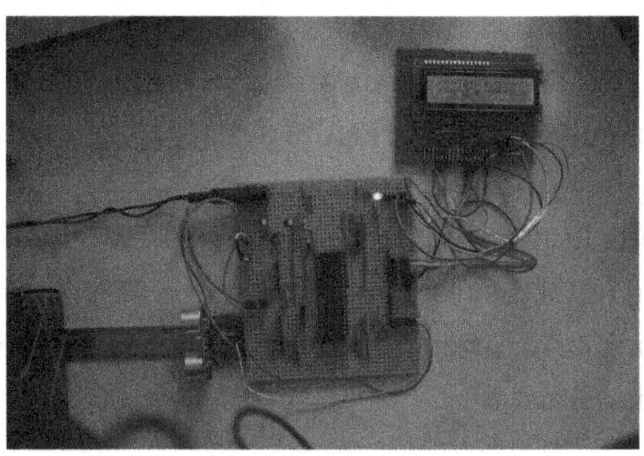

Figure 6-3. *The ultrasonic program*

Figure 6-4 shows the circuit diagram for the ultrasonic program.

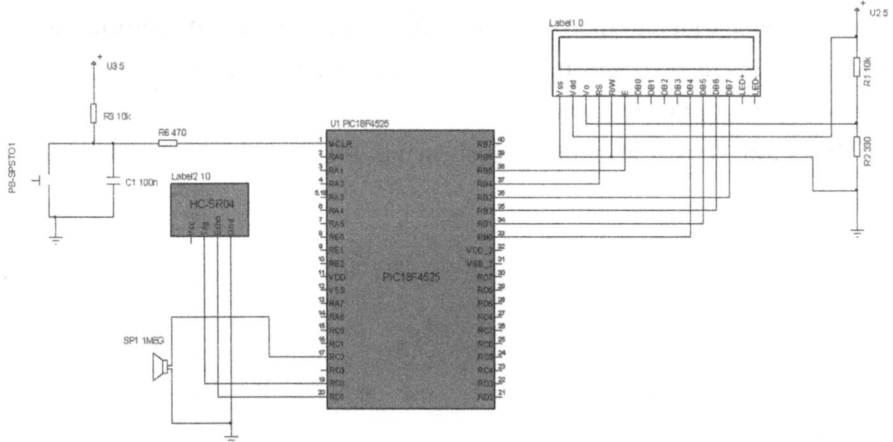

Figure 6-4. *The circuit diagram for the ultrasonic sensor and buzzer*

We could use this distance-sensing program to sound an alarm when the sensor came too close to an obstruction. This would involve using a buzzer connected to one of the outputs of the PIC. That is what we do with lines 75 and 76. In line 75, this is done with the following instruction:

if (distance < 10) PORTCbits.RC0 = 1;

This tests to see if the distance is less than 10cm. If it is, then set bit 0 of PORTC to a logic '1'. This will turn on an active buzzer that is connected to that bit; see the circuit diagram in Figure 6-4.

On line 76 we have the else instruction:

else PORTCbits.RC0 = 0;

This is carried out if the test in the instruction on line 75 is not true and it will turn the active buzzer off. In this way, the program can act as a simple rear-parking sensor.

The DHT11 Humidity and Temperature Sensor

This is a device that can be used to monitor the humidity and temperature in a room. This next program will look at using this sensor and then display the results on our LCD.

The actual sensor we will use is shown in Figure 6-5.

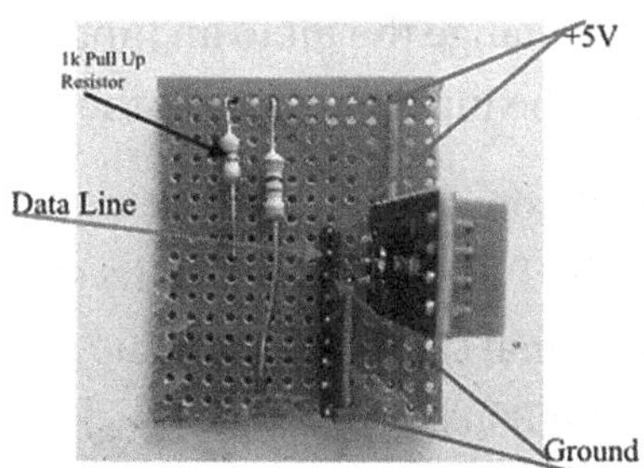

Figure 6-5. *The DHT11 sensor on my vero board with a pull up resistor on the data line*

Communicating with the DHT11

The DHT11 has three pins; some may have four but the fourth is normally left unconnected, as shown in Figure 6-5.

Communication uses just one pin, the data pin. We can connect this pin to any bit of any of the ports on the PIC. We will use bit 0 of PORTD. The process by which the PIC communicates with the DHT11 is as follows:

1. We must first wait at least 1 second after power-up before attempting to communicate with the DHT11. This is to let all the internal circuitry of the sensor settle down.

2. The PIC can then send a start signal to the DHT11. This is done by loading the bit with a logic '0' and keeping it at a logic '0' for 18ms. Note that at this point the bit must be set as an output.

3. After the 18ms, the PIC must load a logic '1' on the bit and keep it a logic '1' for 20μs to 40μs. We will keep it high for 30μs. This is termed the wait time to allow the DHT11 to get ready to respond.

4. We should now change the bit to an input, as the DHT11 will now be inputting data to the PIC.

5. The DHT11 will now send a response signal to the PIC to inform the PIC it has received its start signal. This response signal sends the data line low for 54µs and then high for 80µs.

6. The DHT11 will now send 40 bits of data in five sets of 8 bits. The five sets are in the following order:

    a. Set 1 is the integer part of the humidity reading.

    b. Set 2 is the fractional part of the humidity reading.

    c. Set 3 is the integer part of the temperature reading.

    d. Set 4 is the fractional part of the temperature reading.

    e. Set 5, the final part, is a "checksum" byte, which is simply the binary sum of the first four parts. This checksum is used to validate the reception of the data being sent.

7. The data consists of binary logic '0' and logic '1', and these are represented as voltage states on the data line as follows:

    a. A logic '0' is represented by the data line being held at 0V for 54µs and then at logic high; 5V or 3.3V, for 24µs.

    b. A logic '1' is represented by the data line being held at 0V for 54µs and then at logic high; 5V or 3.3V, for 70µs.

8. After sending the five sets of data, the DHT11 will drive the data line low for 54ms and then send it high. This is an end-of-frame signal.

9. Having received the data from the DHT11 and saved each of the five sets or bytes of data, the PIC must sum the first four bytes of data to create its own "checksum".

10. Having created its own checksum the PIC must compare it with the fifth byte, which is the checksum from the DHT11, to confirm they are the same.

If they are the same, the PIC can use the data; if they are not the same, the PIC cannot use the data.

This helps create an algorithm for the program. The basis of the algorithm is as follows:

- The PIC sends the start signal.
- The PIC then looks for the response signal, which is a low period for 54μs followed by a high period on the data line for 80μs. This can be achieved by waiting for a period of around 40μs and checking to see if the data line is low. It should be. Then, wait a further 80μs and check to see if the data line is high. It would still be high only if the DHT11 is sending a response signal, not a logic '0' or logic '1' (see the respective timing diagrams Figure 6-6). Note that it is unlikely to be an end-of-frame signal, as no data has been sent from the DHT11.
- Now that the PIC has confirmed that the DHT11 has received the start signal, the PIC can now wait for the first eight-bit set of data. This can be achieved as follows:
    - Wait for the logic on the data line to go high, as any data, be it logic '0' or logic '1', starts with a 54μs period of 0V on the data line.

- Now wait around 30μs and check the logic level on the data line.
- If it has now gone to 0V, it means the data must have been a logic '0', as the line is held high for only 24μs.
- If the data line is still high, then it means the data was a logic '1'. The PIC should now wait for the data line to go low.
- Either way, if the data is a '0' or a '1', this first bit must be saved as the MSB in a memory location to be used later. We will use an array to save all 40 bits of data in five separate memory locations.

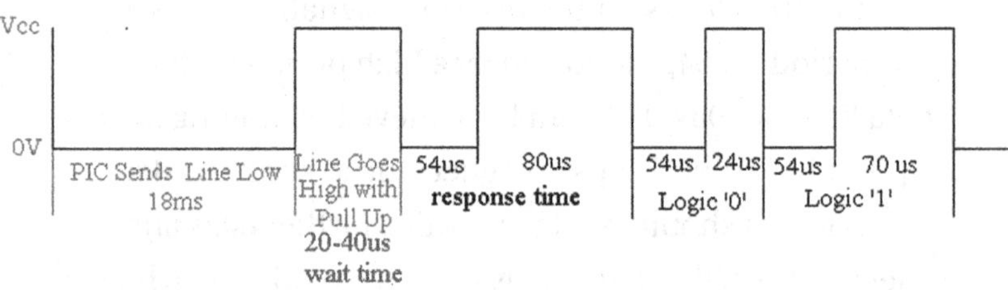

***Figure 6-6.** The timing waveform for communicating with the DHT11*

Figure 6-6 shows that the only difference between the logic '0' and the logic '1' transmitted by the DHT11 is that the high time period for the logic '0' is 24μs, whereas for the logic '1' it is 70μs. Therefore, we simply have to get the PIC to wait until the line goes high and then after say 30μs check to see if the line is still high. If it is, then the DHT11 must be transmitting a logic '1'. If it has already gone low, then it must be transmitting a logic '0'. This is what we do in the program.

The Use of a Pull Up Resistor

One thing you must do is connect the data output of the DHT11 to VCC via a pull up resistor. This is to ensure that when the DHT11 is not switching the output low, the output does go high. The pull up resistor is there to limit the current through the device when the DHT11 does switch the output to 0V. This is shown in the circuit diagram for this project.

Checking the Timing of the Pulses

We need to create some accurate timings, and it would be useful to check that they are accurate and last for the required time period.

A simple method would be to write a small program that makes an LED on an output flash at the required time period. The listing for a simple test program we could use to do this is shown in Listing 6-2.

Listing 6-2. A Simple Program to Test the Period of a Square Wave

```
/*
* File:   dht11Prog.c
Author: H. H. Ward
*
Created on 30 December 2020, 16:29
*/
#include <xc.h>
#include <conFigInternalOscNoWDTNoLVP.h>
void main ()
{
PORTA = 0;
PORTB = 0;
PORTC = 0;
```

```
14.   PORTD = 0;
15.   TRISA = 0b00000000;
16.   TRISB = 0x00;
17.   TRISC = 0b00000000;
18.   TRISD = 0x00;
19.   ADCON0 = 0x00;
20.   ADCON1 = 0x0F;
21.   OSCCON = 0b01110000;
22.   OSCTUNE = 0b10000000;
23.   T0CON = 0b11000111;
24.   T1CON = 0b00010001;
25.   while (1)
26.   {
27.   Flash: PORTDbits.RD0 ^=1;
28.   TMR1 = 0;
29.         while (TMR1 < 25);
30.   goto Flash;
31.   }
```

The concept is that timer1 has been set to count at a frequency of 1MHz. That means that it counts once every 1µs. The program for the DHT11 needs to create a 30µs, a 54µs, and a 70µs time period.

In line 27 of the listing, we make the LED connected to bit 0 of PORTD respond to an Exclusive OR, EXOR function with a logic '1.' This means that if the logic on RD0 is currently at a logic '0,' then when we EXOR it with a logic '1,' RD0 will go to a logic '1.' Then, the next time we EXOR it with a logic '1,' RD0 will go to a logic '0' (see the following EXOR truth table).

B	A	F
0	0	0
0	1	1
1	0	1
1	1	0

EXOR Truth Table

This table shows that the output 'F' will be a logic '1' only when A OR B is a logic '1', not when A AND B are logic '1'.

Lines 28 and 29 create the time delay to generate the required time period. We set the TMR1 register to 0 so that it starts to count from 0. Then in line 29, we get the micro to do nothing while the value in TMR1 is less than 25. You might think that we should use 30, as a count of 30 would take 30μs. However, we have to try and account for the time required to carry out the instructions in lines 28 to 30. It will take a finite time to carry these instructions out.

Now, to check that the time period is the required 30μs and not the written 25μs, we can use an oscilloscope to measure the signal at RD0 on the PIC. The setup for this is shown in Figure 6-7.

Figure 6-8 shows the display on the oscilloscope. It is possible to see that the mark time is 0.029ms or 29μs: still slightly out. Also, we can see that the rise and fall time of the square wave is not instantaneous.

Now look at Figure 6-9, which shows the display on the oscilloscope when we are trying to achieve an 18ms, or 0.018s, mark time. You can see that the mark time is the required 18ms. We can also see that the waveform looks sharper as the fall and rise times look quicker. Well, they are not any quicker, as the rise and fall times are due to the switching time of the outputs, not the software. It looks sharper because these rise and fall times are much smaller compared to the 18ms mark time. With the 0.029ms mark time, the rise and fall times are long enough in proportion to be visible.

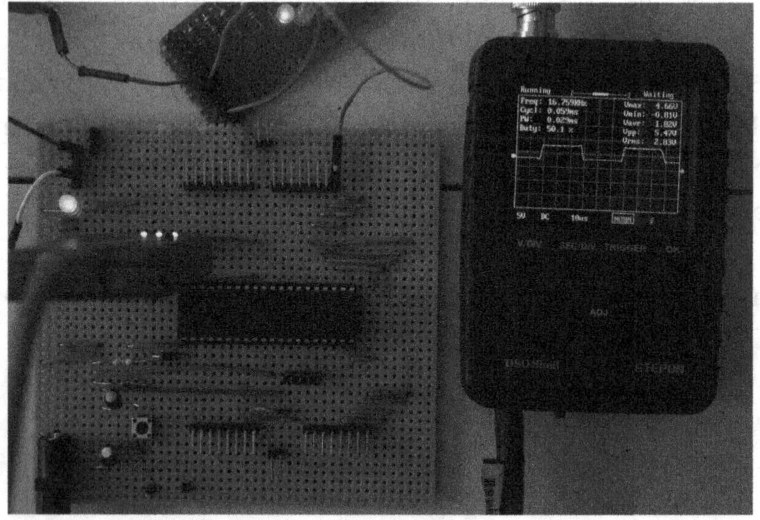

***Figure 6-7.** Using an oscilloscope to check the timing of the pulse*

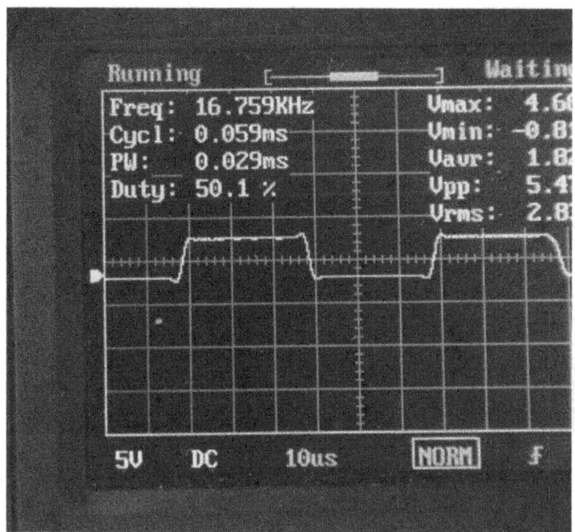

Figure 6-8. *The oscilloscope display for the 29µs mark time*

The change to the program listing to test the 18ms mark time is shown here.

```
Flash: PORTDbits.RD0 ^=1;
TMR0 = 0;
while (TMR0 < 141);
goto Flash;
```

Here we are using timer0, which we have set up to count at a frequency of 7812.5Hz, which has a time period of 128µS.

At that frequency, it would take 140.625 counts to create an 18ms delay. We have used a value of 141. We don't need to use a smaller value here because the time taken to carry out the instructions in the while statement will only be very small compared with the 18ms delay. With respect to the 30µs delay, the time taken to carry out the while instructions is not small compared to the 30µs delay we want to create. Just something you may need to consider when creating accurate delays.

Figure 6-9 shows the oscilloscope display of the 18ms delay.

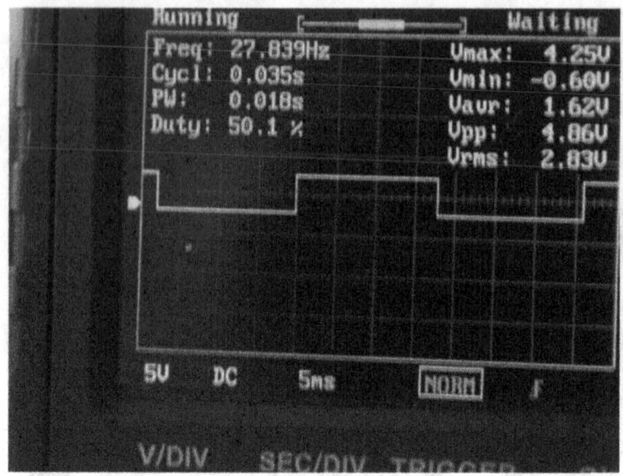

***Figure 6-9.** The oscilloscope display for the 18ms mark time*

Now that we have our fairly accurate delays, we can write the full program. The complete code for the DHT11 humidity and temperature sensor is shown in Listing 6-3.

Listing 6-3. DHT11 Program

```
/*
* File:   dht11Prog.c
Author: H. H. Ward
*
Created on 30 December 2020, 16:29
*/
#include <xc.h>
#include <conFigInternalOscNoWDTNoLVP.h>
#include <4bitLCDPortb.h>
#include <stdio.h>
//some definitions
#define datapin PORTDbits.RD0
#define dataddr TRISDbits.RD0
```

```
//some variables
unsigned char n, m, response = 0, mychecksum, valid = 0;
unsigned char mess[30], *messpointer;
//some subroutines
void debounce ()
{
TMR0 = 0;
while (TMR0 < 100);
}
void delay (unsigned char t)
{
for (n = 0; n < t; n ++)
{
TMR0 = 0;
while (TMR0 < 255);
}
}
void displayreading(float dp)
{
sprintf(str, "%.1f", dp);
writeString(str);
}
void main ()
{
PORTA = 0;
PORTB = 0;
PORTC = 0;
PORTD = 0;
TRISA = 0b00000000;
TRISB = 0x00;
TRISC = 0b00000000;
```

```
TRISD = 0x00;
ADCON0 = 0x00;
ADCON1 = 0x0F;
OSCCON = 0b01110000;
OSCTUNE = 0b10000000;
T0CON = 0b11000111;
T1CON = 0b00010001;
messpointer = mess;
setUpTheLCD ();
clearTheScreen ();
writeString ("DHT11 Humid Temp");
line2 ();
delay (31);
getreading:  dataddr = 0;
datapin = 0;
TMR0 = 0;
while (TMR0 < 141);
datapin = 1;
TMR1 = 0;
while (TMR1 < 25);
dataddr = 1;
TMR1 = 0;
while (TMR1 < 40);
if (datapin == 0)
{
TMR1 = 0;
while (TMR1 < 75);
if (datapin == 1 response = 1;
TMR1 = 0;
while (TMR1 < 45);
}
```

```
else response = 0;
if (response == 1)
{
for (m = 0; m < 5; m++)
{
for (n= 0; n < 8; n++)
{
while (!datapin);
TMR1 = 0;
while (TMR1 < 25);
if (datapin == 0)
{
mess[m]&= ~(1<<(7-n));
}
else
{
mess[m]|=(1<<(7-n));
while (datapin);
}
}
}
mychecksum =(mess[0]+mess[1]+mess[2]+mess[3]);
if (mychecksum - mess[4] == 0) valid = 1;
else valid = 0;
clearTheScreen ();
writeString ("Humidity = ");
displayreading(mess[0]);
lcdData = 0X25;
lcdOut();
line2 ();
writeString ("Temp = ");
```

```
107. displayreading (mess[2]);
108. writeString(" OC");
109. }
110. else writeString ("no response");
111. delay(155);
112. goto getreading;
113. }
```

Analysis of Listing 6-3

Most of the instructions have already been described. I will explain the principal operation of the program and any new instructions.

The main principle of the program is that the PIC will initialize communication with the DHT11. The DHT11 will then send back the 40 bits of data that can be used to relay the humidity and temperature readings from the sensors. We will create an array called “mess”, where we can store the data being sent back. The 40 bits will make up five bytes of data. The first four bytes have the two readings, and the last byte is the result of adding the first four bytes together, by the DHT11, before they are transmitted to the PIC. This result is termed the “checksum”, and the PIC must create its own checksum by adding the first four bytes together that the PIC receives. The PIC must then compare its checksum with the fifth byte it has received to confirm that the data received is valid. If the two checksums are not the same, then an error, termed “Checksum Error”, has occurred and the data is not used.

Line 58 getreading: dataddr = 0;

We have defined the label “dataddr” to mean the bit TRISDbits.RD0 (i.e., bit 0 in the TRIS register for PORTD) on line 13. This bit will control the direction of data through bit 0 of PORTD. With this instruction, we are setting the logic in that bit to 0. This makes bit 0 on PORTD an output.

We are using the label “getreading” here because later in the program, in line 112, we force the PIC to go back to this line using that label.

Lines 59 to 66 get the PIC to initiate communication with the DHT11. This is done by sending the logic on bit 0 of PORTD low (i.e., a logic '0'). Then, with lines 60 and 61, we create the 18ms delay. Then, in line 62, we send the logic on bit 0 of PORTD high (i.e., a logic '1'). Next, with lines 63 and 64, we create a 30μs delay. This is the wait time, which should be between 20μs and 40μs.

With line 65, we change the direction of data through bit 0 of PORTD to input.

Now, with lines 66 and 67, we create a 40μs delay. Then, on line 68, we check to see if the DHT11 has sent the data line low. If this has happened, then it would be the start of the response from the DHT11 telling us it had received the initialization request from the PIC. The PIC would then move into the loop defined by the curly brackets between lines 69 and 78.

If the data line on bit 0 of PORTD had not gone low, and the test on line 68 were untrue, then the DHT11 is not responding correctly and the PIC would have to go to line 79, where it loads the variable response with 0.

If the line had gone low, and the test on line 68 were true, we would then wait around 75μs (lines 70 and 71). Then, we check to see if the DHT11 has allowed the line to be pulled high (i.e., **line 72 if (datain == 1);**). If it has gone to a logic '1', then this would be the correct response signal from the DHT11, and we can remember this response by loading the variable response with 1 (see Figure 6-6).

In lines 73 and 74, we run a 45μs delay, which would take us into the first 54μs low of any data signal being sent to the PIC from the DHT11, be it a logic '1' or a logic '0'.

If test on line 68 were true, we would not carry out the else statement on line 76 because we would ignore the else statement associated with that if test. Instead, we can carry on and in line 80 we check again that the response from the DHT11 was good. We now know the DHT11 will send five blocks of eight bits of data. Therefore, we will load the array "mess" that we created in line 16, with the data that follows.

We start by creating an outer "for do loop" with the variable 'm,' which makes the PIC loop five times (i.e., m = 0, m = 1, m = 2, m = 3, and m = 4). This is used to store the next eight bits that arrive on the data pin into the first, m = 0, of five locations in the array "mess". The eight bits to be stored in this first location in the array will start to arrive on the data pin.

We now create an inner "for do loop" in line 81 which loops eight times to look at the data coming into the PIC from the DHT11. It will store these eight bits of data into the location in the array controlled by the variable 'm,' which at present (i.e., the first run-through of the outer "for do loop") is 0.

By now, we should be well inside the 54μs time period when the DHT11 has sent the data line into a low state (see Figure 6-6). Therefore, on line 83 we wait for this logic low state to finish; that is, while (!datain); while datain is a logic '0' do nothing. Then we create a 30μs delay with lines 84 and 85. Then, on line 86, we ask if the data line has gone back to low from the DHT11. If it has, then it means the data the DHT11 has just sent was the code for a logic '0' (see the timing diagram in Figure 6-6).

If the test on line 86 were true and the DHT11 had just sent a logic '0,' then the PIC would carry out the instruction on line 88. We will look at how this instruction works later in the analysis.

If the test on line 86 were not true, this would mean the data line is still high, at a logic '1,' and then the PIC would carry out the instruction on line 92; we will look at this instruction later. Also, it would mean the DHT11 is sending the code for a logic '1.' Note that if the test on line 86 were true, then the PIC would ignore all the instructions on lines 90 to 94 inclusive. It would then go back to line 83, as 'n' would still be less than 8.

This inner loop would repeat eight times and so receive the first of the five bytes the DHT11 would be sending. The PIC would then go through the outer loop to store the second byte of data in the second location in the array mess.

This whole process is carried out a total of 40 times, in which the PIC will store the 40 bits of data in the five memory locations in the array. Each memory location stores one byte of data.

In line 97, the PIC creates its own checksum by adding the 32 bits of data in the first four memory locations in the array. The results are stored in the variable "mychecksum".

In line 98, we subtract this result from the eight bits in the last memory location stored in the array. This is how the PIC will compare the two checksums. This is done to check the validity of the data received. If the result of the subtraction is zero, then the data is valid.

With the instruction on line 98:

if (mychecksum - mess[4] == 0) valid = 1;

We are setting up a test to see if the subtraction produces a zero result. If the test is true, then we load the variable "valid" with 1. The PIC would then skip the instruction on line 99.

If the test on line 98 is untrue, then the PIC will carry out the instruction on line 99:

else valid = 0;

This loads the variable valid with the value 0.

Line 100 clears the LCD screen of any characters and sends the cursor back to the beginning of the first line.

Line 101 simply displays "Humidity =" on the LCD.

Line 102 calls the subroutine display reading and sends the ASCII that is stored in the first location in the array "mess" to the LCD. This is the integer part of the humidity reading.

Next, with lines 103 and 104, the PIC sends the value 0X25, which is the ASCII for the '%' sign, to be displayed on the LCD.

After that, lines 106 to 109 send the temperature reading that is stored in the third location in the array "mess" to the LCD.

Note that on line 77 we have the following instruction:

if (response == 1)

This sets up a test to see if the data in the variable response is equal to 1. If the result of the test is true, then the PIC will carry out all the instructions between the curly brackets on lines 78 and 109. Note that the PIC would also ignore the instruction on line 110:

else writeString ("no response");

However, if the test on line 77 is untrue (i.e., the value in response is not 1), then the PIC will ignore all the instructions between line 78 and 109 and carry out the instruction on line 110, where it simply sends the message "no response" to the LCD.

Line 111 delay(155);

This calls the subroutine delay and sends the value of 155 up to it. This will create a delay of around 2 seconds.

Line 112 goto getreading;

This makes the PIC go to line 58, where it starts the whole process again.

I hope this description does explain how the instructions achieve the desired result. It is rather a complex process and you may need to read through it and examine Figure 6-6 a few times. However, I hope it shows that once you fully understand what it is you are trying to achieve with the PIC, then it is simply a matter of finding the instructions you need and learning how to implement them. This only comes with understanding and experience. I hope this book will give you some of that.

However, I do feel that there are two instructions that warrant some more detailed analysis. They are the following:

Line 88 mess[m]&= ~(1<<(7-n));

This is inside the nested for do loops that are used to load the 40 bits of data into the first five memory locations in the array. This particular instruction will be carried out if the data being sent is a logic '0' to be stored as one of the eight bits of data being sent by the DHT11. It will be stored in one of the five memory locations in the array "mess".

The 'm,' which starts off with a value of zero, is used to control which memory location in the array we are storing the following eight bits into. We have already determined whether the data is the code for a logic '0' or a logic '1.' If it is a logic '0,' then the PIC will carry out this instruction. What we are doing here is ANDING the bits in the specified memory location in the array with an inversion of a logic '1' that has been shifted seven times to the left, if n = 0. If we assume this is the first pass through this loop, then m will be 0 and also n will be 0. This means we will be ANDING all the bits in the first memory location in the array, with the inversion of a logic '1' that has been shifted to the MSB of an eight-bit number. This means we will be ANDING whatever is in the first memory location of the array with a logic '0' at the MSB. The logic '1' in the part **~(1<<(7-n))** becomes a logic '0' because of the inversion part of this instruction signified by the '~' in front of the bracket. It is shifted to the left, to put this first bit into the MSB position of the specified memory location, by the 7-n part of the instruction. As this is the first time this inner loop has been executed, then n would = 0 and so we shift this bit seven places to the left.

If we now assume we come to the same instruction the second time in the loop, then n = 1 and this instruction will result in bit 6 of the first memory location in the array becoming a logic '0' also.

Note that a logical AND operation with one bit being a logic '0' as in this case after the inversion, and the other bit either a logic '1' or a logic '0,' would always result in a logic '0.' This is what we want to store in this occurrence.

This assumes that the code being sent from the DHT11 represents a logic '0.' However, if it represents a logic '1,' then the PIC would skip lines 87, 88, and 89 and carry out the following instruction.

Line 92 mess[m]|=(1<<(7-n));

This time, there is no inversion part in the instruction. This is because we can simply use the '1' that is shifted.

This time, were are using the logical OR instruction as signified with the symbol '|='. This will perform a logical OR with the contents of the memory location specified and the '1' that has been shifted left the required number of times specified by the '7-n' part of the instruction. Note that a logical OR operation with one bit being a logic '1' as in this case, and the other bit either a logic '1' or a logic '0', would always result in a logic '1'. This is what we want to store in this occurrence.

I appreciate that this is a wordy description of the instructions but they are rather complex. However, it is an interesting solution to a challenging problem: that of loading a memory location with an unknown series of eight bits.

To help explain how this and other complex instructions work, I have tried to simulate this and many other logic operations in the last chapter of this book. I hope they will help you. Also it will help explain how you can use the MPLABX software to debug your programs.

Figure 6-10 shows the DHT11 program working.

Figure 6-10. *The DHT11 program working*

Summary

In this chapter, we have studied how the ultrasonic sensor operates and how it can be programmed with the PIC. We have also learned how the DHT11 humidity and temperature sensor can be programmed to work with the PIC.

In the next chapter, we will learn how to use two types of numeric keypads to give you some security on your entry doors. We will also look at how to program a dot matrix display.

As always, I hope you are finding these chapters informative and challenging as well as exciting and useful.

CHAPTER 7

Working with Keypads

In this chapter, we will program two types of keypads to provide us with security on entry to our house or room. The first keypad will be a 3-by-4 pad using the more traditional type keys on them. A typical board is shown in Figure 7-1.

***Figure 7-1.** The traditional keypad board*

The other keyboard is the slimmer membrane type and is a 4-by-4 keypad. This is shown in Figure 7-2.

H. H. Ward, *Programming Arduino Projects with the PIC Microcontroller*,
https://doi.org/10.1007/978-1-4842-7230-5_7

Figure 7-2. *The 4 × 4 membrane keypad*

The final section in this chapter will look at using an 8-by-8 dot matrix display to display numbers or letters. The matrix display is shown in Figure 7-3. The program to control this display will use the Max7219 driver IC. To use this IC, we will investigate the use of a two-dimensional array.

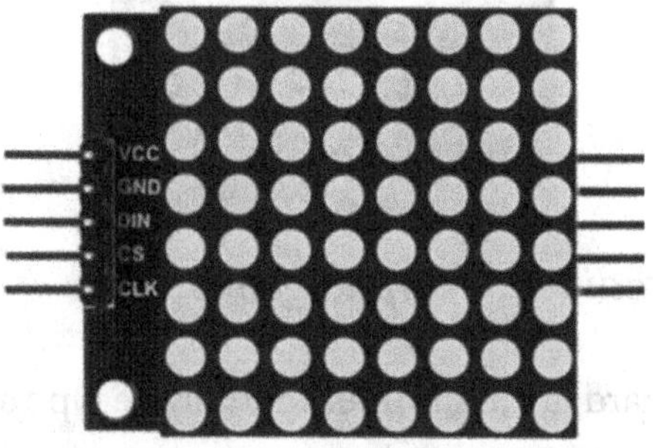

Figure 7-3. *The 8 × 8 dot matrix display*

After reading this chapter, you will have learned how to use these keypads and why we need pull up or pull down resistors. You will also have learned how to implement a two-dimensional array to load a dot matrix display with data and how to use the Max7219 driver chip.

Traditional 3 × 4 Keypad Entry

With this program, we will use a 3-by-4 numeric keypad to control entry into a room. The program will allow the user to set a four-digit numerical code that will have to be matched by anyone wanting to enter the room. Any person trying to enter the room will have three attempts at entering the correct code. If the third attempt is unsuccessful they will be locked out.

The program will use the LCD to display messages to the user. The LCD will be connected to PORTB, and we will use the 4bitLCDPortb.h header file to control it. We will also use the conFigInternalOscNoWDTNoLVP.h, which means we will be using the internal oscillator set at 8Mhz.

The numeric keypad that we will use in this program is shown in Figure 7-4.

Figure 7-4. *The 3 × 4 keypad module*

This is a module made by Matrixmultimedia; it has a nine-pin D-type connector that allows it to be connected to a prototype board. The circuit diagram for the board is shown in Figure 7-5.

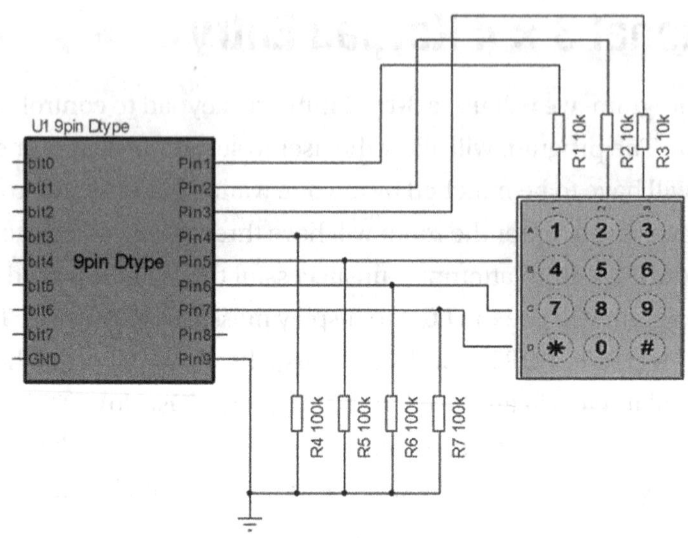

Figure 7-5. *The 3 × 4 keypad circuit diagram*

There are three internal resistors, R1, R2, and R3, to limit the current applied to the switches. There are four pull down resistors, R4, R5, R6, and R7, to ensure the logic goes to logic '0' when the switches are not pressed.

The Need for Pull Up or Pull Down

Figure 7-6 shows the basic circuit of a 4-by-4 keypad. However, the principle of operation is the same with the 3-by-4 keypad.

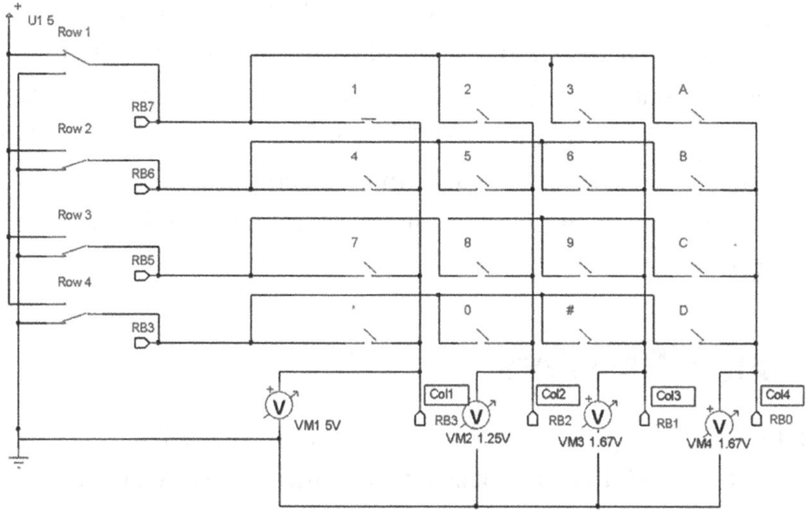

***Figure 7-6.** The basic circuit for the keypad active high*

The basic concept is that you would turn on just one of the switches connected to the four rows. Really, the rows would be connected to outputs of the PIC, and the PIC would send 5V (i.e., a logic '1') or 0V (a logic '0'), depending upon whether the device is active high or active low respectively, onto the relevant output and so onto the relevant row. In Figure 7-6, we are showing that only row 1 is connected to 5V, while all the other three rows are connected to 0V. We now simply monitor the inputs to the PIC that come from each of the columns. If any of the four inputs to the PIC go to 5V (i.e., a logic '1'), then this would mean one of the four keypad buttons on that row must have been pressed. In Figure 7-6 we can see that there is 5V on the RB3 input, which is connected to column 1. As we know the layout of the keypad, we can interpret this as being the key labeled '1' on the keypad.

The problem we will have is what will be the voltage on the other inputs connected to columns 2, 3, and 4. The simulation software "Tina" shows them as 1.25V, 1.67V, and 1.67V. In the arrangement shown in Figure 7-6, those three inputs to the PIC are what we would call "floating".

In reality, we could not say what voltage would be present on the inputs. They could float to a logic '1' or a logic '0.' We would ideally want the unconnected inputs to the PIC to float to a logic '0' so that we would detect only one logic '1' at the four inputs. This is because only one key had been pressed. In any electronics, especially microelectronics, we should never leave an input floating, because it's Murphy's Law that they would float to the wrong logic.

Pull Down Resistors

The solution to the problem, with circuit shown in Figure 7-6, is that on all the inputs to the PIC that are not switched to the active level, which in this case is active high (a logic '1'), we must pull their inputs to the opposite logic. In this case, we must pull the inputs down to a logic '0.'

To do this, we need to change the circuit to the arrangement shown in Figure 7-7.

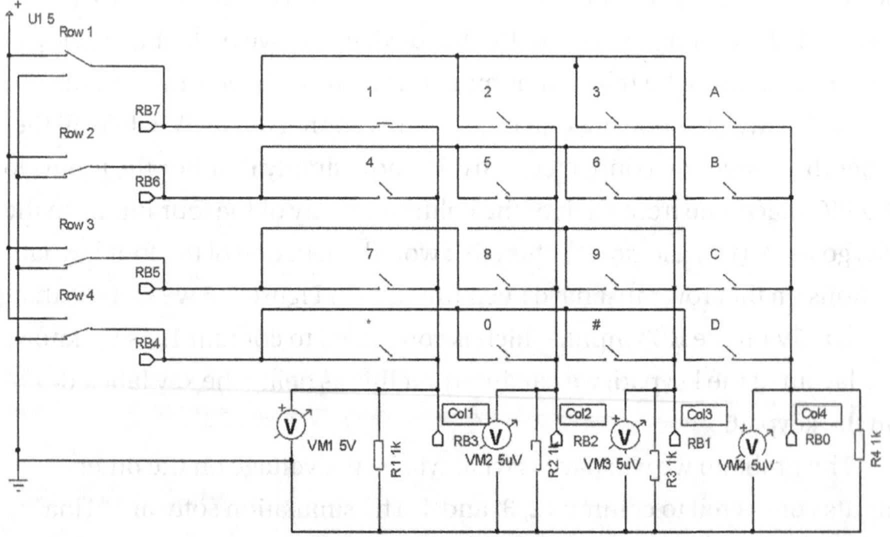

***Figure 7-7.** The keypad circuit with pull down resistors*

With this arrangement, all four inputs to the PIC have a path to ground or 0V via the 1kΩ resistors. If the switches on the rows are as shown in Figure 7-7, then there is no current flowing through any of the 1kΩ resistors connected to the three inputs RB0, RB1, and RB2, as they are open circuited. This means that there can be no voltage dropped across them, and so the voltage at those inputs is 5μV or logic '0', as shown in Figure 7-7. The voltage at the input RB3 is at 5V because the switch on row 1 is closed and so the 5V is connected to row 1. This then supplies the 5V, logic '1', directly onto input RB3 via the switch on keypad '1' as shown.

So why do we have the 1kΩ resistors between the inputs and ground? This is simply to limit the current flowing through the switches of the keypad. If there were no resistance, there then we would be putting a short to ground across the 5V, and we would most likely set the keypad on fire. A 1kΩ resistor would limit the current to around 5mA. This arrangement is termed using pull down resistors. You could use higher-value resistors to limit the current further; 100kΩ would reduce the current to around 50μA.

Pull Up Resistors

With some keypads, we can use the opposite logic (i.e., active low). Really, the choice of active low or active high is up to us and how we connect the basic keypad in the circuit. Sometimes active low is more preferable than active high. This is how we will connect the membrane keypad in the second program. The circuit arrangement is shown in Figure 7-8.

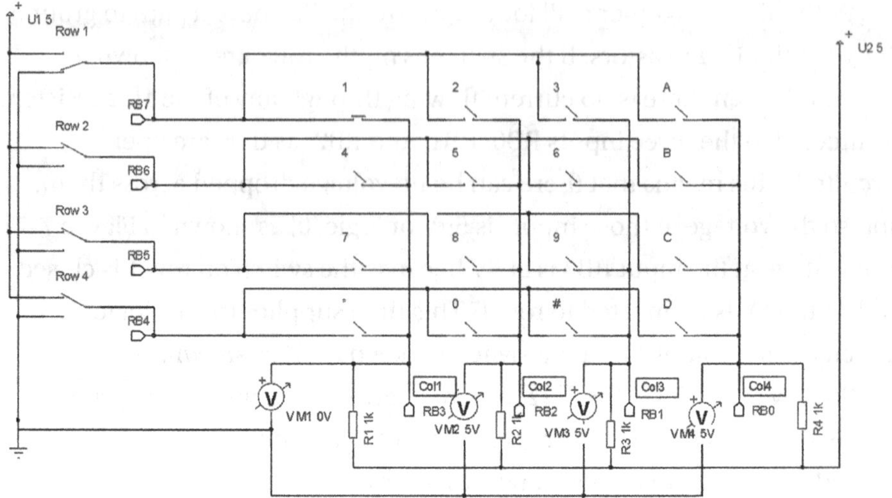

Figure 7-8. *The basic keypad with pull up resistors*

With this arrangement, it is still the key numbered '1' that has been pressed, but now we are looking for a logic '0' (i.e., 0V) at the input. The only input at 0V is RB3, as expected. With this arrangement, the four resistors are now connected to +5V. Now if no current flows through the resistors, the inputs go to 5V, as no voltage is dropped across their respective resistors. The only switch that has a path to ground is switch '1', and so only input RB3 goes to 0V.

Again, the resistors are required to limit the current that would flow through the switches to 5mA.

This arrangement is termed using pull up resistors. As this is the most preferred arrangement, all the PICs from Microchip have these pull resistors connected to one of the PORTS within the PIC. With the PIC18F4525, all inputs on PORTB have these pull up resistors available to us. If we use these internal pull up resistors at the inputs on PORTB, it means we won't have to add them externally in our circuit design. We can enable their use or disable their use depending on our preference.

The circuit for the keyboard program is shown in Figure 7-9.

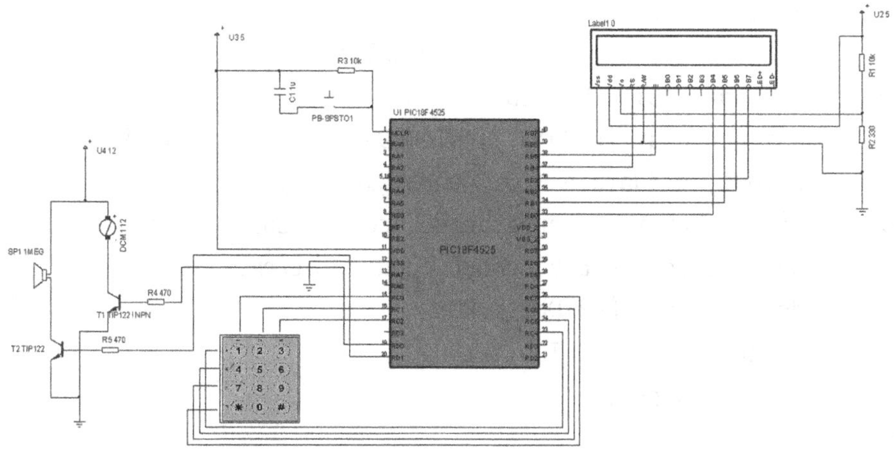

Figure 7-9. *The circuit diagram for the keyboard program*

Traditional Keypad Program

As we will be using the module for Matrixmultimedia shown in Figure 7-4, we will not require any pull up or down resistors because the module uses pull down resistors on all four inputs. This means that the keypad is used in the active high arrangement. This means that we expect the inputs to go to a logic '1' when the key is pressed and logic '0' when the key is not pressed.

The complete code is shown in Listing 7-1.

Listing 7-1. Traditional 3 × 4 Keypad

```
/*
* File:   keypadCodedProg.c
Author: H H Ward
A program to control entry to a room
Written for the PIC18f4525*
Created on 23 December 2020, 13:09
*/
```

```
#include <xc.h>
#include <conFigInternalOscNoWDTNoLVP.h>
#include <4bitLCDPortb.h>
unsigned char lcdData, lcdTempData, rsLine, datain, dataout, olddatain = 0, newdatain = 0;
unsigned char n, count, code, code0, code1, code2, code3, codea, codeb, codec, coded, attempts=0;
#define motor PORTDbits.RD0
#define buzzer PORTDbits.RD1
void debounce ()
{
TMR0 = 0;
while (TMR0 < 100);
}
void delay (unsigned char t)
{
for (n = 0; n < t; n ++)
{
TMR0 = 0;
while (TMR0 < 255);
}
}
void setCode ()
{
PORTCbits.RC0 = 1;
PORTCbits.RC1 = 0;
PORTCbits.RC2 = 0;
{
if (PORTCbits.RC4 == 1)
{
debounce ();
```

```
if (PORTCbits.RC4 == 1)
{
lcdData = 0x31;
lcdOut();
code = 0x31;
}
while (PORTCbits.RC4 == 1);
}
if (PORTCbits.RC5 == 1)
{
debounce ();
if (PORTCbits.RC5 == 1)
{
lcdData = 0x34;
lcdOut();
code = 0X34;
}
while (PORTCbits.RC5 == 1);
}
if (PORTCbits.RC6 == 1)
{
debounce ();
if (PORTCbits.RC6 == 1)
{
lcdData = 0x37;
lcdOut();
code = 0x37;
}
while (PORTCbits.RC6 == 1);
}
```

```
if (PORTCbits.RC7 == 1)
{
debounce ();
if (PORTCbits.RC7 == 1)
{
lcdData = 0x2A;
lcdOut();
code = 0x2A;
}
while (PORTCbits.RC7 == 1);
}
}
PORTCbits.RC0 = 0;
PORTCbits.RC1 = 1;
PORTCbits.RC2 = 0;
{
if (PORTCbits.RC4 == 1)
{
debounce ();
if (PORTCbits.RC4 == 1)
{
lcdData = 0x32;
lcdOut();
code = 0x32;
}
while (PORTCbits.RC4 == 1);
}
if (PORTCbits.RC5 == 1)
{
debounce ();
```

```
if (PORTCbits.RC5 == 1)
{
lcdData = 0x35;
lcdOut();
code = 0x35;
}
while (PORTCbits.RC5 == 1);
}
if (PORTCbits.RC6 == 1)
{
debounce ();
if (PORTCbits.RC6 == 1)
{
lcdData = 0x38;
lcdOut();
code = 0x38;
}
while (PORTCbits.RC6 == 1);
}
if (PORTCbits.RC7 == 1)
{
debounce ();
if (PORTCbits.RC7 == 1)
{
lcdData = 0x30;
lcdOut();
code = 0x30;
}
while (PORTCbits.RC7 == 1);
}
}
```

```
PORTCbits.RC0 = 0;
PORTCbits.RC1 = 0;
PORTCbits.RC2 = 1;
{
for (n = 0; n < 3; n++)
{
if (PORTCbits.RC4 == 1)
{
debounce ();
if (PORTCbits.RC4 == 1)
{
lcdData = 0x33;
lcdOut();
code = 0x33;
}
while (PORTCbits.RC4 == 1);
}
if (PORTCbits.RC5 == 1)
{
debounce ();
if (PORTCbits.RC5 == 1)
{
lcdData = 0x36;
lcdOut();
code = 0x36;
}
while (PORTCbits.RC5 == 1);
}
if (PORTCbits.RC6 == 1)
{
debounce ();
```

```
if (PORTCbits.RC6 == 1)
{
lcdData = 0x39;
lcdOut();
code = 0x39;
}
while (PORTCbits.RC6 == 1);
}
if (PORTCbits.RC7 == 1)
{
debounce ();
if (PORTCbits.RC7 == 1)
{
lcdData = 0x23;
lcdOut();
code = 0x23;
}
while (PORTCbits.RC7 == 1);
}
}
}
}
void getCode()
{
PORTCbits.RC0 = 1;
PORTCbits.RC1 = 0;
PORTCbits.RC2 = 0;
{
if (PORTCbits.RC4 == 1)
{
debounce ();
```

```
if (PORTCbits.RC4 == 1)
{
lcdData = 0x2A;
lcdOut();
code = 0x31;
}
while (PORTCbits.RC4 == 1);
}
if (PORTCbits.RC5 == 1)
{
debounce ();
if (PORTCbits.RC5 == 1)
{
lcdData = 0x2A;
lcdOut();
code = 0X34;
}
while (PORTCbits.RC5 == 1);
}
if (PORTCbits.RC6 == 1)
{
debounce ();
if (PORTCbits.RC6 == 1)
{
lcdData = 0x2A;
lcdOut();
code = 0x37;
}
while (PORTCbits.RC6 == 1);
}
if (PORTCbits.RC7 == 1)
```

```
{
debounce ();
if (PORTCbits.RC7 == 1)
{
lcdData = 0x2A;
lcdOut();
code = 0x2A;
}
while (PORTCbits.RC7 == 1);
}
}
PORTCbits.RC0 = 0;
PORTCbits.RC1 = 1;
PORTCbits.RC2 = 0;
{
if (PORTCbits.RC4 == 1)
{
debounce ();
if (PORTCbits.RC4 == 1)
{
lcdData = 0x2A;
lcdOut();
code = 0x32;
}
while (PORTCbits.RC4 == 1);
}
if (PORTCbits.RC5 == 1)
{
debounce ();
if (PORTCbits.RC5 == 1)
{
```

```
lcdData = 0x2A;
lcdOut();
code = 0x35;
}
while (PORTCbits.RC5 == 1);
}
if (PORTCbits.RC6 == 1)
{
debounce ();
if (PORTCbits.RC6 == 1)
{
lcdData = 0x2A;
lcdOut();
code = 0x38;
}
while (PORTCbits.RC6 == 1);
}
if (PORTCbits.RC7 == 1)
{
debounce ();
if (PORTCbits.RC7 == 1)
{
lcdData = 0x2A;
lcdOut();
code = 0x30;
}
while (PORTCbits.RC7 == 1);
}
}
PORTCbits.RC0 = 0;
PORTCbits.RC1 = 0;
```

```
PORTCbits.RC2 = 1;
{
for (n = 0; n < 3; n++)
{
if (PORTCbits.RC4 == 1)
{
debounce ();
if (PORTCbits.RC4 == 1)
{
lcdData = 0x2A;
lcdOut();
code = 0x33;
}
while (PORTCbits.RC4 == 1);
}
if (PORTCbits.RC5 == 1)
{
debounce ();
if (PORTCbits.RC5 == 1)
{
lcdData = 0x2A;
lcdOut();
code = 0x36;
}
while (PORTCbits.RC5 == 1);
}
if (PORTCbits.RC6 == 1)
{
debounce ();
if (PORTCbits.RC6 == 1)
{
```

```
lcdData = 0x2A;
lcdOut();
code = 0x39;
}
while (PORTCbits.RC6 == 1);
}
if (PORTCbits.RC7 == 1)
{
debounce ();
if (PORTCbits.RC7 == 1)
{
lcdData = 0x2A;
lcdOut();
code = 0x23;
}
while (PORTCbits.RC7 == 1);
}
}
}
}
void main ()
{
PORTA = 0;
PORTB = 0;
PORTC = 0;
PORTD = 0;
TRISA = 0b00010000;
TRISB = 0x00;
TRISC = 0b11110000;
TRISD = 0x00;
ADCON0 = 0x00;
```

```
ADCON1 = 0x0F;
OSCCON = 0b01110000;
OSCTUNE = 0b10000000;
T0CON = 0b11000111;
setUpTheLCD ();
clearTheScreen ();
writeString ("Set your code");
line2 ();
code = 0x25;
while (code == 0x25) setCode ();
code0=code;
code = 0x25;
while (code == 0x25) setCode ();
code1=code;
code = 0x25;
while (code == 0x25) setCode ();
code2=code;
code = 0x25;
while (code == 0x25) setCode ();
code3=code;
clearTheScreen ();
enter: writeString ("Input Code");
line2 ();
delay(10);
code = 0X25;
while (code == 0X25) getCode ();
codea = code;
code = 0x25;
while (code == 0X25) getCode ();
codeb = code;
code = 0x25;
```

```
while (code == 0X25) getCode ();
codec = code;
code = 0x25;
while (code == 0X25) getCode ();
coded = code;
delay (30);
clearTheScreen();
if ((code0 == codea)&(code1 == codeb)&(code2 == codec)&
(code3 == coded))
{
writeString ("Code OK Enter");
attempts = 0;
motor = 1;
buzzer = 1;
delay(120);
motor = 0;
buzzer = 0;
clearTheScreen ();
goto enter;
}
else
{
if (attempts < 2)
{
clearTheScreen ();
writeString ("Incorrect Code");
line2();
writeString ("Try again");
count = 0;
delay (30);
clearTheScreen ();
```

```
406.  attempts++;
407.  goto enter;
408.  }
409.  clearTheScreen ();
410.  writeString("Locked Out");
411.  attempts = 0;
412.  motor = 0;
413.  delay(240);
414.  clearTheScreen ();
415.  goto enter;
416.  }
417.  }
```

Analysis of Listing 7-1

The program is split into two parts. The first part allows the user to set the four-digit code for the door lock. The second part allows the user to input the code to gain entry. The program will then check the four-digit code the user entered against the stored entry code set earlier. If the two codes are the same, the program will drive a solenoid connected to one of the PIC's outputs to open the door. It will also sound off a buzzer, connected to another output on the PIC, as an audio signal to come in. Then, after a short period of time, the two outputs will turn off.

If the code entered by the user is incorrect, the user will have two further attempts before being locked out. An LCD screen will be used to display appropriate messages to the user.

The program uses the "setCode" subroutine between lines 28 and 180, to allow the user to set the entry code. It then uses the "getCode" subroutine, between lines 181 and 333, to scan the keypad waiting for a key to be pressed to gain entry. The operation of the keypad has been described previously. The three columns are connected to plus 5V via the three outputs of the PIC (see Figure 7-9). In this program, those three outputs are connected to RC0, RC1, and RC2.

Each of the three columns have four keypads which when pressed connect the 5V from the particular column to the input that is connected to the row that the key sits on; that is, row 0 is connected to one input of the PIC, which in the program is RC4; row 1 is connected to RC5; row 2 is connected to RC6; and row 3 is connected to RC7.

The principle of operation is that if RC0 outputs the 5V, while RC1 and RC2 are at 0V, and if RC4 input goes to a logic '1', then the number '1' on the keypad must have been pressed.

Similarly, if RC0 outputs the 0V, while RC1 is at 5V and RC2 is at 0V, and RC6 input goes to a logic '1', then the number 8 on the keypad must have been pressed.

Switch Bounce

One problem with any type of switch is the fact the switch will physically bounce. This is due to Newton's First Law: every action has an equal and opposite reaction. This means that when we force the switch to close, there is an equal force set up within the switch that will try to open it. To us humans, this switch bounce does not cause us any problems, as the bouncing action stops well before we can detect it. However, microcontrollers operate a lot faster than we do, and this switch bounce becomes a real problem. To help appreciate the problem, we can look at Figure 7-10.

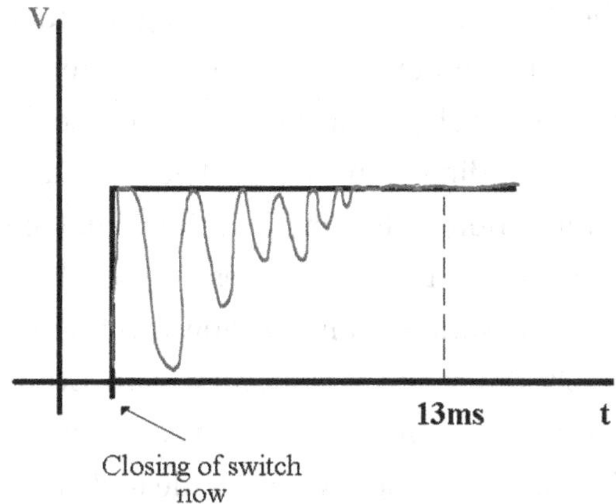

Figure 7-10. *The bouncing voltage from a switch at any input*

The black line is the ideal voltage response when the switch closes. The red line is only to give the impression of what the voltage, across the switch, does when you close the switch; it swings low and then high for some time. The logic levels, upon which a micro responds, have the following voltage ranges:

- Logic '0' is 0V to 0.8V at the input.
- Logic '1' is 2V to 5V at the input.
- Logic '0' is 0V to 0.4V at the output.
- Logic '1' is 2.7V to 5V at the output.

The micro would actually think that the logic at the input had gone to a logic '1' many times during this bounce time. However, the programmer expects the logic to go to logic '1' once only, as he only presses the button once.

There are a few practical ways engineers can try to overcome this problem. However, we as programmers will add some program instructions to overcome this issue.

The principle behind this approach is to recognize that someone has pressed the switch, as the input will go to a logic '1'. The PIC will then wait a small amount of time and check the input again to see if it has really gone to a logic '1' before responding to the action. The small amount of time is to allow this bouncing action to die down, as shown in Figure 7-10, and so ensure the PIC doesn't see the many times the logic bounces between logic '0' and logic '1'. A reasonable time to allow this bouncing action to die down is approximately 13ms. This is what we will do. Every time the input from the switch goes high, we will wait around 13ms and then check to see if the input is really at a logic '1' before we decide to do anything about it. In this way, the program sees that the input goes high only once, instead of thinking it has gone high three or four times, as shown in Figure 7-10.

We should also appreciate that the same type of switch bounce occurs when the input is switched from high to low. This means we should apply the debounce subroutine in those instances as well.

The debounce subroutine is written between lines 15 and 19 (see Listing 7-1). This subroutine can also be used to overcome noise on an input. Noise on an input, or switch, is where an input picks up a voltage spike that makes the micro think the input has gone to a logic '1'. However, in reality the input has not gone high.

The subroutine uses the normal delay approach, but this time it is limited to one wait of 100 clock cycles for TMR0. This creates approximately a 13ms delay.

There are no real new instructions to analyze with this program, but I will discuss some of the more interesting ones here.

Line 353 code = 0x25;

This loads the variable code with the value 0x25. This is the ASCII for the character '%'. This character is not one that is on the keypad, which means the variable code cannot be loaded with this value from the keypad.

Line 354 while (code == 0x25) setCode ();

This instruction is why we loaded the variable code with 0x25 in the previous instruction. The idea is to keep the PIC in the subroutine setCode until the user has entered a character they want to use, in this case, as the first digit in the code. The test in the instruction will only become untrue when the user has pressed a key on the keypad. When the user presses a key, the test is untrue, as the variable code will have been loaded with the ASCII for the key that had been pressed. This means that the PIC will not carry out the instruction on this line and so it will not call the subroutine to set the code. The PIC will go on to the next instruction.

Line 355 code0 = code;

This will load the variable code0 with the data that has been loaded into the variable code from within the subroutine setCode, when the user pressed a key. This will be stored as the first digit (i.e., digit 0) of the four-digit entry code.

This action is repeated a further three times in lines 356 to 365 to get the remaining three digits of the set entry code (i.e., code1, code2, and code3).

The same approach is used in lines 369 to 380 to allow the user to try entering an entry code to come in. These codes will be stored in the variables codea, codeb, codec, and coded.

Line 383 if ((code0 == codea)&(code1 == codeb)&(code2 == codec)&(code3 == coded))

This creates an if test is true, do what I say type test that tests four separate actions. The test is testing to see if the four digits entered in to gain entry are the same (i.e., equal to the set code entered in with the setCode subroutine). If all four are the same, then the PIC will carry out the instructions between lines 384 and 394.

Line 386 attempts = 0;

This is just to make sure that the variable "attempts" is loaded with the value 0. This is to ensure that the next user has three attempts to get the entry code correct.

Line 395 else

This is creating the list of instructions that the PIC will carry out if the test on line 383 is untrue. Note that if the test is true, then the PIC will not get to this instruction on line 395 because the PIC will have carried out the instruction on line 393, which forces the PIC to the label "enter" that is on line 366.

The instructions that the PIC will carry out with this else instruction are written between lines 396 and 416. Note that this is why there is no semicolon after the else at the end of line 395. The instruction does not end until line 416. However, the compiler does not need a semicolon at the end of line 416.

Line 397 if (attempts < 2)

This test is to see if the value in the variable attempts is less than 2. If the test is true, as it should be if this is the first try by the user to enter the correct code, the PIC will carry out the instructions between lines 398 and 408. This is how we allow the user only three attempts, 0, 1, and 2, to enter the correct code.

Lines 409 to 415 are what the PIC does if the user has had three failed attempts to enter the correct code.

Line 415 goto enter;

This forces the PIC to go back to line 366, where the label "enter" is. This makes the program go through the cycle of allowing the user to enter in the correct entry code. Note that line 393 does the same operation.

I hope there is no need for any further analysis, as the instructions have been looked at in previous programs. I think this is a very useful program, and I hope you guys might try and use it to restrict entry into your bedrooms.

Figure 7-11 does show the program working with my homemade prototype board. Note that I have made a cable to connect to the nine-pin D-type connector on the keypad.

Figure 7-11. *The traditional keypad program*

The Membrane 4 × 4 Keypad

This keypad works in a similar fashion to the 3-by-4 keypad we have just looked at, except there is one major difference. It is that when you press any key on the membrane, you are actually sending the input to the PIC low. This is termed "active low". The concept of how this keyboard works has been examined using Figure 7-8. With the membrane keypad using active low inputs, I have decided to use the internal pull up resistors within the PIC. That is why I have connected the membrane keypad to PORTB. However, that means that I will have to connect the LCD to another PORT. I have connected it to PORTD. This also means I cannot use the header file for the LCD, as with that header file the LCD is connected to PORTB (see Listing 7-2).

Listing 7-2. Membrane 4 × 4 Keypad

```
/*
* File:   keypadCodedProg.c
Author: H H Ward
This uses the membrane 4by4 keypad that is active low
Created on 23 December 2020, 13:09
*/
#include <xc.h>
#include <conFigInternalOscNoWDTNoLVP.h>
//some definitions
#define firstbyte      0b00110011
#define secondbyte     0b00110011
#define fourBitOp     0b00110010
#define twoLines       0b00101100
#define incPosition    0b00000110
#define cursorNoBlink  0b00001100
#define clearScreen     0b00000001
#define returnHome      0b00000010
#define lineTwo         0b11000000
#define doBlink         0b00001111
#define shiftLeft       0b00010000
#define shiftRight      0b00010100
#define shdisright      0b00011100
#define lcdPort         PORTD
#define eBit            PORTDbits.RD5
#define RSpin           PORTDbits.RD4
//some variables
unsigned char n, lcdData, lcdTempData, rsLine, dataIn;
char str[80];
char lcdInitialise [8] =
```

```
{
firstbyte,
secondbyte,
fourBitOp,
twoLines,
incPosition,
cursorNoBlink,
clearScreen,
returnHome,
};
//some subroutines
void sendData ()
{
lcdTempData = (lcdTempData << 4 | lcdTempData >>4);
lcdData = lcdTempData & 0x0F;
lcdData = lcdData | rsLine;
lcdPort = lcdData;
eBit = 1;
eBit = 0;
TMR0 = 0; while (TMR0 < 20);
}
void lcdOut ()
{
lcdTempData = lcdData;
sendData ();
sendData ();
}
void setUpTheLCD ()
{
TMR0 = 0; while (TMR0 <255);
n = 0;
```

```
rsLine = 0X00;
while (n < 8)
{
lcdData = lcdInitialise [n];
lcdOut ();
n ++;
}
rsLine = 0x10;
}
void line2 ()
{
rsLine = 0X00;
lcdData = lineTwo;
lcdOut ();
rsLine = 0x10;
}
void clearTheScreen ()
{
rsLine = 0X00;
lcdData = clearScreen;
lcdOut ();
rsLine = 0x10;
}
void sendcursorhome ()
{
rsLine = 0X00;
lcdData = returnHome;
lcdOut ();
rsLine = 0x10;
}
```

```
void shiftcurleft ( unsigned char l)
{
for (n = 0; n < l; n ++)
{
rsLine = 0X00;
lcdData = shiftLeft;
lcdOut ();
rsLine = 0x10;
}
}
void shiftcurright (unsigned char r)
{
for (n = 0; n < r; n ++)
{
rsLine = 0X00;
lcdData = shdisright;
lcdOut ();
rsLine = 0x10;
}
}
void writeString (const char *words)
{
while (*words)
{
lcdData = *words;
lcdOut ();
*words ++;
}
}
unsigned char lcdData, lcdTempData, rsLine, datain,
dataout, olddatain = 0, newdatain = 0;
```

```
unsigned char n, count, code, code0, code1, code2,
code3, codea, codeb, codec, coded, attempts=0;
//#define motor PORTDbits.RD0
//#define buzzer PORTDbits.RD1
#define row4    PORTBbits.RB4
#define row3    PORTBbits.RB5
#define row2    PORTBbits.RB6
#define row1    PORTBbits.RB7
#define col4    PORTBbits.RB0
#define col3    PORTBbits.RB1
#define col2    PORTBbits.RB2
#define col1    PORTBbits.RB3
#define motor   PORTCbits.RC0
#define buzzer  PORTCbits.RC1
void debounce ()
{
TMR0 = 0;
while (TMR0 < 100);
}
void delay (unsigned char t)
{
for (n = 0; n < t; n ++)
{
TMR0 = 0;
while (TMR0 < 255);
}
}
void setCode ()
{
row1 = 0;
row2 = 1;
```

```
row3 = 1;
row4 = 1;
{
if (col1 == 0)
{
debounce ();
if (col1 == 0)
{
lcdData = 0x31;
lcdOut();
code = 0x31;
}
while (col1 == 0);
}
if (col2 == 0)
{
debounce ();
if (col2 == 0)
{
lcdData = 0x32;
lcdOut();
code = 0X32;
}
while (col2 == 0);
}
if (col3 == 0)
{
debounce ();
if (col3 == 0)
{
lcdData = 0x33;
```

```
lcdOut();
code = 0x33;
}
while (col3 == 0);
}
if (col4 == 0)
{
debounce ();
if (col4 == 0)
{
lcdData = 0x41;
lcdOut();
code = 0x41;
}
while (col4 == 0);
}
}
row1 = 1;
row2 = 0;
row3 = 1;
row4 = 1;
{
if (col1 == 0)
{
debounce ();
if (col1 == 0)
{
lcdData = 0x34;
lcdOut();
code = 0x34;
}
```

```
while (col1 == 0);
}
if (col2 == 0)
{
debounce ();
if (col2 == 0)
{
lcdData = 0x35;
lcdOut();
code = 0X35;
}
while (col2 == 0);
}
if (col3 == 0)
{
debounce ();
if (col3 == 0)
{
lcdData = 0x36;
lcdOut();
code = 0x36;
}
while (col3 == 0);
}
if (col4 == 0)
{
debounce ();
if (col4 == 0)
{
lcdData = 0x42;
lcdOut();
```

```
code = 0x42;
}
while (col4 == 0);
}
}
row1 = 1;
row2 = 1;
row3 = 0;
row4 = 1;
{
if (col1 == 0)
{
debounce ();
if (col1 == 0)
{
lcdData = 0x37;
lcdOut();
code = 0x37;
}
while (col1 == 0);
}
if (col2 == 0)
{
debounce ();
if (col2 == 0)
{
lcdData = 0x38;
lcdOut();
code = 0X38;
}
while (col2 == 0);
```

```
}
if (col3 == 0)
{
debounce ();
if (col3 == 0)
{
lcdData = 0x39;
lcdOut();
code = 0x39;
}
while (col3 == 0);
}
if (col4 == 0)
{
debounce ();
if (col4 == 0)
{
lcdData = 0x43;
lcdOut();
code = 0x43;
}
while (col4 == 0);
}
row1 = 1;
row2 = 1;
row3 = 1;
row4 = 0;
{
if (col1 == 0)
{
debounce ();
```

```
if (col1 == 0)
{
lcdData = 0x2A;
lcdOut();
code = 0x2A;
}
while (col1 == 0);
}
if (col2 == 0)
{
debounce ();
if (col2 == 0)
{
lcdData = 0x30;
lcdOut();
code = 0X30;
}
while (col2 == 0);
}
if (col3 == 0)
{
debounce ();
if (col3 == 0)
{
lcdData = 0x23;
lcdOut();
code = 0x23;
}
while (col3 == 0);
}
if (col4 == 0)
```

```
{
debounce ();
if (col4 == 0)
{
lcdData = 0x44;
lcdOut();
code = 0x44;
}
while (col4 == 0);
}
}
}
}
void getCode ()
{
row1 = 0;
row2 = 1;
row3 = 1;
row4 = 1;
{
if (col1 == 0)
{
debounce ();
if (col1 == 0)
{
lcdData = 0x2A;
lcdOut();
code = 0x31;
}
while (col1 == 0);
}
```

```
if (col2 == 0)
{
debounce ();
if (col2 == 0)
{
lcdData = 0x2A;
lcdOut();
code = 0X32;
}
while (col2 == 0);
}
if (col3 == 0)
{
debounce ();
if (col3 == 0)
{
lcdData = 0x2A;
lcdOut();
code = 0x33;
}
while (col3 == 0);
}
if (col4 == 0)
{
debounce ();
if (col4 == 0)
{
lcdData = 0x2A;
lcdOut();
code = 0x41;
}
```

```
while (col4 == 0);
}
}
row1 = 1;
row2 = 0;
row3 = 1;
row4 = 1;
{
if (col1 == 0)
{
debounce ();
if (col1 == 0)
{
lcdData = 0x2A;
lcdOut();
code = 0x34;
}
while (col1 == 0);
}
if (col2 == 0)
{
debounce ();
if (col2 == 0)
{
lcdData = 0x2A;
lcdOut();
code = 0X35;
}
while (col2 == 0);
}
```

```
if (col3 == 0)
{
debounce ();
if (col3 == 0)
{
lcdData = 0x2A;
lcdOut();
code = 0x36;
}
while (col3 == 0);
}
if (col4 == 0)
{
debounce ();
if (col4 == 0)
{
lcdData = 0x2A;
lcdOut();
code = 0x42;
}
while (col4 == 0);
}
}
row1 = 1;
row2 = 1;
row3 = 0;
row4 = 1;
{
if (col1 == 0)
{
debounce ();
```

```
if (col1 == 0)
{
lcdData = 0x2A;
lcdOut();
code = 0x37;
}
while (col1 == 0);
}
if (col2 == 0)
{
debounce ();
if (col2 == 0)
{
lcdData = 0x2A;
lcdOut();
code = 0X38;
}
while (col2 == 0);
}
if (col3 == 0)
{
debounce ();
if (col3 == 0)
{
lcdData = 0x2A;
lcdOut();
code = 0x39;
}
while (col3 == 0);
}
```

```
if (col4 == 0)
{
debounce ();
if (col4 == 0)
{
lcdData = 0x2A;
lcdOut();
code = 0x43;
}
while (col4 == 0);
}
}
row1 = 1;
row2 = 1;
row3 = 1;
row4 = 0;
{
if (col1 == 0)
{
debounce ();
if (col1 == 0)
{
lcdData = 0x2A;
lcdOut();
code = 0x2A;
}
while (col1 == 0);
}
if (col2 == 0)
{
debounce ();
```

```
if (col2 == 0)
{
lcdData = 0x2A;
lcdOut();
code = 0X30;
}
while (col2 == 0);
}
if (col3 == 0)
{
debounce ();
if (col3 == 0)
{
lcdData = 0x2A;
lcdOut();
code = 0x23;
}
while (col3 == 0);
}
if (col4 == 0)
{
debounce ();
if (col4 == 0)
{
lcdData = 0x2A;
lcdOut();
code = 0x44;
}
while (col4 == 0);
}
}
}
```

```
void main ()
{
PORTA = 0;
PORTB = 0;
PORTC = 0;
PORTD = 0;
TRISA = 0b00010000;
TRISB = 0b00001111;
TRISC = 0b00001111;
TRISD = 0x00;
ADCON0 = 0x00;
ADCON1 = 0x0F;
OSCCON = 0b01110000;
OSCTUNE = 0b10000000;
INTCON2 = 0b00000000;
T0CON = 0b11000111;
setUpTheLCD ();
clearTheScreen ();
writeString ("Coded Automation");
line2 ();
code = 0x25;
while (code == 0x25) setCode ();
code0=code;
code = 0x25;
while (code == 0x25) setCode ();
code1=code;
code = 0x25;
while (code == 0x25) setCode ();
code2=code;
code = 0x25;
while (code == 0x25) setCode ();
```

```
code3=code;
clearTheScreen ();
enter: writeString ("Input Code");
line2 ();
delay(10);
code = 0X25;
while (code == 0X25) getCode ();
codea = code;
code = 0x25;
while (code == 0X25) getCode ();
codeb = code;
code = 0x25;
while (code == 0X25) getCode ();
codec = code;
code = 0x25;
while (code == 0X25) getCode ();
coded = code;
delay (30);
clearTheScreen();
if ((code0 == codea)&(code1 == codeb)&(code2 == codec)&(code3 == coded))
{
writeString ("Code OK Enter");
attempts = 0;
motor = 1;
buzzer = 1;
delay(120);
motor = 0;
buzzer = 0;
clearTheScreen ();
goto enter;
}
```

```
615.	else
616.	{
617.	if (attempts < 2)
618.	{
619.	clearTheScreen ();
620.	writeString ("Incorrect Code");
621.	line2();
622.	writeString ("Try again");
623.	count = 0;
624.	delay (30);
625.	clearTheScreen ();
626.	attempts++;
627.	goto enter;
628.	}
629.	clearTheScreen ();
630.	writeString("Locked Out");
631.	attempts = 0;
632.	motor = 0;
633.	delay(240);
634.	clearTheScreen ();
635.	goto enter;
636.	}
637.	while (1);
638.	}
```

Lines 10 to 119 are the instructions for the LCD. To make the inputs and outputs more readable, I have defined the outputs as rows and the inputs as columns (see lines 124 to 131). The only real difference is that to switch three rows off and one row on, we set the one row to a logic ‘0’ and the other rows to logic ‘1’ (see lines 149 to 152). Also, the inputs are looking for them to change to a logic ‘0’ instead of a logic ‘1’. This is because this keypad has been set up as active low.

Again, I hope there is no need for any further analysis and that you do find this program useful.

Figure 7-12 shows the membrane keypad program working with my homemade prototype board.

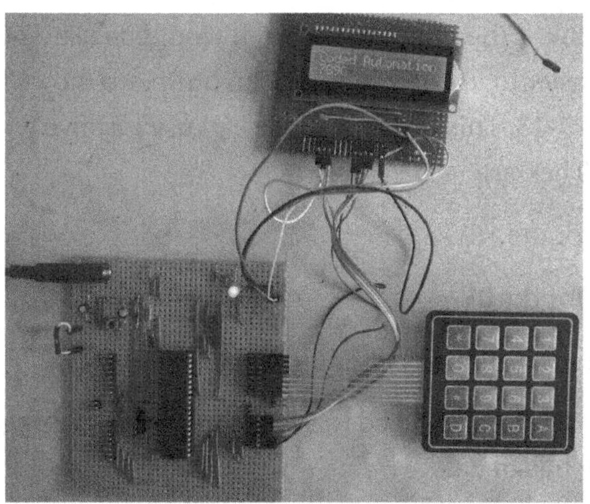

Figure 7-12. *The membrane keypad program*

The 8 × 8 Dot Matrix Board

This is the final project in this chapter. The dot matrix board is shown in Figure 7-13.

Figure 7-13. *The 8 × 8 dot matrix board*

The Max7129 driver chip, which is shown on the board, can be used to enable the matrix to be driven from just five wires from the PIC. There are also five more terminals on the other side of the board to enable the board to be cascaded with other matrix boards.

The Max7219 Driver IC

Before we look at the program listing, it would be useful to look at this IC. To make it easier to use, the IC has been built into the PCB board as shown in Figure 7-13. This does mean we can use just five wires to use the matrix display. They are

- VCC for the +5V
- GND for the 0V
- DIN for the data to be sent to the display
- CS or Load; this is used to synchronize the latching of the 16 bits of data
- Clk to synchronize the operation of the display

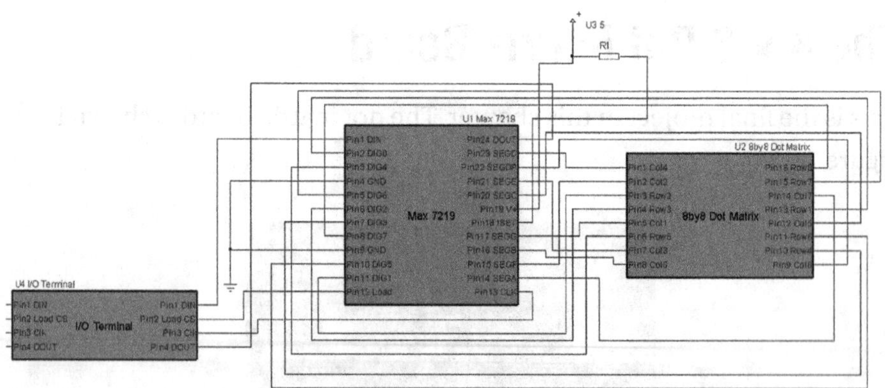

***Figure 7-14.** The basic interface circuit of the Max7219 with the dot matrix display*

We can use the PIC to control the display on the dot matrix without using the Max7219 driver. However, using the driver requires just 3 outputs from the PIC, whereas using the PIC would use up 16 outputs. The only issue with using the driver is communicating with it. This is done serially with the DIN and DOUT lines. The load and clock lines are used to synchronize when the data is latched. Communication can be achieved by using the SPI protocol or by controlling the input of the individual bits. We will use the latter method, as we will not be looking at the SPI protocol until chapter 10. Also, as we will not be cascading any displays to our display, we do not need to connect to the DOUT pin of the Max7219. That is why we use the five pins of the module shown in Figure 7-13, as they are basically all we need.

Figure 7-14 shows the basic arrangement for connecting the Max driver to the dot display. It also shows the DIN, Load/CS, and Clk inputs to the diver. These three inputs will come from the PIC, and they will be used to control the sending of data to the Max7219.

Writing to the Max7219

As we are not going to use any SPI protocol, we need to understand how the 7219 will receive information. One type of information will be control information that sets the 7219 up as we want to use it. The other type of information will be data that tells the 7219 which LEDs in the matrix we want to turn on to create our display.

All information is sent in two bytes of eight bits. Each bit is latched into the internal shift register in the 7219 when the clk signal goes high. This also means that the clock signal must be low before the bit is sent to the 7219. This clock signal can be synchronized to a clock as with the SPI module, or it can be imitated in software. We will be doing the latter.

When the second byte has been sent (i.e., when all 16 bits have arrived in the 7219), the load signal is sent high to signify this and latch the two bytes into the 7219. This then means that the load signal must be low when we start to send the 16 bits to the 7219. How we achieve this should become apparent when we analyze the program listing.

Just a few more concepts before we look at the program. The first thing the program must do is configure the Max7219 as to how we are going to use it. Inside the 7219 there are five control registers:

- The shutdown register: this puts the IC into shutdown or not shutdown.
- The mode register: this sets up how the IC decodes the data being sent to be displayed.
- The intensity register: this sets up how we control the brightness of the display.
- The scan-limit register: this sets up how the digits are scanned to be displayed.
- The display test register: this is used to put the display into normal mode or test mode.

When we are writing control information to the registers, we must first tell the 7219 which register we are writing to and then which command byte we want to write to the register.

When we are sending data as to what we want to display, it will be sent again in two bytes. These will control which LED on which column we want to turn on. Again, how we achieve this should become clearer as we analyze Listing 7-3.

Listing 7-3. Dot Matrix Display

```
/* File:   64DotMatrixBoard.c
Author: H. H. Ward
Using the 7219 matrix controller
Created on 01 February 2019, 16:36
*/
#include <xc.h>
#include <conFigInternalOscNoWDTNoLVP.h>
```

```
#define decodeModeReg     0b00001001
#define intensityReg     0b00001010
#define scanLimitReg     0b00001011
#define shutdownReg     0b00001100
#define displayTestReg     0b00001111
#define disableDecode     0b00000000
#define codeB0         0b00000001
#define codeB4         0b00001111
#define codeB8         0b11111111
#define brightMax     0b00001111
#define scanAll         0b00000111
#define normalOperation     0b00000001
#define shutdown     0b00000000
#define noTest         0b00000000
#define maxin         PORTCbits.RC0
#define maxload         PORTCbits.RC1
#define maxclk         PORTCbits.RC2
#define nzero        maxWrite (0,0x00); maxWrite(1,0x08); maxWrite(2,0x14); maxWrite(3,0x22); maxWrite(4,0x26); maxWrite(5,0x2A); maxWrite(6,0x32); maxWrite(7,0x14); maxWrite(8,0x08);
#define none         maxWrite (0,0x00); maxWrite (1,0x08); maxWrite (2,0x18); maxWrite (3,0x28); maxWrite (4,0x08); maxWrite (5,0x08); maxWrite (6,0x08); maxWrite (7,0x08); maxWrite (8,0x3E);
#define ntwo         maxWrite (0,0x00); maxWrite(1,0x1C); maxWrite(2,0x22); maxWrite(3,0x22); maxWrite(4,0x02); maxWrite(5,0x3C); maxWrite(6,0x20); maxWrite(7,0x20); maxWrite(8,0x3E);
```

```
#define nthree      maxWrite (0,0x00); maxWrite (1,0x38); maxWrite (2,0x04); maxWrite (3,0x04); maxWrite (4,0x04); maxWrite (5,0x1C); maxWrite (6,0x04); maxWrite(7,0x04); maxWrite(8,0x38);
#define nfour       maxWrite (0,0x00); maxWrite (1,0x04); maxWrite (2,0x0C); maxWrite (3,0x14); maxWrite (4,0x24); maxWrite (5,0x7C); maxWrite (6,0x04); maxWrite (7,0x04); maxWrite (8,0x3F);
unsigned char n, row, col;
unsigned const char show [62][9]=
{
{0x00,0x08,0x14,0x22,0x26,0x2A,0x32,0x14,0x08}, //0
{0x00,0x08,0x18,0x28,0x08,0x08,0x08,0x08,0x3E}, //1
{0x00,0x1C,0x22,0x22,0x02,0x3C,0x20,0x20,0x3E}, //2
{0x00,0x3C,0x04,0x04,0x04,0x1C,0x04,0x04,0x3C}, //3
{0x00,0x04,0x0C,0x14,0x24,0x7C,0x04,0x04,0x3F}, //4
{0x00,0x3C,0x20,0x20,0x3C,0x04,0x04,0x3C,0x00}, //5
{0x00,0x3C,0x20,0x20,0x3C,0x24,0x24,0x3C,0x00}, //6
{0x00,0x3E,0x02,0x02,0x04,0x08,0x10,0x20,0x00}, //7
{0x00,0x1C,0x22,0x22,0x1C,0x1C,0x22,0x22,0x1C}, //8
{0x00,0x1C,0x22,0x22,0x22,0x1E,0x02,0x02,0x1E}, //9
{0x00,0x10,0x28,0x44,0x44,0x7C,0x44,0x44,0x44}, //A
{0x00,0x70,0x48,0x48,0x70,0x48,0x44,0x44,0x78}, //B
{0x00,0x1C,0x20,0x40,0x40,0x40,0x20,0x1C,0x00}, //C
{0x00,0x70,0x48,0x44,0x44,0x44,0x48,0x70,0x00}, //D
{0x00,0x78,0x40,0x40,0x70,0x40,0x40,0x78,0x00}, //E
{0x00,0x78,0x40,0x40,0x70,0x40,0x40,0x40,0x00}, //F
{0x00,0x38,0x44,0x40,0x58,0x44,0x44,0x38,0x00}, //G
{0x00,0x44,0x44,0x44,0x7C,0x44,0x44,0x44,0x00}, //H
{0x00,0x7C,0x10,0x10,0x10,0x10,0x10,0x7C,0x00}, //I
{0x00,0x00,0x3E,0x08,0x08,0x08,0x48,0x38,0x10}, //J
```

```
{0x00,0x44,0x48,0x50,0x60,0x50,0x48,0x44,0x00}, //K
{0x00,0x70,0x20,0x20,0x20,0x20,0x22,0x3C,0x00}, //L
{0x00,0x41,0x63,0x55,0x49,0x41,0x41,0x41,0x00}, //M
{0x00,0x42,0x62,0x52,0x4A,0x46,0x42,0x42,0x00}, //N
{0x00,0x18,0x24,0x42,0x42,0x42,0x24,0x18,0x00}, //O
{0x00,0xF8,0x44,0x44,0x78,0x40,0x40,0xE0,0x00}, //P
{0x00,0x18,0x24,0x42,0x42,0x42,0x24,0x1C,0x02}, //Q
{0x00,0xF0,0x48,0x44,0x48,0x70,0x50,0x48,0xE4}, //R
{0x00,0x30,0x48,0x40,0x30,0x08,0x48,0x30,0x00}, //S
{0x00,0x7C,0x94,0x10,0x10,0x10,0x10,0x38,0x00}, //T
{0x00,0xE4,0x64,0x64,0x64,0x64,0x24,0x18,0x00}, //U
{0x00,0x41,0x41,0x22,0x22,0x14,0x14,0x08,0x00}, //V
{0x00,0x81,0x81,0x42,0x5A,0x24,0x24,0x24,0x00}, //W
{0x00,0x82,0x44,0x28,0x10,0x28,0x44,0x82,0x00}, //V
{0x00,0x82,0x44,0x28,0x10,0x20,0x40,0x80,0x00}, //Y
{0x00,0xFE,0x04,0x08,0x10,0x20,0x40,0xFE,0x00}, //Z
{0x00,0x30,0x48,0x04,0x3C,0x44,0x44,0x3E,0x00}, //a
{0x00,0x40,0x40,0x40,0x78,0x44,0x44,0x78,0x00}, //b
{0x00,0x00,0x18,0x20,0x40,0x40,0x20,0x18,0x00}, //c
{0x00,0x08,0x08,0x08,0x18,0x28,0x28,0x18,0x00}, //d
{0x00,0x30,0x48,0x48,0x30,0x40,0x48,0x30,0x00}, //e
{0x00,0x18,0x24,0x20,0x78,0x20,0x20,0x70,0x00}, //f
{0x00,0x18,0x24,0x24,0x18,0x04,0x24,0x18,0x00}, //g
{0x00,0x20,0x20,0x20,0x38,0x24,0x24,0x24,0x00}, //h
{0x00,0x20,0x00,0x20,0x20,0x20,0x20,0x70,0x00}, //i
{0x00,0x08,0x00,0x08,0x08,0x08,0x48,0x38,0x10}, //j
{0x00,0x20,0x20,0x24,0x28,0x30,0x28,0x24,0x00}, //k
{0x00,0x20,0x60,0x20,0x20,0x20,0x20,0x78,0x00}, //l
{0x00,0x00,0x00,0x00,0x66,0x5A,0x42,0x42,0x00}, //m
{0x00,0x00,0x00,0x18,0x64,0x42,0x42,0x42,0x00}, //n
{0x00,0x00,0x00,0x18,0x24,0x24,0x24,0x18,0x00}, //o
```

```
{0x00,0x00,0x00,0x38,0x24,0x38,0x20,0x20,0x20}, //p
{0x00,0x00,0x18,0x24,0x24,0x1C,0x04,0x06,0x04}, //q
{0x00,0x00,0x58,0x24,0x20,0x20,0x20,0x20,0x00}, //r
{0x00,0x00,0x18,0x24,0x20,0x18,0x04,0x38,0x00}, //s
{0x00,0x10,0x38,0x10,0x10,0x10,0x14,0x08,0x00}, //t
{0x00,0x00,0x64,0x24,0x24,0x24,0x14,0x0A,0x00}, //u
{0x00,0x00,0x00,0xC2,0x44,0x28,0x10,0x00,0x00}, //v
{0x00,0x00,0x00,0x82,0x44,0x54,0x28,0x28,0x00}, //w
{0x00,0x00,0x00,0x44,0x28,0x10,0x28,0x44,0x00}, //x
{0x00,0x00,0x00,0x44,0x28,0x10,0x20,0x40,0x00}, //y
{0x00,0x00,0x00,0x78,0x08,0x10,0x20,0x78,0x00}  //z
};
void delay (unsigned char t)
{
for (n = 0; n < t; n ++)
{
TMR0 = 0;
while (TMR0 < 250);
}
}
void sendByte(char info)
{
for(n = 0 ; n < 8 ; n ++ )
{
maxclk = 0;
maxin = ( (info << n) & 0x80 ) ? 1 : 0; //send bits to max MSB of byte first this test to see if the bit ANDED with 0X80 is true. If it is then bit is '1' if not bit is '0'
maxclk = 1;
}
}
```

```
void maxWrite(char add,char data)
{
maxload = 0;
sendByte(add);
sendByte(data);
maxload = 1;
}
void maxSetup()
{
maxWrite(decodeModeReg,disableDecode);
maxWrite (intensityReg,brightMax);
maxWrite(scanLimitReg,scanAll);
maxWrite(shutdownReg,normalOperation);
maxWrite(displayTestReg,noTest);
}
void main ()
{
PORTA = 0;
PORTB = 0;
PORTC = 0;
PORTD = 0;
TRISA = 0b00000111;
TRISB = 0x00;
TRISC = 0b00000000;
TRISD = 0b00000010;
ADCON0 = 0b00000000;
ADCON1 = 0b00001111;
ADCON2 = 0b00111001;
OSCCON = 0b01110100;
OSCTUNE = 0b10000000;
T0CON = 0b11000111;
```

```
maxSetup ();
while (1)
{
maxWrite( 0, 0x00);
maxWrite( 1, 0x66);
maxWrite( 2, 0x66);
maxWrite( 3, 0x66);
maxWrite( 4, 0x7E);
maxWrite( 5, 0x7E);
maxWrite( 6, 0x66);
maxWrite( 7, 0x66);
maxWrite( 8, 0x66);
delay (60);
maxWrite( 0, 0x00);
maxWrite( 1, 0xC3);
maxWrite( 2, 0xC3);
maxWrite( 3, 0xC3);
maxWrite( 4, 0xDB);
maxWrite( 5, 0x5A);
maxWrite( 6, 0x7E);
maxWrite( 7, 0x66);
maxWrite( 8, 0x24);
delay (60);
nzero;
delay (60);
none;
delay (60);
ntwo;
delay (60);
nthree;
delay (60);
```

```
175. nfour;
176. delay (60);
177. for (row = 0; row < 62; row  ++)
178. {
179. for(col = 0; col < 9; col++)
180. {
181. maxWrite( col, show[row][col]);
182. }
183. delay (60);
184. }
185. }
186. }
```

Analysis of Listing 7-3

The newest part of this program is the two-dimensional array set up between lines 31 and 95.

Line 31 unsigned const char show [62] [9] =

This instruction creates the array. It is done in a similar fashion to the single array we created in chapter 4. However, the difference is that we have added a second square bracket. The two dimensions of the array align to rows and columns in the array. The first square bracket [62] sets up the number of rows in the array, and the second square bracket [9] sets up the number of columns in the array. We are again including the "=" equal sign with the instruction. That is because we are going to define what is stored in the array with this instruction. The contents of each row in the array are listed with the opening and closing curly brackets that follow. We are using the term "const" as in const char to ensure that the contents in the array cannot be changed.

Line 33 {0x00,0x08,0x14,0x22,0x26,0x2A,0x32,0x14,0x08},

This is the first line within the two curly brackets that define the contents of the whole array. This is defining what is stored in the first row of the array. The nine hexadecimal numbers are what are stored in the nine columns of the first row of the array.

Lines 34 to 94 define what is stored in the remaining rows of the two-dimensional array.

Creating the Data for Each Row in the Two-Dimensional Array

The data in these rows is what we will send to the dot matrix display to display what we want to show on it. If we draw up a map of the display, we could interpret what the data would be to display any character we want. This option is looked at in Figure 7-15.

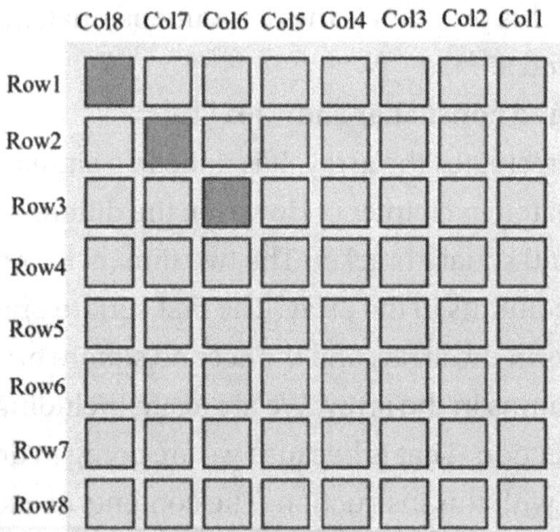

Figure 7-15. *The 8 × 8 dot matrix grid*

Top row is row 1, and each row has eight cells. We can turn each cell on by indicating a logic '1' in the cell we want to light and a logic '0' in those we don't want to light. This means to light just the last cell in row 1 as shown in Figure 7-15, the eight binary number would be 0b1000 0000 or 0X80 in hexadecimal.

The data for row 2 would be 0b0100 0000 or 0X40.

For row 3, it would be 0b0010 0000 or 0X20.

For the remaining five rows, the data would be 0b0000 0000 or 0X00. Therefore, the complete data to produce the display shown in Figure 7-15 would be as follows:

0x80, 0x40, 0x20, 0x00, 0x00, 0x00, 0x00, 0x00.

If you are not too sure about binary and hexadecimal numbers, there is a section in the appendix that explains how to convert decimal numbers to binary and binary numbers to hexadecimal.

This approach would take you some time to create a range of characters you may want to display. An alternative method would be to use a program that could convert your dot matrix pattern to the list of hexadecimal numbers you need for each row in the array that displays the characters you want. One such program that I have used is the PixeltoMatrix program. This is free to download from the Internet. I have used the program to create the binary code for the letter "H" at the beginning of the program. The Form1 is shown in Figure 7-16.

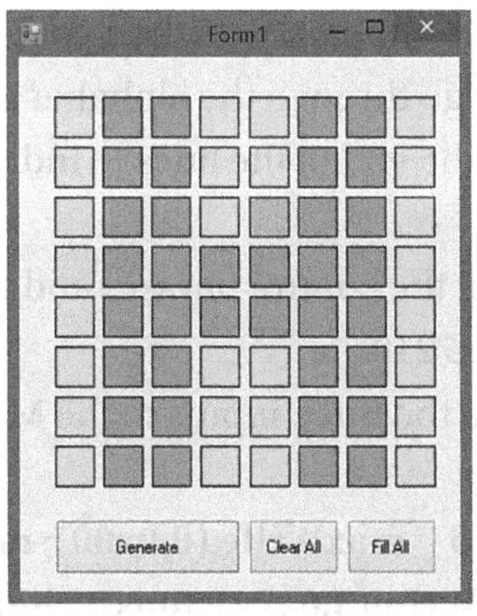

***Figure 7-16.** The Form1 drawn by me in the PixeltoMatrix program*

***Figure 7-17.** The Form2 with the eight bytes of data to display the "H"*

Figure 7-17 shows the Form2 that is created when you click the generate button on the Form1 display. This will list the eight binary and hexadecimal values to create the symbol you want, the H in this case, for you to store in the array. There is one issue I have found, and that is that you need to add an extra byte at the beginning of the list. This is the 0X00 that I have added here.

0x00, 0x66, 0x66, 0x66, 0x7E, 0x7E, 0x66, 0x66, 0x66.

I have used this PixeltoMatrix program to create a list of nine bytes for the 62 rows in the array "show". When the program accesses this array, the display will show the numbers 0 to 9, then go through the alphabet in capital letters, and finally go through the alphabet in lowercase letters. I have used comments on the end of the lines to indicate what character that row will display.

Lines 8 to 21 define all the control phrases and their binary values that are used to set up the Max7219.

Lines 22 to 24 allocate the three inputs to the Max7219 to the bits on PORTC.

Line 25 #define nzero maxWrite (0,0x00); maxWrite(1,0x08); maxWrite(2,0x14); maxWrite(3,0x22); maxWrite(4,0x26); maxWrite(5,0x2A); maxWrite(6,0x32); maxWrite(7,0x14); maxWrite(8,0x08);

This is defining what the phrase "nzero" means. When the compiler sees the phrase "nzero", it knows I mean the list of nine instructions with their bytes of data that follow. These nine instructions call the subroutine "maxWrite" and send the nine bytes needed to display a "0", with a line through the naught, on the matrix. On line 167, there is the phrase "nzero". This gets the PIC to call the subroutine 'maxWrite' and send the parameters defined on line 25 to the subroutine 'maxWrite' for the first byte of data. The PIC then calls the subroutine again for the following eight bytes of data as defined on line 25.

Lines 26 to 29 do the same for the numbers 1, 2, 3, and 4.

This is an example of using the define to link a series of instructions to a phrase that has a name linking it to the instructions (i.e., nzero means the **n**umber **zero**).

Lines 96 to 103 create our usual variable delay subroutine.

Line 104 void sendByte (char info)

This is creating a subroutine that will be used to send a byte to the DIN pin of the Max7219. I have called the output of the PIC that connects to this DIN pin "maxin". This subroutine expects the PIC to send a byte to it when it is called from the program. The subroutine will then load this byte into the local variable "info" to be used in the subroutine.

Line 106 for (n = 0; n < 8; n ++)

This sets up a normal for do loop that is carried out eight times, once for each bit in the byte that has been loaded into "info".

Line 107 maxclk = 0;

This puts a logic '0' onto the output pin RC2 on PORTC (see line 24). This is connected to the clk input of the Max7219. This means we are sending the clock to a logic '0'. This is getting the clk input ready to go back to a logic '1' to latch the first bit into the 7219.

Line 108 maxin = ((info << n) & 0x80) ? 1 : 0;

This is quite an involved instruction. It is performing an action detailed within the normal brackets and then testing if the action results in a true outcome. It then tells the PIC what logic to put onto the output pin "maxin" depending upon the outcome of the test.

The action that is listed between the outer brackets is **(info << n) & 0x80)**. What this does is perform a logic AND with the contents of the variable "infor" and the number 0X80, but after the contents in that variable have been shifted to the left. The number of bits that the contents of the variable are shifted is controlled by the value in the variable 'n.'

To help explain the operation of this instruction, we will assume that the information loaded into the variable "info" when the subroutine was called is 0x66 or 0b01100110 in binary.

If we now assume this is the first run-through of the for do loop in the subroutine, then n = 0.

This means we will not shift the data in the variable info (i.e., shift it 0 places to the left).

This then means the two bytes that will be ANDED will be

	Bit 7	Bit 6	Bit 5	Bit 4	Bit 3	Bit 2	Bit 1	Bit 0
Info after being shifted	0	1	1	0	0	1	1	0
0x80	1	0	0	0	0	0	0	0
Result	0	0	0	0	0	0	0	0

This will result in the test being untrue.

You should appreciate that we are only testing bit 7 of the variable info. Really, only when bit 7 is a logic '1' will the test be true.

So what happens now that the result is untrue? You can see that there is the following after the brackets:

? 1 : 0

The question mark relates to the test part of the instruction. The '1' is the logic that the pin maxin goes to if the test is true.

The '0' after the colon is what the pin maxin goes to if the test is untrue.

This means that the pin maxin goes to a logic '0' as the result of the test being untrue.

After the PIC has carried out this instruction once, the PIC carries out the next instruction.

Line 110 maxclk = 1;

This will set the clk pin high, which is the signal for the Max7219 to latch the data at the DIN pin to the register in the 7219. Note that at this moment in time this will be the msb, bit 15 of the 16-bit data register inside the 7219.

Now the PIC goes back to line 105, where it increments the value in n. Now n = 1, which is still less than 8, so the PIC goes to line 106, where it resets the clk line to logic '0'.

Now when we carry out the instruction on line 107, the data in infor is shifted one place to the left. This means that the logical AND operation is as follows;

	Bit 7	Bit 6	Bit 5	Bit 4	Bit 3	Bit 2	Bit 1	Bit 0
Info after being shifted	1	1	0	0	1	1	0	0
0x80	1	0	0	0	0	0	0	0
Result	1	0	0	0	0	0	0	0

The AND operation produces a true result, and so the pin maxin is sent to a logic '1'. This means that the logic on DIN on the 7219 is sent to a logic '1'.

Now when the PIC sends the clk high, as with line 109, the 7219 latches the logic '1' but now into bit 14 of the data register inside the 7219.

The cycle repeats until n = 8. The final result would be that bits 15 to 8 of the data register in the 7219 will have the same data as was loaded into the variable info. In this case it would be

0b01100110xxxxxxxx

Note that the remaining eight lower bits have not been loaded yet.

So this instruction will split a byte of data up into its eight single bits and send them one at a time to the DIN pin of the 7219. This is a very complex instruction which has required a detailed explanation of how it works. I hope you can follow the explanation without too much trouble.

Line 113 void maxWrite(char add,char data)

This sets up a subroutine that will write two byes of data to the 7219. It expects the PIC to send up two bytes of info to the subroutine. These will be loaded into the two local variables add and data.

The first variable, add, will be the address of the control register the data is to be written to if the info is for a control command. However, if the info is a character to be displayed, then the add will be the row number of the matrix, and the data will be the column number.

Line 115 maxload = 0;

This sets the logic on the maxload pin to logic '0'. This is to get the load pin of the 7219 ready to go to a logic '1' to latch the full 16 bits to the 7219 and get it to respond to them.

Line 116 sendByte (add);

This calls the subroutine sendByte to send the first byte of the two bytes required, to the 7219. This sends the information loaded into the variable add when the maxWrite subroutine was called. We have looked at how this subroutine, sendByte, splits a byte up into the single eight bits and sends them to the 7219. This will be the high byte.

Line 117 sendByte (data);

This calls the subroutine sendByte to send the second byte of the two bytes required to the 7219. This sends the information loaded into the variable data when the maxWrite subroutine was called. This uses the sendByte subroutine again, and it will be the low byte.

With these two instructions, we can send the full 16 bits of the command instruction or the data to be displayed instruction to the 7219.

Line 118 maxload = 1;

This sets the logic on the maxload pin of the 7219 to a logic '1.' This is the action needed to get the 7219 to latch the 16 bits into the register and respond to them.

Line 120 void maxSetup ()

This sets up a subroutine that is used to send the commands to set up the Max7219 as we want it.

Lines 122 to 126 send the commands for the following actions:

- set up the 7219 to disable the decode,
- set for maximum brightness,
- set to scan all inputs,
- use normal operation,
- and have no test action.

Lines 128 to 143 create the main loop and set up the PIC as normal.

Line 144 maxSetup ();

This is the first real action of the program, and it is to call the setup subroutine and set up the 7219 as per the subroutine.

Line 145 while (1)

This sets up the for every loop so that the PIC does not carry out the instructions on lines 130 to 144 again.

Lines 147 to 155 call the subroutine maxWrite and send the information to display the symbol "H" on the dot matrix.

Line 156 delay (60);

This just creates a delay of approximately 2 seconds.

Lines 157 to 166 do the same for the symbol "W."

Line 167 nzero;

This is the phrase that was defined in line 25. The PIC will now carry out the instructions listed in that line, which send the symbol 0 to the display.

Line 168 to 176 do the same for the numbers 1, 2, 3, and 4 but with a 2-second delay between them.

Line 177 for (row = 0; row < 62; row ++)

This sets up an outer loop that will be used to access the two-dimensional array "show" created between lines 31 and 95.

Line 179 for(col = 0; col < 9; col++)

This sets up the inner loop that will be used to access the columns for each of the rows in the array "show".

Line 181 maxWrite(col, show[row][col]);

This accesses the array "show" and sends the information to the subroutine maxWrite. The value of row varies from 0 to 62 and so this accesses all rows in the array. The value of col varies from 0 to 9, so that the PIC can access each of the columns in the array as the row value changes from 0 to 62.

Line 181 sends the col number to control which column in the matrix display we are writing to. Then with the show[row][col], it selects which byte from the array "show" it will display on the current column in the matrix display. The row number stays at 0 initially, while the col number increments until it reaches the value of 9 as the PIC cycles through the inner loop. This ensures that the PIC retrieves the nine bytes of data for the first character to be displayed on the matrix display. Then the PIC goes to the outer loop, where it increments the value in row to 1. The PIC then repeats the inner loop, whereby it gets the nine bytes from the array show to display the next character. The PIC then goes back to line 177 and so repeats the whole process 62 times. In this way, the PIC can cycle through all the rows in the array and so get all the nine bytes from all 62 rows of the array show.

Line 183 delay (60);

This calls a 2-second delay between displaying each character.

I hope you have been able to follow the analysis of this program, as it is quite a complex program which is covering some new and challenging concepts.

Figure 7-18 shows the program working.

Figure 7-18. *Program working*

Summary

In this chapter, we have studied how we can use two types of keyboards and use the max7219 to drive the display on an 8-by-8 dot matrix display. We have learned how to set up and use a two-dimensional array. We have also learned how we can manipulate the bits in a byte of data and send them out on an output of the PIC one bit of a time.

In the next chapter, we will learn how we can use a Bluetooth device and a simple motion sensor.

CHAPTER 8

Using Bluetooth with PIR Motion Sensors

In this chapter, we will learn about Bluetooth communication. We will study how the PIC18F4525 can use a suitable Bluetooth device to send and receive instructions from your mobile phone. We will create a project where we can control some devices in our home from our mobile phone. We will also look at using the HC-SR501 PIR motion sensor. We will program the PIC to display a message on the LCD when the sensor senses some movement.

After reading this chapter, you will know how to use the UART (Universal Asynchronous Receive and Transmit) for serial communication and how to use the PIC to communicate with a simple Bluetooth device, the HC-06. You will also see how to use a suitable terminal software terminal to program the HC-06 using AT commands and be able to make use of the PIR motion sensor.

The HC-06 Module

This is the Bluetooth device that we will be using in this project. Unlike the HC-05, the HC-06 can only act as a slave, which means it can't initiate communication. It can communicate with the master via wireless Bluetooth, which we will use to connect to our phone. We will use the

H. H. Ward, *Programming Arduino Projects with the PIC Microcontroller*,
https://doi.org/10.1007/978-1-4842-7230-5_8

UART module on the PIC to allow the HC-06 to pass data between the phone and the PIC. The HC-06 can transmit and receive commands and data up to a range of around 10m.

We will use the default settings for the HC-06. However, if we wanted to change these settings, the module uses the AT command set; note that AT simply stands for Attention, to allow us to make some changes. We will look at this later in the chapter.

Matching 5V to 3.3V

The HC-06 can be supplied with a standard 5V supply; however, the TX and RX are really suitable only for 3.3V. However, as 3.3V is still within the acceptable range of a logic '1' for TTL, then there is no problem simply connecting the TX output of the HC-06 to the RX input of the PIC. There is an issue when you pass the output of the PIC, which is from the TX pin of the PIC, to the RX of the HC-06. This is because the 5V TTL logic needs to be reduced to 3.3V. This can be done via a simple voltage divider network. This is shown in the circuit diagram set up in Figure 8-1.

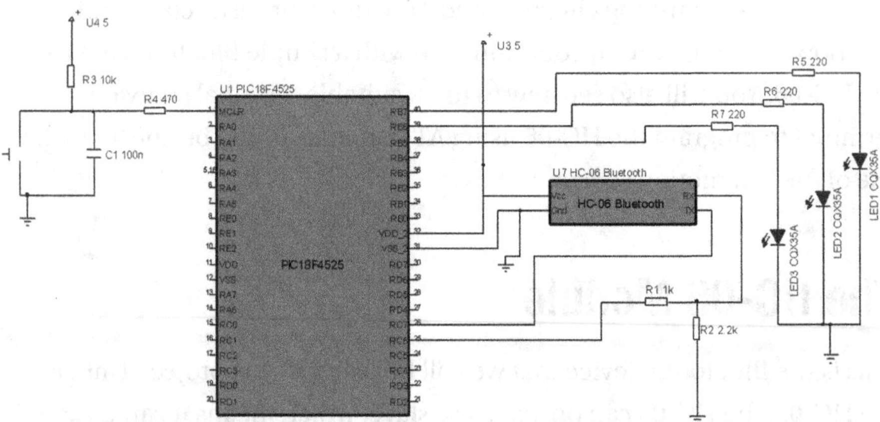

Figure 8-1. The circuit for the HC-06 Bluetooth device

The voltage divider network uses the concept that the voltage across the 2.2k resistor, R2 in the circuit diagram, can be calculated as follows:

$$V_{R2} = \frac{V_{IN} R_2}{R_1 + R_2}$$

$$\therefore V_{R2} = \frac{5 \times 2.2E^3}{1E^3 + 2.2E^3} = \frac{11E^3}{3.2E^3} = 3.438V$$

Close enough to the maximum of 3.3V at the input of the HC-06.

The HC-06 can communicate with a mobile phone wirelessly using either an app you have developed or a ready-made app. There are a variety of phone apps that you can use to test this setup. The app I have used in this project is simply called "Bluetooth Terminal".

The Default Settings of the HC-06

The HC-06 comes with the following default settings:

- Name: linvar
- Password: 1234 (or 0000)
- Type: Slave
- Baud Rate: 9600 with eight data bits, no parity, and one stop bit

There is also an on-board LED which flashes repeatedly when the module is not paired to a device. Once the module is paired, the LED stays on constantly.

The HC-05 Bluetooth Module

The other common Bluetooth module is the HC-05. You can easily identify the HC-05 and the HC-06, as the main physical difference between the two is that the HC-06 only has four terminals and it does not have a button on it. See Figure 8-2.

The HC-05 module can be used to communicate with the PIC, or any device, using the SPI, or the UART module. It also supports communication using USB.

The pins of the HC-05 module are as follows:

1. VCC. This is the positive supply, which is 5V. Note that the module has its own on-board 3.3V regulator.
2. GND. This is the ground pin.
3. TXD. This is the output from the module, which should be connected to the RX pin of the UART.
4. RX. This is the input to the module, which should be connected to the TX pin of the UART.
5. EN. This is the enable pin. When this pin is connected to VCC, the module is always enabled. If this pin is connected to GND, the module is disabled. Note that if it is left unconnected, which is termed floating, it usually floats high and so it will be enabled, but it is not really advisable to do this.
6. STATE. This is a status indicator pin. This pin goes LOW when the module is not connected to any device. When the module is paired with any device, this pin goes HIGH. There is also an on-board LED which flashes repeatedly when the module is not paired to a device.

There is a button on the module, and this is used to configure the module in AT command mode.

The HC-05 Bluetooth module can be configured in two modes of operation:

- Command mode. In this mode, AT commands can be sent to configuring various settings and parameters of the module such as the following:
    - firmware information
    - change UART baud rate
    - change module name
    - set it as either master or slave (etc.)
    - An important point about HC-05 module is that it can be configured as master or slave in a communication pair. In order to select either of the modes, you need to activate the command mode and send appropriate AT commands.
- Data mode. In this mode, the module is used for communicating with other Bluetooth devices (i.e., data transfer happens in this mode).

The HC-05 comes with the following default settings;

- Name: HC-05
- Password: 1234 (or 0000)
- Type: Slave
- Mode: Data
- Baud Rate: 9600 with eight data bits, no parity, and one stop bit

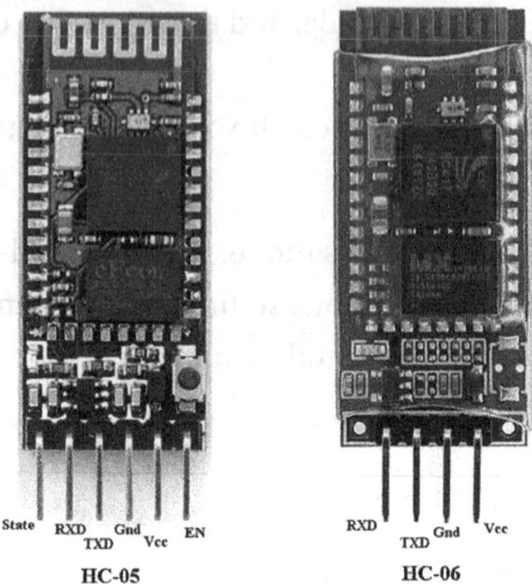

Figure 8-2. *The HC-05 and HC-06 Bluetooth modules*

Connecting the PIC to a Mobile Phone via the HC-06

The first program that we will look at will use the HC-06 module to allow our PIC to communicate with a mobile phone. The idea behind the project is that we have three sets of lights wired up externally to the house. We have a PIC set up outside the house that will take commands from our mobile phone, via the HC-06, to control the three sets of lights (Listing 8-1). The circuit diagram for this program is shown in Figure 8-1.

Listing 8-1. HC-06 Program

```
/*
* File:   blueToothControlProg.c
Author: H. H. Ward
Written for the PIC18f4525
Created on 12 May 2021, 13:38
*/
//some includes
```

```
#include <xc.h>
#include <conFigInternalOscNoWDTNoLVP.h>
//some definitions
#define DecLights       PORTDbits.RD7
#define IceLights       PORTDbits.RD6
#define FloLights       PORTDbits.RD5
//some variables
unsigned char n, deviceValue;
//some subroutines
void delay (unsigned char t)
{
for (n = 0; n < t; n ++)
{
TMR0 = 0;
while (TMR0 < 255);
}
}
void sendDeviceChar(char byte)
{
TXREG = byte;
while(!TXIF);
while(!TRMT);
}
void sendDeviceString(const char* string)
{
while(*string)
sendDeviceChar(*string++);
}
void broadcastDevice()
{
TXREG = 13;
```

```
delay (30);
}
char receiveDeviceChar()
{
while (!RCIF);
if(OERR)
{
CREN = 0;
CREN = 1;
}
if(RCIF==1) return RCREG;
else return 0;
}
void main(void)
{
PORTA = 0;
PORTB = 0;
PORTC = 0;
PORTD = 0;
TRISA = 0X01;
TRISB = 0x00;
TRISC = 0b10000000;
TRISD = 0x00;
ADCON0 = 0x00;
ADCON1 = 0x0F;
OSCTUNE = 0b10000000;
OSCCON = 0b01110000;
T0CON = 0b11000111;
TXSTA = 0b00100000;
RCSTA = 0b10010000;
BAUDCON = 0b00000000;
```

```
SPBRG  =12;
sendDeviceString("Ready to go");
sendDeviceChar (0x0A);
sendDeviceString("Waiting for your instruction");
sendDeviceChar (0x0A);
sendDeviceString("Press 0 to turn Off Declights");
sendDeviceChar(0x0A);
sendDeviceString("Press 1 to turn ON Declight");
sendDeviceChar (0x0A);
sendDeviceString("Press 2 to turn Off Ice lights");
sendDeviceChar(0x0A);
sendDeviceString("Press 3 to turn On Ice lights");
sendDeviceChar(0x0A);
sendDeviceString("Press 4 to turn Off Floral lights");
sendDeviceChar(0x0A);
sendDeviceString("Press 5 to turn On Floral lights");
sendDeviceChar(0x0A);
while(1)
{
deviceValue = receiveDeviceChar();
if ( deviceValue == '0')
{
DecLights = 0;
sendDeviceString("DecLights Off");
sendDeviceChar (0x0A);
}
if (deviceValue == '1')
{
DecLights = 1;
sendDeviceString("DecLights On");
sendDeviceChar(0x0A);
```

```
}
if (deviceValue == '2')
{
IceLights = 0;
sendDeviceString("Ice Lights Off");
sendDeviceChar(0x0A);
}
if (deviceValue == '3')
{
IceLights = 1;
sendDeviceString("Ice Lights On");
sendDeviceChar(0x0A);
}
if (deviceValue == '4')
{
FloLights = 0;
sendDeviceString("Floral Off");
sendDeviceChar(0x0A);
}
if (deviceValue == '5')
{
FloLights = 1;
sendDeviceString("Floral On");
sendDeviceChar(0x0A);
}
}
}
```

The UART

The PIC 18f4525 has two UARTs; for a fuller analysis of how the UART works, read chapter 11, as that chapter explores using the UART. In this chapter, we will learn how to set the control registers to use the UART. UART stands for Universal Asyncronous Receiever and Transmiter.

Analysis of Listing 8-1

The main principle of the program is that the PIC sends the message to the mobile phone via the HC-06 requesting that the phone tells the PIC what it should do. The phone then simply sends a number between 0 to 5 back to the PIC. The PIC then interprets these numbers as one of six instructions that it must carry out.

Lines 1 to 9 are the standard instructions that have been looked at before.

Lines 10 to 13 define some useful phrases to represent the actual inputs at the respective switches.

Lines 14 and 15 declare some variables that we will use in the program.

Lines 17 to 24 declare the normal variable delay subroutine.

Line 25 void sendDeviceChar(unsigned char byte)

This creates a subroutine that will send a single character to the device that is connected using the UART1 of the PIC18f4525. It will expect a value to be sent up to the subroutine which is of the type "unsigned char". This means that we could be expecting a value between 0 and 255. This value would be copied into the local variable "byte".

Line 27 TXREG = byte;

This copies the data in the variable byte to the TXREG of the UART. This will start the process of sending the data to the device connected to the UART. In this case, that is the HC-06 the Bluetooth module. The term TXREG stands for the transmit register. The term TX stands for transmit. TXIF stands for transmit interrupt flag.

Line 28 while (!TXIF);

This makes the PIC wait until the interrupt flag, the TXIF, of the UART goes to a logic '1'. This will only go to a logic '1' when the TXREG becomes empty after its contents are moved into the TSR shift register of the UART.

Line 29 while (!TRMT);

This makes the PIC wait until the transmit bit, TMRT, goes to a logic '1'. This will happen when the last bit of the data has been shifted out of the TSR, the UART transmit shift register.

In this way, these two instructions make the PIC wait until the UART has successfully transmitted the data to the device connected to it.

Line 31 void sendDeviceString(unsigned char*string)

This creates a subroutine that will send a string of characters to the device connected to the UART. This subroutine expects the address of where the first character of the string will be temporarily saved in an array. This address is stored into the local pointer *string.

Line 33 while (*string)

This creates a test that is true as long as the pointer *string is not pointing to the address in the array that has the null character. The "null" character denotes the end of the string.

Line 34 sendDeviceChar (*string++);

This makes the PIC call the subroutine "sendDeviceChar". The character that the pointer *string is currently pointing to will be sent up to that subroutine. This will be the first character in the string that needs sending. The '++' at the end means that the PIC will increment the value of the pointer *string when it comes back from the subroutine. In this way, the pointer will be pointing to the next character in the string that wants to be sent.

This will continue until the pointer is pointing to the "null" character that signifies the end of the string. This null character will not be transmitted.

Line 36 void broadCastDevice ()

This creates a subroutine to send the CR (carriage return) character to the device. This may be required by some Bluetooth devices to force them to send a character to the master.

Line 38 TXREG = 13;

This is the ASCII value in decimal for the CR character. The value 13 is 13 in decimal. Note that decimal is the default radix for MPLABX, and we are not changing the radix by adding "0X" for hexadecimal or "0b" for binary.

Line 39 delay (30);

This calls the delay subroutine and sends the value 30 to be copied into the local variable 't'. This creates an approximately 1-second delay. This is to allow the device to settle down after receiving the CR character.

Line 41 char receiveDeviceChar()

This creates a subroutine to receive a character from the device connected to the UART. In this case, that device will be the HC-06, which has received the byte that is to be passed onto the PIC from the mobile phone.

This expects to send a variable of type char back to the program when it completes the subroutine.

Line 43 while (!RCIF);

This simply makes the PIC wait until the UART's receive interrupt flag (RCIF) goes high. This will happen when its RXREG is filled with data. Note that the program is not using interrupts, so we are using this interrupt flag just as signal that the UART has received data from the HC-06.

Line 44 if (OERR)

This test is to see if the OERR bit of the UART has been set to a logic '1'. This will happen if an overrun error has happened. The instructions on lines 45 to 48 are what the PIC should do if the OERR bit is set.

Line 46 CREN = 0;

This disables the UART reception. This will clear the OERR bit.

Line 47 CREN = 1;

This re-enables the UART reception.

Line 49 if (RCIF == 1) return RCREG;

The term RCIF stands for the Receieve Interrupt Flag and RCREG is the Receieve register in the PIC.

This tests to see if the RCIF flag bit has gone to a logic '1'. This happens when the RCREG becomes filled with data from the device connected to the UART.

If the flag has been set, then the PIC will carry out the return RCREG part of this instruction. This will make the PIC break away from the subroutine and send the data that is in the RCREG back to the main program. You should note that when we set up this subroutine, we use the keyword "char" instead of the normal "void". This is because we know we want to send a byte of data back to the main program. Note also that when we call this subroutine, we will insert the variable that we want to load this byte into in the beginning of the call instruction. The instruction on line 89 is an example of this.

Line 50 else return 0;

This is what the PIC should do if the preceding test was untrue. It simply ends the subroutine and sends the value 0 back to where it was called from.

Line 52 creates the main loop and lines 54 to 66 set up the SFRs of the PIC as normal.

Line 67 TXSTA = 0b00100000;

We will use the UART to communicate with the HC-06. This means we must set the UART up for use. This instruction enables the transmit function of the UART by setting bit 5 to a logic '1'.

Line 68 RCSTA = 0b10010000;

This sets bit 7 to a logic '1', which enables the serial port and sets the direction of data through the RX and TX pins accordingly. It also sets bit 4 to a logic '1', which enables the UART to receive data from the external device.

Line 69 BAUDCON = 0b00000000;

This sets all the bits in this SFR to logic '0.' More importantly, it sets the BRG16 bit to logic '0,' which sets up the BRG (baud rate generator) to work in eight-bit mode. This means the SPRGH, the high byte of the baud rate register pair, is ignored. This will be explained more in chapter 11.

Line 70 SPBRG = 12;

This loads the SPBRG, the low byte of the register pair that stores the number for the BRG. In line 69, we told the PIC to ignore the high byte, and so it is the value in this register, the SPBRG register, that sets the baud rate for the UART. Chapter 11 details what the baud rate is and how we set it. For now, you should know this value of 12 sets the baud rate to 9600. This is the same baud rate of the HC-06.

Line 71 sendDeviceString ("Ready to go");

This calls the subroutine to send a string of characters to the mobile phone via the HC-06; the characters are ready to go. Note that the PIC actually sends the ASCII for each of the characters in the message.

Line 72 sendDeviceChar (0X0A);

This calls the subroutine to send a single character to the mobile phone via the HC-06. The char to be sent is the ASCII character for CR and so moves the display on the mobile phone to the beginning of the next line.

Lines 73 to 86 simply send more strings of characters and CRs to the mobile phone. These are to show the user what number they need to send to the PIC, via the HC-06, to turn on and off the three sets of lights.

Lines 87 to 126 set up a forever loop so that the PIC constantly only carries out the following instructions.

Line 89 deviceValue = receiveDeviceChar ();

This calls the subroutine "receiveDeviceChar", which makes the PIC check to see if a message has been sent from the mobile phone. It will load the result, which will be sent back from the subroutine, into the variable deviceValue. We will test to see how the value in this variable is used to determine what the PIC is being told to do. In chapter 11, we will look at using an interrupt when receiving data into the UART.

Line 90 if (deviceValue == '0');

This is the first of six "if this then do that" type tests to determine what the PIC is being told to do. This is testing to see if the value in the variable deviceValue is '0'. If it is, the test will be true and the PIC must carry out the lines set out between the opening and closing curly brackets. If the value is not '0', then the PIC must move onto the next test on line 96.

Line 92 DecLights = 0;

This simply loads a logic '0' onto bit 7 of PORTD, which has been defined as the label DecLights in line 11, and turns off one of the sets of lights.

Line 93 sendDeviceString ("Declights off");

This calls the subroutine sendDeviceString and sends the phrase "Declights off" to the mobile phone via the HC-06.

Line 94 sendDeviceChar (0X0A);

This calls the subroutine to send a single character to the mobile phone via the HC-06. The char to be sent is the ASCII character for CR and so moves the display on the mobile phone to the beginning of the next line.

Lines 102 to 125 repeat the previous procedure but for the other five possible values and their respective actions.

I hope this analysis helps you to understand how this program works. Note that I have not included the lines with the opening and closing curly brackets, as I hope by now you appreciate why they are needed and how they work.

An Important Distinction

Before we end this analysis, I feel I should clarify what happens in the current program when the PIC uses the receiveDeviceChar subroutine, something it is currently doing constantly, even when no command has been sent to the PIC.

On line 50, we see that the else instruction will return with the value 0. The problem, you might say, is that in line 90 we say that if deviceValue is '0' then we should turn the declights off. So why is this not happening when no button has been pressed and the subroutine returns the value 0? Surely this subroutine will be constantly sending 0 back to be loaded into the variable deviceValue. The reason why this does not turn off the declights is because 0 is not the same as '0'. I have not just forgotten to add the ' '. In line 50, we will load the variable deviceValue with the decimal value of 0, which is 0b00000000 in binary. This is actually the ASCII for the 'null' character, not the ASCII for the value '0'. In a way, the 'null' character tells the PIC to do nothing, which means the PIC will not respond to 0b00000000 (i.e., the 'null' character). In line 90, we are actually looking for the ASCII value for number or value '0', which is 0b00110000 in eight-bit binary; see the ASCII table in the appendix. It is a very subtle difference but a very important one. I hope this explanation clears up that small concern if you had one. If you didn't, then I hope it deepens your understanding of ASCII. Also, when we look at Listing 8-2, where we use interrupts, this will not be an issue.

I hope that even though this program is simply turning lights on or off, it can easily be adapted. The lights are just outputs, and so there is no reason why you could not change the outputs to say a solenoid lock on your drive gates and a motor to drive the gates open or closed. In this way, you could use your mobile phone to open your gates or anything else, your bedroom door perhaps. This program becomes much more exciting.

Using the Mobile APP Bluetooth Terminal

There are many apps that you can use to connect your phone to your Bluetooth devices. I will use the Bluetooth terminal HC-05. I do think the app is quite self-explanatory. Therefore, I will leave any explanation of how to use the app and move on to writing commands to the HC-06.

Changing the PIN on the HC-06

As we will be using the HC-06 to allow us to control some lights and so forth in our home, we will want to add some security. This is to ensure that only we, and not some random person passing nearby, can control our HC-06 and so our devices. The simplest way to achieve this would be to change the PIN number of the HC-06 module that is attached to our PIC. The following section will show you how to connect the HC-06 to your laptop and change the PIN number using either Tera Term or PuTTY terminal software.

The method by which you connect your HC-06 to your laptop or PC depends upon whether or not it has a serial COM port. Most modern laptops don't have one, and so you will need a USB-to-serial adapter. There are a few modules you can use to connect to the USB of your laptop and communicate with the HC-06 or HC-05 Bluetooth module. This will then enable programming HC-06 via a terminal software such as Tera Term or PuTTY. I will discuss how to use a USB-to-serial module and program the HC-06 using both Tera Term and PuTTY.

The Moyina USB-to-serial converter shown in Figure 8-3 is one possible module you can use. This uses a genuine FTDI USB UART IC 'FT232RL'. It produces TX, RX, CTS, RTS, VCC, and GND, all available as TTL logic levels or 3.3V logic levels. This makes it a very useful interface that will enable the terminal software on your PC to talk to any UART device, such as that on your PIC microcontroller or the HC-06/05 module.

In this chapter, we will use it to program our HC-06 Bluetooth module. As this works on 3.3V logic, then we must set the Moyina to 3.3V logic. There is a switch on the module to give us this option, but take care, as it may not be advisable to switch it to 3.3V. One other issue you must understand is that the TX is an output from the Moyina module, and this will become an input on the RX pin of the HC-06. Also the RX on the Moyina module is an input that will come from the TX of the HC-06.

However, you cannot use the USB to serial converter set up as 3.3V VCC. You need to ensure that it is set to 5V VCC so that it can be used to supply the HC-06 with the 5V supply it needs. This means that the RX and TX, and also the RTS and CTS, will be at TTL 5V logic. This means that the TX output from the USB serial converter must be passed through the resistor divider network, to bring the 5V down to the 3.3V, before it is fed to the RX input on the HC-06. The correct connections for this approach is shown in Figure 8-3. Note that the USB to serial converter is switched to 5V VCC.

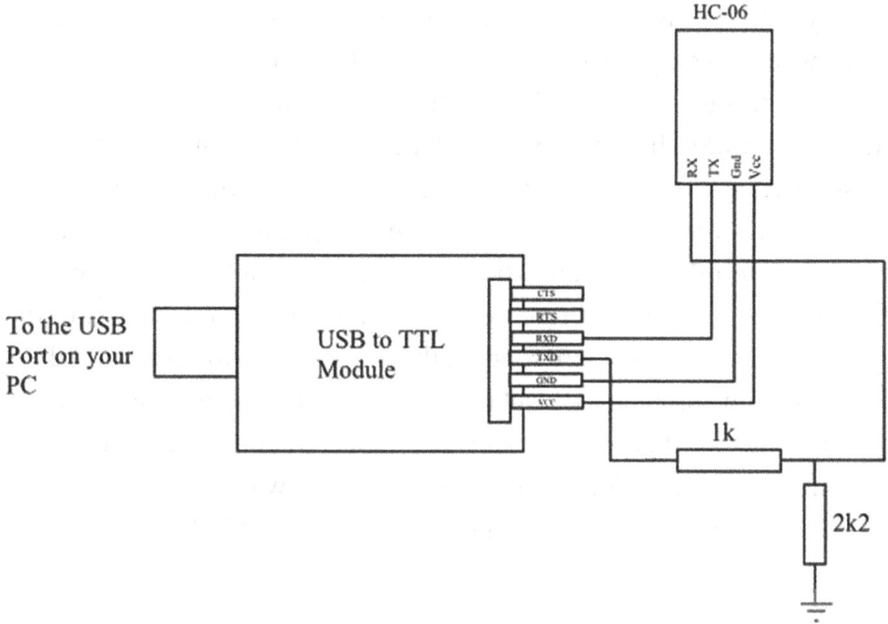

Figure 8-3. *The setup to connect the HC-06 to your laptop*

With the HC-06 connected as shown in Figure 8-3, we can use the terminal software Tera Term or PuTTY to program the HC-06 using AT commands. The following is a description of how to program the HC-06 in this way.

Using AT Commands

All commands have to be written in capital letters. The timing for commands to be entered is critical. This is set at about 1 second. This means you have to type the full command in the terminal software you are using in 1 second. Not bad if it is simply AT. However, with any other command, this is extremely difficult. One way around this is to use a terminal software which allows you to type in the full command before you send the command to the device, such as the serial monitor, as in the Arduino environment. However, we will be using either PuTTY or Tera Term as our terminal program. These programs are available as downloads from the Internet for free. These two terminal programs do not allow us to type the full command before sending them. Therefore, to get around this 1-second timing problem, we will write the command we want to send to the device in a word processing software, then copy and paste them into the terminal software. Notepad is fine for this, but I will use Word.

The AT commands that are available to us are listed in Table 8-1.

***Table 8-1.** AT Commands for the HC-06*

Command	Comments
AT	This will simply check that you are correctly connected to your device. You should get the response OK
AT+VERSION	This will simply get the following response: LinvorV1.n (n is the version number)
AT+BAUDx	With this command, you can change the baud rate for your device. You should replace the 'x' with the number from the following list that corresponds to the baud rate you want. The response you get back will be: OK(whatever baud rate you selected)
AT+NAMExxxxxxx	This allows you to change the name of the device, where you replace the xxxxx with the name you want to use. The response you get back will be: OKsetname.........
AT+PINxxxx	This allows you to change the password on the HC-06. You should replace the 'xxxx' with a four-digit number for the PIN you want. The response will be: OKsetpin
The following commands are available if the version number is greater than 5.	
AT+PO	These commands allow you to choose what type of parity checking you want. PO means Parity ODD The response you get back will be: OK ODD

(continued)

Table 8-1. (continued)

Command	Comments
AT+PE	PE means Parity Even The response you get back will be: OK EVEN
AT+PN	PN means Parity None The response you get back will be: OK NONE Note that parity is a basic method of validating data transmitted and received.

Using Tera Term to Change the PIN

The first method we will go through is to use the Tera Term software. You should have connected your HC-06 to the USB serial converter, as shown in Figure 8-3. Now connect the USB to an empty USB port on your PC or laptop. You can now start the Tera Term software, and you should see the following once you have clicked the serial option (see Figure 8-4).

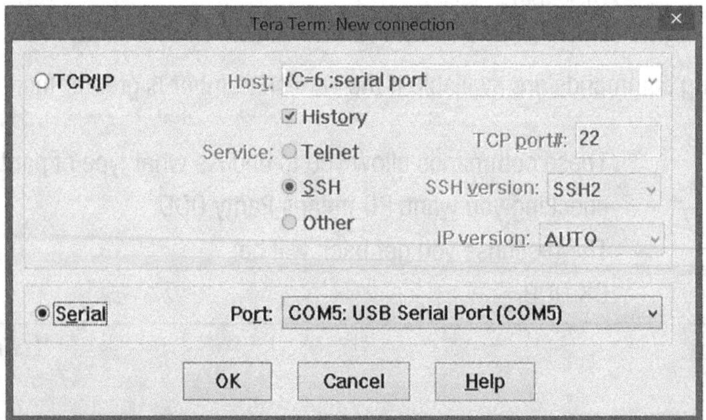

Figure 8-4. *The COM port in Tera Term*

If your version of Tera Term is different and it does not find the COM port you have connected your USB-to-serial converter to, you will need to run Windows "Device Manager" to find the COM port it is connected to. Depending upon which version of Windows you are using, you may be able to find "Device Manager" by simply clicking the right mouse button while positioning the mouse on the Windows icon in your taskbar. You should then see a pop-up window with an option to start "Device Manager". When you do run "Device Manager", you should see the following window appear (see Figure 8-5). You can then look down the options and find the option for ports (COM & LPT). This is shown in Figure 8-5.

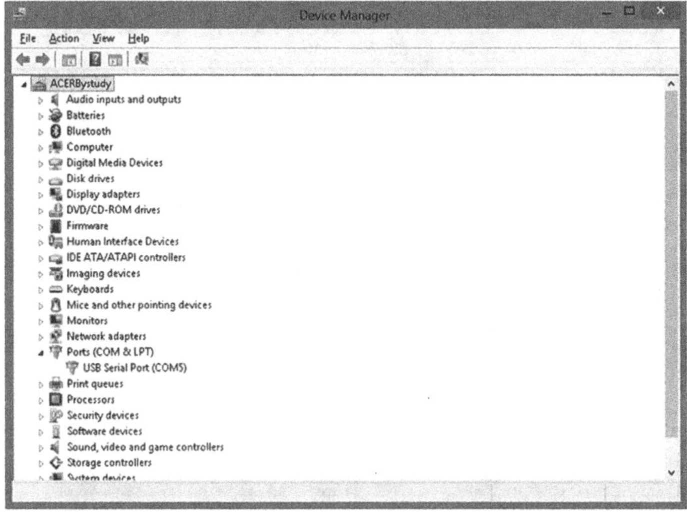

Figure 8-5. *The device manager window showing the COM port connection*

We are going to transmit the following commands to the HC-06:

AT

AT+VERSION

AT+PINXXXX

The first command is just to confirm that we have a successful connection to the HC-06. The response should be as shown in Figure 8-6 (i.e., OK). To do this, you must copy the characters 'AT' to the clipboard. To paste this command into the Tera Term, you simply need to position the mouse cursor at the beginning of the first line on the screen and click the right button on the mouse. If, as I have, you have set up the Tera Term to not use a local echo, whereby the Tera Term software will display the commands you send on the screen, you will not see the AT command, but after a slight delay you should see the word "OK" displayed. This will have been sent by the HC-06 and so it confirms the communication is working. This is shown in Figure 8-6.

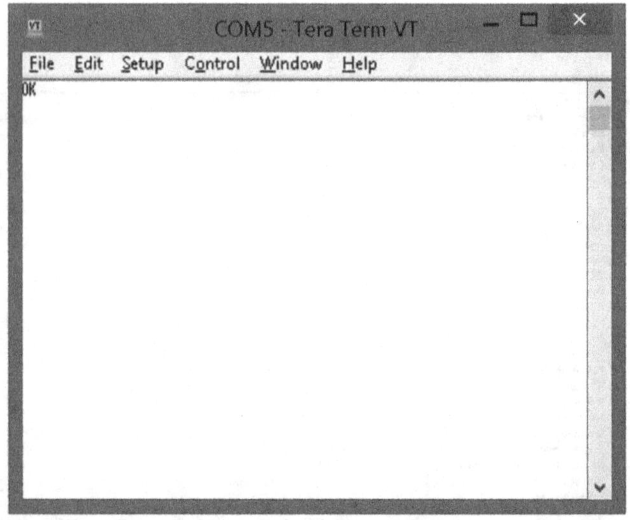

Figure 8-6. *The OK response from the HC-06*

If you now copy and paste the AT+VERSION command, you will get the response as shown in Figure 8-7. Note that to keep my display clean, I got the Tera Term software to clear the screen before I sent the new command. If you don't, then there will be two OKs, as the previous OK will still be there.

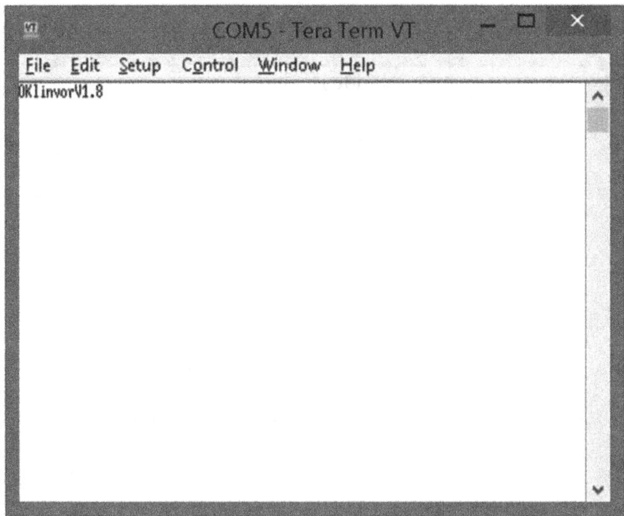

Figure 8-7. *The next response from the HC-06*

Now to change the PIN number or password on your HC-06, you need to copy and paste the following command: AT+PINXXXX. You must replace the 'XXXX' with a four-digit number of your choice. Again I have cleared the display before I sent this command. The HC-06 will respond as shown in Figure 8-8.

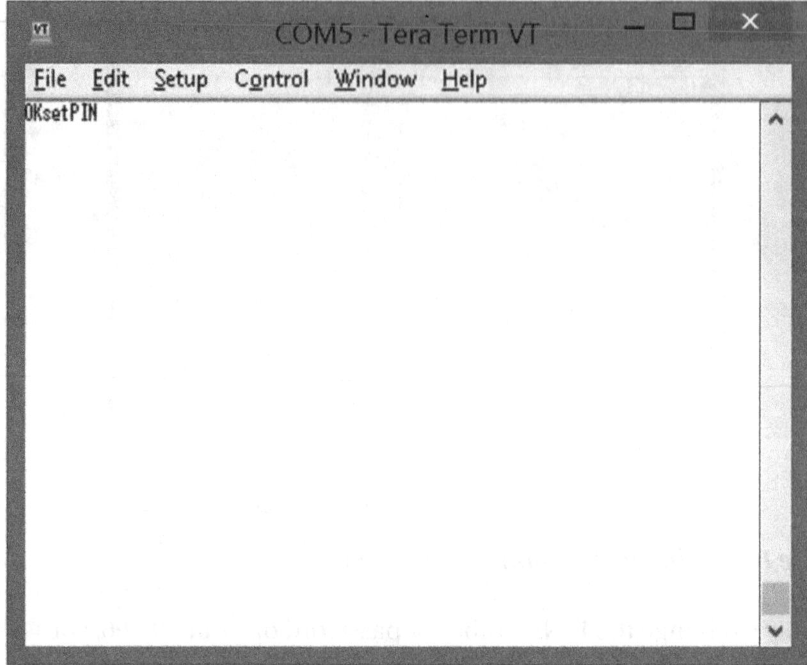

Figure 8-8. *Changing the PIN number*

So we have now changed the PIN number so that if anyone else finds the HC-06 as a nearby Bluetooth device, they will not be able to pair with it because they do not know the PIN number.

Now we will consider how we can change the name of the HC-06 and see what happens, just because we can. To do this, we must copy the following command and paste it into the Tera Term software:

AT+NAME ....

Note that we must replace the dots ..... with whatever we want to name the HC-06. When you paste this into the software, you will get the response as shown in Figure 8-9.

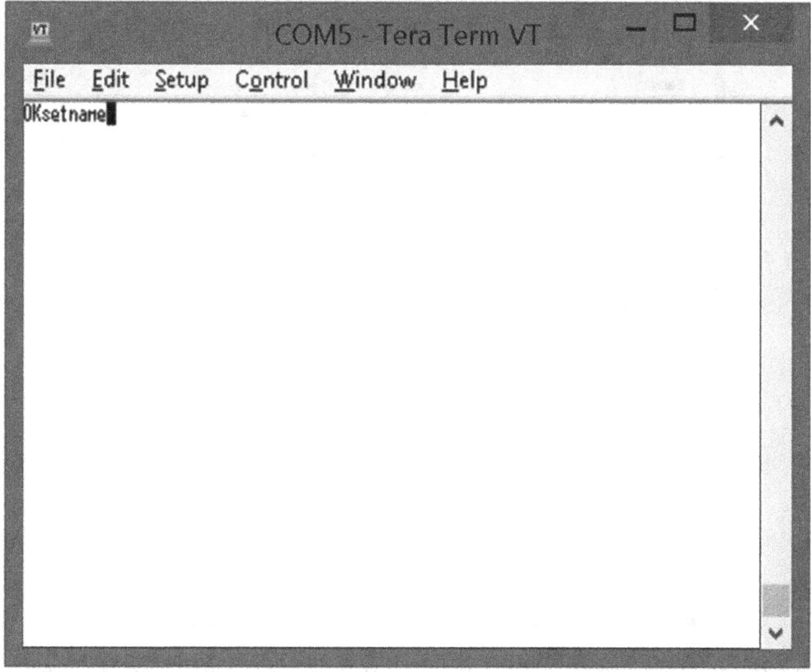

Figure 8-9. *Changing the name*

Now when you pair the HC-06 with your phone and it connects, you will see the name displayed on the screen of your phone. Note that you will need to input the correct PIN number to pair your phone with the HC-06.

Using PuTTY to Program the HC-06

The other software you can use to allow your laptop to work as a terminal is PuTTY. This is freely available to download from the Internet.

When you first open it, you should select the serial option and set it up as shown in Figure 8-10.

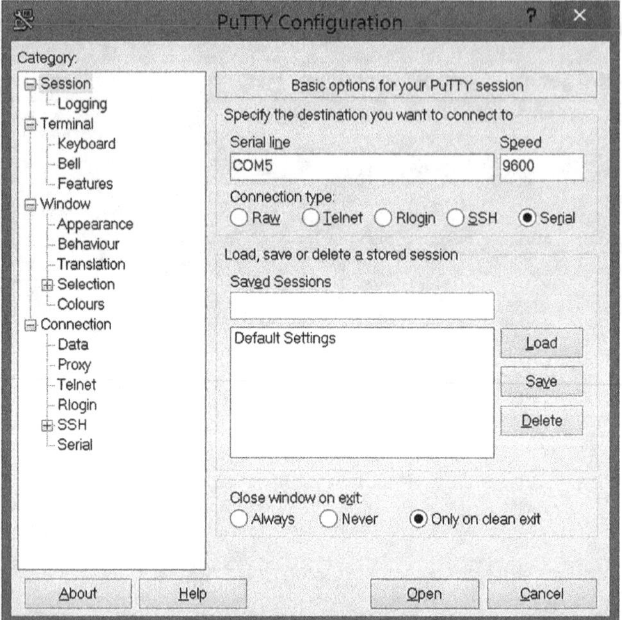

Figure 8-10. *Setting PuTTY up to communicate with the HC-06*

Note that you should confirm which port the USB to serial module is connected to. Once you have set up the software correctly as shown in Figure 8-10, you should click the open option. The terminal screen as shown in Figure 8-11 will appear.

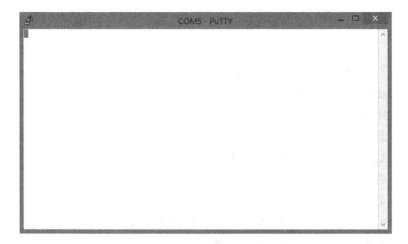

Figure 8-11. *The opening screen for PuTTY*

You should now cut and paste the AT commands in the same way as we did with the Tera Term software. You should get the same responses.

However, I must add that sometimes this approach does not work. It may be because of the time delay, but I am not sure. So you may have to use the Tera Term software. However, in the next section we will look at using a more reliable method.

Programming the HC-06 with AT Command from the PIC Micro

I hope you are now fast becoming a PIC embedded programmer. Also, as I did find, the terminal software was a bit unreliable. I think we should try an alternative approach. Therefore, in this program we are going to see how we can configure the HC-06 by sending the AT commands from the PIC. In this way, we don't need the Tera Term or PuTTY software. The program listing is shown in Listing 8-2.

Listing 8-2. Write AT Commands to the HC-06 Using Your PIC Micro

```
/*This is a program to send AT commands to the HC-06 using the PIC 18F4525
Written by H H Ward dated 12/05/21.
It uses the LCD to show the responses from the HC-06 to the commands sent to it
*/
#include <xc.h>
#include <conFigInternalOscNoWDTNoLVP.h>
#include <4bitLCDPortb.h>
unsigned char lcdData, lcdTempData, rsLine, datain, dataout, olddatain = 0, newdatain = 0;
unsigned char n, count, m;
unsigned char mess[30], *messpointer;
#define repeatButton PORTCbits.RC0
#define incButton   PORTCbits.RC1
#define decButton   PORTCbits.RC2
#define setButton   PORTCbits.RC3
#define RTS PORTDbits.RD0
#define CTS PORTDbits.RD1
void shortdelay ()
{
TMR0 = 0;
while (TMR0 < 255);
}
void debounce ()
{
TMR0 = 0;
while (TMR0 < 100);
}
```

```
void delay (unsigned char t)
{
for (n = 0; n < t; n ++)
{
TMRO = 0;
while (TMRO < 255);
}
}
void sendDeviceString(const char* meshw)
{
while(*meshw)
{
TXREG = (*meshw++);
shortdelay ();
}
}
void showResponse ()
{
count = 0;
while (count == 0);
for (n = 0; n <count; n++)
{
lcdData = mess[n];
lcdOut ();
}
}
char receiveDeviceChar(void)
{
while (!RCIF);
if(OERR)
{
```

```
CREN = 0;
CREN = 1;
}
if(RCIF==1) return RCREG;
else return 0;
}
void interrupt  isr1 ()
{
if (PIR1bits.RCIF == 1)
{
RCIF = 0;
mess[count]=RCREG;
count++;
}
}
void main ()
{
PORTA = 0;
PORTB = 0;
PORTC = 0;
PORTD = 0;
TRISA = 0b00010000;
TRISB = 0x00;
TRISC = 0b10000001;
TRISD = 0x02;
ADCON0 = 0x00;
ADCON1 = 0x0F;
OSCCON = 0b01110000;
OSCTUNE = 0b10000000;
T0CON = 0b11000111;
INTCON = 0b11000000;
```

```
PIE1bits.RC1IE = 1;
TXSTA = 0b00100000;
RCSTA = 0b10010000;
BAUDCON = 0b00000000;
SPBRG = 12;
messpointer = mess;
setUpTheLCD ();
clearTheScreen ();
writeString ("Coded transmit");
line2 ();
while (1)
{
while (!repeatButton);
debounce ();
while (repeatButton);
sendDeviceString ("AT");
shortdelay ();
showResponse ();
while (!repeatButton);
debounce ();
while (repeatButton);
clearTheScreen ();
sendDeviceString ("AT+VERSION");
shortdelay ();
showResponse ();
while (!repeatButton);
debounce ();
while (repeatButton);
clearTheScreen();
sendDeviceString ("AT+NAMEherb");
shortdelay ();
```

```
120.    showResponse ();
121.    while (!repeatButton);
122.    debounce ();
123.    while (repeatButton);
124.    clearTheScreen();
125.    sendDeviceString ("AT+PIN5653");
126.    shortdelay ();
127.    showResponse ();
128.    delay (10);
129.    }
130.    }
```

Analysis of Listing 8-2

The idea behind this program is to run it when you want to change the settings on the HC-06. Then you would run the program of Listing 8-1 to use your mobile phone and the HC-06 to control some devices in your home.

This program uses an interrupt that is initiated every time the PIC's UART receives data from the HC-06. The data that the PIC would receive will be the expected responses from the HC-06 to the AT commands sent from the PIC. As this data may be a string of characters, then the program uses an array called 'mess' to store the characters as they are received by the PIC. We will then display these responses as they arrive on the LCD.

Lines 1 to 16 are the normal comments, includes, defines, and variables type instructions that we have looked at before.

Lines 17 to 21 create a short delay, of approximately 33ms, that is used to give the HC-06 time to respond to the commands sent by the PIC.

Lines 22 to 26 create the debounce subroutine, which is used to allow the switch inputs to settle down once they have been pressed. This to ensure we don't see the input going to a logic '1' multiple times.

Lines 27 to 34 create the normal variable delay.

Lines 35 to 42 create the void sendDeviceString(const char* meshw) subroutine, which is used to send a string of characters to the HC-06. We have looked at this subroutine in Listing 8-1; the only difference is that I have changed the name of the pointer.

Line 43 showResponse ()

This creates a subroutine that gets the PIC to display the response from the HC-06 on the LCD.

Line 45 count = 0;

This loads this variable with the value 0. This gets the variable ready for the while loop that follows.

Line 46 while (count == 0);

At first look, this instruction looks incorrect. As in line 45, we set count to 0, and with line 46 we are making the PIC do nothing while count is 0, as it is now. Therefore, the PIC should get stuck here forever. However, you should appreciate that we have called this subroutine almost immediately after sending an AT command to the HC-06. We know the HC-06 will send a response back to the PIC after a short delay of around 1 second. The PIC would be at this instruction, on line 46, just before the HC-06 sends its response. When the HC-06 has started to send its response the UART's RCIF will be set. This means the PIC will go to the ISR (interrupt service routine) between lines 64 and 72, and carry out the instructions there. In line 70, the PIC increments the value in count. Therefore, when the PIC returns back from the ISR to this instruction, on line 46, count will no longer be 0 and so the PIC will move onto line 47.

Line 47 for (n = 0; n <count; n++)

This sets up a standard "for do loop" that will be carried out as long as 'n' is less than count.

Line 49 lcdData = mess[n];

This loads the variable lcdData with the contents of the memory location in the array mess indicated by the value in the variable 'n.' At the moment, as this is the first run through the "for do loop" n = 0.

Therefore, the contents of the first location in the array 'mess' will be copied into lcdData.

Line 50 lcdOut ();

This sends the data in the variable lcdData to the LCD.

This loop continues until the variable 'n' equals the variable 'count'. In this way, the PIC will send all the characters in the array 'mess' to the LCD. Note that in the ISR, the array 'mess' is filled with the characters sent back to the PIC from the HC-06.

Lines 53 to 63 set up a subroutine that receives a character from the HC-06. This has been analyzed in Listing 8-1.

Lines 64 to 72 are the instructions of the ISR. This is a special subroutine that is called from within the fetch and execute cycle. This is looked at more in chapter 11.

Line 66 if (PIR1bits.RCIF == 1)

This is an if type test that checks to see if it was the RCIF that caused the interrupt. This is the only interrupt active, so it must be. The RCIF will be set when the HC-06 sends data to the UART in the PIC.

Line 68 RCIF = 0;

This sets the interrupt flag back to logic '0' so that it can be set again when the PIC receives the next byte from the HC-06. Also, if we didn't set it back to logic '0', then it would continually cause an interrupt even though it shouldn't, as no new byte has yet been received.

Line 69 mess[count]=RCREG;

As this is the first run-through of this interrupt, then count = 0. This means that this instruction will load the first memory location in the array 'mess' with the contents of the RCREG. This will be the byte we have just received from the HC-06.

Line 70 count ++;

This simply increments the variable count. This means that when the PIC returns to the response subroutine, the PIC can move onto line 47.

Lines 73 to 87 are the normal instructions to set the PIC up.

Line 88 INTCON = 0b11000000;

As bit 7 is a logic '1', then the GIE (Global Interrupt Enable) is enabled. Also as bit 6 is a logic '1', then the PIE (Peripheral Interrupt Enable) bit is also enabled. These two bits must be enabled if we want to use the peripheral interrupts of the PIC such as the UART receiver.

Line 89 PIE1bits.RC1IE = 1;

This enables the particular interrupt, that for the UART1 receiver.

Lines 90 to 100 are fairly standard instructions we have already looked at.

Line 101 while (!repeatButton);

This is waiting for the logic on this input to go to a logic '1' before the program carries on. This is so that we can control when the PIC sends the AT command to the HC-06.

Line 102 debounce ();

This calls the subroutine to ensure that the PIC does not think the input has gone to a logic '1' more than once.

Line 103 while (repeatButton);

This makes the PIC wait until the logic at this input has gone back to a logic '0'.

Line 104 sendDeviceString ("AT");

This calls the sendDeviceString subroutine and sends the first AT command. The HC-06 should respond with the message "OK".

Line 105 shortdelay ();

This calls the shortdelay subroutine to give the HC-06 time to receive the AT command.

Line 106 showResponse ();

This calls the subroutine to show how the HC-06 has responded to the AT command. Note that when the HC-06 sends the first byte of its response, the RCIF will be set, forcing the PIC to go to the ISR.

Lines 107 to 127 get the PIC to send the other AT commands and display the HC-06 responses.

I hope you can see that this program can send commands to the HC-06. I also think it is more reliable than using the terminal software programs Tera Term and PuTTY. I am not sure why, but the PIC does not fail to get a response. However, the terminal software does sometimes fail to get a response from the HC-06.

The HC-SR501 PIR Motion Sensor

This is a relatively inexpensive device for detection of motion within an area around the sensor. Its simplicity of use makes it quite attractive. Basically, it can be viewed as a switch connected to the PIC. When the sensor detects motion in the area around it, the switch can be said to close. This is because the output will go to around 3.3V, which is enough to be seen as a logic '1' in TTL. When there is no motion, the output goes to a low voltage around 0V. You can easily get the PIC to do a number of things when this "switch" closes.

It's not important to understand how the sensor actually detects motion, but there are some things you should know about how the PIR works.

The connections of the PIR sensor are shown in Figure 8-12.

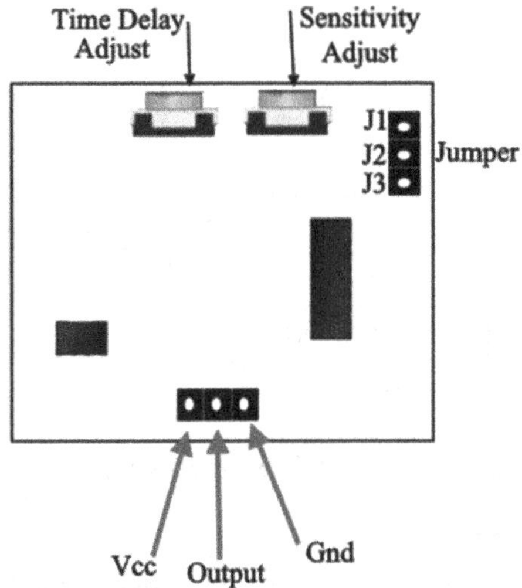

Figure 8-12. *The connections of the PIR viewed from underneath*

The Trigger Mode Select

This has two possible selections:

- Single trigger: This is when the jumper connects J1 to J2. With this selection, the time delay starts immediately when the first motion is detected. Further detection cannot happen until this time delay has completed.
- Repeatable trigger: This is selected when J2 connects with J3. In this mode, the time delay starts again if motion is detected, but it can also start while a time delay is still running.

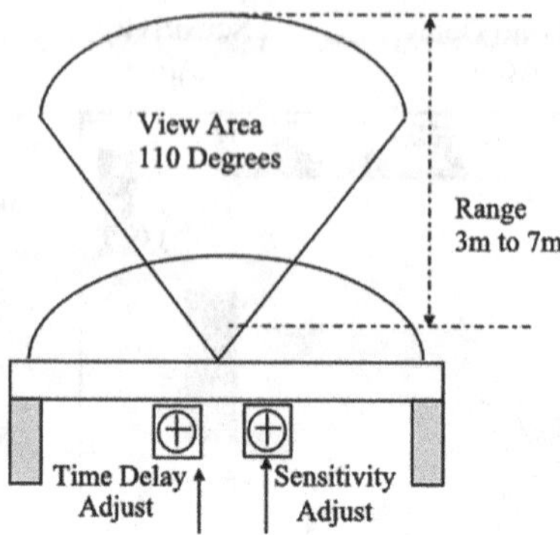

Figure 8-13. *The range of the PIR motion sensor*

The Range or Sensitivity

To adjust the sensitivity, turning the control knob fully clockwise reduces the range to 3m (see Figure 8-13).

When the control knob is turned fully anticlockwise, the range increases to a maximum of 7m.

The Time Delay

To adjust the time delay, which sets the time the output remains high, turning the control knob fully clockwise increases this time to a maximum of 5 minutes. Turning it fully anticlockwise reduces the time to a minimum of 3 seconds. Note that when motion is detected, the output will go high and remain high until this time delay has completed. Then it will go low for around 3 seconds before it can detect motion again. Therefore, the normal signal from the output will be as shown in Figure 8-14.

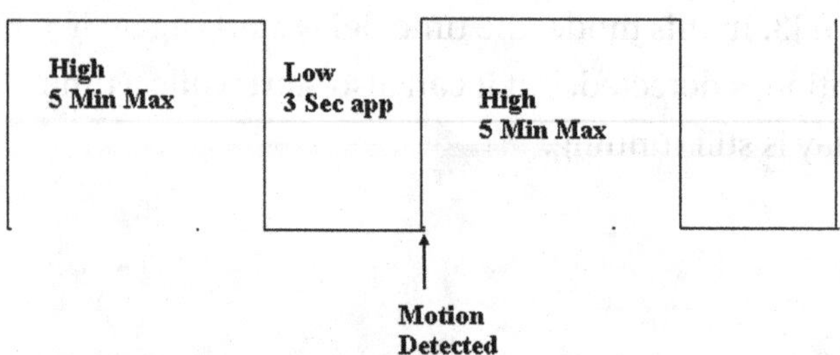

Figure 8-14. *A representation of the output from the PIR motion sensor*

The output will stay high for the delay time you set with the adjustment control. Then the output will go low for a minimum of 3 seconds. Then when the next motion is sensed, the output will go high again. This is with the trigger set to single mode using the jumper shown in Figure 8-12. However, if you set the jumper to repeatable trigger, then the output could be triggered to go high again and start the time delay you set at any point in the output shown in Figure 8-14.

The program listing for the PIR program is shown in Listing 8-3.

Listing 8-3. HC S501 PIR Motion Sensor

```
/*c
* File:   pirMotionProg.c
Author: H. H. Ward
written for the PIC18F4525
Created on 12 May 2021, 09:45
*/
#include <xc.h>
#include <conFigInternalOscNoWDTNoLVP.h>
#include "4bitLCDPORTD.h"
#define pir PORTBbits.RB0
#define ledout PORTCbits.RC0
void delay (unsigned char t)
{
for (n = 0; n < t; n ++)
{
TMR0 = 0;
while (TMR0 < 255);
}
}
void main(void)
{
```

```
PORTA = 0;
PORTB = 0;
PORTC = 0;
PORTD = 0;
TRISA = 0X01;
TRISB = 0b00000001;
TRISC = 0b10000000;
TRISD = 0x00;
ADCON0 = 0x00;
ADCON1 = 0x0F;
OSCTUNE = 0b10000000;
OSCCON = 0b01110000;
T0CON = 0b11000111;
setUpTheLCD ();
while (1)
{
while (pir)
{
ledout = 1;
writeString ("Intruder");
}
clearTheScreen ();
ledout = 0;
PORTCbits.RC1 = 1;
delay (15);
PORTCbits.RC1 = 0;
delay (15);
}
}
```

Analysis of Listing 8-3

There are no real new instructions. One real change is that I am using a new header file for the LCD.

Line 9 #include "4bitLCDPORTD.h"

This is the new header file, except that the only part that is new is that I have changed the reference to the PORT from PORTB to PORTD. This has an effect on the following instructions:

```
#define lcdPort                PORTD
#define eBit                   PORTDbits.RD5
#define RSpin                  PORTDbits.RD4
```

Everything else remains the same as before. This shows a real advantage of using the #define directive.

I am using the following instructions on lines 38 to 42 to control what happens when the PIR detects any motion.

```
while (pir)
{
    ledout = 1;
        writeString ("Intruder");
}
```

The input on bit 0 of PORTB, defined as pir in line 10, will go high. Then while it is high, the PIC will light the LED on bit 0 of PORTC, defined as ledout in line 11. It will also write the phrase "Intruder" to the LCD. As the word "Intruder" is eight characters, this will repeat the phrase exactly twice on each line, displaying the phrase four times on the LCD.

When the output of the PIR goes low, then 'pir' input will no longer be a logic '1' or high, and so the PIC will break out of the while loop and then carry out the following on lines 43 and 44.

```
clearTheScreen ();
ledout = 0;
```

This resets the output on the LCD and turns the LED off.

Lines 45 to 48 simply make an LED on bit 1 of PORTC flash on and off at half-second intervals.

I hope this brief analysis is enough to explain how the program works.

***Figure 8-15.** The PIC communicating with my mobile via Bluetooth*

***Figure 8-16.** The PIC programming the HC-06 with AT commands*

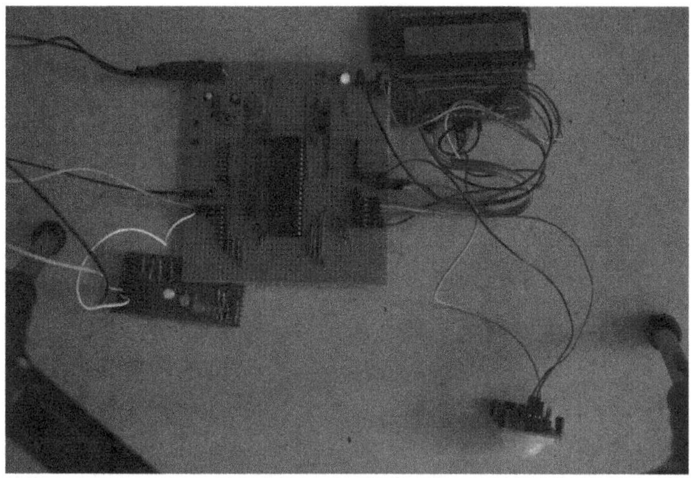

Figure 8-17. *The PIR sensor detecting motion*

Figures 8-15, 8-16, and 8-17 show the three programs working with the homemade prototype board.

Summary

In this chapter, we made some inroads into home automation. We have studied how you can use a HC-06 Bluetooth device to communicate with a PIC. We have learned how to program the HC-06 with AT commands using a terminal software and also from a PIC program. We have used a simple PIR motion sensor to detect some basic movement and get a PIC to respond.

In the next chapter, we will look at using the SPI communication module in the PIC to communicate with the TC72 temperature sensor and another PIC.

CHAPTER 9

Communication

In this chapter, we will look at the MSSP (master synchronous serial port) of the 18F4525 PIC. We will concentrate on the SPI (serial peripheral interface). We will learn how it works and then use it to interface with the TC72 temperature sensor from microchip.

We will learn how the TC72 formats negative temperatures and how we can manipulate binary numbers using 2's complement to read negative temperatures.

We will look at two methods for displaying binary values on the LCD, one of which will be using the sprintf function. We will then make a comparison of the two approaches.

We will finally look at using two PICs to communicate with each other using the SPI module. This will involve setting one as the master and the other as a slave.

After reading this chapter, you will be able to set up the SPI module. You will be able to use the TC72 temperature sensor to read temperature readings with a resolution of 0.25. You will be able to manipulate binary numbers to read negative values.

H. H. Ward, *Programming Arduino Projects with the PIC Microcontroller*,
https://doi.org/10.1007/978-1-4842-7230-5_9

Getting the PIC to Communicate with Other Devices

One aspect that makes the PIC extremely useful is its ability to communicate with other devices. These devices can be anything from some simple extra memory, or another PIC, or devices that let the PIC monitor and control a system outside the PIC. To save I/O pins and extra cables, most PICs use serial communication; however, some of the larger PICs, such as 32-bit PICs, do incorporate a parallel port which can be used for communication over a short distance.

The 18F4525, like most PICs, has three basic methods of serial communication:

- SPI, one of the simplest ways of implementing serial communications.
- I^2C (inter-integrated circuit)
- UART (universal asynchronous receive and transmit device).

This chapter will look at using the SPI module on the 18F4525.

The SPI and the I^2C modes of communication operate from the MSSP module of the PIC; these will be looked at in chapter 10.

After reading this chapter, you will be able to use the SPI module of a PIC.

The SPI Mode

This is a synchronous method of communication between a master, usually a microcontroller such as a PIC, and at least one other device. The fact that it is synchronous means that a clock signal is used to synchronize all the operations. The SPI must have at least two devices, as one will be the master, which will produce the clock signal and any other control signals, while the other will be the slave. The master can talk to more than one slave, but if this is to happen, the master must produce a control signal that will select which slave the master is talking to by turning that slave on and all the other slaves off.

With SPI communication, there are three main connections which connect the master to each slave, with a fourth one being a chip select (CS) needed if there is more than one slave the master is communicating with. The three main connections are the following:

- The SCK. This is the line that distributes the clock signal to the slaves.
- The SDO. This is the Data Out from either the master or the slave. This line actually connects to the Data In on the other device.
- The SDI. This is the Data In for either the master or the slave.
- The connections are shown in Figure 9-1.

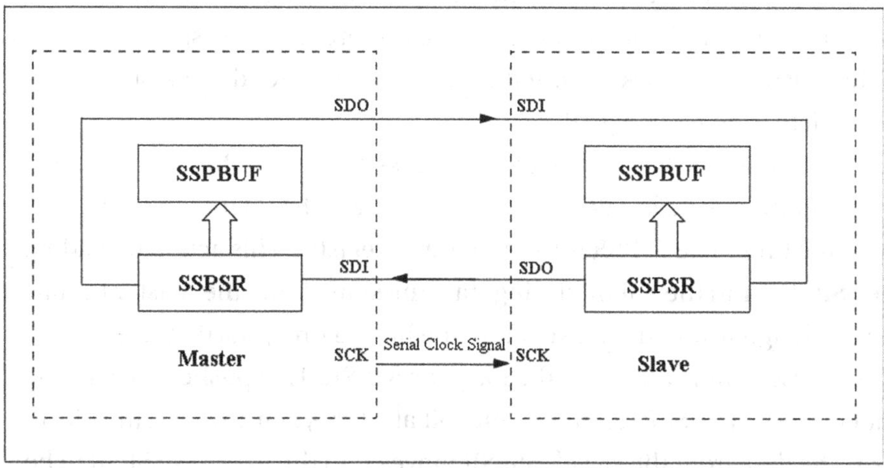

Figure 9-1. *The connections for the SPI module*

Table 9-1 helps explain what the abbreviations in Figure 9-1 mean.

Table 9-1. *Table of the MSSP Module*

Abbreviation	Meaning
MSSP	Master Synchronous Serial PORT module
SSP	Synchronous Serial Port
SSPBUF	SSP Buffer (a register that is a temporary store for data)
SSPSR	SSP Shift Register (a register that shifts the data in or out one bit at a time)
SSPSTAT	SSO Status Register (which shows the current state of the SSP module)
SSPCON1	Control Register 1 for the SSP module
SSPCON2	Control Register 2 for the SSP module

The SPI communication is a synchronized communication system, where all communication is synchronized to a clock signal sent out from the master to a slave, or all slaves if there is more than one slave connected to the master. The clock is started when the master sends data out; until then, there is no clock signal.

The master must initialize the transmission cycle. When the master is transmitting data, the data goes into the SSPBUF and into the SSPSR at the same time. The SSPSR is the serial shift register. This action of loading the SSPBUF and the SSPSR during transmission allows the master to start the clock signal, and data is sent out one bit at a time, starting with the MSB (most significant bit) in the master's SSPSR. This pushes the current data in the slave's SSPSR out of it one bit at a time, starting with the MSB also. The data from the slave's SSPSR moves into the master's SSPSR to be received by the master, while the transmitted data from the master moves into the slave's SSPSR. This circulating action continues until the master has sent out all of the eight bits that were in its buffer. This then means that the eight bits that were in the master's SSPBUF have gone into the slave's SSPBUF, and the eight bits that were in the slave's SSPBUF have gone into the master's SSPBUF, via their respective shift registers. This means that as the master sends out data to the slave, the slave will send some data to the master. This data from the slave may or may not be useful, but the master will get some data from the slave.

Another important thing to become aware of is that if the slave needs to send data to the master (i.e., if the master wants to read data from the slave), the master must send eight bits first to the slave to start the clock signal and so start this circulating operation. These eight bits that have been sent from the master would be useless information and the slave would simply ignore it. The slave cannot initiate any communication.

The Buffer Full (BF) Flag in the SSPSTAT Register

The SSPSTAT register is a register that can indicate the current state of the SPI. There is a full description of this SFR (special function register) later in this chapter. In this section we will look at the BF bit (buffer full bit), or flag. As its name suggests, this bit, sometimes called a flag, can be used to indicate if the SSPBUF is full, BF = '1,' or it is not full, BF = '0.'

The filling of the master's SSPBUF can be done in two ways; either way will set the BF flag to a logic '1.' The two ways are as follows:

- The master loading the buffer with data it wants to send to the slave, which could be
    - Commands to the slave.
    - Addresses of where to write to or read from.
    - Information to write to the slave.
- The slave automatically fills the master SSPBUF with the circulating action.

However, there are two circumstances when the slave fills the master's SSPBUF in this way, which are as follows:

1. When the master is writing to the slave. In this instance, the data circulating back from the slave will be nonsense and the master must empty its SSPBUF by reading the nonsense into the dummy variable. We need only one dummy variable, as its contents don't need to be saved.

2. When the master is reading data from the slave. In this instance the circulating data from the slave will be useful, and so the master must empty the SSPBUF by reading this useful data into a useful variable.

You should appreciate that reading the master's SSPBUF, or clocking the first bit out of the buffer in the circulating action to the slave, will clear the BF flag. The flag will stay at a logic '0' until the SSPBUF is filled with eight new bits.

The SPI method of communication is the simplest form, as it is only eight bits circulating in a prescribed manner. There is no protocol that sets out how the message is constructed, and there is no error checking. There are just binary bits that fill the respective buffer. You, as a programmer, must determine when those bits are useful and when they can be discarded.

Synchronizing the Sequence

I have stated that the process is synchronized to a clock signal created by the master. However, we need to appreciate what a clock signal is and how we can use it to synchronize operations. A typical clock signal is shown in Figure 9-2.

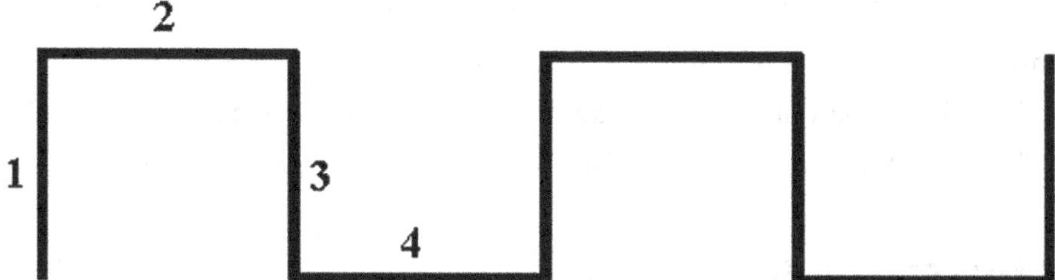

Figure 9-2. *A typical clock signal*

The purpose of this clock signal is to synchronize when the master and the slave will be triggered or told to carry out their actions. Figure 9-2 shows that there are four points on the clock signal when this triggering can happen. They are identified as follows:

- Trigger point '1' is termed positive edge triggering.
- Trigger point '2' is termed high-level triggering.
- Trigger point 3 is termed negative edge triggering.
- Trigger point 4 is termed low-level triggering.

It should be clear that the edge triggering is the more precise triggering point, as it lasts for only an instant. That is why it is most common to use edge triggering, either positive or negative. The programmer must set the trigger point of the clock signal to be the same as that for the slave device. Some slave devices can work with any trigger point, and so the master can set it to whatever the master feels like. However, we will look at using the positive edge of the clock signal, and therefore the master controlling the operations must set up its clock synchronization accordingly.

There are two control registers that the PIC uses to set up how the MSSP module works. They are as follows:

SSPSTAT (Synchronous Serial Port Status register).

SSPCON1 (Synchronous Serial Port Control register 1).

Note that if the MSSP module is used in I²C mode, there is an extra control register, the SSPCON2.

To help explain how we can use these registers to set up the PIC for SPI mode, we will look at the two registers and see what each bit controls.

SSPSTAT Register

This is shown in Table 9-2.

Table 9-2. *The SSPSTAT Register*

Bit 7	Bit 6	Bit 5	Bit 4	Bit 3	Bit 2	Bit 1	Bit 0
SMP	CKE	D/A	P	S	R/W	UA	BF

To fully appreciate what these bits control, you should understand that the PIC can be in master mode where it is the master to the other slave devices. However, it can also be a slave to another PIC or master. Therefore, the PIC could be in master mode or slave mode, and this will affect the operation of some of the control bits.

Bit 7 the SMP the Sample Bit

When the PIC is in master mode:

A logic '1' means input data is sampled at the end of output time.

A logic '0' means input data is sampled at the middle of output time.

When the PIC is in slave mode:

This bit must be cleared (i.e., set to a logic '0').

Bit 6 the CKE the SPI Clock Select Bit

A logic '1' means the transmit occurs on transition from active to idle clock state.

A logic '0' means the transmit occurs on transition from idle to active clock state.

However, the CKP (Clock Polarity Select) bit in the SSPCON1 register determines what polarity or logic level the idle state is, and so what the polarity of the active state is. This means these two bits must be decoded together to appreciate what they do. This is shown in Table 9-3.

Bit 5 the D/A Data or Address Bit

This bit is only used in I²C mode, so read as logic '0'.

Bit 4 the P Stop Bit

This bit is only used in I²C mode, so read as logic '0'.

Bit 3 the S Start Bit

This bit is only used in I²C mode, so read as logic '0'.

Bit 2 the R/W Read Write Bit

This bit is only used in I²C mode, so read as logic '0'.

Bit 1 the UA Update Address Bit

This bit is only used in I²C mode, so read as logic '0'.

Bit 0 the BF Buffer Full Status Bit

A logic '1' means receive complete and the SSPBUF is full.

A logic '0' means receive not complete and the SSPBUF is empty.

The SSPCON1 Register

This is shown in Table 9-3.

Table 9-3. *The SSPCON1 Register*

Bit 7	Bit 6	Bit 5	Bit 4	Bit 3	Bit 2	Bit 1	Bit 0
WCOL	SSPOV	SSPEN	CKE	SSPM3	SSPM2	SSPM1	SSPM0

Bit 7 the WCOL Write Collision Detect Bit

A logic '1' means the SSPBUF has been written to while it is still transmitting the previous data. Once this bit has been set, it must be cleared in software.

A logic '0' means no collision.

Bit 6 the SSPOV Receive Overflow Bit

An overflow can only occur when operating in slave mode. This bit will be set if a new byte of data is received while the SSPBUF is still holding the previous data. Once this bit has been set, it must be cleared in software.

Bit 5 the SSPEN the MSSP Enable Bit

A logic '1' enables the MSSP and configures the SCK, SDO, SDI, and SS pins as serial port pins.

A logic '0' disables the MSSP and set the pins as normal I/O.

Bit 4 the CKP the Clock Polarity Select Bit

This is the bit that is used in conjunction with the CKE pin.

A logic '1' means the idle state is a logic '1' or high level.

A logic '0' means the idle state is a logic '0' or low level.

Bits 3, 2, 1, and 0 set out the use of the MSSP according to Table 9-4.

Table 9-4. *Bits 3, 2, 1, and 0 of the SSPCON1 Register*

Bit 3	Bit 2	Bit 1	Bit 0	Operation of the MSSP
0	1	0	1	SPI in slave mode, clock on SCK, SS disabled normal I/O
0	1	0	0	SPI in slave mode, clock on SCK, SS enabled
0	0	1	1	SPI in master mode, clock is TMR2/2
0	0	1	0	SPI in master mode, clock is FOSC/64
0	0	0	1	SPI in master mode, clock is FOSC/16
0	0	0	0	SPI in master mode, clock is FOSC/4

It is important to get the logic of the control pins, CKP and CKE, correct, as you could lose bits in the data written to or read from the slave.

- The logic state expressed as active is vaguely referenced in the data sheet. The SPI modes are Microchip's method for standardizing these settings, and the two most popular modes are '1 1' and '0 0'.

The setting of these two bits, CKP and CKE, is quite difficult to define, and sometimes you may need to go through some trial and error to determine the correct setting. There are only eight possible combinations, so it shouldn't take too long.

We can now decide what data must be written to the two SFRs.

Setting the SSPSTAT Register

We need to set the master to sample the data at the end of the output time so that the slave samples it in the middle. We also need to ensure the synchronization is on the positive edge triggering of the clock signal. This means we need to set the SMP bit to a logic '1' so we sample the data at the end. We know we need to set the CKE bit to a logic '0' so transmission occurs from idle to active. Bits 5, 4, 3, 2, and 1 are only used in I^2C mode, so set these to a logic '0'. Bit 0 is the BF bit, which we should set to a logic '0' at this moment in time. The PIC then controls the setting of that bit. Therefore, the eight-bit data we need to write to the SSPSTAT register is

0b10000000 in binary of 0X80 in hexadecimal.

Setting The SSPCON1 Register

Bits 7 and 6 are signals from the PIC, so set them to a logic '0' now. Bit 5 enables the MSSP, so set this to a logic '1' now to turn the MSSP on. Bit 4 is the CKP which we want to set to a logic '0', which sets the idle state to logic '0'. This then, with the setting of the CKP bit, sets us up to use positive edge triggering. Bits 3, 2, 1, and 0 must be set to logic '0' (see Table 9-4) to set the MSSP to SPI in master mode; clock is FOSC/4. This means that the eight-bit data to be written to the SSPCON1 register is

0b00100000 in binary or 0X20 in hexadecimal.

However, you must make sure the MSSP is turned off before you write to the SSPSTAT register, so you could simply write 0 to the SSPCON1 register, then load the SSPSTAT register with 0X80, and then load the SSPCON1 register with 0X20.

This aspect of synchronizing the operation is not easy to understand, and we will look at it later as we run the program.

Using the SPI to Read from the TC72

The TC72 is a temperature sensor that conforms to the SPI mode of communication for communicating to a master. This means that we can use the SPI module to read a temperature reading from it and use the PIC as the master to communicate with it.

Operating Modes for the TC72

The TC72 can be operated in two modes. One mode is the single-shot mode whereby the master requests a reading from the TC72 and the TC72 responds by sending the two bytes that represent the temperature, then going into shutdown mode.

The other mode is the continuous mode, whereby the TC72 will measure the temperature once every 150ms.

The temperature is represented by a ten-bit number with 2's complement format for negative values; see the appendix for an explanation of 2's complement. The ten-bit would be stored in two eight-bit registers. The address for the registers are as follows:

0X02 for the high byte

0X01 for the low byte

The resolution of the temperature is 0.25°C per bit, giving a temperature range of 127°C to -127°C. However, the specified range of the TC72 is -55°C to 125°C.

The high byte register holds the signed bit number representation of the integer part of the temperature. This means that bit 7 of the high byte is used to state the "sign", positive or negative, of the value. The low byte holds the decimal or fractional part of the temperature.

This gives the programmer the choice of just reading the high byte at address 0X02 and ignoring any decimal points, or reading both registers to give a reading to two decimal places. It only uses two decimal places as the low six bits, bit 0 to bit 5 of the low byte, are not used.

When the temperature goes negative, the binary value goes into 2's complement mode and the programmer needs to perform a 2's complement on the binary number presented to them, to determine what the negative value really is.

The Registers of the TC72

There are three registers that can be accessed to use the TC72. They are listed and explained in Table 9-5.

Table 9-5. *The Registers of the TC72*

Register Name	Register Address
Control	0X00
Low byte of temperature reading	0X01
High byte of temperature reading	0X02

The control register can be written to that the TC72 can be put into either a write mode or a read mode. It is bit 7 of the eight-bit address that is used to differentiate between these two modes. Bit 7 is set to a logic '1' for writing to it and a logic '0' for reading from it.

You can write to the control register to send the appropriate instructions to put the TC72 into the single-shot or continuous mode as described earlier. The following are the binary values that need to be sent to the TC72 to do that:

- 0b1000 0000 or 0X80. This is to tell the TC72 you want to write to the control register. This must be done before any instruction is sent to the TC72.

- 0b00010001 or 0X11. This is the instruction to set up the TC72 into single-shot mode. Note that the TC72 will automatically shut down after each temperature measurement.
- 0b00000000 or 0b00010000 puts the TC72 into continuous mode. Note that you should wait at least 150ms before trying to read the temperature again with this mode of operation.

The Algorithm for Using the TC72

Now that we have some idea of how the TC72 works, we should think about the program. After the PIC is configured, it must be initialized, which includes setting up the SPI module. Note that the TC72 does not require a specific triggering to be specified for it so the triggering will be set by the master, and in this case it will be set for positive triggering.

Turn the TC72 on by sending its CE (Chip Enable) pin to a logic '1'.

Write to the control register to put the TC72 into the required mode. Normally, send the data 0b10000000 or 0X80 to the TC72 to let it know you want to write to the control register.

Then send the code to put it into your desired mode, usually 0b00010001 or 0X11, to put it into single-shot mode.

Then turn the TC72 off and wait 150ms.

Then turn the TC72 back on and send the address you want to read from. If, as is usual, you send the address of the high byte, which is 0X02, the TC72 will send the data from that register and then open the address of the low byte automatically, waiting to send it to the master.

The master needs to put some rubbish data into its buffer after sending the address 0X02 to enable the TC72 to send the high byte of the temperature to the master. The master must then put a second byte of rubbish into its buffer to enable the TC72 to send the low byte of the temperature to the master.

The TC72 can now be turned off by sending the CE pin to a logic '0'.

Displaying the Temperature Reading

The program will now have two eight-bit variables that represent the current temperature readings from the TC72 device (Listing 9-1). I have called the two variables "thigh", which holds the high byte and "tlow", which holds the low byte. The problem is how to get the two eight-bit binary numbers to be displayed as temperatures on the LCD. There are two approaches we can use to solve this problem. This program uses a method to display the readings that I have produced myself. This method is to split the readings up into units, tens, and hundreds as well as tenths and hundredths, a method I have used before but one that produces a long section of coding.

The other method, which is used in Listing 9-2, uses the sprintf function to display floats (i.e., numbers that have an integer part and a fractional part).

Listing 9-1. Reading from the TC72

```
/*
* File:   tempSensor|SPI.c
Author: hward
*
Created on 02 November 2017, 11:02
*/
#include <xc.h>
#include <4bitLCDPortb.h>
#include <conFigInternalOscNoWDTNoLVP.h>
//some variables
unsigned char count, dummy, thigh, tlow, huns, tens,
units, decten, dechun, thigh, tlow, negbit = 0;
```

```
//some subroutines
void delay(unsigned char t)
{
for (n = 0; n < t; n++)
{
TMRO = 0;
while (TMRO < 195);
}
}
void convert ()
{
decten = 0x30;
dechun = 0x30;
if (tlow == 0b01000000)
{
decten = (0x32);
dechun = (0x35);
}
if (tlow == 0b10000000)
{
decten = (0x35);
dechun = (0x30);
}
if (tlow == 0b11000000)
{
decten = (0x37);
dechun = (0x35);
}
if (thigh & 0b10000000)
{
negbit = 1;
```

```
tlow = ~tlow +1;
PORTA = thigh;
PORTD = tlow;
decten = 0x30;
dechun = 0x30;
if (tlow == 0b01000000)
{
thigh = ~thigh;
decten = (0x32);
dechun = (0x35);
}
if (tlow == 0b10000000)
{
thigh = ~thigh;
decten = (0x35);
dechun = (0x30);
}
if (tlow == 0b11000000)
{
thigh = ~thigh;
decten = (0x37);
dechun = (0x35);
}
if (tlow == 0b00000000)
{
thigh = ~thigh+1;
decten = (0x30);
dechun = (0x30);
}
}
if (thigh >= 0 && thigh < 10)
```

```
{
units = (thigh + 48);
tens = 48;
huns = 48;
}
if (thigh >= 10 && thigh < 20)
{
units = (thigh -10 + 48);
tens = ( 1 + 48);
huns = 48;
}
if (thigh >= 20 && thigh < 30)
{
units = (thigh -20 + 48);
tens = ( 2 + 48);
huns = 48;
}
if (thigh >= 30 && thigh < 40)
{
units = (thigh -30 + 48);
tens = ( 3 + 48);
huns = 48;
}
if (thigh >= 40 && thigh < 50)
{
units = (thigh -40 + 48);
tens = ( 4 + 48);
huns = 48;
}
if (thigh >= 50 && thigh < 60)
{
```

```
units = (thigh -50 + 48);
tens = ( 5 + 48);
huns = 48;
}
if (thigh >= 60 && thigh < 70)
{
units = (thigh -60 + 48);
tens = ( 6 + 48);
huns = 48;
}
if (thigh >= 70 && thigh < 80)
{
units = (thigh -70 + 48);
tens = ( 7 + 48);
huns = 48;
}
if (thigh >= 80 && thigh < 90)
{
units = (thigh -80 + 48);
tens = ( 8 + 48);
huns = 48;
}
if (thigh >= 90 && thigh < 100)
{
units = (thigh -90 + 48);
tens = ( 9 + 48);
huns = 48;
}
if (thigh >= 100 && thigh < 110)
{
units = (thigh -100 + 48);
```

```
tens = ( 0 + 48);
huns = (1+ 48);
}
if (thigh >= 110 && thigh < 120)
{
units = (thigh -110 + 48);
tens = ( 1 + 48);
huns = (1+48);
}
if (thigh >= 120 && thigh < 130)
{
units = (thigh -120 + 48);
tens = ( 2 + 48);
huns = (1+48);
}
if (negbit == 1) writeString ("Temp is -");
else writeString ("Temp is ");
if (huns == 48) goto distens;
lcdData = huns;
lcdOut ();
distens: if (tens == 48 && huns == 48) goto disunits;
lcdData = tens;
lcdOut ();
disunits: lcdData = units;
lcdOut ();
lcdData = 0X2E;
lcdOut ();
lcdData = decten;
lcdOut ();
lcdData = dechun;
lcdOut ();
```

```
lcdData = 0XDF;
lcdOut ();
lcdData = 0X43;
lcdOut ();
lcdData = 0X20;
lcdOut ();
lcdData = 0X20;
lcdOut ();
negbit = 0;
}
void main ()
{
PORTA = 0;
PORTB = 0;
PORTC = 0;
PORTD = 0;
TRISA = 0;
TRISB = 0;
TRISC = 0b00010000;
TRISD = 0;
ADCON0 = 0;
ADCON1 = 0X0F;
OSCCON = 0X74;
T0CON = 0XC7;
SSPCON1 = 0X00;
SSPCON1bits.CKP =1;
SSPSTAT = 0b00000000;
SSPSTATbits.CKE = 0;
SSPCON1bits.SSPEN =1;
setUpTheLCD ();
while (1)
```

```
{
units = 0;
writeString ("TC72 TEMP Sensor");
line2 ();
PORTCbits.RC0 = 1;
SSPBUF = 0X80;
while (!SSPSTATbits.BF);
dummy = SSPBUF;
SSPBUF = 0X11;
while (!SSPSTATbits.BF);
PORTCbits.RC0 = 0;
dummy = SSPBUF;
delay(7);
PORTCbits.RC0 = 1;
SSPBUF = 0X02;
while (!SSPSTATbits.BF);
dummy = SSPBUF;
SSPBUF = 0x00;
while (!SSPSTATbits.BF);
thigh = SSPBUF;
SSPBUF = 0x00;
while (!SSPSTATbits.BF);
tlow = SSPBUF;
PORTCbits.RC0 = 0;
convert ();
sendcursorhome ();
}
}
```

The circuit diagram for the program is shown in Figure 9-3. The circuit uses two pull up resistors on the SDO and SDI lines. This is just to ensure the lines do go high when they are supposed to.

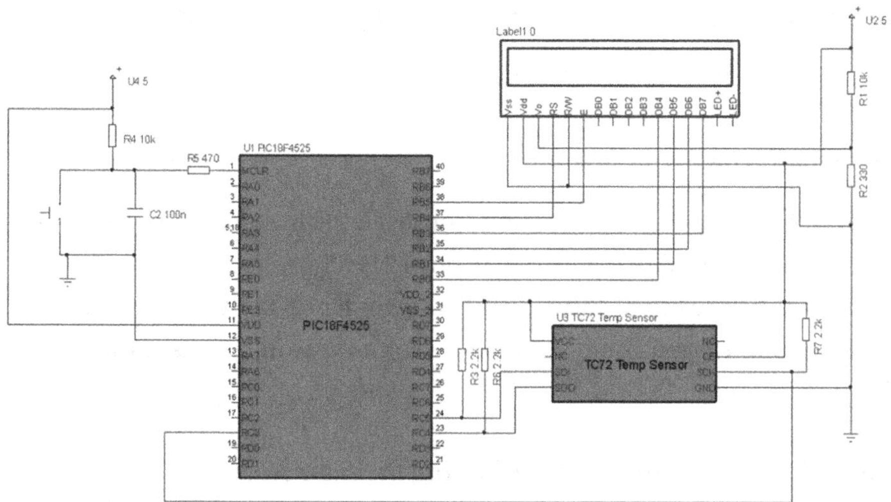

Figure 9-3. *The circuit for the SPI communication with the TC72*

Binary Numbers

Before we start the analysis of Listing 9-1, I think it might be useful to look at binary numbers and how they work.

We should really all see numbers as digits set out in a series of columns. The problem is that with our normal number system, the denary number system, we are so used to using it that we don't show the columns. Consider the number 225.5. This number is shown in columns in Table 9-6.

Table 9-6. *The Number 225.5 with Columns*

Hundreds	Tens	Units		Tenths
2	2	5	.	5

Another way of showing the columns would be to use the base number raised to a number. Our base number is 10, and the number it is raised by relates to the number of the column. This concept is shown in Table 9-7.

Table 9-7. *The Number 225.5 Shown Using the Base Number 10*

10^2	10^1	10^0		10^{-1}
2	2	5	.	5

Table 9-7 shows the title for the columns in the base number, 10 for the denary system, raised to a power. The power is related to the position of the column. If we weren't showing the fractional part of the number after the decimal point, you could see that the columns would be as shown in Table 9-8.

Table 9-8. *The Denary Columns Using the Base Number 10*

Ten Thousands	Thousands	Hundreds	Tens	Units
10^4	**10^3**	**10^2**	**10^1**	**10^0**
		2	2	5

The heading for the columns is shown in its name and how it relates to the base number. The first column has the power 0 as we start from 0. In the other columns, the power simply increments as we move to the left.

The process by which this number equals 225 is that there are

$2(100) + 2(10) + 5(1) = 225.$

We are so used to the denary system that we don't look at numbers in this way. However, all number systems work in the same way.

Now let's look at the binary number system. The base number for the binary system is '2', as there are only two digits allowed: 0 and 1. Therefore, if we use the same approach to show the titles for headings of the columns, we have those as shown in Table 9-9.

Table 9-9. *The Binary Number System*

Sixteens	Eights	Fours	Twos	Units
2^4	2^3	2^2	2^1	2^0

If we now extend the columns to show the fractional part, we have Table 9-10:

Table 9-10. *Fractional Binary Numbers*

Sixteens	Eights	Fours	Twos	Units	0.5	0.25
2^4	2^3	2^2	2^1	2^0	2^{-1}	2^{-2}

In the binary system, the number can be made up of either 1 in the column or 0 in the column added to the others. Consider Table 9-11:

Table 9-11. *An Example Binary Number*

Sixteens	Eights	Fours	Twos	Units	0.5	0.25
2^4	2^3	2^2	2^1	2^0	2^{-1}	2^{-2}
0	0	1	1	0	1	0

This number has no (16s), no (8s), 1 (4s), 1 (2s), 0 (1s), 1 (0.5s), and 0 (0.25s). Therefore, if we add all the values with a logic '1' in the column, we get the number 4+2+0.5 = 6.5.

This shows that 00110.10 is the binary for 6.5.

Consider the next example shown in Table 9-12.

Table 9-12. Another Binary Example

Sixteens	Eights	Fours	Twos	Units	0.5	0.25
2^4	2^3	2^2	2^1	2^0	2^{-1}	2^{-2}
1	0	1	0	0	1	1

This number is made up of 1 (16) + 1 (4) + 1 (0.5) + 1 (0.25) and therefore is 16 + 4 + 0.5 + 0.25 = 20.75.

Adding Binary Numbers

We just need to see what happens when we add binary numbers. There are a few examples shown here:

	Bit 1	Bit 0
	0	0
add		1
result	0	1

In this first example, we are simply adding 1 to 0 in binary. It should be obvious that the result is just 1.

	Bit 1	Bit 0
	0	1
add		1
result	1	0

In this second example, we see that 1 + 1 does not produce a result of 2, as the digit 2 is not allowed in binary. What happens is that 0 and 1 carry into the next column, just like what happens when we add 1 to 9 in the denary system: we get 0 in the units column and 1 in the tens column.

Now in the second column, bit 1, we get 0 + 1 = 1. This is how we get the result as shown.

Now consider the following:

	Bit 1	Bit 0
	1	1
add		1
result	0	0

Again, the addition in the first column would produce the result of 0 in that column. Also, a 1 would be carried onto column bit 1, where again the addition of 1 + 1 would produce the result 0. However, as this is a two-bit number that can only go from 0 to 3, there is no third column to put the carry into. Therefore it will be simply lost.

I am not going to go any further into looking at number systems. There is a section in the appendix that does all that. However, what I hope you can appreciate is how we can add binary numbers together and how we can convert binary to decimal. This basic understanding will, I hope, help you understand the following analysis about receiving negative values from the TC72.

Analysis of Listing 9-1

Lines 1 to 6 are just the standard type comments. Lines 7, 8, and 9 are the standard include files.

Line 11 sets up the eight-bit memory locations for all the variables we will use in the program. Note that we don't need to declare the variable 'n' even though it is used as a global variable in the program. This is because it is declared in the header file for the LCD.

Lines 13 to 20 create our standard variable time delay.

Line 21 convert ()

This sets up a subroutine that will convert binary numbers that are used to describe a value that has both integer and fractional parts into the ASCII for the different parts of the number. This is so that the value can be displayed on the LCD.

This is a long subroutine which ends at line 176. When we are happy that this subroutine works, we could look at making it a header file that we could use for other instances instead of using the sprintf function.

Line 23 decten = 0x30;

Line 24 dechun = 0x30;

We are going to split the fractional part of the display into two columns. One will display the tenths value; this uses the variable 'decten'. The other will display the hundredths; this will use the variable 'dechun'. We are loading both these variables with the value 0x30, which is the ASCII for 0. I am using the term "dec" to indicate these are the fractional parts.

Reading the Temperature from the TC72

To appreciate how the next few instructions work, we need to appreciate how the TC72 sends the temperature readings back to the PIC. The TC72 uses a ten-bit number to represent the temperature reading. The definition of the TC72 is 0.25°C. This means it will be sending back data that consists of the integer part and the fractional part of the reading. The integer part of the reading is sent back in the whole eight bits of the high byte. The fractional part is sent back in just bit 7 and bit 6 of the low byte. The remaining bits of the low byte are not used at all. An example of the temperature reading is shown in Table 9-13.

Table 9-13. *A Temperature Reading of 11.75*

High Byte	Low Byte	Temperature Reading
0 0 0 0 1 0 1 1	1 1	11.75

I hope you can now understand how the binary number is 11.75 in decimal. Just to make sure the decimal number is made up of

1(8) + 1(2) + 1(1) + 1(0.5) + 1(0.25)

= 8 +2 +1 + 0.5 + 0.25 = 11.75.

I am only showing bit 7 and bit 6 of the low byte, as these are the only bits we use.

It is the fact that we are only using the first two decimal places, which gives the TC72 a resolution of 0.25, as this is the smallest value we can use.

What the program must do is examine the low byte to determine the fractional part of the reading. When this low byte is sent to the PIC, its value is stored in the tlow variable (see line 220).

The next three tests are there to determine what bits 7 and 6 of the tlow variable, which has been loaded with the value of the lowbyte in line 220, are set to. They then load the appropriate value into the variables decten and dechun.

Line 25 if (tlow == 0b01000000)

This is simply testing to see if bit 6 has gone to a logic '1'. If it has, the result of the test will be true, and this means the fractional part is 0.25. Therefore, the PIC carries out lines 27 and 28, where it loads them with the correct ASCII to display 25. Note that the ASCII for 2 is 0X32 and 5 is 0X35.

Lines 30 to 34 to do the same but this time for the value 0.50.

Lines 35 to 39 do the same but now for the value 0.75.

You should appreciate that only one of the preceding three tests will be true. Of course, the variable tlow could have 0b00000000 in it. If it does, then decten and dechun will stay set to 0X30 as in lines 23 and 24.

Line 40 if (thigh & 0b10000000)

This is a test that performs a logic AND with bit 7 of the variable 'thigh' and the logic '1' in the binary number 0b10000000. The result of the test will be true if bit 7 of 'thigh' is a logic '1'. If it is true, the PIC will carry out the instructions between lines 41 and 72. This is a test to see if the temperature reading is a negative value. This is because we are using signed number representation where bit 7 is used to signify if the number is negative. A logic '1' on bit 7 means the number is negative.

Examples of the 2's Complement Process

Before we go any further with this analysis, I think it would be useful to look at the use of 2's complement, especially how we can manipulate binary numbers to create and solve 2's complement representation. All computers and microcontrollers use 2's complement to express negative numbers. I hope the following examples will help explain how this whole process works and how we can read negative temperatures from the TC72. However, before we go through the examples it might be useful to see how the 2's complement of binary numbers works.

To create a 2's complement, we must invert all the bits and add 1. Let's look at a simple example: expressing –7 in eight-bit binary.

The process is that the micro will receive the 2's complement of 7, which is shown in row 4 of Table 9-14. The PIC will recognize that the number should be negative, as bit 7 is a logic '1'. Now the PIC must find out what the value of the negative number is. To do this, the PIC must create a 2's complement on the binary number it has just got. This is done on rows 6 and 7. The final result is the number 7, shown in row 8. Now the PIC knows the negative number has a value of 7 (i.e., –7).

Note that rows 1, 2, and 3 show the initial process of creating the 2's complement of 7. Row 4 is the 2's complement of 7 in eight-bit binary. Note that you must use all eight bits. There are more examples in the appendix.

Table 9-14. *An Example of 2's Complement for -7*

Bit 7	Bit 6	Bit 5	Bit 4	Bit 3	Bit 2	Bit 1	Bit 0	
0	0	0	0	0	1	1	1	7 in decimal
1	1	1	1	1	0	0	0	Invert all bits
							1	
1	1	1	1	1	0	0	1	This is the 2's complement to describe –7 Note that bit 7 is a logic '1'
To get the real number, the PIC must do another 2's complement								
0	0	0	0	0	1	1	0	Invert all bits
							1	Add 1
0	0	0	0	0	1	1	1	The result is back to 7.

Now we will look at some examples of how the TC72 will send the values -1.00, -1.25, 1.50, and 1.75. This is to determine when we need to carry a logic '1' on the 'thigh' variable. This is because we separate the ten bits into the two variables 'thigh' and 'tlow', as the TC27 only sends eight bits at a time. Therefore, the carry cannot go onto 'thigh' automatically; the program has to add it when needed.

The first example looks at what happens when the reading is -1.00.

High Byte								Low Byte		
b7	b6	b5	b4	b3	b2	b1	b0	b7	b6	
0	0	0	0	0	0	0	1	0	0	This is the 10-bit binary for 1.00
1	1	1	1	1	1	1	0	1	1	This the 10-bit number inverted
									1	Now add 1
1	1	1	1	1	1	1	1	0	0	The result of the TC72 performing its 2's complement. Note that bit 7 of high byte is a logic '1'. This is sent to the PIC and stored in thigh and tlow.
0	0	0	0	0	0	0	0	1	1	Now the PIC will invert both parts
									1	Now add 1. This action does produce a carry to pass on to the high byte. Therefore, in the program, we need to invert the thigh and add 1 to it
0	0	0	0	0	0	0	1	0	0	The binary number is back to 1.0

I hope you can see how the process works and that we have to invert the variable 'thigh' and add '1' to it at the same time. This will be done in line 68.

The next example is for -1.25.

High Byte	Low Byte		
0 0 0 0 0 0 0 1	0	1	1.25
1 1 1 1 1 1 1 0	1	0	The TC72 will perform its 2's complement. Note that bit 7 of high byte is a logic '1'
		1	Now add 1
1 1 1 1 1 1 1 0	1	1	The result of the TC72 performing its 2's complement. Note that bit 7 of high byte is a logic '1'. This is sent to the PIC and stored in thigh and tlow.
0 0 0 0 0 0 0 1	0	0	We now invert the result
		1	Now add 1. This action does not produce a carry to pass on to the high byte. Therefore, in the program, we only need to invert the thigh.
0 0 0 0 0 0 0 1	0	1	The binary number is back to 1.25

Now when the PIC added the 1 to PIC's inversion, in row6, there was no carry to pass on to the high byte. Therefore in the program we simply need to invert the variable 'thigh.' This is done in line 50.

Now consider the operation on the number -1.50.

High Byte								Low Byte		
0	**0**	**0**	**0**	**0**	**0**	**0**	**1**	**1**	**0**	**This is the 10-bit binary for 1.5**
1	**1**	**1**	**1**	**1**	**1**	**1**	**0**	**0**	**1**	This the 10-bit number inverted
									1	Now add 1
1	**1**	**1**	**1**	**1**	**1**	**1**	**0**	**1**	**0**	The result of the TC72 performing its 2's complement. Note that bit 7 of high byte is a logic '1'. This is sent to the PIC and stored in thigh and tlow.
0	**0**	**0**	**0**	**0**	**0**	**0**	**1**	**0**	**1**	We now invert the result
									1	Now add 1. This action does not produce a carry to pass on to the high byte. Therefore, in the program, we only need to invert the thigh.
0	**0**	**0**	**0**	**0**	**0**	**0**	**1**	**1**	**0**	The binary number is back to 1.5

Again there is no carry to pass on to the high byte. So we need to just invert the variable 'thigh.' This is done in line 56.

Now consider the final possibility: the number -1.75. Note that this is the last possible value in the fractional part. The integer part can be any value, really; it will not change the process.

High Byte								Low Byte		
b7	b6	b5	b4	b3	b2	b1	b0	b7	b6	
0	0	0	0	0	0	0	1	1	1	This is the 10-bit binary 1.75
1	1	1	1	1	1	1	0	0	0	This the 10 bit number inverted
									1	Now add 1
1	1	1	1	1	1	1	0	0	1	The result of the TC72 performing its 2's complement. Note that bit 7 of high byte is a logic '1'. This is sent to the PIC and stored in thigh and tlow.
0	0	0	0	0	0	0	1	1	0	We now invert the result
									1	Now add 1. This action does not produce a carry to pass on to the high byte. Therefore, in the program, we only need to invert the thigh.
0	0	0	0	0	0	0	1	1	1	The binary number is back to 1.75

Again there is no carry to pass on to the high byte. So we need to just invert the variable 'thigh.' This is done in line 62.

This is quite a bit to go through, but it does cover all four possible fractional numbers. It then hopefully explains what we have to do in the program and how the relevant instructions carry them out.

Note that in each of the four responses we are also loading the variable decten and dechun with the relevant values to display the appropriate ASCII on the LCD.

Line 72 is the end of the instructions that must be carried out if the reading from the TC72 is negative. The next section of instructions between lines 73 and 150 are a series of tests to see if the value stored in the variable 'thigh' is between a range of values. These are used to determine what numbers need to be stored in the units, tens, and hundreds columns of the display.

Line 73 if (thigh >= 0 && thigh < 10)

This is a test to see if the value in 'thigh' is between 0 and 9. The thigh > = 0 test is to see if the value is greater than or equal to 0. The thigh < 10 test is to see if 'thigh' is less than 10.

If the result of the test is true, the PIC will carry out the instructions between lines 74 and 78.

Line 75 units = (thigh + 48);

This loads the variable "units" with the value that is in 'thigh,' which will be a value between 0 and 9, to 48. This will make the variable have a value between 48 and 57. These are the ASCII values, in decimal, for the digits 0 to 9.

Line 76 tens = 48;

Line 77 tens = 48;

These load the variable tens and huns with the value 48, which is the ASCII for 0 in decimal. We could have used 0X30 but I wanted to show you that we could describe ASCII values in decimal.

This means if these were displayed, the LCD would show 000 to 009 for the integer part of the display.

Line 79 if (thigh >= 10 && thigh < 20)

This test to see if the value in 'thigh' is between 10 and 20.

Line 81 units = (thigh –10 + 48);

If the test was true, then the value in 'thigh' must be between 10 and 19. This means the units must be between 0 and 9. Therefore, we must –10 from 'thigh' before we add the 48. For example, if the thigh was 12, then with this instruction, units would equal (12 – 10) = 2 + 48 = 50, which is the ASCII for 2.

Line 82 tens = (1 + 48);

This just loads the variable tens with 49, which is the ASCII for '1' in decimal.

Line 83 huns = 48;

This loads huns with the ASCII for '0'.

These instructions would mean that if these values were displayed, the LCD would show 010 to 019.

Lines 85 to 149 carry out the same procedures to determine the correct values for the variable units, tens, and huns to ensure the LCD displays the correct values.

Line 151 if (negbit == 1) writeString ("Temp is -");

This is a test to see if the variable negbit has a value of '1' in it. This would have been loaded into the variable in line 42 if the reading from the TC72 had been negative. If the test is true, the PIC sends the phrase "Temp is -" to the LCD.

If the test were untrue, the PIC would carry out line 152, where it would send the phrase "Temp is". If the test in line 151 is true, then the PIC skips the instruction on line 152.

Line 153 if (huns == 48) goto distens;

This is a test to see if the variable huns has a value of 48, the ASCII for '0', in it. If it has, then we don't need to display this '0' on the screen. Therefore, if the test is true, then the PIC will jump to the label distens.

Line 154 and 155 will send the ASCII stored in the variable huns if the test in line 153 were not true (i.e., the value in huns is not '0').

Line 156 distens: if (tens == 48 && huns == 48) goto disunits;

This test to see if the value in both tens and huns is 48, which would be true if they were both storing the ASCII for '0'. If this is true, then we would not want to display the two 0s before the units. Therefore, the PIC would jump to the label disunits. Line 156 is where the label distens is and so where the PIC would go if the test on line 153 were true.

If this test were untrue, then the PIV would carry out the instructions on lines 157 and 158.

Line 159 disunits: lcdData = units;

This is where the label disunits is. Here we load the variable lcdData with the variable units.

Line 160 is where we send that data to the LCD.

Line 161 is where we load the ASCII for the decimal point. This is then sent to the LCD with line 162.

Lines 163 to 166 send the data in the variables dectens and dechuns to the LCD.

Lines 167 to 174 send the characters °C to the LCD with a space between them.

Line 175 reloads the negbit with the value 0 to reset it.

This then ends the subroutine to convert the binary values into ASCII values that can be displayed in the correct positions on the LCD.

Lines 177 to 190 are the usual instructions to set up the PIC as normal.

Line 191 SSPCON1 = 0X00;

This loads this control register with all logic '0's. This sets the SSPEN, the SSP Enable, bit in the to a logic '0'. This disables the SSP module. We do this before we write to the control registers.

Line 192 SSPCON1bits.CKP =1;

This sets this bit to a logic '1', which sets the idle state of the clock to high. This gets the PIC ready for negative edge triggering.

Line 193 SSPSTAT = 0b00000000;

This loads the SSPSTAT register with all logic '0's. This sets the SMP to logic '0', which means the PIC samples the data in the middle of the data output time. It also sets the CKE to a logic '0', which means the transmit occurs on a transition from idle to active. This is negative edge triggering.

The other bits in the SSPSTAT register are only used in I^2C communication.

Line 194 SSPSTATbits.CKE = 0;

This sets the CKE bit to a logic '0'.

Line 195 SSPCON1bits.SSPEN =1;

This simply turns the SSP module on.

Line 196 setUpTheLCD ();

This calls the subroutine to set up the LCD.

Line 197 while (1)

This sets up the forever loop.

Line 199 units = 0;

This simply loads the variable units with 0.

Line 200 writeString ("TC72 TEMP Sensor");

This calls the subroutine writeString to send the characters stated between the quotation marks to the LCD.

Line 201 line2 ();

This calls the subroutine to send the cursor to the beginning of line 2 on the LCD.

Line 202 PORTCbits.RC0 = 1;

This puts a logic '1' on this bit of PORTC. This output is connected to the CS pin of the TC72 temperature sensor. Therefore, this will turn the TC72 on.

Line 203 SSPBUF = 0X80;

This loads the SSPBUF of the PIC, which is the master, with the data 0X80. Once the SSPBUF is loaded with the eight bits 0b10000000, the master starts the clock and the cycling action of the SPI starts. The binary value 0b10000000 tells the TC72 that we want to write to it.

Line 204 while (!SSPSTATbits.BF);

This gets the PIC to do nothing while the buffer flag, or BF Flag, is a logic '0'. Note that as soon as the master starts to send the data to the TC72, or any slave device, this flag will go to a logic '0'. The flag won't go back to a logic '1' until the SSPBUF has been refilled with eight bits of data. This new eight bits of data will have come from the slave device (i.e., the TC72 in this case). Therefore, this instruction makes the PIC wait until the master has received eight bits back from the slave.

Line 205 dummy = SSPBUF;

In this first instance, the eight bits sent back from the slave will be nonsense. However, we must empty the SSPBUF before it can be refilled by the PIC. This instruction empties the SSPBUF into a temporary location called dummy.

Line 206 SSPBUF = 0X11;

This writes the instruction 0b00010001 to the TC72. This puts it into single-shot mode.

Line 207 waits for the TC72 to fill the SSPBUF with more nonsense.

Line 208 PORTCbits.RC0 = 0;

This sends the CS pin on the TC72 low and so turns it off.

Line 209 gets rid of the nonsense the TC72 has just sent back.

Lone 210 delay (7);

This calls the delay subroutine and sends the value 7 to be loaded into the local variable 't' in that subroutine. This creates a 200ms delay, which is needed to ensure that the TC72 does respond to the command we have just sent.

With line 211, we turn the TC72 back on.

Line 212 SSPBUF = 0X02;

This loads the SSPBUF with the address of the data 0X02. This action also gets the PIC to start the cycle to send this data to the TC72. This is the address of the high byte of the temperature reading that the PIC wants to read from. Note that bit 7 is a logic '0', which tells the TC72 we want to read from it.

Line 212 will force the slave to send more nonsense back to the PIC. Line 213 waits for that data to load in the PIC's SSPBUF.

Line 214 allows the PIC to get rid of this nonsense byte. However, after the TC72 has emptied its SSPBUF of the nonsense it has just sent back, the TC72 will load the value of the temperature reading that was stored in the address 0X02. This then gets the TC72 ready to send this reading back to the master.

Line 215 SSPBUF = 0x00;

This loads the PIC's SSPBUF with the data 0x00. This has no meaning but it must be loaded into the PIC's SSPBUF to start the SPI cycling process. This will force the TC72 to send the contents of its SSPBUF to the PIC. However, this will not be nonsense; it will be the temperature reading from the high byte of the TC72.

Line 216 gets the PIC to wait until its SSPBUF has been filled.

Line 217 thigh = SSPBUF;

This loads the variable 'thigh' with the data in the SSPBUF. This is the integer part of the current temperature reading from the TC72.

Line 218 reloads the PIC's SSPBUF with data that has no meaning. This starts the SPI cycling process, and the TC72 will send back to the PIC what was now in the SSPBUF of the TC72. This will be the fractional part of the temperature reading that was stored in the low byte address, OX01. Note that the TC72 loaded this into its SSPBUF automatically after it had sent the previous high byte to the PIC.

Line 220 tlow = SSPBUF;

After waiting for the SSPBUF in the PIC to load with the new data from the TC72, the PIC loads the contents of the SSPBUF into the variable 'tlow'. The PIC now has the integer part of the temperature reading in the variable 'thigh'. It also has the fractional part of the reading in the variable 'tlow'.

Line 221 simply turns the TC72 off, as we have finished with it for now.

Line 222 convert ();

This calls the subroutine convert. This subroutine will convert the binary numbers in 'thigh' and 'tlow' into ASCII that can be displayed correctly on the LCD.

Line 223 sendcursorhome ();

This calls the subroutine to send the cursor to the start of the first line on the LCD.

Lines 224 and 225 are the closing curly brackets of the while (1) and main loops.

This has been, in parts, a complex analysis, but I hope you have found it useful. I hope it shows you that to write a program to control any device, you need to fully understand how that device works. Then, to come up with the instructions to do the work, you may have to call upon a thorough understanding of some basic operations. But that is the challenge and excitement of embedded programming.

One final item I should mention is that I sometimes add some extra instructions to help in debugging the program. I have done that with this listing, and I have left them in to show you the concept of how I do this. The two instructions are

Line 44 PORTA = thigh;

Line 45 PORTD = tlow;

I have inserted these two instructions so that I could monitor what is actually going into these two important variables. I could then see if they were what I thought they should be. This is quite a useful idea that I use a lot in debugging my programs. I thought you might like the idea.

The next program will use the same SPI interface to control the same TC72 temperature sensor, but it will use the sprintf function to send the data to the LCD. I am including this program just so that you can make a comparison between the two approaches. The comparison we will make is in how much memory the two approaches will use. To that end, I have looked at the memory usage of this first approach. It is displayed in the screenshot shown in Figure 9-4.

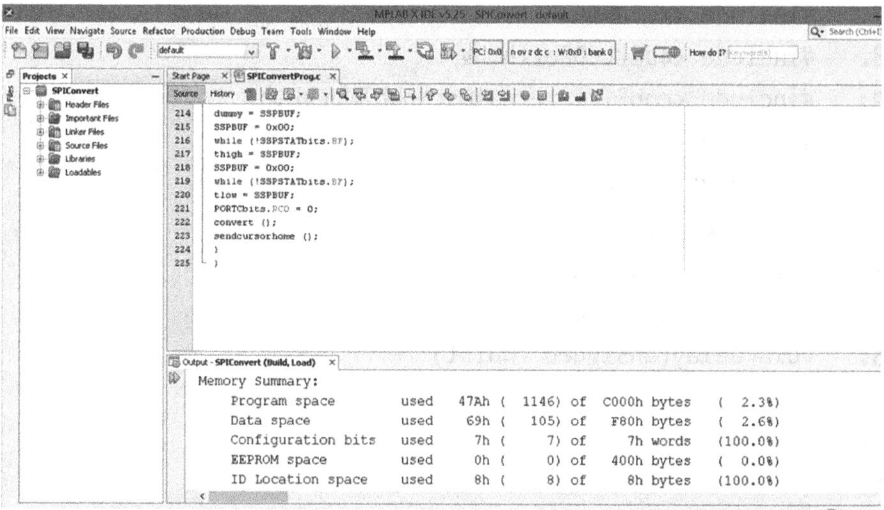

Figure 9-4. *The screen showing memory usage for the convert method*

We will discuss this figure later when we compare the two methods.

Using the Sprintf Function

The sprintf function is a freely available function written to convert decimal values into the ASCII and then send them to a LCD. It is with the studio.h header file. Listing 9-2 is the alternative program for displaying the temperature reading from the TC72 temperature sensor. We will compare this approach with the one shown in Listing 9-1.

Listing 9-2. TC72 Program Using the Sprintf Function

```
/*
 * File:   tempSensor|SPI.c
Author: hward
*
Created on 02 November 2017, 11:02
*/
```

```
#include <xc.h>
#include <4bitLCDPortb.h>
#include <conFigInternalOscNoWDTNoLVP.h>
#include <stdio.h>
//some variables
unsigned char dummy, thigh, tlow ;
float sysTemperature, decvalue;
//some subroutines
void delay(unsigned char t)
{
for (n = 0; n < t; n++)
{
TMR0 = 0;
while (TMR0 < 225);
}
}
void displayTemp(float dp)
{
sprintf(str, "%.2f OC   ", dp);
writeString(str);
}
void displayTempNeg(float dp)
{
sprintf(str, "-%.2f OC   ", dp);
writeString(str);
}
void main ()
{
PORTA = 0;
PORTB = 0;
PORTC = 0;
```

```
PORTD = 0;
TRISA = 0;
TRISB = 0;
TRISC = 0b00010000;
TRISD = 0;
ADCON0 = 0;
ADCON1 = 0X0F;
OSCCON = 0X74;
T0CON = 0XC7;
SSPCON1 = 0X00;
SSPCON1bits.CKP =1;
SSPSTAT = 0b00000000;
SSPCON1bits.SSPEN =1;
setUpTheLCD ();
while (1)
{
writeString ("The Temp is");
line2 ();
PORTCbits.RC0 = 1;
SSPBUF = 0X80;
while (!SSPSTATbits.BF);
dummy = SSPBUF;
SSPBUF = 0X11;
while (!SSPSTATbits.BF);
PORTCbits.RC0 = 0;
dummy = SSPBUF;
delay(7);
PORTCbits.RC0 = 1;
SSPBUF = 0X02;
while (!SSPSTATbits.BF);
dummy = SSPBUF;
```

```
SSPBUF = 0x00;
while (!SSPSTATbits.BF);
thigh = SSPBUF;
SSPBUF = 0x00;
while (!SSPSTATbits.BF);
tlow = SSPBUF;
PORTCbits.RC0 = 0;
decvalue = 0;
if (thigh & 0b10000000)
{
tlow = ~tlow + 1;
if (tlow == 0b01000000)
{
decvalue = 0.25;
thigh = (~thigh);
}
if (tlow == 0b10000000)
{
decvalue = 0.5;
thigh = (~thigh);
}
if (tlow == 0b11000000)
{
decvalue = 0.75;
thigh = (~thigh);
}
else if (tlow == 0b00000000)
{
decvalue = 0;
thigh = (~thigh +1);
}
```

```
100.    sysTemperature = thigh + decvalue;
101.    displayTempNeg(sysTemperature);
102.    }
103.    else
104.    {
105.    if (tlow == 0b01000000) decvalue = 0.25;
106.    if (tlow == 0b10000000)  decvalue = 0.5;
107.    if (tlow == 0b11000000)  decvalue = 0.75;
108.    sysTemperature = thigh + decvalue;
109.    displayTemp(sysTemperature);
110.    }
111.    sendcursorhome ();
112.    }
113.    }
```

Analysis of Listing 9-2

There are really no new instructions to look at, but we will look at the difference between this listing and Listing 9-1.

The convert subroutine in Listing 9-1 has been removed, as we are using the sprintf function to display the readings.

The first sprintf subroutine, named displayTemp, is between lines 23 and 27. Most of the instructions have already been looked at; however, we can look at the following instruction:

Line 25 sprintf(str, "%.2f OC ", dp);

This is the normal sprintf function, but I have included the 'OC' (for degrees Celsius) inside the brackets. Placing it after the %.2f means that the function will display the reading value first and then the 'OC'. I have inserted some empty spaces after the 'OC' so that as the display changes when we go from units, to tens and units, and then to hundreds, tens, and units and back again, the display does rub out any spare 'OC' characters. Try removing these spaces and see what happens.

The number 2 after the '%.' defines the number of values after the decimal point. This is set for two places after the decimal point.

The sprintf subroutine, named displayTempNeg, is between lines 28 and 32. This is the same except it is for displaying negative readings.

Line 30 sprintf(str, "-%.2f OC ", dp);

This instruction accommodates the negative display by adding the '-' minus sign. This is placed between the two quotation marks but before the '%.2f,' as we want to display the minus sign before the temperature readings.

The next main change in the listing is between lines 78 and 100. We will look at some of the changes here.

Line 79 tlow = ~tlow + 1;

The first thing we do is perform the 2's complement on the variable 'tlow.' This is because, as the reading is now negative, the TC72 would have performed its own 2's complement before it sent both the high byte and the low byte to the PIC. This was also done in Listing 9-1.

Now follow four "if" type tests on the data now stored in 'tlow.'

Line 80 if (tlow == 0b01000000)

This test is to see if the data in 'tlow' is 0b01000000. If the test is true, the PIC will carry out the following two instructions. As there are two instructions (i.e., more than one), they need to be listed between opening and closing brackets.

Line 82 decvalue = 0.25;

This loads the variable decvalue with the value 0.25. The variable decvalue has been declared as a float type, because it will store numbers with decimal points, in line 13. This variable is used to store the fractional part of the reading so that it can be added to the total value later.

Line 83 thigh = (~thigh);

This simply inverts the binary number in the variable thigh. Note that we don't add the 1 as in a full 2's complement. The reasoning for this has been described in the analysis of Listing 9-1.

Lines 85 to 89 do the same for the 0.5 value.

Lines 90 to 94 do the same for the 0.75 value.

Line 95 else if (tlow == 0b00000000)

This is the test we carry out if none of the previous three tests are true. This is to manage the display when the fractional part is 0.

Line 97 decvalue = 0;

This loads decvalue with the value 0.

Line 98 thigh = (~thigh +1);

This performs a complete 2's complement on the variable 'thigh'; note that we do add the '1.' The reasoning for this has been explained in the analysis of Listing 9-1.

Line 100 sysTemperature = thigh + decvalue;

This now loads the float type variable "sysTemperature" with the contents of 'thigh,' the integer part of the reading, but with the contents of decvalue, the fractional part of the reading, added to it. This now gets the variable sysTemperature ready to be sent to the display.

Line 101 displayTempNeg(sysTemperature);

This calls the subroutine displayTempNeg and sends the variable sysTemperature up to it. Inside that subroutine, the contents of the variable displayTempNeg are loaded into the local variable 'dp.' This is then used in the sprintf function.

Lines 104 to 110 are carried out if the temperature reading sent back from the TC72 is not negative. The first three lines, 105, 106, and 107, check the contents of the variable 'tlow' to determine if they need to change the contents of decvalue to either 0.25, 0.5, or 0.75. Note that there is no need to perform a 2's complement, either full or partial, on the variable 'thigh,' as the reading is positive not negative.

Line 109 displayTemp(sysTemperature);

After adding the 'thigh' and the 'decvalue' together in line 108, the PIC calls the subroutine 'sysTemperature' to display the positive reading.

Line 111 sendcursorhome ();

Finally, this calls the subroutine to send the cursor back to the beginning of the display.

We will look at the memory usage of this approach. Figure 9-5 is the screenshot displaying this memory usage.

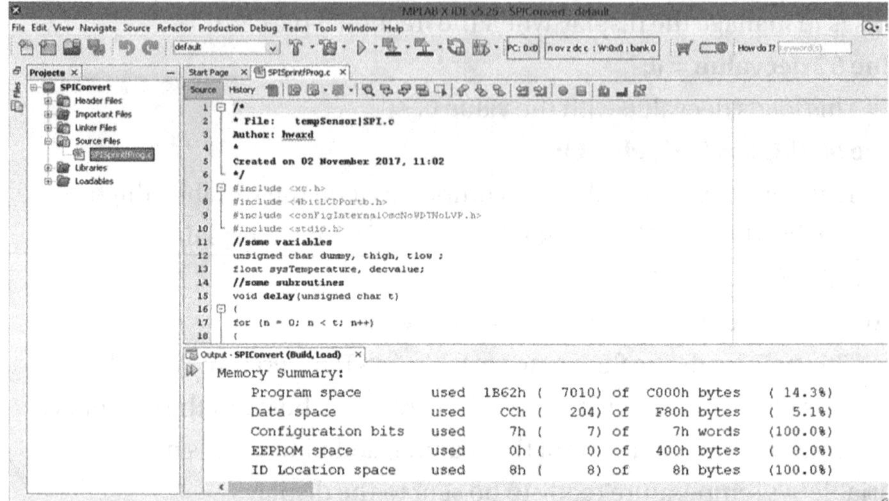

***Figure 9-5.** The screen showing memory usage for the sprintf method*

Comparing the Two Approaches

Whenever we have two or more approaches to doing something, we should compare the two and then, hopefully, come up with a decision as to which approach is best.

When we first look at the two approaches, which I will call "convert" for Listing 9-1 and "sprintf" for Listing 9-2, we can see that convert uses 225 lines of programming, whereas sprintf uses 113. Surely this suggests that the sprintf is much more efficient, as it uses approximately 50% lines of programming compared to convert.

Well, you should appreciate that in using the sprintf function, which is inside the stdio.h header file, the linker program, inside MPLABX, will look for that header file and add it to the program instructions that it needs from that header file, when the compiler compiles it. Therefore, this simple line count may not be the best way to compare the two approaches. A better approach would be to look at how much of the PIC's memory do the two approaches use. MPLABX does show us the memory usage when we compile the program. This is shown in the output window. You may have to scroll up a bit in that window to find it.

I have shown the memory usage for both programs in Figures 9-4 and 9-5. They show the following results:

```
Memory Summary:
    Program space        used   47Ah (  1146) of  C000h bytes   (  2.3%)
    Data space           used    69h (   105) of   F80h bytes   (  2.6%)
    Configuration bits   used     7h (     7) of     7h words   (100.0%)
    EEPROM space         used     0h (     0) of   400h bytes   (  0.0%)
    ID Location space    used     8h (     8) of     8h bytes   (100.0%)
```

Figure 9-6. *Memory usage convert*

```
Memory Summary:
    Program space        used  1B62h (  7010) of  C000h bytes   ( 14.3%)
    Data space           used    CCh (   204) of   F80h bytes   (  5.1%)
    Configuration bits   used     7h (     7) of     7h words   (100.0%)
    EEPROM space         used     0h (     0) of   400h bytes   (  0.0%)
    ID Location space    used     8h (     8) of     8h bytes   (100.0%)
```

Figure 9-7. *Memory usage sprintf*

By comparing these usages in Figures 9-6 and 9-7, we can see that the convert uses 2.6% of program space and 2.3% of data space, whereas the sprintf uses 14.3% of program space and 5.5% of data space. My explanation for this difference is that the convert approach is very precise, in that I only consider the actions that I know are needed to do what I want. However, the sprintf has to be much more versatile, as it cannot guarantee what is going to be asked of it. However, I do think that the convert approach is much more efficient, as the sprintf uses around 550% more memory. I won't say this is definitive proof, but I am convinced; you guys can make your own mind up.

Really, I do think you can only become a better embedded programmer if you write all your own instructions. It is worth the effort, and really it's not too much of an effort in any case.

Using the PIC18f4525 as the Slave

This final program, on using the SPI, will look at using two PICs to communicate with each other using the SPI module. This will require one PIC being set up as the master and the other PIC being set up as the slave.

The slave's program will just keep an LED, connected to bit 0 of PORTD, flashing on for half a second and off for half a second. The slave will respond when the master PIC wants to send data to the slave. When the master sends data to the slave, the slave will display this data on the LCD connected to PORTB.

The master will have just one function, which is when one of four switches are momentarily sent to a logic '1', the data 3, 4, 5, or 6 will be sent to the slave. To verify what data has been sent and received, the master will display the data to be sent to the slave on the LCD connected to PORTB, and it will display the data the slave sends back to the master, which is really rubbish, on PORTD.

Listing 9-3 is the master program, and Listing 9-4 is the slave program.

Listing 9-3. The Master Program

```
/*
File: PIctoPICSPIProg.c
Author: H Ward
Created on 06 June 2021, 17:18
*/
#include <xc.h>
#include <conFigInternalOscNoWDTNoLVP.h>
```

```
#include <4bitLCDPortb.h>
//some definitions
    #define sspin           PORTCbits.RC2
    //some variables
    unsigned char n, dummy, setTime = 9;
    unsigned char rxData[12];
    void setupMSSP ()
    {
    SSPCON1bits.SSPEN =0;
    SSPSTAT = 0b00000000;
    SSPSTATbits.SMP = 0;
    SSPSTATbits.CKE = 0;
    SSPCON1 = 0X00;
    SSPCON1bits.CKP =0;
    SSPCON1bits.SSPEN =1;
    }
    void sendToSlave (unsigned char spiData)
    {
    send: SSPBUF = spiData;
    if (SSPCON1bits.WCOL)
    {
    SSPCON1bits.WCOL = 0;
    goto send;
    }
    while (!SSPSTATbits.BF);
    PORTD = SSPBUF;
    }
    void delay (unsigned char t)
    {
    for (n = 0; n < t; n++ )
```

```
{
TMR0 = 0;
while (TMR0 < 255);
}
}
//The main program
void main ()
{
PORTA = 0;
PORTB = 0;
PORTC = 0;
PORTD = 0;
TRISA = 0b00001111;
TRISB = 0x00;
TRISC = 0b10010000;
TRISD = 0x00;
ADCON0 = 0b00000000;
ADCON1 = 0b00001111;
OSCTUNE = 0x80;
OSCCON = 0x70;
T0CON = 0XC7;
setupMSSP ();
setUpTheLCD ();
sspin = 0;
writeString ("The Master");
while (1)
{
line2 ();
delay (7);
if (PORTAbits.RA0) setTime = 3;
if (PORTAbits.RA1) setTime = 4;
```

```
69.        if (PORTAbits.RA2) setTime = 5;
70.        if (PORTAbits.RA3) setTime = 6;
71.        lcdData  = setTime + 48;
72.        lcdOut();
73.        sendToSlave (setTime);
74.        }
75.        }
```

Analysis of Listing 9-3

There are no real new instructions, so we will look at the more important ones.

There is a subroutine to set up the MSSP module. This is defined within lines 14 and 23. Line 16 turns the module off so that it can be configured.

Line 20 SSPCON1 = 0X00;

This ensures all the bits in the SSPCON1 register are set to logic '0'. This sets this PIC to operate as a master; bits 3, 2, 1, and 0 are all logic '0'. It also sets the idle state, as the low level, bit CKP, bit 4, is a logic '0'.

Line 21 SSPCON1bits.CKP =0;

This is not really needed, but it shows you how you can change the state of just this one bit.

Line 22 SSPCON1bits.SSPEN =1;

This just turns the module back on.

Lines 24 to 34 set up a subroutine to send data to the slave. It expects the program to send a byte of data to the subroutines when it is called. This will then be loaded into the local variable spiData. This will be used in the subroutine.

Line 26 send: SSPBUF = spiData;

This creates the label "send", which is used in the subroutine. It then loads the SSPBUF with the data in the variable spiData. This action will then start the SPI cycle.

Line 27 if (SSPCON1bits.WCOL)

This checks to see if a collision has occurred. If a collision has occurred, then this bit will go to a logic '1' automatically. A collision occurs if data is attempted to be loaded onto the SSPBUF while the PIC is still transmitting the last byte of data. The PIC would then carry out the two instructions listed between lines 28 and 31.

Line 29 SSPCON1bits.WCOL = 0;

This simply clears the WCOL bit.

Line 30 goto send;

This sends the PIC back to line 26.

Line 32 while (!SSPSTATbits.BF);

This gets the PIC to wait until the slave has filled the SSPBUF with the byte it sends back to the PIC in the SPI cycle.

Lines 67 to 70 test to see if any of the four switches at the inputs have gone to a logic '1'. If any have, then their respective values will be loaded into the variable setTime.

Line 71 lcdData = setTime + 48;

This loads a copy of the data in the variable setTime but adds the value 48 to it before doing so. The number 48 is the ASCII for 0. In hexadecimal, this is 0X30. This is required to ensure that the data sent to the LCD in the next instruction will be the correct ASCII for the required number to be displayed.

Line 72 lcdOut ();

This calls the subroutine lcdOut, which sends the data in lcdData to be displayed on the LCD.

Line 73 sendToSlave (setTime);

This calls the subroutine and sends the data stored in the setTime variable to the slave.

The slave PIC is shown in Listing 9-4.

Listing 9-4. Slave Program

```
/*This is a basic program to use the SPI module in the PIC 18F4525 to write
to a pic18f4525 that is used as a slave
u1 is the master U2 is the slave
Written by H H Ward dated 06/06/21. */
#include <xc.h>
#include <conFigInternalOscNoWDTNoLVP.h>
#include <4bitLCDPortb.h>
//some definitions
#define sspin           PORTCbits.RC2
//some variables
unsigned char dummy, setTime, dataTemp;
unsigned char rxData[12];
void setupMSSP ()
{
SSPCON1bits.SSPEN =0;
SSPSTAT = 0b00000000;
SSPSTATbits.SMP = 0;
SSPSTATbits.CKE = 0;
SSPCON1 = 0b00000100;
SSPCON1bits.CKP =0;
SSPCON1bits.SSPEN =1;
}
void delay (unsigned char t)
{
for (n = 0; n < t; n++ )
{
TMR0 = 0;
while (TMR0 < 255);
}
```

```
}
//The main program
void main ()
{
PORTA = 0;
PORTB = 0;
PORTC = 0;
PORTD = 0;
TRISA = 0b00100000;
TRISB = 0x00;
TRISC = 0b10011000;
TRISD = 0x00;
ADCON0 = 0b00000000;
ADCON1 = 0b00001111;
OSCTUNE = 0x80;
OSCCON = 0x70;
T0CON = 0XC7;
setupMSSP ();
setUpTheLCD ();
writeString ("The Slave");
while (1)
{
PORTBbits.RB0 ^=1;
delay(15);
line2 ();
if(BF)
{
dataTemp = SSPBUF ;
SSPBUF = 0XFF;
lcdData = dataTemp + 0X30;
lcdOut();
```

```
61.    }
62.    }
63.    }
```

Analysis of Listing 9-4

This is fundamentally the same as Listing 9-3. Here are the important instructions.

Line 19 SSPCON1 = 0b00000100;

It is bits 3, 2, 1, and 0 that set the mode of operation for the MSSP module; see Table 9-4. It sets this PIC up as the slave device.

Lines 52 PORTDbits.RD0 ^=1;

This gets the PIC to perform a logical EXOR operation with the state of bit 0 of PORTD and a logic '1'. This will set the bit to a logic '1' if it is currently at a logic '0'. It would also be set it to a logic '0' if it was currently at a logic '1'. This simply makes the bit flash.

Line 53 delay (15);

This calls the delay subroutine and loads the value 15 into the local variable 't' inside the subroutine. This will create an approximately 0.5-second delay.

Line 55 if (BF)

This asks if the SSPBUF has been filled. This would have happened if the master had sent data to the slave.

Line 57 dataTemp = SSPBUF;

This stores the data that was sent by the master into the variable dataTemp.

Line 58 SSPBUF = 0XFF;

This loads the SSPBUF with data 0XFF. This is the rubbish that will be sent to the master when the master starts the SPI cycle again.

Line 59 lcdData = dataTemp + 0X30;

This loads the variable lcdData with the value in the variable dataTemp but with the value 0X30 added to it first. This gets the PIC ready to send the correct ASCII for the number to be displayed.

Line 60 lcdOut ();

This sends the data to the LCD.

I hope the analysis is enough for you to understand how these programs work.

The circuit for this PIC-to-PIC program is shown in Figure 9-8, and Figure 9-9 shows the program working. The only real difference is that I have used the PICDEM board for the master and so I have had to use bit 0 of PORTB for the flashing LED (see line 52 in the program listing).

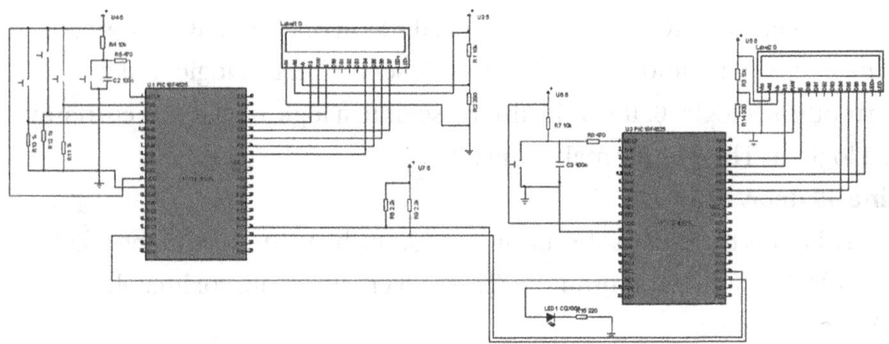

***Figure 9-8.** The circuit for PIC-to-PIC using SPI*

The two resistors R6 and R9 are there as pull ups to ensure the SDO and SDI lines do pull up the logic '1' correctly.

Figure 9-9. *The PIC-to-PIC communication using SPI*

Summary

In this chapter, we have studied how you can set up the MSSP module to operate with the SPI communication between a master and a slave. We have learned how the TC72 temperature sensor works and can communicate to a PIC using the SPI interface. We have studied 2's complement and how it can be used to represent negative numbers. We have studied how 2's complement can be implemented with a PIC program and how it allows the PIC to deal with negative readings from the TC72.

We then went on to learn how we can set the PIC up as a slave and so communicate with another PIC which was set up as its master. I hope you have found this chapter useful and appreciate the importance of understanding the instructions you use.

In the next chapter, we will look at the two other methods of communication with PIC: I^2C and the UART. We will use the PIC to use the TC74 temperature sensor and some external EEPROM. Both devices will use the I^2C protocol.

CHAPTER 10

Using the I^2C Protocol

In this chapter, we are going to look at using the I^2C communication protocol. We will study the 24LC256, a serial EEPROM that uses I^2C, and the TC74, a temperature sensor that also uses the I^2C protocol. We will create a program that will communicate with both these devices using the PIC as the master device.

After reading this chapter, you will know how the I^2C protocol works and how to set it up with the PIC. You will also learn how to use the TC74 temperature sensor and how to use the 24LC256 EEPROM. You should also learn what an EEPROM is and why we use them.

I^2C Communication Protocol

I^2C stands for inter-integrated circuit, a protocol designed by Phillips back in 1982. It is a synchronous serial communication setup that only uses two wires: the SDA and the SCL. That is why it is sometimes referred to as TWI (two-wire interface). It can be served by multiple masters and have multiple slaves on the bus. A simple setup is shown in Figure 10-1.

H. H. Ward, *Programming Arduino Projects with the PIC Microcontroller*,
https://doi.org/10.1007/978-1-4842-7230-5_10

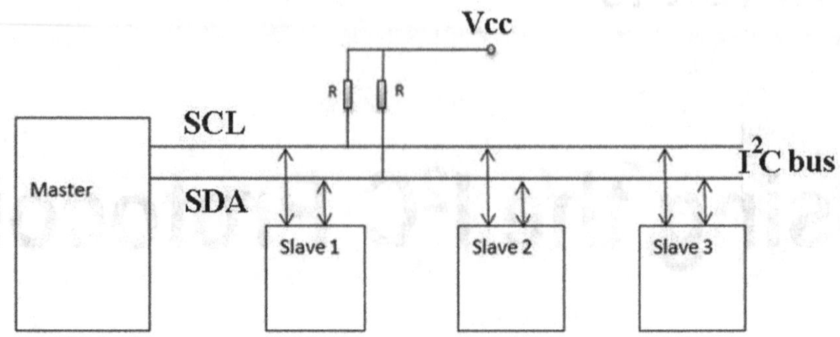

Figure 10-1. *A typical I²C bus*

The fact that it requires only two wires is an advantage over the SPI communication system we looked at in chapter 9. However, there are some extra aspects that make this protocol more rigorous.

EEPROM

The EEPROM is used for permanent storage of data. This EEPROM is an external device, but some PICS, and the PIC18F4525 is one of them, have some internal EEPROM memory. The term EEPROM comes initially from ROM (read-only memory). This was used for storing the BIOS programs of the system. They use nonvolatile memory, which is memory that does not lose its data when the power is removed.

The ROM then went to PROM (programmable ROM). This meant it could be programmed by the user, as well as the manufacturer, with data that would be permanently stored.

Then we went to EPROM, which added the term "erasable". This now meant the program or data could be erased so that you could reprogram it. The only problem with the EPROM was that you had to use an ultraviolet light to erase it.

Finally, we have reached EEPROM, which adds the term "electrically". This means the memory could be erased by sending the appropriate electrical signal to it. This now made the EEPROM a very useful type of memory, as it can be used for permanent storage of important data you don't want to lose if the power is removed. However, you can now easily change the contents, making it much more useful.

24LC256 EEPROM

This is a 32k by eight-bit serial EEPROM manufactured by Microchip. It conforms to the I²C protocol and comes in an eight-pin dual inline package as well as other packages. The packages are shown in Figure 10-2.

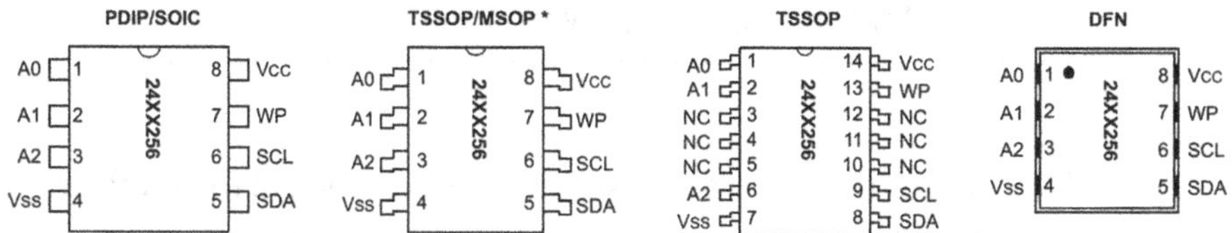

Figure 10-2. *The available packages for the 24LC256*

We will use the PDIP dual inline package.

The pin usage is detailed in Table 10-1.

Table 10-1. The Pin Usage for the 24LC256 EEPROM

Pin Number	Usage
1	A0: the first of the three address lines
2	A1: the second of the three address lines
3	A2: the third of the three address lines
4	VSS: the ground terminal
5	SDA: the data terminal; it can be input for data coming into the device and output for data going out of it
6	SCL: the clock input terminal
7	WP: the write protect terminal
8	VCC: the positive supply terminal

The 24LC256 uses the three address lines A0, A1, and A2 to enable a maximum of eight EEPROMs to be addressed separately from the same master.

The WP can be used to prevent any accidental writing to the EEPROM. This pin is active high, which means if it is at a logic '1,' then the EEPROM cannot be written to.

The 24LC256 needs only two connections to communicate with the master. They are

- The SCL, which supplies the clock signal from the master to the slave.
- The SDA, which acts as the data input to the 24LC256 when the master is writing to it. It also acts as the data output when the 24LC256 is sending data to the master.

Writing to the EEPROM

To write to the 24LC256, the master must send a start bit, which is a transition from high to low while the clock signal is high. This start bit is followed by a control byte. The first four bits of this byte will be the control code, which is 1010. The next three bits are the address bits of the EEPROM: A0, A1, and A2. They must match the logic that is connected to these three address pins on the actual EEPROM. The final bit is used to determine if the master will be writing to the EEPROM or reading from it. If this bit is a logic '1,' then the master will be reading from the EEPROM. If this bit is a logic '0,' then the master will be writing to the EEPROM. As we are writing to the EEPROM, this bit must be a logic '0.'

The selected slave will now generate an acknowledge bit which sends the SDA line low, while the ninth clock pulse that master generates is high. This acknowledge bit will be created after each byte has been transmitted from the master.

The master will now send the high byte of the 16-bit address that it wants to write to or read from. Note that as this is a 32KB device, it really only needs 15 address lines. This means that the MSB of this high byte is of no importance. The slave will again acknowledge this byte.

The master then sends the low byte of the address and the slave acknowledges this byte.

The master will now send the byte of data that it wants to write to the selected address. The slave will acknowledge this byte.

The master now sends a stop bit, which is a low-to-high transition of the SDA line, while the SCL line is high.

This sequence of actions for the write operation is shown in Figure 10-3.

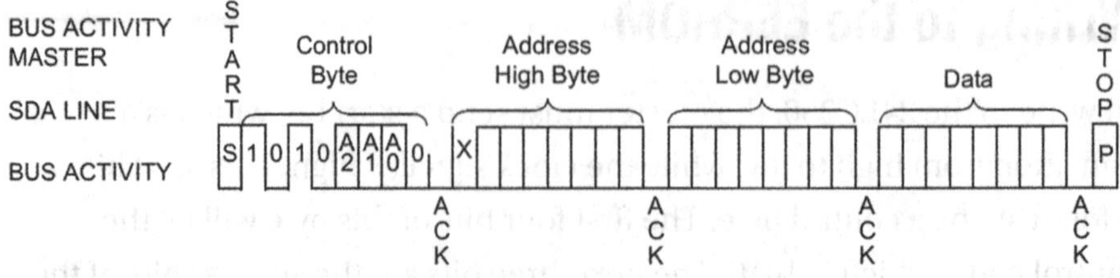

Figure 10-3. *The write operation*

You can write to more than one address in the EEPROM at a time by simply sending more data after the acknowledgment of the first data and before the master sends the stop bit. The EEPROM will automatically open up the next memory location after each byte of data has been written to it.

Reading from the EEPROM

The master will first send the same start bit, followed by the control byte with the address of the slave. The final bit of this control byte is set to logic '0', as with a write operation. This is still a write operation because the master must first write the address of where it wants to start the read operation from.

After the slave has acknowledged the control byte, the master will send the high byte and low byte of this address the master wants to start reading from. Now the slave will send an acknowledge bit, after which the master must send a new start bit. This is followed by the same control and slave address information. However, the final bit of this new control byte is set to a logic '1', signifying the master wants to read from the address that has just been sent to the slave.

Then, after the slave has acknowledged this new control byte, the slave will put the requested data on the SDA bus. This data is followed by a NOT acknowledge bit and the master then sends a stop bit. This read operation is shown in Figure 10-4.

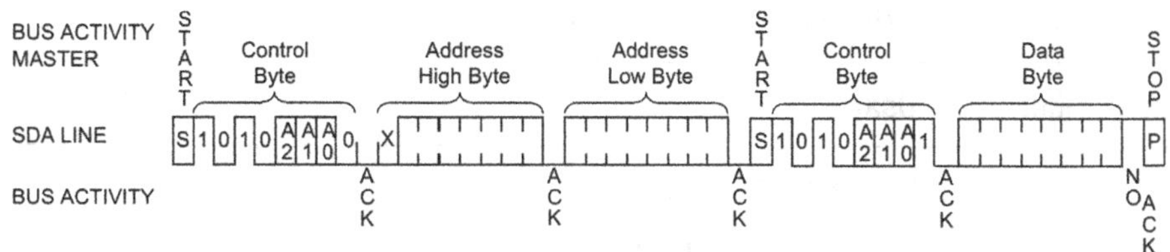

Figure 10-4. *The read operation*

Again, you can read from more than one address at a time by simply requesting more data before you send the NOT ack and stop bit. The EEPROM will automatically open up the next memory location after each byte of data has been read from it.

TC74 Temperature Sensor

This is a temperature sensor manufactured by Microchip. It comes in a five-pin TO22 package, which is the type I use, or a five-pin SOT-23A package. These are shown in Figure 10-5.

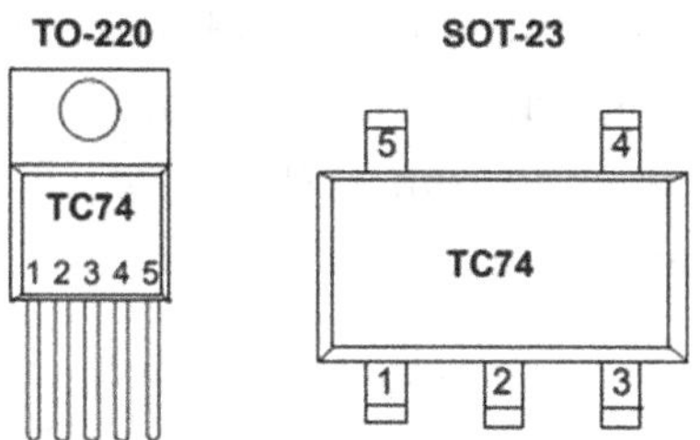

Figure 10-5. *The packaging for the TC74*

The pin usage is detailed in Table 10-2.

Table 10-2. The Pin Usage for the TC74

Pin Number	Usage
1	NC: No connection
2	SDA: Data in and out
3	GND Note: with the TO-220 the outer tab is connected to ground
4	SCL: The clock input
5	VCC: The positive supply

Communication is similar to that of the EEPROM and normally it is just a read operation. However, there may be times when you need to write to the TC74.

Reading the Temperature

To read the current temperature that the TC74 has just acquired, the master must write the code 0X00 to the TC74. This means that the master must first tell the TC74 it is writing a command. Then, the master must tell the TC74 it wants to be reading from it. The TC74 will then respond with the temperature reading. The process is as follows:

1. The master sends a start bit to the slave.
2. The master then sends the seven-bit address of the TC74. This defaults to 1001 101. There are seven other addresses, but these must be set up by Microchip.
3. The master then sets the eighth bit of the address byte to a logic '0' to indicate it is writing to the TC74.

4. The master then waits for the acknowledge bit from the slave.
5. The master then sends the command byte 0X00.
6. The master then waits for the acknowledge bit from the slave.
7. The master then issues another start bit.
8. This is then followed with the 1001 101 address, byte, but this time the eighth bit is set to a logic '1' to indicate the master wants to read from the TC74.
9. The master then waits for the acknowledge bit.
10. The TC74 will then send eight bits that represent the temperature reading.
11. The master must respond with the NOT acknowledge bit and the stop bit.

This process is shown in Figure 10-6.

S	Address	WR	ACK	Command	ACK	S	Address	RD	ACK	Data	NACK	P
	7 Bits			8 Bits			7 Bits			8 Bits		
	1001 101	0		0000 0000			1001 101	1				

Figure 10-6. *Reading the temperature*

Using I²C with 24LC256 and TC74

Listing 10-1 will demonstrate how this protocol can be used to communicate with a serial EEPROM and a temperature sensor.

Listing 10-1. I^{2}C Protocol

```
/*
* File:   12cEEPROMPIC18F4525Prog.c
Author: Mr H. H. Ward
*
Created on 25 July 2018, 13:19
*/
#include <xc.h>
#include <stdio.h>
#include <conFigInternalOscNoWDTNoLVP.h>
#include <4BitLCDDemoBoard.h>
// declare any variables
unsigned char a,b, i, disData, temp, tempr, thigh, tlow, adhigh, adlow;
float sysTemperature;
unsigned char rxData[12];
unsigned char dataout [8] =
{
0x41,
0x6E,
0x6E,
0x2C,
0x57,
0x61,
0x72,
0x64,
};
//declare any subroutines
void ms13delay (unsigned char (t))
```

```
{
for (n = 0; n <t; n++)
{
TMR0 = 0;
while (TMR0 < 255);
}
}
void MSSP2CInit()
{
SSPCON1 = 0x28;
SSPCON2 = 0x00;
SSPSTAT = 0x00;
SSPADD =  0x13;
TRISCbits.RC3 = 1;
TRISCbits.RC4 = 1;
}
void MSSP2Cidle()
{
while ((SSPSTAT & 0x04) || (SSPCON2 & 0x1F));
}
void MSSP2Cwait()
{
while(!PIR1bits.SSPIF);
PIR1bits.SSPIF=0;
}
void MSSP2CStart()
{
MSSP2Cidle();
SSPCON2bits.SEN = 1;
}
```

```
void MSSP2CStop()
{
MSSP2Cidle();
SSPCON2bits.PEN = 1;
}
void MSSP2CRestart()
{
MSSP2Cidle();
SSPCON2bits.RSEN = 1;
}
void MSSP2CNACK()
{
MSSP2Cidle();
SSPCON2bits.ACKDT = 1;
SSPCON2bits.ACKEN = 1;
}
void MSSP2CWrite(unsigned char data)
{
MSSP2Cidle();
SEND: SSPBUF=data;
MSSP2Cidle();
while(SSPCON2bits.ACKSTAT)
{
SSPCON2bits.RSEN=1;
MSSP2Cwait();
goto SEND;
}
}
//-----------------------------------------------------
```

```
unsigned char MSSP2Cread()
{
SSPCON2bits.RCEN=1;
while(!BF);
SSPCON2bits.RCEN=0;
return SSPBUF;
}
unsigned char MSSP2CreadNAck()
{
SSPCON2bits.RCEN=1;
while(!BF);
SSPCON2bits.RCEN=0;
SSPCON2bits.ACKDT=1;
SSPCON2bits.ACKEN=1;
MSSP2Cwait();
return SSPBUF;
}
void writeToEEPROM(unsigned char adhigh, unsigned char
adlow, unsigned char edata)
{
MSSP2Cidle();
MSSP2CStart();
MSSP2CWrite(0xA0);
MSSP2CWrite(adhigh);
MSSP2CWrite(adlow);
MSSP2CWrite(edata);
MSSP2CStop();
//ms13delay (2);
}
```

```
unsigned char readFromEEPROM(unsigned char adhigh,
unsigned char adlow)
{
MSSP2CIdle();
MSSP2CStart();
MSSP2CWrite(0XA0);
MSSP2CWrite(adhigh);
MSSP2CWrite(adlow);
MSSP2CRestart();
MSSP2CWrite(0xA1);
temp = MSSP2CreadNAck ();
MSSP2CStop();
return temp;
}
void displayTemp(float dp)
{
sprintf(str, "%.1f OC   ", dp);
writeString(str);
}
void displayTempNeg(float dp)
{
sprintf(str, "-%.1f OC   ", dp);
writeString(str);
}
void main()
{
PORTA = 0;
PORTB = 0;
PORTC = 0;
PORTD = 0;
TRISA = 0XFF;
```

```
TRISB = 0;
TRISC = 0;
TRISD = 0;
ADCON0 = 0;
ADCON1 = 0X0F;
OSCCON = 0X74;
T0CON = 0XC7;
setUpTheLCD ();
MSSP2CInit();
writeString ("Hello EEPROM");
line2 ();
adhigh = 0x01;
for(adlow=0,b=0;adlow<8;adlow++)
{
a = dataout [b];
writeToEEPROM(adhigh,adlow, a);
ms13delay (3);
b++;
}
for(adlow=0, b=0;adlow<8;adlow++)
{
disData = readFromEEPROM(adhigh,adlow);
rxData [b] = disData;
ms13delay (10);
lcdData = rxData[b];
lcdOut ();
}
ms13delay(30);
while (1)
{
clearTheScreen ();
```

```
176.    writeString ("Temp is");
177.    line2 ();
178.    MSSP2CIdle ();
179.    MSSP2CStart ();
180.    MSSP2CWrite (0x9A);
181.    MSSP2CWrite (0x00);
182.    MSSP2CRestart();
183.    MSSP2CWrite(0x9B);
184.    thigh = MSSP2CreadNAck ();
185.    MSSP2CStop();
186.    if (thigh & 0b10000000)
187.    {
188.    thigh = (~thigh + 1);
189.    sysTemperature = thigh;
190.    displayTempNeg(sysTemperature);
191.    }
192.    else
193.    {        sysTemperature = thigh;
194.    displayTemp(sysTemperature);
195.    }
196.    ms13delay(61);
197.    }
198.    }
```

Analysis of Listing 10-1

Lines 1 to 6 are the standard comments.

Line 7 to 10 are the usual includes; however, on line 8 we are including a new header the stdio.h header file. This is required for the sprintf function we will use to display the temperature on the LCD. Note that as the prototype board I am using for this program is the PICdem2 plus board, the include file for the LCD, on line 10, is <4BitLCDDemoBoard.h>.

On line 12, we set up some variables of type unsigned char, and on line 13, we set up a float type variable named sysTemperature. This is to give us the option of using a number with some numbers after a decimal point. However, the TC74 has a maximum resolution of 1°C, so a float is not really required.

Line 14 unsigned char rxData[12];

This sets up an empty array of 12 memory locations. This will be used to store the data read back from the EEPROM. However, this will limit the number of characters we can receive back from the EEPROM to 12. If you need more, then you will have to increase this value here.

Line 15 unsigned char dataout [8] =

This sets up an array of eight memory locations and loads them with the following eight ASCII values. These eight ASCII values will spell out the phrase Ann Ward, my wife's name. This may have the same issue as with line 14.

Lines 27 to 34 create a subroutine to create a variable delay that has a minimum delay time of 13ms.

Line 35 void MSSP2CInit()

This sets up the first of a series of subroutines that will be used by the MSSP (master synchronous serial port) for I²C operation. This first subroutine will initialize the MSSP.

Line 37 SSP1CON = 0X28;

This loads the SSP1CON register with 0b00101000. This means the SSPEN bit is a logic '1', which turns on the MSSP module. The CKP bit is not used in I²C mode. Then, bit 3 is a logic '1' and bits 2, 1, and 0 are all logic '0', which sets the MSSP to I²C mode, with the clock being the oscillator divided by (4 × (SSPADD + 1)). We will look at this later.

Line 38 SSP2CON = 0x00;

This loads all the bits in the SSP2CON register with logic '0'. This basically turns all aspects off. We will look at the use of these bits later.

Line 39 SSPSTAT = 0X00;

This loads all the bits in the SSPSTAT register with logic '0'. This basically turns all aspects off. We will look at the use of these bits later.

Line 40 SSPADD = 0X13;

This loads the SSPADD with 0x13. To appreciate what this does, we need to understand that for the 24LC256 EEPROM, the maximum frequency of the clock signal is 100kHz or 400kHz. We will use 100kHz. In line 37, we choose the selection to set the clock frequency of the I²C module to be the oscillator divided by (4 × (SSPADD + 1)). In line 150, we set the oscillator frequency to be 8Mhz. Therefore, to divide this down to 100kHz, we must divide the 8Mhz by 80. This value of 80 will be made up of 4 × (SSPADD +1)). This means that the value in the SSPADD register must be 19. This is 13 in hexadecimal. That is why we are loading the SSPADD register with 0X13.

Line 41 TRISCbits.RC3 = 1;

Line 42 TRISCbits.RC4 = 1;

These two lines set the respective bits to input.

Line 44 void MMSP2Cidle ()

This creates a subroutine that is used to check that the I²C module is idle. This should be done before you attempt any operation so as to avoid any collisions on the bus.

Line 46 while ((SSPSTAT & 0x04) || (SSPCON2 & 0x1F));

The first test checks to see if the master is transmitting data. The second test checks to see if an acknowledge, or receive enable, or a stop, or a repeat start, or a start is active. If any of these tests result in a true, then the PIC must wait until they become untrue (i.e., the I²C is doing nothing).

Line 48 void MSSP2Cwait()

This sets up a subroutine that makes the PIC wait until the MSSP2 module has finished.

Line 50 while(!PIR1bits.SSPIF);

This makes the PIC wait until the interrupt flag of the MSSP module, the PIR1bits.SSPIF, goes to a logic '1'. This will happen when the master receives the full eight bits of data from the slave. Note that we are not using this action to generate an interrupt, as we are not enabling any interrupts. We are using it just to see if the master has received the full data from the slave.

Line 51 PIR1bits.SSPIF = 0;

This resets the interrupt flag back to logic '0' so that we can test for it going back to a logic '1' after the next eight bits have been received from the slave. Note that this interrupt flag does not reset back to logic '0' automatically.

Line 53 void MSSP2CStart()

This is a subroutine to generate the start bit required to transmit data to the slave.

Line 55 MSSP2idle ();

The first thing we do inside this MSSP2start subroutine is call the MMSP2idle subroutine. This is so that we can make sure the MMSP is not still doing something.

Line 56 SSPCON2bits.SEN = 1;

The next thing we do is set bit 0 of the SSPCON2 control register to a logic '1'. This generates the start bit of the sequence.

Line 58 void MSSP2CStop()

This creates a subroutine that generates the stop bit.

Line 60 MSSP2idle ();

The first thing we do inside this MSSP2Stop subroutine is call the MMSP2idle subroutine. This is so that we can make sure the MMSP is not still doing something.

Line 61 SSPCON2bits.PEN = 1;

The next thing we do is set bit 2 of the SSPCON2 control register to a logic '1'. This generates the stop bit of the sequence.

Line 63 void MSSP2CRestart()

This creates a subroutine that generates the restart bit. This may be required if we had created a collision.

Line 65 MSSP2idle ();

The first thing we do inside this MSSP2CRestart subroutine is call the MMSP2idle subroutine. This is so that we can make sure the MMSP is not still doing something.

Line 66 SSPCON2bits.RSEN = 1;

The next thing we do is set bit 1 of the SSPCON2 register. This resends the start bit.

Line 68 void MSSP2CNACK()

This creates a subroutine to generate the NOT acknowledge that the master will send to the slave at the end of transmission.

Line 70 MSSP2idle ();

The first thing we do inside the MSSP2CNACK subroutine is call the MMSP2idle subroutine. This is so that we can make sure the MMSP is not still doing something.

Line 71 SSPCON2bits.ACKDT = 1;

The next thing we do is set up the Not acknowledge pulse.

Line 72 SSPCON2bits.ACKEN = 1;

This starts the clocking to transmit the NACK to the slave.

Line 74 void MSSP2CWrite(unsigned char data)

This sets up a subroutine to write a byte of data to the slave.

Line 76 MSSP2idle ();

The first thing we do inside this MSSP2CWrite subroutine is call the MMSP2idle subroutine. This is so that we can make sure the MMSP is not still doing something.

Line 77 SEND: SSPBUF = data;

We are creating a label named "SEND", as we may need to go to this line in the program from somewhere else. The next thing we do is load the SSPBUF with the data to be sent to the slave. Note that data is a local variable for this subroutine. When we call this subroutine, we must send some information that will be loaded into this local's variable-called data.

Line 78 MSSP2idle ();

The next thing we do is call the subroutine MSSP2idle to make sure we wait until the PIC is idle.

Line 79 while (SSPCON2bits.ACKSTAT)

This tests to see if the slave has sent back an acknowledge signal. If it had, then the logic on the ACKSTAT bit would have gone low. If it is still a logic '1', then no acknowledgment has been sent and the result of this test will be true. The micro would then have to carry out the following instructions listed within the curly brackets.

Line 81 SSPCON2bits.RSEN = 1;

This sets the RSEN, ReSend ENable bit, to a logic '1'. This enables the PIC to try resending the same data again. This is needed, as the slave has not sent the ACKSTAT bit to a logic '0'. This would be the signal to tell the master the slave has received the data sent by the master.

Line 82 MSSP2wait ();

This calls the MSSP2wait subroutine to make the PIC wait until it has stopped.

Line 83 goto SEND;

This makes the PIC go back to line 77, where it will try to send the data again. This makes use of labels in our programs.

Line 87 unsigned char MSSP2Cread()

This creates a subroutine that will read what is on the I^2C bus. It will send a variable of type unsigned char, back to where the subroutine was called from.

Line 89 SSPCON2bits.RCEN = 1;

The first thing we do is set bit 3 of the SSPCON2 SFR. This is the ReCieve ENable pin of the MSSP. This enables the MSSP to receive data on the I^2C bus.

Line 90 while (!BF);

This test to see if the BF (buffer full) flag of the SSPSTAT SFR is a logic '0'. If it is, then the SSPBUF of the master is not yet full and the slave is still sending data. Therefore, the PIC must do nothing until the SSPBUF is full.

Note that this format identifies the actual bit without using the SSPSTATbits.BF approach as used before. It is really a personal preference as to which approach you use. I prefer to include the SFR reference, as it reminds me which SFR the actual bit is associated with.

Line 91 SSPCON2bits.RCEN = 0;

As soon as the BF bit goes to a logic '1', the PIC can move on to this instruction. This will actually turn off the ability for the MSSP2C to receive data. It also means that the master has read the eight bits from the slave into its SSPBUF. Therefore, we can end the subroutine.

Line 92 return SSPBUFF;

This ends the subroutine with the return instruction and sends the data in the SSPBUF as the unsigned char it has to send back to where it was called from.

Line 94 unsigned char MSSP2CreadNAck()

This creates a subroutine to read data from the slave. This subroutine will also create the NOT Acknowledgment signal. At the end of the subroutine, the PIC will send a variable back to where it was called from.

Line 96 SSPCON2bits.RCEN = 1;

This sets this bit to a logic '1' and so enables the module to receive data from the slave.

Line 97 while (!BF);

This gets the PIC to wait for its SSPBUF to fill with data from the slave.

Line 98 SSPCON2bits.RCEN = 0;

This now disables the receive mode of I^2C module.

Line 99 SSPCON2bits.ACKDT=1;

This sets bit 5 of the SSPCON2 SFR. This puts a logic '1' on this pin, which is NOT Acknowledge signal.

Line 100 SSPCON2bits.ACKEN=1;

This sets bit 4 of the SSPCON2 SFR. This initiates the acknowledge sequence on the SDA and SCL pins. This will transmit the data on the ACKDT bit.

Line 101 MSSP2wait ();

This calls the wait subroutine.

Line 102 return SSPBUF;

This ends the subroutine with the return instruction and sends the data in the SSPBUF, as the unsigned char it has to send back to where it was called from.

Line 104 void writeToEEPROM (unsigned char adhigh, unsigned char adlow, unsigned char edata)

This creates a subroutine for writing to the EEPROM. It will expect three variables of type unsigned char to be sent to it when it is called. The three variables are

- adhigh: This will hold the number for the high byte of the address in the EEPROM we want to write to.
- adlow: This will hold the number for the low byte of the address in the EEPROM we want to write to.
- edata: This will hold the data that we want to write to the address we have just specified.

Line 106 MSSP2idle ();

This calls the basic subroutine to make sure the I^2C bus is not busy.

Line 107 MSSP2CStart();

This calls the subroutine to send the start signal to the slave.

Line 108 MSSP2Write(0XA0);

This calls the subroutine to write to the EEPROM. It sends the data 0XA0 up to it. 0XA0 makes up the control byte that has to be sent first to the EEPROM. This is 0b10100000 in binary where the 0b1010 is the four-bit control code for read and write operations. Then bits3, 2, and 1 are all logic '0,' as this is the address of this particular EEPROM. Note that the three address pins A2, A1, and A0 are all tied to logic '0.' The final bit, which is bit 0, is used to tell the EEPROM the master is either writing to or reading from the EEPROM. A logic '0' on this bit means the master wants to write to the

EEPROM, which is what we want to do now, whereas a logic '1' on this bit means the master wants to read from the EEPROM.

Line 109 MSSP2Write(adhigh);

This now writes the high byte of the 16-bit address we want to write to.

Line 110 MSSP2Write(adlow);

This now writes the low byte of the 16-bit address we want to write to.

Line 111 MSSP2Write(edata);

Now we have told the EEPROM the address in it that we want to write to, and we can write the actual data we want to write there. Note that after this data has been written there, the EEPROM will make the next address available to be written to automatically. In this way, the master needs only send the next byte of data.

Line 112 MSSP2Stop ();

This calls the subroutine to send the stop bit to the slave.

Line 114 unsigned char readFromEEPROM(unsigned char adhigh, unsigned char adlow)

This creates a subroutine to read from the EEPROM. It expects two bytes to be sent up to when it is called. The first byte is the high byte of the first address we want to start reading. The second is the low byte.

Lines 116 to 121 are the same as with the write to EEPROM subroutine. You will note that the control byte on line 119 is the same as we are writing to the EEPROM to tell it the address of the first byte of data we want to read.

Line 122 MSSP2Restart ();

This calls the restart subroutine, as we want to send a second start signal.

Line 123 MSSP2Write (0XA1);

This sends another control byte to the EEPROM, but this time bit 0 is a logic '1'. This is because we now want to read from the address we have just sent.

Line 124 temp = MSSP2ReadNAck ();

This calls the subroutine to read from the address but also send a Not acknowledgment to the slave. Note that the variable temp is what will be loaded with the data sent back from this subroutine. This means that the final contents of the SSPBUF will be loaded into temp at the end of the subroutine. This is how you make use of the return instruction on line 101.

Line 125 MSSP2Stop ();

This calls the MSSP2Stop subroutine to create a stop signal.

Line 126 return temp;

This ends the subroutine and returns with the value temp.

Line 128 void displayTemp(float dp)

This creates a subroutine that will be used to send a variable of type float, basically a number with decimals, to the LCD. It will expect a value to be sent up to it that will be loaded into the local variable dp.

Line 130 sprintf(str, "%.1f OC ", dp);

This calls the function sprintf, which is in the header file stdio.h. This is an open source header file that contains various functions that are freely available to programmers.

It will use a variable str that is part of the stdio.h file. The "%.1f" is used to set how many decimal places are used in the display. The number '1' means I will use only one decimal place. The OC are the characters to show the reading is in degrees centigrade. The dp at the end is the variable into which the data that was sent up to the subroutine when it was called will be loaded.

Line 131 writeString (str);

This calls the subroutine writeString, which is in my header file 4BitLCDDemoBoard.h. It sends the data in the variable str to that subroutine.

Line 133 displayTempNeg(float dp)

This creates the same type of subroutine as the one before, but this time it is used for displaying negative temperature values. The difference is in line 135, where a minus sign is included as shown here: sprintf(str,

"-%.1f OC ", dp);sprintf(str, -"%.1f", dp);. In this instruction, we have added a '-' sign that will be displayed in front of the reading on the LCD.

Lines 139 to 151 are the standard setup instructions in the main loop.

Line 152 setUpTheLCD ();

This calls the subroutine to set up the LCD.

Line 153 MSSP2Init ();

This calls the subroutine to set up the MSSP module into I²C communications.

Lines 154 and 155 write to the LCD and then send the cursor to the beginning of the second line on the LCD.

Line 156 adhigh = 0X01;

This loads the desired value of the high byte of the address into the variable adhigh.

Line 157 for (adlow=0,b=0;adlow<8;adlow++)

This sets up a for do loop that first loads the two global variables adlow and 'b' with the value zero. It then asks whether the variable 'adlow' is less than 8, which it will be as it has just been set to zero. This makes the PIC carry out the instructions in the loop, and at the end, it will increment the value of the variable 'adlow'. It will then ask whether adlow is less than 8.

This makes the PIC carry out the loop instructions eight times.

Line 159 a = dataout [b];

This is the first instruction in the for do loop. It will load the global variable 'a' with the contents of the first memory location in the array dataout. This is because the variable 'b' inside the [] brackets has the value '0' in it at this moment in time. Note that the contents of the array dataout were defined in lines 16 to 25.

Line 160 writeToEEPROM (adhigh,adlow, a);

This calls the writeToEEPROM subroutine, sending the three variables up to it that it is expecting:

- 'adhigh' is the byte that contains the high byte of the address we want to write to. This is set to 0X01 in line 155.
- 'adlow' is the byte that contains the low byte of the address we want to write to. As this is the first run-through the loop, the byte will be 0 as set in line 157. However, this will increment every time we go through the loop.
- 'a' is the byte that is loaded with the data we want to store in the EEPROM. As this is the first run-through the loop, this data will be the data stored in the first (i.e., 0) location of the array dataout. However, this will increment every time we go through the loop.

These three bytes will be loaded into the local variables of the subroutine; see line 104.

Line 160 13msdelay (3);

This calls the variable delay subroutine and runs through it three times, creating an approximately 40ms delay. This allows the write operation to complete.

Line 161 b++;

This increments the value in the variable 'b'. This is needed so that in line 159 the contents of the next memory location in the array dataout will be loaded into the variable 'a'.

In this way, the whole contents of the array dataout, which spells "Ann Ward", will be written to the specified address in the EEPROM.

Lines 164 to 171 create a similar for do loop, but this time it is used for reading the same data back from the same memory locations and storing it in the array rxdata. It then displays the data on the LCD.

The most interesting instruction is the following:

Line 165 disData = readFromEEPROM(adhigh,adlow);

This makes use of the fact that when creating the subroutine, unsignedchar readFromEEPROM(unsigned char adhigh, unsigned char adlow), we used the term "unsigned char" in the declaration. This meant that this subroutine would be sending back a variable, using the return keyword, of type unsigned char, to be used by the call instruction: "return temp;". In this case, the call would load this variable, temp, into the variable disData.

The reason I am explaining all this is because if you are not going to connect a variable to the call instruction for the subroutine, then you should use the term "void" in the declaration of the subroutine. Also, you would not need the "return" instruction at the end of the subroutine.

As a thought, there is a saving of one instruction line in this section of programming. Can you think what it is? I will show you at the end of this chapter.

Line 172 13msdelay (30);

This creates a delay of approximately 1 second.

Line 173 while (1)

The first phase of the program is completed, in that we have written data to the EEPROM and then read it back and displayed it on the LCD. The next phase is to constantly monitor the temperature using the TC74, a temperature sensor that uses the I^{2}C protocol.

This instruction sets up a forever loop to make sure we don't run any of the previous instructions again.

Line 175 clearTheScreen ();

This calls the subroutine to clear all data from the LCD display and send the cursor to the first position on the first line (i.e., the "home" position). This subroutine is in my header file

Line 176 writeString ("Temp is");

This writes the string "Temp is" to the LCD.

Line 177 line2 ();

This calls the subroutine that moves the cursor on the LCD to the beginning of line 2. This is to get it ready to display the temperature.

Line 178 MSSP2idle ();

This calls the subroutine to check that the I²C bus is not doing anything.

Line 179 MSSP2Start ();

This calls the subroutine to generate the start bit.

Line 180 MSSP2Write (0X9A);

This calls the subroutine to write the data 0X9A to the TC74. The value 0X9A in hexadecimal is 0b10011010 in binary; refer to the appendix for notes on converting hex to binary and so on. The data 1001 101x is the default address of the TC74. There can be seven other addresses, but to use one of these you must set it up with Microchip, who manufactures the TC74. The LSB, bit 0, which is shown as a don't care 'X', dictates whether or not the master is writing to or reading from the TC74. If this bit is a logic '0', as it is with this instruction, then the master wants to write to the TC74. A logic '1' would mean the master wants to read from the TC74.

Line 181 MSSP2Write (0X00);

This calls the MSSP2Write subroutine and sends the data 0X00 to the TC74. This is the address of the register that the master will be reading from next, and it is the address of where the temperature will be stored after the TC74 has acquired it.

These two instructions together prepare the TC74 to send the current temperature reading to the master.

Line 182 MSSP2Restart ();

This calls the restart subroutine to generate another start signal.

Line 183 MSSP2Write (0X9B);

This calls the write subroutine again, but this time it will send the default address but with bit 0 set to a logic '1'. The value 0X9B in hexadecimal is 0b10011011 in binary; refer to the appendix for notes on converting hex to binary and so on. This is to tell the TC74 it wants to read from the TC74 and read from the address it sent last (i.e., address 0X00).

Line 184 thigh = MSSP2ReadNAck ();

This calls the read subroutine with the no Acknowledgment. This will load the 'thigh' variable with the data this subroutine sends back when it finishes. In this way, the temperature reading of the TC74 will be loaded into the variable 'thigh.' Note that we won't use the tlow, as we did with the TC72, as the definition of the TC74 is ± 1°C. We don't need decimal values. Also, we only need one eight-bit register.

Line 185 MSSP2Stop ();

This calls the subroutine to generate the stop bit.

This now ends the reading of the TC74.

Line 186 if (thigh & 0b10000000)

This is testing to see if the temperature reading is negative. To understand how this instruction works, you must appreciate that the TC74 represents a negative value using a 2's complement on the actual binary number of the value. In doing so, it ensures that bit 7 of the binary number will be a logic '1.'

This instruction does a logical AND operation with each individual bit of the two values. The only AND operation that will result in a logic '1' will be between bit 7 of the 'thigh' variable and bit 7 of the binary number 0b10000000. In this way, the instruction is testing to see if bit 7 of the 'thigh' variable is a logic '1.' If it is a logic '1,' then the result of the test is true, and it means the value sent is a 2's complement of a negative value.

This action is called bit testing.

Line 188 thigh = (~thigh + 1);

This is the first of a series of instructions the PIC must carry out if the test on line 186 was true. This performs a 2's complement of the value in 'thigh.' This is done by inverting all the bits in 'thigh'; the '~' is the C instruction to invert the bits. It will then add 1 to the result to complete the 2's complement operation. In doing this, the binary number now in 'thigh' will be the actual value of the temperature, but we know it is negative and we must display the '-' sign in front of it.

Line 189 sysTemperature = thigh;

This loads a copy of the value in 'thigh' into the variable sysTemperature.

Line 190 displayTempNeg (sysTemperature);

This calls the subroutine to display a negative value and sends the data in the variable sysTemperature up to that subroutine.

Line 192 else

This creates the statement of what the PIC should do if the test on line 186 was untrue. Note that the PIC will only carry out these instructions if the result of the test was untrue. If the result of the test was true, the PIC would jump over these instructions and go to line 197.

Line 193 sysTemperature = thigh;

This loads a copy of 'thigh' into sysTemperature, but we now know this value is positive.

Line 194 displayTemp (sysTemperature);

This calls the subroutine to display the temperature with no negative sign in front of it.

Line 195 13msdelay (61);

This creates a 2-second delay.

I hope the analysis does help you understand how to use I^2C comms with the PIC micro.

Figures 10-7 and 10-8 show the program working. I am using the PIC demo board, as I don't have a TC74 and a 24LC256. However, I hope you can see that the program works.

Figure 10-7. *The display showing data from the EEPROM*

Figure 10-8. *The temperature reading from the TC74*

That Little Thought

Harken back to lines 166 and 167:

- disData = readFromEEPROM(adhigh,adlow);
- rxData [b] = disData;

These can be merged together as follows:

rxData[b] = readFromEEPROM(adhigh,adlow);

This would work just as well and save a line of programming. The subroutine has the return instruction at the end. That return instruction would simply load the location in the array, rxData, that is indicated by the value in the variable 'b' with the data the subroutine would return with.

Summary

In this chapter, we have studied how the PIC uses the I^{2}C protocol to communicate to external devices. We have also studied how the one master can communicate with two slaves.

We have looked at how the 24LC256 EEPROM can be used to permanently store data externally and how it can be written to and read from.

We have learned how to use the TC74 to monitor temperature and how it can be controlled by a PIC.

In the next chapter, we will look at the final communication module that is in the PIC18F4525. That is the UART: the Universal Asynchronous Receive and Transmit chip.

CHAPTER 11

Using the UART

In this chapter, we are going to study the Universal Asynchronous Receive and Transmit (UART) module of the PIC18f4525. This is a very versatile module that a lot of systems use. We will look at how the UART can be used to communicate with an external terminal using a terminal software program such as Tera Term. We will communicate with the terminal using no handshaking and then with handshaking.

After reading this chapter, you should understand what the UART does and how to use it in a variety of situations.

UART at a Glance

UART is a circuit that is used in most microprocessors that communicate with the outside world. This is because the inside world of the micro communicates to itself using a parallel bus system. This makes communication much quicker than serial communications.

However, this requires a lot of tracks. The first parallel buses were only four bits wide, as micros communicated in nibbles of data. Nowadays the buses are up to 64 bits wide, which means they communicate 16 times faster, even if they were to use the same clock, which they don't.

With the outside world, we can't afford to have cables that have 64 wires in them. The early printers did use what were called ribbon cables, which were 8 or 16 bits wide but restricted in length to around 3m maximum. So, to keep costs down, communication in the outside world has been done serially using only two wires.

H. H. Ward, *Programming Arduino Projects with the PIC Microcontroller*,
https://doi.org/10.1007/978-1-4842-7230-5_11

This means we needed a device that would change the parallel inside the micro to serial outside. Also change the serial outside to the parallel inside the micro. This is the UART; which has PISO(parallel in and serial out) shift registers and SIPO(serial in and parallel out) shift registers.

This means that it is essential, even now, for the would-be embedded programmer to understand how we can use the UART. In this chapter, you will learn that and how to apply it.

Unlike the SPI module, this type of communication is asynchronous, which means it is not synchronized to a clock and so there is no need for a clock signal. Indeed, with the UART you only really need two wires, which connect to the transmit, TX, and the receive, RX, pins on the PIC. You can, if you so wish, use what is termed "Handshaking" whereby you add an RTS(ready to transit) and a CTS(clear to send) signal between each device; however, this will tie up more I/O pins and require more cabling.

To show how to use the UART, I will go through a program that does the following:

1. An LCD will display the following message: "Coded Uart".
2. The main program will then simply get an LED to flash at 1-second intervals.
3. However, there will be a terminal connected to the PIC which, when a character is typed in at the terminal, will send that character to the PIC via the UART.
4. When the PIC receives the character, an interrupt will be initiated and the PIC will display that character on the LCD.

5. The PIC will then send the numbers 1 through 9 out to the terminal, which will display them on itsdisplay.

6. As each character is displayed on the terminal, the PIC also sends the start new line instruction so that each new character is displayed on a new line.

Note that this program will not use any handshaking between the terminal and the PIC.

We will use a laptop running a terminal software, such as Tera Term or PuTTY, to act as the terminal. This means we can use the laptop's keyboard to enter in the characters.

The circuit for this project is shown in Figure 11-1.

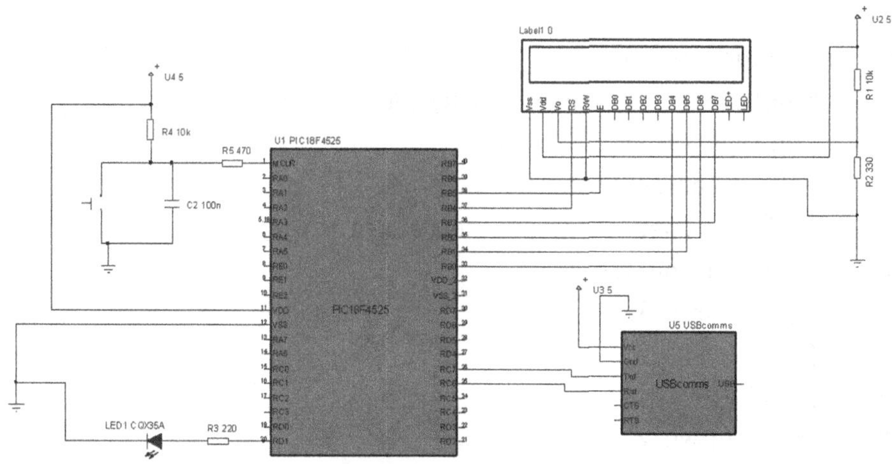

***Figure 11-1.** The circuit for the UART program*

The USB comm's symbol on the circuit diagram is the USB to serial com port converter, which is used to connect the laptop to the UART inside the PIC. The code for this project is shown in Listing 11-1.

Listing 11-1. The UART Program

```
/*This is a basic program to control the LCD and the UART using the PIC 18F4525
Written by H H Ward dated 02/04/16.
modified 24/06/16 to include running from an interrupt whilst main program is simply flashing an led
the ISR sends out the character received at the uart back to a terminal and then sends the numbers 1 to 9
inserting a line after each number has been sent to the terminal.
The program also echos the character received onto the LCD connected to the pic.
using the LCD connected to PORTB
*/
#include <xc.h>
 #include <conFigInternalOscNoWDTNoLVP.h>
 #include <4bitLCDPortb.h>
 //some variables
 unsigned char n, count, newdatain = 0;
 //the subroutines
 void shortdelay ()
 {
 TMR0 = 0;
 while (TMR0 < 255);
 }
 void delay (unsigned char t)
 {
 for (n = 0; n < t; n ++)
 {
 TMR0 = 0;
```

```
while (TMR0 < 255);
}
}
void interrupt  isr1 ()
{
if (PIR1bits.RCIF == 1)
{
PIR1bits.RCIF = 0;
newdatain = RCREG;
lcdData = newdatain;
lcdOut ();
TXREG = newdatain;
shortdelay ();
TXREG = 0x0a;
shortdelay ();
for (n = 0x30; n < 0x3A; n++)
{
TXREG = 0X0A;
shortdelay ();
TXREG = 0x0D;
shortdelay ();
TXREG = n;
shortdelay ();
TXREG = 0x0A;
}
}
}
void main ()
{
PORTA = 0;
PORTB = 0;
```

```
PORTC = 0;
PORTD = 0;
TRISA = 0X01;
TRISB = 0x00;
TRISC = 0b10000000;
TRISD = 0x00;
ADCON0 = 0x00;
ADCON1 = 0x0F;
OSCTUNE = 0b10000000;
OSCCON = 0b01110000;
T0CON = 0b11000111;
INTCON = 0b11000000;
PIE1bits.RC1IE = 1;
TXSTA = 0b00100000;
RCSTA = 0b10010000;
BAUDCON = 0b00000000;
SPBRG = 12;
setUpTheLCD ();
clearTheScreen ();
writeString ("Coded Uart");
line2 ();
while (1)
{
PORTDbits.RD1 = PORTDbits.RD1^1;
delay (20);
}
}
```

Interrupts and How They Work

Perhaps, before we go any further, it might be useful to explain a bit about interrupts. An interrupt would make the PIC carry out a special subroutine that you must write, termed an ISR(interrupt service routine). This subroutine will contain a list of instructions that the PIC must carry out before returning back to the main program. However, you do not have to write any instructions that will call this special subroutine. How then does the PIC know when it should run this ISR, the special subroutine? The answer is that the PIC is checking to see if an interrupt that would force the PIC to run the ISR has happened every time the PIC carries out any instruction. Inside the "Fetch and Execute" cycle, which happens with every instruction, the PIC checks a special bit called the "interrupt flag", even if an interrupt has not been raised. This interrupt flag can be set by a whole range of events, and one of them is the UART receiving data from an external source. However, to use these interrupt sources, you as the programmer have to enable them. There are ten registers used in the control of the interrupts with the PIC18f4525. Other PICs will have more or less. For the PIC18f4525 they are as follows:

1. INTOCON The Interrupt Control Register
2. INTCON2 The Interrupt Control Register2
3. INTCON3 The Interrupt Control Register3
4. PIR1 Peripheral Interrupt Request Control Register1
5. PIR2 Peripheral Interrupt Request Control Register2
6. PIE1 Peripheral Interrupt Enable Control Register1
7. PIE2 Peripheral Interrupt Enable Control Register2
8. IPR1Interrupt Priority Request Control Register1

9. IPR2Interrupt Priority Request Control Register2
10. ROCN Reset Control Register

The process by which we control interrupts is not as complicated as the list of control registers suggests. I will run through the basic concept here, but as we use more interrupts, I will explain more about them then.

There are two basic groups of interrupts:

- Global, which covers all the external but also all interrupts.
- Peripheral, which are internal from all the peripheral modules of the PIC, such as
  - Timers
  - Capture Compare and PWM (i.e., CCP 1 and 2 modules)
  - UART 1 and modules
  - I^2C module
  - MSSP modules

To use any interrupt, we have to enable the global interrupts, which is done by setting bit 7, GIE bit, on the INTCON register to a logic '1'. Then, to enable any peripheral interrupts, we have to set bit6, PIE bit, of the INTCON register as well. This is done in Listing 11-1 in

Line 67 INTCON = 0b11000000;

The action of these two bits depends upon the setting of the IPEN bit. This is the Interrupt Priority Enable bit, which is bit7 of the RCON register. This bit enables the PIC to give some interrupts priority over interrupts that may already be running. We will not be using this option in this program. We will discuss its use later.

As well as setting these two bits, GIE and PIE, to use any peripheral interrupt, as we do in this program, we have to set the enable bit for that particular interrupt. With the PIC18F4525, there are so many peripheral devices that can be the cause of an interrupt. There are two peripheral enable registers: PIE1 and PIE2. As we are using the fact that a reception of data into the RXREG, receiver register of the UART, we need to enable that interrupt. This is done in Listing 11-1 in

Line 68 PIE1bits.RC1IE = 1;

Each peripheral or global interrupt will have a bit that will go to a logic '1' when that peripheral or global interrupt wants to cause an interrupt. These bits are termed the flags, and for the peripheral interrupts, they are listed in the two peripheral request registers PIR1 and PIR2. When a device sends data to the UART, then the PIC automatically sets this bit, PIR1bits. RCIF, to a logic '1'. Note that this happens every time the UART receives data, but to ensure that this action generates an interrupt, the appropriate peripheral enable bit must have previously been set. As we have done that, with line 68, then when the RCIF bit goes to a logic '1' an interrupt will be generated, and the interrupt flag, which is checked in the "Fetch and Execute Cycle", will go to a logic '1'.

What happens then is that the PIC will stop what it is doing immediately and go to the ISR to carry out the instructions inside the ISR.

You might think that we could do the same with an ordinary subroutine. But the PIC will only carry out the subroutine call if it is at that line in the program. With an interrupt, the PIC will go to the ISR from wherever it is in the program. This is because the interrupt flag is checked every time the PIC gets an instruction, regardless of what the instruction is. In this way, the PIC will never miss an interrupt that has been enabled.

I hope this brief explanation of what interrupts are and how they work has helped you to understand the use of interrupts. Now we will get back to analyzing the program listing.

Analysis of Listing 11-1

Many of the instructions have been analyzed in previous chapters, so I will restrict the analysis to new and important instructions.

Lines 16 to 19 create a short delay of around 33ms. This is required because there needs to be a small delay between sending data to the terminal.

Lines 20 to 27 create our standard variable delay. This is used in the main program on line 80.

Line 28 void interrupt isr1 ()

This creates the ISR. Note that I am using version 1.35 of the XC8 compiler software. Later versions may require a different instruction here to create the ISR.

Line 30 if (PIR1bits.RCIF == 1)

It is quite normal to have more than one source of interrupts enabled in a program. If that is so, as they all use the same ISR, then the first thing you should do is determine which source has caused the interrupt. That is what this instruction is doing. The instruction is an if type test to see if the receiver in the UART caused the interrupt(i.e., if its bit, the RCIF bit, has gone to a logic '1'). Of course, in this program it must have, but if there were other sources you would add the same if type test bit to test if their interrupt flag was set to a logic '1.'

Line 32 PIR1bits.RCIF = 0;

This clears the interrupt flag associated with the reception of the UART1. This is done to ensure it does not initiate any further interrupts until we are ready and also to get it ready to go to a logic '1' if the UART1 receives new data.

Line 33 newdatain = RCREG;

This loads the data in the RCREG, which has just been filled with data that had come from the terminal, into the variable 'newdatain.'

Line 34 lcdData = newdatain;

This moves a copy of that data into the variable lcdData, ready to send it to the LCD. I could have saved a line by writing lcdData = RCREG, but I wanted to use the newdatain variable on line 36 to echo the data back to the terminal later.

Line 35 lcdOut ();

This calls the subroutine lcdOut, which is in the header file 4bitLCDPortb.h. This will send the data received from the terminal to be displayed on the LCD.

Line 36 TXREG = newdatain;

This loads the data we have just received from the terminal into the UART's transmit register, TXREG. This will start the process to transmit the data to the terminal. In this way, we can echo the character back onto the terminal. Note that I will turn off the facility for the terminal to automatically echo its characters to the screen.

Line 37 shortdelay ();

This calls the subroutine for the short delay required by the terminal to allow it to deal with the data we have just sent before we do anything else connected with the terminal.

Line 38 TXREG = 0X0a;

This loads the ASCII for line feed into the TXREG. This will send this ASCII to the terminal and the terminal will move to the next line directly under where the cursor is now. Note that it will not return the cursor to the beginning of the next line. The letter 'a' is the hexadecimal for 1001 or 9. It does not matter if you use lowercase or uppercase 'A'; either will do the same.

Line 39 shortdelay ();

Just another short delay.

Line 40 for (n = 0x30; n < 0x3A; n++)

This sets up a "for do loop". It sets the initial value for the variable 'n' to 0x30. This is the ASCII for the number '0'. It will test to see if n is less than 0x3A, which is the ASCII for '10'. It will go through the "for do loop", incrementing the value of 'n' each time, until n is 0X3A. When n = 0X3A, the PIC will break out of this for do loop.

Line 42 TXREG 0x0A;

This sends this character to the terminal. This will get the terminal to send the cursor of the terminal down to the next line on the screen.

Line 33 shortdelay ();

Just another short delay.

Line 44 TXREG 0x0D;

This sends the ASCII to send the cursor back to the beginning of the current line. In this way, these two instructions on lines 42 and 44 combine together to move the cursor on the terminal screen to the beginning of the next line on the screen.

As an exercise, comment out this line 44 and see what happens.

Line 45 shortdelay ();

Just another short delay.

Line 46 TXREG = n;

This sends the actual number stored in the variable 'n' to the terminal. In this way, we send the numbers 0 to 9 to the terminal displaying them at the beginning of new lines on the screen.

Line 47 shortdelay ();

Just another short delay.

Line 48 TXREG 0x0A;

This sends an extra empty line on the screen between the numbers 0 to 9.

Line 52 void main ()

This is the start of the main program.

Lines 54 to 66 set up the normal aspects of the PIC.

Line 67 INTCON = 0b11000000;

This sets bits 7 and 6 to a logic '1'. This enables both the global and peripheral interrupts. This is needed, as we are using the UART interrupt, which is a peripheral device. However, we must still enable the global interrupts as well.

Line 68 PIRE1bits.RC1IE = 1;

This enables the UART to generate interrupts. Note that the PIC18f4525 has two UARTs, hence the number '1'. Also, there are quite a few peripheral devices that can cause interrupts, and so we need two peripheral interrupt enable registers.

Line 69 TXSTA = 0b00100000;

This sets bit5 of the TXSTA(transmit status) register. This enables the UART to transmit data.

Line 70 RCSTA = 0b10100000;

This sets bits 7 and 5 of the RCSTA(receive status)register. Bit 7 enables the serial PORT and sets the correct direction of the RX and TX pins. Bit 5 enables the reception aspect of the UART.

Line 71 BAUDCON = 0b00000000;

This clears all the bits in the BAUDCON(baud rate control)register. Importantly, bit3 is a logic '0', which sets the UART up for eight-bit baud rate generator; so it only uses the SPBRG register and ignores the SPBRGH register.

Line 72 SPBRG = 12;

This loads the low byte, SPBRG, of the baud control value with 12. This number is what is required to produce a baud rate of 9600. See the note on the baud ratelater in this chapter.

Most of the remaining instructions have been looked at inearlier analysis.

This program listing shows how you can get the PIC18F4525 to communicate with a terminal with a keyboard, such as a PC, using the UART. Really, any system that has a UART can be used to communicate with the PIC in this way. One thing this program does assume is that the user is careful in sending the information. It does not take account of any collisions that may occur; that needs some additions to the program. It does not use any form of verifying that the data sent and received are the same.

What the main program does is simply flash the LED at 0.5-second intervals. However, if the terminal connected to the UART on the PIC sends a character to the PIC, an interrupt occurs and the PIC breaks off from the main program and carries out the instructions in the ISR.

Figure 11-2 shows what is displayed on the terminal software when the user types the character "H" on the laptop. I have turned off the automatic echo function of the Tera Term software. It is the PIC that echoes the "H" to be displayed here. Then, the PIC sends the numbers 0 to 9 to be displayed as shown in Figure 11-2.

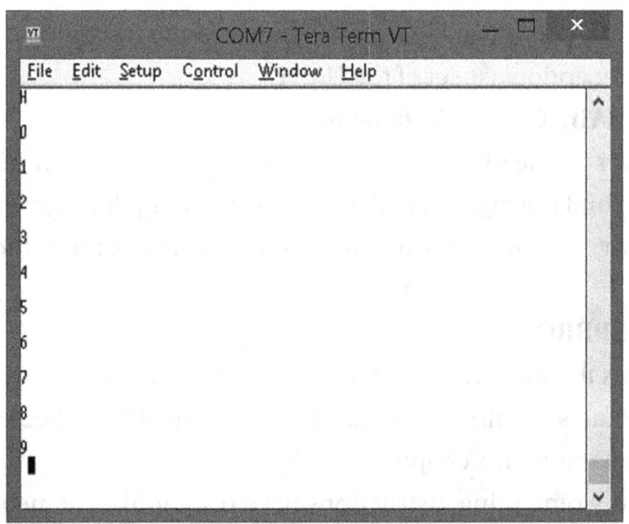

***Figure 11-2.** The display on the Tera Term software*

Figure 11-3 shows the corresponding display on the LCD connected to the PIC.

Figure 11-3. *The corresponding display on the LCD*

The Baud Rate

In serial communication, all data is sent one bit at a time. The number of bits that can be sent in 1 second determines the speed of the system. The baud rate is a term given for the number of bits per second the communication system is set to. A typical value for the baud rate is 9600. This simply means that 9600 bits are sent in 1 second. There are a number of different standard baud rates, such as the following:

- 110
- 300
- 600
- 1200
- 2400
- 4800
- 9600
- 14400

- 19200
- 38400
- 57600
- 115200
- 230400
- 460800
- 921600

For most serial communications, a baud rate must be set up for the operation to communicate successfully. This means the PIC must have a method by which it can be set to any one of the standard baud rates. The main formula that the PIC uses for this is given in Equation 11-1.

$$BaudRate = \frac{Fosc}{Mode(n+1)}$$ **Equation 11-1 The Baud Rate Equation**

The following defines the terms:

- *Fosc* = Frequency of oscillation.
- *Mode* is just a number which will be either 64,16, or 4 depending on the mode setting of the BRG and ESUART (see Table 11-2).
- *n* is a number depending upon the required baud rate. This number is stored in the BRGH and BRG register pair.

Table 11-1 shows the UART settings.

***Table 11-1.** The Settings for the UART*

Configuration Bits		BRGH	BRG	ESUART	Baud Rate
SYNC	BRG16 Bit Bit 3 of BAUDCON	Bit 2 of TXSTA	Mode	Mode	Formula
0	0	0	8 bit	Asynchronous	$\frac{Fosc}{64(n+1)}$
0	0	1	8 bit	Asynchronous	$\frac{Fosc}{16(n+1)}$
0	1	0	16 bit	Asynchronous	
0	1	1	16 bit	Asynchronous	$\frac{Fosc}{4(n+1)}$
1	0	x	8 bit	Synchronous	
1	1	x	16 bit	Synchronous	

When using Equation 11-1, you would normally know the baud rate you want to use as well as the oscillator frequency. You would also know if you were using 8 bit or 16 bit and the mode setting of the BRG and ESUART. This means that Equation 11-1 must be rearranged for *n*(the number to be loaded into the register pair). Equation 11-2 is the rearranged expression.

$$n = \frac{Fosc}{Mode \times BaudRate} - 1$$ **Equation 11-2 'n' The Number For the Register Pair**

As an example to show how this works, we will assume the required baud rate is 9600 and the oscillator frequency is 8Mhz. The mode number will be 64, as we are using the UART in eight-bit asynchronous mode with BRGH and BRG16 both set to logic '0' (see lines 71 and 72 in Listing 11-1).

Putting the numbers into Equation 11-2 gives

$$n = \frac{8E^6}{64 \times 9600} - 1$$
$$\therefore n = 12.0208$$

Therefore, let $n = 12$, as it must be an integer because it has to be stored in the register pair BRGH and BRG. This means that0 is stored in the SPBRGH(this is the high byte of the number n), and 12, in decimal, is stored in the SPBRG. This was done in lines 71 and 72 of Listing 11-1. The reason we need a register pair is that if *Fosc* were 20Mhz and the mode number were 4, then for a baud rate of 9600 we would get a value for n of 519.8. This would round up to 520 and it would be 0b1000001000 in binary. This needs ten bits (i.e., two eight-bit registers).

The actual values to be stored in the register pair will depend upon the settings you have chosen for your PIC program, such as the Oscillator frequency and the Mode used in the baud rate generator. However, I hope the precedinginformation explains how to set up and use the UART for your PIC.

Using Tera Term

This is a free software that allows you to use your PC as a terminal that can be used to send and receive data. The version I am using is detailed in Figure 11-4.

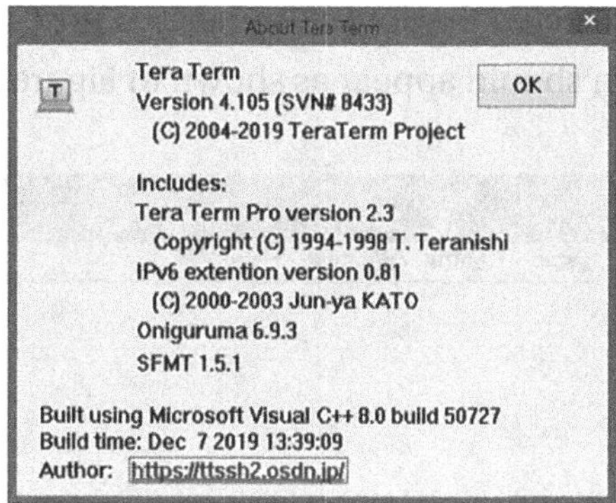

Figure 11-4. *The version of Tera Term*

When using this software, I used Moyina USB to serial converter to connect the PIC to my laptop. This is because my laptop does not have a serial com port.

To use the Tera Term software, click the icon for Tera Term. The software will start with the opening screen as shown in Figure 11-5.

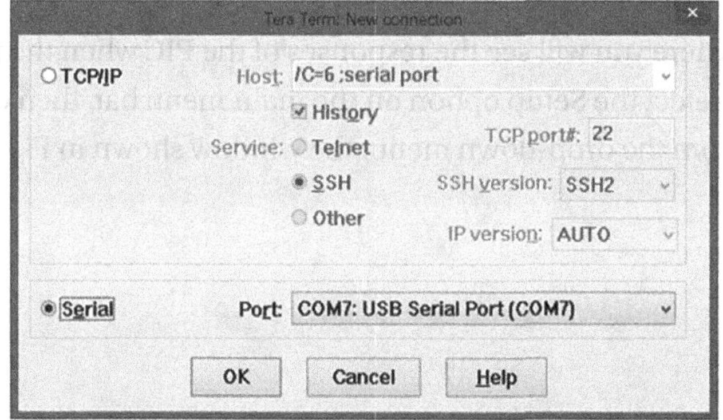

Figure 11-5. *The opening screen of Tera Term*

If you click the serial option, as shown in Figure 11-5, the software should automatically find the correct com port that your USB converter is connected to. This is shown in Figure 11-5. If it doesn't or it finds the wrong com port, then you may have to use Device Manager to find the correct com port.

Once you have selected the correct serial com port and clicked OK, the main terminal screen should appear as shown in Figure 11-6.

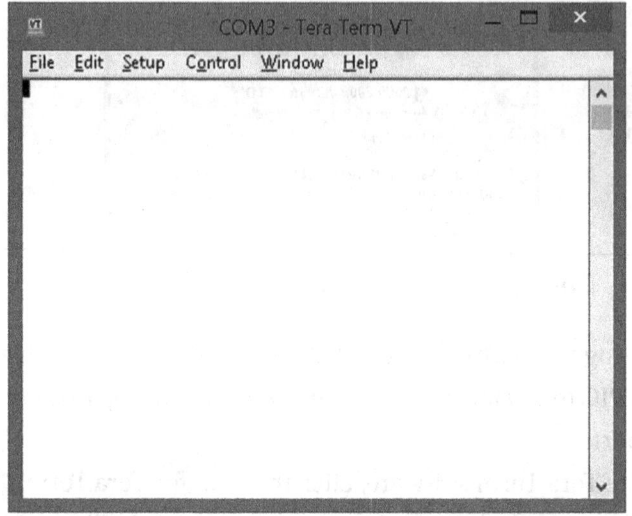

***Figure 11-6.** The main screen of Tera Term*

This is where you will see the responses of the PIC when the program runs. If you select the Setup option on the main menu bar, then choose serial port from the drop-down menu, the window shown in Figure 11-7 will appear.

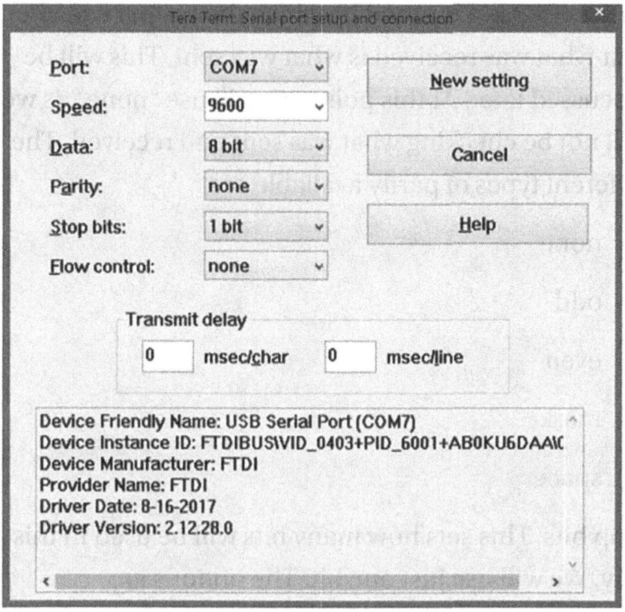

Tera Term: Serial port setup and connection

Port:	COM7	New setting
Speed:	9600	
Data:	8 bit	Cancel
Parity:	none	
Stop bits:	1 bit	Help
Flow control:	none	

Transmit delay
0 msec/char 0 msec/line

Device Friendly Name: USB Serial Port (COM7)
Device Instance ID: FTDIBUS\VID_0403+PID_6001+AB0KU6DAA\C
Device Manufacturer: FTDI
Provider Name: FTDI
Driver Date: 8-16-2017
Driver Version: 2.12.28.0

Figure 11-7. *The serial port setup screen*

This should confirm the correct com port but will also give you the option of setting some other parameters as detailed here:

- Speed. This sets the desired baud rate in bits per second. The most common baud rate is 9600, and this is the one we are using in our program. There are quite a few other possible baud rates.
- Data. This sets the number of bits used to be sent as data. We will use eight bits.

- Parity. This is a method by which the system can check that what was received is what was sent. This will be discussed later. At this point, we will use "none", as we will not be checking what was sent and received. The different types of parity available are
    - none
    - odd
    - even
    - mark
    - space
- Stop bits. This sets how many bits will be used in this way. We will use just one bit. The options are
    - 1
    - 1.5
    - 2
- Flow control. This is used to ensure it is safe to send data to and fro. If you try to send data when the system is not ready, you may cause a collision and the data will not be sent but you may think it has. This is sometimes referred to as "Handshaking". The options available are
    - none, which is what we will use for now
    - Xon/Xoff software control
    - RTS/CTS, which are quite popular, and we will use these in our next UART program;this is hardware control
- DSR/DTR. This is hardware control.

The only other aspect of the software you may want to set up is the actual terminal window. If you select the first option of terminal from the drop-down menu that is presented when you click "setup", you will be presented with the window shown in Figure 11-8.

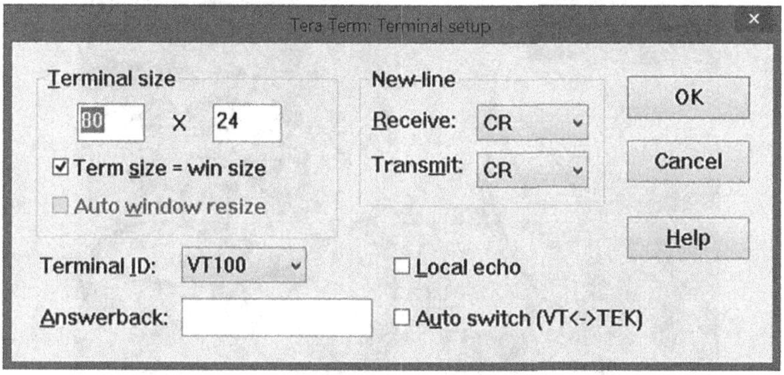

Figure 11-8. *The setupterminal window*

You can leave this with the default setting but the ones you might want to change are as follows:

Terminal size: This is set at 80 characters wide and 24 lines deep at present.

Newline: Both for receiving and for transmitting, the default setting is CR. This means that to move the cursor to the start of a new line, you must send the ASCII for both the LF and the CR individually. This is what we will do in our program. These can be set up so that sending just the ASCII for LF or CR will produce the same effect.

If you tick the box alongside the local echo, then the terminal will send the character that it is transmitting to its screen automatically. However, we want the PIC to echo the character back to the terminal screen; therefore, we have left this unchecked.

Hopefully, this explanation will help you set up the Tera Term software,so you can run the program in the practical situation as shown in Figure 11-1. You should appreciate that with the software Tera Term running, whatever you type on your laptop's keyboard will be transmitted to the PIC.

Figures11-9 and 11-10 show the responses to the UART communication.

Figure 11-9. *The UART program working with the home made board*

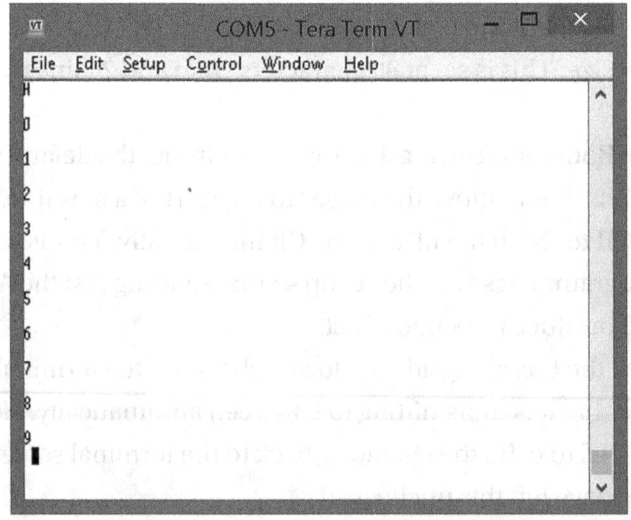

Figure 11-10. *The display on Tera Term when talking to the PIC via the UART*

Using Handshaking

There may be instances where the PIC may be writing to the terminal when the terminal is not ready or when the terminal is trying to write to the PIC. Indeed, if you try typing to the PIC from the terminal too quickly, the program might hang; try it and see what happens.

One method that we can use to try and avoid this is termed "Handshaking". This is when the terminal and the PIC, or whatever we are trying to communicate to, signal to each other that it is clear to send(CTS) and ready to send(RTS). In this next program, we will look at implementing this (Listing 11-2).

Listing 11-2. UART with Handshaking

```
/*This is a basic program to control the LCD and the UART using the PIC 18F4525
 Written by H H Ward dated 02/04/16.
 * modified 24/06/16 to include running from an interrupt whilst main program is simply flashing an led
 * the ISR sends out the character received at the uart back to a terminal and then sends the numbers 0 to 9
 * inserting a line after each number has been sent to the terminal.
 * The program also echos the character received onto the LCD connected to the pic.
 * Note the program has the addition of handshaking using the CTS and RTS signals.
 */
#include <xc.h>
#include <conFigInternalOscNoWDTNoLVP.h>
#include <4bitLCDPortb.h>
//some definitions
```

```
#define RTS PORTDbits.RD0
#define CTS PORTDbits.RD1
//some variables
unsigned char n, count, newdatain = 0;
//the subroutines
void shortdelay ()
{
    TMR0 = 0;
    while (TMR0 < 255);
}
void delay (unsigned char t)
{
for (n = 0; n < t; n ++)
{
    TMR0 = 0;
    while (TMR0 < 255);
}
}
void sendDeviceChar(char byte)
{
    TXREG = byte;
    while(!TXIF);
    while(!TRMT);
    shortdelay ();
}
void sendDeviceString(const char* meshw)
{
    RTS = 1;
    while(*meshw)
    {
    while(!TXIF);
```

```
        TXREG = (*meshw++);
        shortdelay ();
        }

    }
     void interrupt  isr1 ()
    {
        if (PIR1bits.RCIF == 1)
                   {
                           RTS = 1;
                           PIR1bits.RCIF = 0;
                           if(OERR)
                               {
                                   CREN = 0;
                                   CREN = 1;
                               }
                           while(!RCIF);
                           newdatain = RCREG;
                           lcdData = newdatain;
                           lcdOut ();
                           PORTA = newdatain;
                           while (CTS);
                           TXREG = newdatain;
                           shortdelay ();
                           TXREG = 0x0a;
                           shortdelay ();
                           for (n = 0x30; n < 0x3A; n++)
                            {
                               TXREG = 0X0A;
                               shortdelay ();
                               TXREG = 0x0D;
```

```
                        shortdelay ();
                        TXREG = n;
                        shortdelay ();
                        TXREG = 0x0A;
                    }
                  RTS = 0;
            }
}
void main ()
{
    PORTA = 0;
    PORTB = 0;
    PORTC = 0;
    PORTD = 0;
    TRISA = 0X00;
    TRISB = 0x00;
    TRISC = 0b10000000;
    TRISD = 0b00000010;
    ADCON0 = 0x00;
    ADCON1 = 0x0F;
    OSCTUNE = 0b10000000;
    OSCCON = 0b01110000;
    T0CON = 0b11000111;
    INTCON = 0b11000000;
    PIE1bits.RC1IE = 1;
    TXSTA = 0b00100000;
    RCSTA = 0b10010000;
    BAUDCON = 0b00000000;
    SPBRG = 12;
    setUpTheLCD ();
    clearTheScreen ();
```

```
106.        writeString ("Coded Handshaking");
107.        sendDeviceString ("Coded Handshaking Working Now");
108.        sendDeviceChar (0X0A);
109.        sendDeviceChar (0X0D);
110.        line2 ();
111.                while (1)
112.                {
113.                    RTS = 0;
114.                    PORTDbits.RD3 = PORTDbits.RD3^1;
115.                    delay (20);
116.                }
117.    }
```

Analysis of Listing 11-2

I will only discuss the differences with this program. The circuit diagram is shown in Figure 11-12.

The first difference is that we have defined bit0 of PORTD as the RTS pin and bit1 as the CTS pin for the PIC. Also we have connected the LED to bit3 of PORTD. If you look at the circuit diagram as shown on Figure 11-12, you can see that the RTS of the PIC is connected to the CTS of the terminal via the USB converter. Also, the CTS of the PIC is connected to the RTS of the terminal. This is because the PIC will tell the terminal it is ready for the terminal to send(RTS)data to the PIC by sending the logic on this line to a logic '0'. This is done in line 113 of the main part of the program. This means that the CTS input of the terminal is telling the terminal it is clear to send (CTS) data to the PIC.

The first thing the program does after writing the message "Coded Handshaking" to the LCD is to send the message "Coded Handshaking Working Now" to the terminal. This is done with the following instruction:

Line107 sendDeviceString ("Coded Handshaking Working Now");

This calls the subroutine 'sendDeviceString' between lines 38 and 48.

Line 38 void sendDeviceString(const char* meshw)

Sets out the subroutine. Inside the normal brackets, we have named a local variable(i.e., one that can only be used in this subroutine) of type const char * meshw. This is a pointer which is used to point to subsequent locations inside an array. The term 'const' is there to ensure that the address passed up to the subroutine cannot be changed by any instruction in the subroutine. The array that it refers to does not have to be set up by us, but it is automatically created when we call the subroutine in line 107.

When we call this subroutine, the pointer will be pointing to the first character within the call instruction on line 107. In this case, this would be 'C'.

Line 40 RTS = 1;

This is to tell the terminal the PIC is NOT ready for the terminal to send data to the PIC. This is because the PIC is going to send data to the terminal.

Line 43 TXREG = (*meshw++);

This loads the TXREG of the UART in the PIC with this first character and sends it to the terminal. At the same time after loading the TXREG, the PIC will increment the contents of the pointer *meshw so that it is now pointing to the next character waiting to be transmitted.

We then call for a short delay to give the terminal time to display the first character.

This whole process repeats until the pointer *meshw is actually pointing to the important "null" character. That null character is automatically added to the data we are trying to send out of the PIC, written between the normal brackets on line 107. This is important because it denotes the end of the message, and the PIC does not transmit it. However, it does end the while test on line 41.

When we return from the subroutine, the PIC sends out the instructions on lines 108 and 109 to send the cursor to the beginning of the next line on the terminal display.

Line 110 line2 ();

This calls the subroutine line2 to send the cursor on the LCD to the beginning of the second line.

Line 111 while (1)

This creates the forever loop.

Line 113 RTS = 0;

This sets the RTS pin to a logic '0,' which allows the terminal to send any data to the PIC.

Line 114 PORTDbits.RD3 = PORTDbits.RD3^1;

This gets the PIC to do a logical EXOR, signified by the symbol '^,' with the current logic on bit3 of PORTD and the logic '1.' This will make the logic on bit3 goto a logic '1' if it is at a logic '0' when the PIC carries out this instruction. If the logic on bit3 was already a logic '1,' then it would go to a logic '0.' Therefore, this instruction will make a LED connected to bit3 flash.

Line 115 delay (20);

This calls the delay subroutine and passes the number 20 to it. This will create a quarter-of-a-second delay between changes of logic on bit3 of PORTD.

When the terminal sends data to the PIC, the UART generates an interrupt. This makes the PIC stop what it is currently doing and goto the ISR listed between lines 49 and 82. As a precaution, we prevent the terminal from sending any more data as we are processing the initial piece of data. This is done by setting the RTS pin to a logic '1'(see line 53). If we were expecting more data from the terminal, then we would need to set this RTS pin to logic '0' as soon as we have dealt with that initial data. However, in this program we send out the numbers 0 to 9 as before. After that, we set the RTS pin back to a logic '0'(see line 80).

Line 55 if(OERR)

This is an if type test to check if the OERR bit is at a logic '1.'

The OERR bit is bit1 of the RCSTAregister for the UART. It will be set to a logic '1' if new data arrives in the receive register of the UART before your program has emptied the previous byte. If your coding is correct, it should not happen. However, if it did, then you must clear the OERR bit and try to receive the new data again.

Lines 61 to 79 have been discussed in the analysis of Listing 11-1.

Line 81 RTS 0;

This resets this bit back to logic '0'. This then tells the terminal that it can send more data to it.

Figure 11-11 shows the display on the Tera Term software with the text and data sent to it from the PIC.

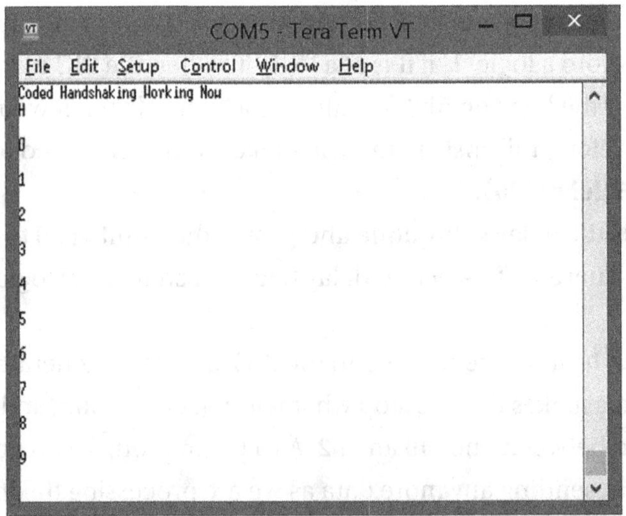

***Figure 11-11.** The screenshot of Tera Term with the inital message from the PIC displayed*

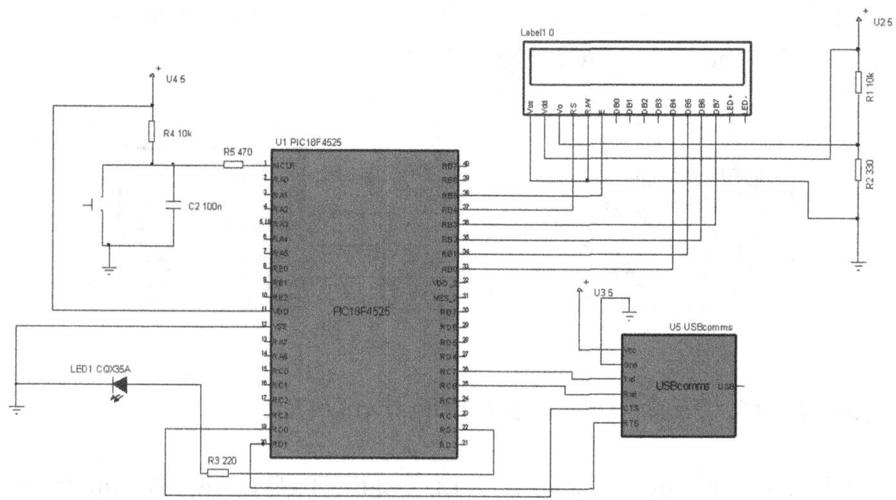

***Figure 11-12.** The UART with handshaking*

I hope this analysis has helped you understand how this program works. The next program will look at using the UART to enable two PICs to talk to each other.

Two PICs Communicate via the UART

In this next exercise, we are going to program two PICs to communicate with each other via the UART. One PIC will be called PIC1 and the other will be called PIC2. I have used my two prototype boards to show this project working practically. PIC1 uses the matrix board with an LCD connected to PORTB. This then uses the header file 4bitLCDPortb.h. PIC2 is on the Microchip demo board, which has the LCD connected to PORTD. This then uses the header file 4bitLCDDemoBoard.h. This means that there are some small differences with the TRIS registers. Another difference is that the RTS on PIC1 is connected to bit0 of PORTD and the CTS is connected to bit1 of PORTD. With respect to PIC2, the RTS is connected to bit0 of PORTB and the CTS is connected to bit1. Note that the RTS on PIC1 is connected to the CTS of PIC2 and the CTS of PIC1 is connected to the RTS of PIC2 (Figure 11-13).

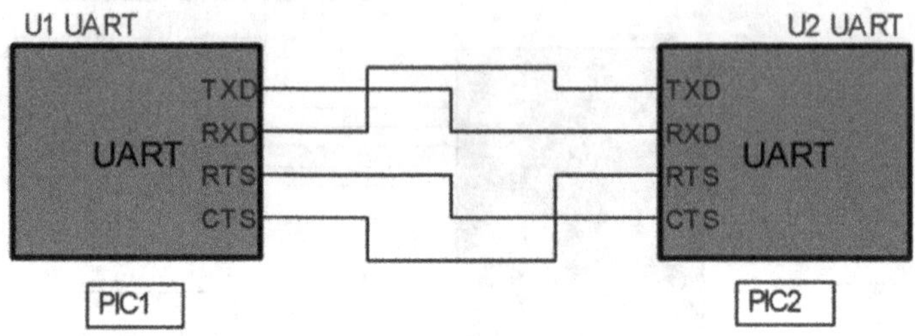

***Figure 11-13.** The connections for the two UARTs*

Note also, as shown in Figure 11-13, that the TXD in PIC1 is connected to the RXD of PIC2 and the TXD is connected to the RXD of PIC2.

Figure 11-14 shows the displays of the two PICs after they have sent and received data to and fro.

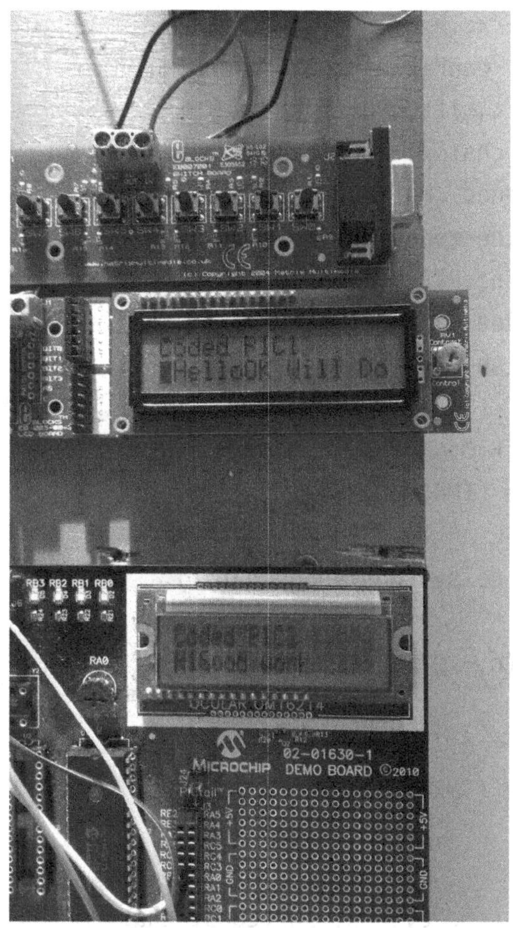

Figure 11-14. *The displays of the two PICs*

The code for the two PICs are shown in Listings 11-3 and 11-4.

Listing 11-3. PIC1

```
/*This is a basic program to use the UART
To communicate with two PICs
This is the program for PIC one
Written by H H Ward for the PIC18F4525
Dated 03/04/2021*/
```

```
#include <xc.h>
#include <conFigInternalOscNoWDTNoLVP.h>
#include <4bitLCDPortb.h>
unsigned char n, count, newdatain = 0;
    unsigned char mess[30], *messpointer;
    #define repeatButton PORTAbits.RA4
    #define RTS PORTDbits.RD0
    #define CTS PORTDbits.RD1
    void shortdelay ()
    {
    TMR0 = 0;
    while (TMR0 < 255);
    }
    void delay (unsigned char t)
    {
    for (n = 0; n < t; n ++)
    {
    TMR0 = 0;
    while (TMR0 < 255);
    }
    }
    void sendDeviceString(const char* meshw)
    {
    while(*meshw)
    {
    while (CTS);
    RTS = 1;
    while(!TXIF);
    TXREG = (*meshw++);
    shortdelay ();
    RTS = 0;
    }
```

```
}
void interrupt  isr1 ()
{
if (PIR1bits.RCIF == 1)
{
RTS = 1;
do
{
if(OERR)
{
CREN = 0;
CREN = 1;
}
while(!RCIF);
newdatain = RCREG;
lcdData = newdatain;
lcdOut ();
shortdelay ();
}while (RCIF);
RTS = 0;
}
}
void main ()
{
PORTA = 0;
PORTB = 0;
PORTC = 0;
PORTD = 0;
TRISA = 0b00010000;
TRISB = 0x00;
TRISC = 0b10000000;
TRISD = 0x02;
```

```
ADCON0 = 0x00;
ADCON1 = 0x0F;
OSCCON = 0b01110000;
OSCTUNE = 0b10000000;
T0CON = 0b11000111;
INTCON = 0b11000000;
PIE1bits.RC1IE = 1;
TXSTA = 0b00100000;
RCSTA = 0b10010000;
BAUDCON = 0b00000000;
SPBRG = 12;
messpointer = mess;
setUpTheLCD ();
clearTheScreen ();
writeString ("Coded PIC1");
line2 ();
while (1)
{
while (!repeatButton);
while (CTS);
sendDeviceString ("Hi");
delay (10);
while (!repeatButton);
while (CTS);
sendDeviceString ("Good work");
delay (10);
while (!repeatButton);
delay (10);
}
}
```

Analysis of Listing 11-3

There are no really new instructions, so I will just discuss the principle of the programs. Both PICs display an opening statement on their LCDs(see line 84). Next, they both go into a forever while loop(see line 86). We start the sequence by PIC1, after waiting for the repeat button to go high(see line 88), will send the first message, "Hi", to PIC2 (see line 90). However, this will only happen if PIC2 has driven the CTS input to PIC1 down to a logic '0'. Both PICs will ensure this happens, as within their respective interrupt routines they ensure that their RTS pin, which is the CTS pin of the other PIC, is sent to a logic '0' (see line 57). Line 91 creates a delay of about 135ms. This is just to make sure the repeatbutton has returned to a logic '0'. Line 92 waits for the repeatbutton to go high again before PIC1 can send out the next message. However, before this happens you should get PIC2 to send its first message.

The process repeats: PIC1 will receive the two messages from PIC2 and it will send its own messages to PIC2(see Figure 11-14 for the two displays).

Listing 11-4. PIC2

```
/*This is a basic program to use the UART
To communicate with two PICs
This is the program for PIC two
Written by H H Ward for the PIC18F4525
Dated 03/04/2021*/
#include <xc.h>
#include <conFigInternalOscNoWDTNoLVP.h>
#include <4bitLCDDemoBoard.h>
unsigned char n, count, newdatain = 0;
      unsigned char mess[30], *messpointer;
      #define repeatButton PORTAbits.RA4
      #define RTS PORTBbits.RB0
```

```
#define CTS PORTBbits.RB1
void shortdelay ()
{
TMR0 = 0;
while (TMR0 < 255);
}
void delay (unsigned char t)
{
for (n = 0; n < t; n ++)
{
TMR0 = 0;
while (TMR0 < 255);
}
}
void sendDeviceString(const char* meshw)
{
while(*meshw)
{
while (CTS);
RTS = 1;
while(!TXIF);
TXREG = (*meshw++);
shortdelay ();
RTS = 0;
}
}
void interrupt  isr1 ()
{
if (PIR1bits.RCIF == 1)
{
RTS = 1;
```

```
do
{
if(OERR)
{
CREN = 0;
CREN = 1;
}
while(!RCIF);
newdatain = RCREG;
lcdData = newdatain;
lcdOut ();
shortdelay ();
}while (RCIF);
RTS = 0;
}
}
void main ()
{
PORTA = 0;
PORTB = 0;
PORTC = 0;
PORTD = 0;
TRISA = 0b00010000;
TRISB = 0x02;
TRISC = 0b10000000;
TRISD = 0x00;
ADCON0 = 0x00;
ADCON1 = 0x0F;
OSCCON = 0b01110000;
OSCTUNE = 0b10000000;
T0CON = 0b11000111;
```

```
INTCON = 0b11000000;
PIE1bits.RC1IE = 1;
TXSTA = 0b00100000;
RCSTA = 0b10010000;
BAUDCON = 0b00000000;
SPBRG = 12;
messpointer = mess;
setUpTheLCD ();
clearTheScreen ();
writeString ("Coded PIC2");
line2 ();
while (1)
{
while (repeatButton);
while (CTS);
sendDeviceString ("Hello");
delay (10);
while (repeatButton);
while (CTS);
sendDeviceString ("OK Will Do");
delay (10);
while (repeatButton);
delay (10);
}
}
```

At this point, there are no real aspects of this program that need analyzing. Figure 11-15 shows the circuit for the PIC-to-PIC UART project.

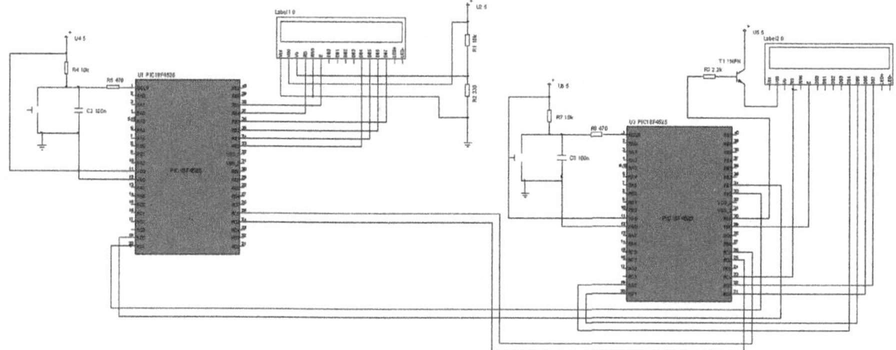

Figure 11-15. *The circuit for the PIC-to-PIC UART project*

Summary

In this chapter, we have studied how the PIC can use the UART to communicate with a terminal device. The same approach can be used for many other devices. We have gone through an initial look at interrupts, learning something about what they are and how the PIC can control and use them.

In the next chapter, we will look at using an interrupt to create a real-time clock (RTC) display on an LCD. We will also look at using the DS1307 module to create an RTC.

CHAPTER 12

Real-Time Clock and Interrupts

In this chapter, we will look at two programs that create a real-time clock (RTC). The first uses an external crystal to provide the synchronization for the clock and the LCD to display the information. It also uses an interrupt to tell the PIC to increment the time. The second will use the DS1307 RTC module.

Finally, we will use the RTC from the first program to run a module with four seven-segment displays to display a digital clock. The display uses the TM1637 driver IC from Titan Micro Electronics. We will also use the display to show the current temperature.

After reading this chapter, you will know how to use an interrupt and an external crystal oscillator to produce an RTC with the PIC18f4525. You will also learn how to use the DS1307 module to do the same. Also, you will be able to use the TM1637 IC to control a series of four seven-segment displays.

H. H. Ward, *Programming Arduino Projects with the PIC Microcontroller*,
https://doi.org/10.1007/978-1-4842-7230-5_12

The RTC Program

I am adding this program because it is a good use of timer1 and its interrupt. The ability to produce an accurate clock program is very useful. It can be used to synchronize events by time and date, and create a calendar. In my second book, we created a clock program, but it was not easy to make it very accurate. The RTC program that we will look at in this chapter is much more accurate and easy to set up.

The program uses an external crystal oscillator that produces a very accurate 32.768kHz frequency output. This oscillator can be set up as the source for timer1. This is one of the four timers that the PIC18f4525 has at its disposal. The control register for timer1 is shown in Table 12-1.

Table 12-1. *The T1CON Control Register*

Bit 7	Bit 6	Bit 5	Bit 4	Bit 3	Bit 2	Bit 1	Bit 0
RD16	T1RUN	T1CKPS1	T1CKPS0	T1OSEN	$\overline{\text{T1SYNC}}$	TMR1CS	TMR1ON

The usage of the bits in the T1CON SFR is as follows.

Bit 7 RD16 (16bit Read/Write Mode Enable bit)

- A logic '1' enables TMR1 as a 16-bit read or write operation.
- A logic '0' enables TMR1 as an eight-bit read or write operation so that you can read or write to the TMR1H, high byte, or TMR1L the low byte.

Bit 6 T1RUN (Timer1 System Clock Status bit)

- A logic '1' means the device clock is derived from the timer1 oscillator. This means the timer1 oscillator must be enabled.

- A logic '0' means the device clock is derived from somewhere else.

Bit 5 T1CKPS1 (Timer1 Clock Prescale Select 1)

- This is used in conjunction with bit 4.

Bit 4 T1CKPS0 (Timer1 Clock Prescale Select 0)

- This is used in conjunction with bit 5. These two bits allow four different divide rates as shown in Table 12-2.

Table 12-2. *The Prescaler Divide Rate*

Bit 5 T1CKPS1	Bit 4 T1CKPS0	Prescale Divide rate
0	0	1:1 No divide
0	1	1:2 Divide by 2
1	0	1:4 Divide by 4
1	1	1:8 Divide by 8

Bit 3 T1OSCEN (Timer1 Oscillator Enable Bit)

- Logic '1' timer1 oscillator is enabled. There is an oscillator circuit on the chip that uses a crystal oscillator that is connected between T1OSI, timer1 OSC input, and T1OSCO, timer1 OSC Output. It is a low-powered circuit that incorporates a 32.768kHz crystal.
- Logic '0' oscillator is disabled.

Bit 2 T1SYNC (Timer1 External Clock Input Synchronization Select Bit)

- The action of this bit is dependent upon the TMR1CS bit. If that bit is a logic '0', then this bit is ignored. If the TMR1CS bit is a logic '1', then the T1SYNC action is as follows:
    - A logic '1' Do not synchronize the external clock input.
    - A logic '0' means synchronize the external clock input.

Bit 1 TMR1CS (Timer1 Clock Source Select Bit)

- A logic '1' external clock from RC0/T1OSCO/T13CKI (on rising edge)
- A logic '0' internal clock (Fosc/4)

Bit 0 TMR1ON (Timer1 On Bit)

- A logic '1' turns timer1 on.
- A logic '0' turns timer1 off.

In this program, we are going to use timer1 to produce an RTC function. To do this, the source for timer1 will be a 32.768kHz crystal that is connected between T1OSI and T1OSO, which are pins 16 and 15 of the PIC. These pins are multiplexed with RC1 and RC0; however, when timer1 is turned on these two pins are set as inputs regardless of their settings with the TRISC SFR. To use this oscillator with timer1, we must do the following:

Set bit 0 to a logic '1' to turn timer1 on.

Set bit 1 to a logic '1' to use the external oscillator as the clock source for timer1.

Set bit 2 to a logic '1' so that we do not synchronize the external clock input.

Set bit 3 to a logic '1' so that the external oscillator circuit is enabled.

Set bits 4 and 5 to logic '0' so that we do not divide the oscillator.

Set bit 6 to a logic '0' so that the device clock is not sourced by timer1 oscillator.

Set bit 7 to a logic '0' so that timer1 register, which holds the current count value for timer1, is made up of two eight-bit registers cascaded together, namely TMR1H and TMR1L

This means that the eight-bit number to be written to T1CON is 0b00001111.

The best way to explain the process of the RTC program would be to go through a program listing. The following program simply displays a 24-hr clock in hours, minutes, and seconds using the RTCC, RTC Circuit (Listing 12-1, Figure 12-1).

Listing 12-1. RTC Program

```
/*
* File:   Real Time Clock.c
Author: H. H. Ward
*Written for the PIC18F4525
Created on 24 August 2020, 12:09
*/
#include <xc.h>
#include <conFigInternalOscNoWDTNoLVP.h>
#include <4bitLCDDemoBoard.h>
unsigned char secunits = 0X30, sectens = 0X30, minunits =
0X30, mintens = 0X30, hourunits = 0X30, hourtens = 0X30;
void delay (unsigned char t)
{
for (n = 0; n < t; n ++)
```

```
{
TMR0 = 0;
while (TMR0 < 255);              //a 30msec delay
}
}
void interrupt isr1 ()
{
secunits ++;
PIR1bits.TMR1IF = 0;
TMR1H = 0X80;
}
void main ()
{
PORTA = 0;
PORTB = 0;
PORTC = 0;
PORTD = 0;
TRISA = 0b00001111;
TRISB = 0b00000000;
TRISC = 0b10010010;
TRISD = 0x00;
ADCON0 = 0b00000000;
ADCON1 = 0b00001111;
OSCTUNE = 0x80;
OSCCON = 0x70;
T0CON = 0XC7;
T1CON = 0b00001111;
INTCON = 0b11000000;
PIE1bits.TMR1IE = 1;
PORTB = 0;
setUpTheLCD ();
```

```
writeString ("Hello");
line2 ();
while (1)
{
if (secunits == 0X3A)
{
secunits = 0X30;
sectens ++;
if ( sectens == 0X36)
{
sectens = 0X30;
minunits ++;
if (minunits == 0X3A)
{
minunits = 0X30;
mintens ++;
if (mintens == 0X36)
{
mintens = 0X30;
hourunits ++;
if(hourunits == 0X3A)
{
hourunits = 0X30;
hourtens ++;
}
}
}
}
if (hourtens == 0X32 & hourunits == 0X34 )
{
hourtens = 0x30;
```

```
hourunits= 0x30;
}
}
line2 ();
lcdData = hourtens;
lcdOut ();
lcdData = hourunits;
lcdOut ();
lcdData = 0x3A;
lcdOut ();
lcdData = mintens;
lcdOut ();
lcdData = minunits;
lcdOut ();
lcdData = 0x3A;
lcdOut ();
lcdData = sectens;
lcdOut ();
lcdData = secunits;
lcdOut ();
lcdData = 0xA0;
lcdOut ();
}
}
```

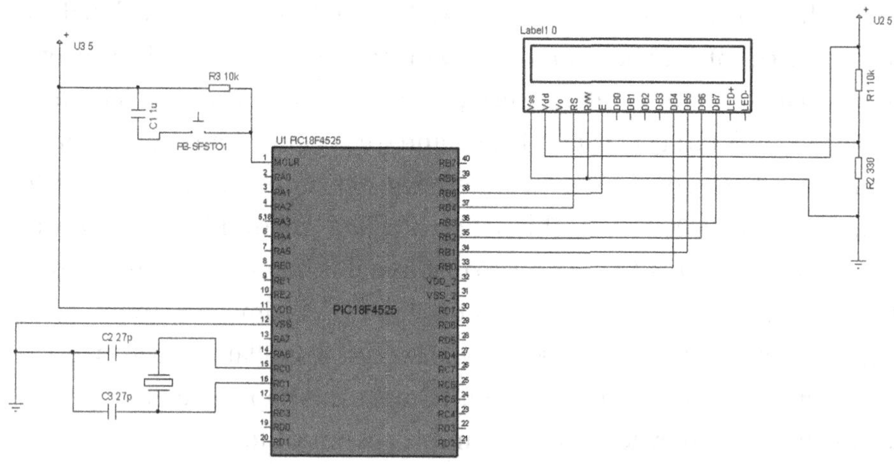

Figure 12-1. *The basic circuit for the RTC*

Analysis of Listing 12-1

I will restrict the analysis to the main principle of the program and any new instructions that are used in the program.

The main principle is that we will use TIMER1, set as a 16-bit timer, to count the clock pulses from the external crystal that is used as the source for timer1. Note that the source for the clock that is used to synchronize the instructions of the program will still be the internal oscillator block set to 8Mhz.

To understand how the process will work, we should appreciate that timer1 will now simply count the clock pulses provided by the very accurate 32.758kHz crystal oscillator. The current count value will be stored in the two eight-bit registers TMR1H and TMR1L, as we have set timer1 to a 16-bit register that can be split into two bytes: TMR1H and TMR1L. This means the maximum value that timer1 can count up to is 65535. Knowing that the oscillator runs at 36.768kHz, then one count will take 30.5176ms. This means that counting from 0 to 65535 will take 65536 × 30.5176ms (i.e., 2 seconds exactly). Therefore, if we only let timer1 count half of the 65536 counts, then it will take 1 second. However, which half should we count, and how do we know that timer1 has counted correctly? To understand the answer, we must ask what happens when timer1 is at 65535, which is 0b1111111111111111, and we get one more count. What happens is that all the bits in the timer1 register simply go back to logic '0' (i.e., 0b0000000000000000). This action is called "rollover", as the value in the register goes from 65535 back to 0. When this happens, the interrupt flag, or bit, for timer1, TMR1IF, is set to a logic '1'. As timer1 is simply counting clock pulses from the 32.768kHz crystal oscillator, it will take 2 seconds for this rollover to happen. To make this happen after only 1 second has passed instead of 2, we simply get timer1 to count the top half of its count (i.e., from 0b1000000000000000 to 0b1111111111111111). At 32.768kHz, this will only take 1 second exactly.

This is what we do, however, to take advantage of the fact that when timer1 "rolls over", we must enable the interrupt for timer1. I have already said that the timer1 interrupt flag will go to a logic '1' when this rollover happens. However, if we don't enable the interrupt action for timer1, this setting of the flag won't cause an interrupt to the PIC. To enable the timer1 interrupt, we must enable all global and peripheral interrupts as well as enabling the actual peripheral interrupt for timer1.

One more thing you need to be aware of is that the interrupt flag, once set, does not automatically reset back to logic '0'. Therefore, you must reset the bit back to logic '0' in your programming or else you will never be able to determine when another rollover occurs.

We could get the program to check to see if the rollover flag had been set; this is called software polling. However, the more efficient way is to use the interrupt, as we know this is checked in the fetch-and-execute cycle every time the micro fetches an instruction. This means we will never miss the rollover at the instant it happens.

We must now write that special subroutine, the interrupt service routine (ISR) so that the PIC knows what to do when timer1 rolls over.

The ISR for the rollover of timer1 is written in lines 19 and 24 of Listing 12-1. All we do in that service routine is increment the variable "secunits". This is the variable that counts the seconds for the 24hr clock.

We also clear the timer1 interrupt flag so that we can detect the next rollover.

Finally, in line 23 we load the timer1 high byte, TMR1H, with the value of 0X80. This means that the timer starts counting from the latter half of its value and so it will take exactly 1 second for timer1 to reach its maximum value and roll over again.

Line 41 is where we enable all global and peripheral interrupts, and line 42 is where we enable the timer1 peripheral interrupts. Note that bit 7, the GIE bit, of the INTCON register, when set to a logic '1', enables the global interrupts. Also bit 6, PIE, enables all peripheral interrupts.

Line 47 while (1)

This sets up the forever loop that displays the time on the LCD. The principle behind controlling the LCD is to split the time up into columns: secs, mins, hours. However, each column will be further split into units and tens. This is why I have created the six variables on line 10:

Line 10 unsigned char secunits = 0X30, sectens = 0X30, minunits = 0X30, mintens = 0X30, hourunits = 0X30, hourtens = 0X30;

At the same time that we declare the variables, we load each variable with the value 0X30. This is ASCII for '0'. Note that in the ASCII table, the numbers 0 to 9 start at 0X30 and the digit 0 is simply replaced with the number between 0 to 9. Pretty sensible, isn't it?

This means we will be splitting the LCD display up into these six columns. Also, between each column we will display the colon ':'. The ASCII for the colon symbol is 0X2A. Now let's look at the instructions in this forever loop.

Line 49 if (secunits == 0X3A)

This is the first thing we do. This is a test to see if the value in the variable secunits has gotten to 0X3A. This is the ASCII for 10. If it has been incremented to 10 within the ISR, then the PIC will carry out the instructions between lines 50 and 78. If it hasn't reached 0X3A, then the PIC will go to line 79, where it starts to send instructions for the LCD display.

Line 51 secunits = 0X30;

Within any column of our display of the denary system, we can only have single digits 0 to 9. This means we cannot display the number 10 in one column. What should happen is the active column goes back to 0 and we carry one over to the next column. That is what happens here. As this is the units column, the units must go back to 0, hence secunits = 0x30 as with this instruction. Also the sectens increments by 1, as with the next instruction.

Line 52 sectens ++;

Line 53 if (sectens == 0X36)

This is testing to see if the variable sectens has just been incremented to a value of 0X36. What we are really testing is whether we are trying to display the number 6 in the tens column of the seconds count for the display. Well, as you know, the seconds go from 0 to 59 and then roll over to 0, with 1 to carry on to the minutes display. This means the sectens must go back to 0 and the minunits must increment by 1. This is what the next two instructions do.

Line 55 sectens = 0X30;

Line 56 minunits ++;

Lines 61 to 72 carry out similar tests and instructions on the remaining columns of the time displayed on the LCD.

Line 73 if (hourtens == 0X32 & hourunits == 0X34)

This is carrying out two tests with the same instruction. It is testing to see if the hourtens is at 2 and at the same time we are trying to display

4 on the hour units. This would mean we are trying to display a time of 24 hrs plus. This can't happen, as 1 second after 23 hrs 59 mins and 59 sec, the display must roll over to 00 hrs 00 mins and 00 sec. The next two instructions zero the hours units and tens. The min and sec will be zeroed in instructions written before these two.

Line 75 hourtens = 0x30;

Line 76 hourunits= 0x30;

Line 79 line2 ();

This calls the subroutine to send the cursor to the beginning of line 2 on the LCD.

Line 80 lcdData = hourtens;

Line 81 lcdOut;

Line 82 lcdData = 0x3A;

Line 83 lcdOut;

These four instructions send the value for the hour columns to the LCD and the ':' colon symbol.

The following lines from 84 to 97 do the same for the mins and sec columns of the display.

I am hoping that there are no more instructions that need any analysis, as we have used them all in previous programs. I also hope that all my analyses, in each of the chapters in the book, give some insight as to how I come up with the design and concepts for my programs. I basically study what it is I have to achieve and then consider what instructions will get me to achieve it. I then see if I can make my coding more efficient.

I hope you will develop your own successful approach. However, I also hope you now realize that it is essential that you fully understand how the systems you want to use work. When you gain that understanding then, with experience, I hope you will find that putting the instructions together to achieve what you want is the easy part. I am saying this now, as I think this next program will show you what I mean.

Figure 12-2 shows the program for the RTC working on my microchip PIC DEM board. I used this board as I didn't have a 32.768kHz crystal. However, the PIC DEM board has one connected already. That is why I have used the <4bitLCDDemoBoard.h>. It is almost the same as the PORTB header file but the LCD PORT is PORTD.

Figure 12-2. *The RTC program*

The DS1307 RTC Module

Listing 12-1 created a 24hr clock display using a 32.768kHz crystal oscillator. However, as it stands that is all it does. I could write a lot more coding to make it do a lot more, including a calendar with day, month, and year, as well as get it to respond to different numbers of days for different months and leap years. However, that would produce a long program listing. Not difficult, just too long to put in this book.

An alternative approach would be to use the DS1307 module. This will perform all the work which I just mentioned in this opening paragraph and a bit more; but you won't need all that coding. A lot of the program is firmware on the module. The drawback, which is not too bad, is that you have to learn how to control it and use it.

Setting Up and Reading from the DS1307

The DS1307 communicates with a microcontroller using the I^2C protocol. We have used the I^2C in chapter 10 with the TC74 temperature sensor. That means we should now have some idea of how to use it already, but we will look at it in more depth here.

The I^2C Protocol

First, it might be useful to explain what a protocol is. Simply put, it is an agreed procedure for recognizing what the transmission of bits between a transmitter and a receiver mean. Once this process has been agreed, the users can then use the protocol with confidence that both the transmitter and receiver can understand the communication between them.

I^2C stands for inter-integrated circuit, and the procedure can be described as follows:

There must be a master device and a slave device. The master can communicate with more than one slave. Also, there can be more than one master in the system. In chapter 10, our master, the PIC, communicated with two slaves, the EEPROM and the TC74 temperature sensor. In this chapter, the PIC will only communicate with one slave, the DS1307 RTC module.

Once communication has been set up, the master can be the transmitter, as when the master is simply writing to the slave. However, it can also be the receiver, as when the master is reading from the slave.

The slave can also be the receiver, as when the master is just writing to the slave, but it can also be the transmitter, as when the master is reading from the slave.

To try and fully explain the I^2C process, we will look at the process when the master is just writing to the slave and then when it is reading from the slave.

Writing to the Slave

The following describes what happens when the master is writing to the slave.

The Start Bit

The first thing the master must do is send a "start" bit to the slave. This means the master must drive the SDA line from high to low while the SCL line is held high.

The Address Bits and Control Bit in the First Byte

The master will then send a byte that contains the address of the particular slave it wants to write to and a control bit that tells the slave it wants to write to it or read from it. This byte is

b7, b6, b5, b4, b3, b2, b1, and b0.

Bits 1 to 7 contain the actual address of the slave the master wants to write to. This gives the master the ability to address 2^7 slaves (i.e., 128, addresses 0 to 127).

A logic '1' in bit 0 means the master wants to read from the slave, and a logic '0' means the master wants to write to the slave.

The address of the DS1307 is set as 0b1101000x. The slave address for the TC74, in chapter 10, was 0b1001101x.

Therefore, as we want to write to the DS1307, the first byte will be 0b11010000 or 0XD0. Note that bit 0 is set to a logic '0', as we are writing to the DS1307.

The Acknowledgment Bit

Then, as the slave is in receiving mode, it must send an acknowledgment bit to confirm to the master it has received the byte. This means the slave must pull the SDA line low while the clock is high. This is the acknowledgment bit.

The Data Byte

The master must now write to the slave a byte of data that contains the memory location in the slave which the master wants to write to first. The slave will load this data into a pointer inside it, which the slave uses to point to the address the master wants to write to. The slave will then send the acknowledgment bit to the master.

The master will now send the data that it wants to write to the address it has just given to the slave. The slave will write the data to that address. Then it will increment the pointer so that it now points to the next memory address. The slave will then send another acknowledgment bit to the master.

The master will send any more data to the slave that it wants to write to it. The slave will respond as before.

The Stop Bit

When the master wants to tell the slave it has finished writing to it, the master must send a stop bit. This is when the master changes the SDA line from low to high when the SCL line is high.

This action can be summed up in Table 12-3.

Table 12-3. *The Process for Writing to the Slave*

Start Bit	Slave Address	R/W bit	Ack	Memory Address	Ack	Data	Ack	Last Data	Ack	Stop Bit
H to L	0b110100x	0	Low	xxxxxxxx	Low	xxxxxxxx	Low	xxxxxxxx	Low	L to H

The shaded cells are the responses from the slave. When we look at the program listing, we will see how the program conforms to this protocol.

Reading from the Slave

Before the master can read from the slave, the master must send to the slave the address of where the master wants to start reading from. This address would be loaded into the pointer in the slave as before. This would be a write operation; therefore, to start the read sequence, the master must do the following:

1. Put a start bit on the SDA line.
2. Send the address and control byte to tell the correct slave the master will be writing to it. In our case this would be the following eight bits:
    a. 0b11010000 bits 7 down to 1 make up the correct address of the slave, and bit 0 is a logic '0' as we are writing to the slave.
3. The slave will then respond with the acknowledgment bit.
4. The master will send the eight bits that details the start address of where the master wants to start reading from. The slave will load its pointer with this address.
5. The slave will respond with the acknowledgment bit.
6. The master will then send the stop bit to finish this initial write operation.
7. The master will now tell the slave it wants to read from the start address it has just sent. This will involve the following operations;

8. The master will send another start bit.

9. The master then sends the address and control bit as follows:

   a. 0b11010001. Bit 0 is a logic '1' as the master is now reading from the slave.

10. The slave will send the acknowledgment bit.

11. The slave now sends the first byte of data from the requested address. Note that if the master did not send an address via an initial write operation, then the slave will send the data from the address that its pointer is currently pointing to. The slave then increments its address pointer.

12. Now, as the master is receiving the data, it must put an acknowledgment on the SDA.

13. After seeing the acknowledgment, the slave will put the data from the next location on the SDA line to send it to the master. The slave increments its address pointer again.

14. The master, after receiving this new data from the slave, must put an acknowledgment bit on the SDA line again.

The NACK or Not Acknowledgment Bit

This process carries on until the master gets the last byte of data it wants from the slave. When the master gets this last byte of data it will put a Not Acknowledgment (NACK) bit on the SDA line. The NACK is recognized as the SDA line being held high while the 9th clock signal is high. This 9th clock cycle is generated by the master after all eight bits have been transmitted. This 9th cycle is reserved for the reception of either the acknowledgment bit or NACK bit.

When the slave sees this NACK bit on the SDA line, it knows not to transmit any more data.

To complete the action, the master will put a stop bit on the SDA line. This whole read action can be summed up in Tables 12-4 and 12-5.

Table 12-4. *The Initial Write to Slave to Set Up the Read Operation*

Start Bit	Slave Address	R/W Bit	Ack	Memory Address	Ack	Stop Bit
H to L	0b110100x	0	low	xxxxxxxx	low	L to H

Table 12-5. *The Read from Slave Operation*

Start Bit	Slave Address	R/W Bit	Ack	Data from Slave	Ack from Master	Last Data	NOT Ack from Master	Stop Bit
H to L	0b110100x	1	Low	xxxxxxxx	low	Xxxxxxxx	High	L to H

The shaded cells are the responses from the slave.

I know this is rather a lot to read through, but once you have gotten your thorough understanding correct, you know you now have a firm basis for writing your program instructions. Listing 12-2 provides the code for using the DS1307.

Listing 12-2. Using the DS1307

```
/*
* File:   I2C DS1307 RTC Module
Author: Mr H. H. Ward
*DS1307 RTC program
```

```
using the PIC18f4525
Created on 25 July 2018, 13:19
*/
#include <xc.h>
#include <stdio.h>
#include <conFigInternalOscNoWDTNoLVP.h>
#include <4BitLCDPortb.h>
// declare any variables
unsigned char sec = 10, min = 0x59, hour = 0x23, day, date = 0x31, month = 0x12, year = 0x20;
//declare any subroutines
void ms13delay (unsigned char (t))
{
for (n = 0; n <t; n++)
{
TMR0 = 0;
while (TMR0 < 255);
}
}
void MSSP2CInit()
{
SSPCON1 = 0x28;
SSPCON2 = 0x00;
SSPSTAT = 0x00;
SSPADD =  0x13;
TRISCbits.RC3 = 1;
TRISCbits.RC4 = 1;
}
void MSSP2Cidle()
{
while ((SSPSTAT & 0x04) || (SSPCON2 & 0x1F));
}
```

```
void MSSP2Cwait()
{
while(!PIR1bits.SSPIF);
PIR1bits.SSPIF=0;
}
void MSSP2CStart()
{
MSSP2Cidle();
SSPCON2bits.SEN = 1;
}
void MSSP2CStop()
{
MSSP2Cidle();
SSPCON2bits.PEN = 1;
}
void MSSP2CRestart()
{
MSSP2Cidle();
SSPCON2bits.RSEN = 1;
}
void MSSP2CNACK()
{
MSSP2Cidle();
SSPCON2bits.ACKDT = 1;
SSPCON2bits.ACKEN = 1;
}
void MSSP2CWrite(unsigned char data)
{
MSSP2Cidle();
SEND: SSPBUF=data;
MSSP2Cidle();
```

```
while(SSPCON2bits.ACKSTAT)
{
SSPCON2bits.RSEN=1;
MSSP2Cwait();
goto SEND;
}
}
//-----------------------------------------------------
unsigned char MSSP2Cread()
{
MSSP2Cidle();
SSPCON2bits.RCEN=1;
while(!BF);
MSSP2Cidle();
ACKDT = (1)?0:1;     //check if ack bit received
ACKEN = 1;           //pg 85/234
MSSP2Cidle();
SSPCON2bits.RCEN=0;
return SSPBUF;
}
unsigned char MSSP2CreadNAck()
{
MSSP2Cidle();
SSPCON2bits.RCEN=1;
while(!BF);
MSSP2Cidle();
SSPCON2bits.RCEN=0;
SSPCON2bits.ACKDT=1;
SSPCON2bits.ACKEN=1;
MSSP2Cwait();
return SSPBUF;
}
```

```
void setclock ()
{
MSSP2Cidle ();
MSSP2CStart ();
MSSP2CWrite (0xD0);
MSSP2CWrite (0);
MSSP2CWrite ((sec/10<<4)+(sec % 10));
MSSP2CWrite (min);
MSSP2CWrite (hour);
MSSP2CWrite (1);
MSSP2CWrite (date);
MSSP2CWrite (month);
MSSP2CWrite (year);
MSSP2CStop();
}
void main()
{
PORTA = 0;
PORTB = 0;
PORTC = 0;
PORTD = 0;
TRISA = 0XFF;
TRISB = 0;
TRISC = 0;
TRISD = 0;
ADCON0 = 0;
ADCON1 = 0X0F;
OSCCON = 0X74;
T0CON = 0XC7;
setUpTheLCD ();
MSSP2CInit();
```

```
clearTheScreen ();
setclock ();
MSSP2Cidle ();
MSSP2CStart ();
MSSP2CWrite (0xD0);
MSSP2CWrite (0);
MSSP2CStop();
while (1)
{
writeString ("Time ");
MSSP2Cidle ();
MSSP2CStart ();
MSSP2CWrite (0xD1);
sec = MSSP2Cread();
min = MSSP2Cread();
hour = MSSP2Cread();
day = MSSP2Cread();
date = MSSP2Cread();
month = MSSP2Cread();
year = MSSP2CreadNAck();
MSSP2CStop();
MSSP2Cidle ();
MSSP2CStart ();
MSSP2CWrite (0xD0);
MSSP2CWrite (0);
MSSP2CStop();
lcdData = ((hour>>4)+0x30);
lcdOut ();
lcdData = ((hour & 0x0F)+0x30);
lcdOut ();
lcdData = 0x3A;
```

```
lcdOut ();
lcdData = ((min>>4)+0x30);
lcdOut ();
lcdData = ((min & 0x0F)+0x30);
lcdOut ();
lcdData = 0x3A;
lcdOut ();
lcdData = ((sec>>4)+0x30);
lcdOut ();
lcdData = ((sec & 0x0F)+0x30);
lcdOut ();
line2();
writeString ("Date ");
lcdData = ((date >>4)+0x30);
lcdOut ();
lcdData = ((date  & 0X0F)+0x30);
lcdOut ();
lcdData = 0x3A;
lcdOut ();
lcdData = ((month >>4)+0x30);
lcdOut ();
lcdData = ((month  & 0X0F)+0x30);
lcdOut ();
lcdData = 0x3A;
lcdOut ();
lcdData = ((year >>4)+0x30);
lcdOut ();
lcdData = ((year  & 0X0F)+0x30);
lcdOut ();
sendcursorhome ();
}
}
```

Analysis of Listing 12-2

The main aspects of the program are as follows:

First, write some values to the DS1307 to set the seconds, minutes, hours, day, date, month, and year values. That is what the following instruction does:

Line 13 unsigned char sec = 10, min = 0x59, hour = 0x23, day, date = 0x31, month = 0x12, year = 0x20;

This sets up seven eight-bit memory locations to store the settings set up in this instruction.

We are loading the relevant variables with the data to display the following initial display on the LCD screen:

Time 23:59:10

Date 31:12:20

This is a specific setting arranged so that in 50 seconds from starting the program, the display should change to:

Time 00:00:00

Date 01:01:21

This would confirm that the firmware on the DS1307 is working correctly. This is what happened with my program. Note that I have not really used the day variable, as this would involve changing the display.

This would mean writing to a series of addresses inside the DS1307. These addresses are detailed in the datasheet for the DS1307. Remember I have told you already that to become an engineer, you must get used to reading datasheets. However, that does assume that the datasheet is well written. Not always the case. Figure 12-3 shows the addresses of the main memory locations we need to use in our program.

ADDRESS	BIT 7	BIT 6	BIT 5	BIT 4	BIT 3	BIT 2	BIT 1	BIT 0	FUNCTION	RANGE
00h	CH	10 Seconds			Seconds				Seconds	00–59
01h	0	10 Minutes			Minutes				Minutes	00–59
02h	0	12 24	10 Hour PM/AM	10 Hour	Hours				Hours	1–12 +AM/PM 00–23
03h	0	0	0	0	0	DAY			Day	01–07
04h	0	0	10 Date		Date				Date	01–31
05h	0	0	0	10 Month	Month				Month	01–12
06h	10 Year				Year				Year	00–99
07h	OUT	0	0	SQWE	0	0	RS1	RS0	Control	—
08h–3Fh									RAM 56 x 8	00h–FFh

Figure 12-3. *The time addresses in the DS1307*

As we know, the slave will increment its pointer every time it puts an acknowledgment bit on the SDA or sends data out to the master; then we need only send the address of the first memory location we want to write to. This would be the address 0x00, which is where the DS1307 stores the seconds value. If we look at Figure 12-3 carefully, we can see that some data is split up into 10s and units, as with "10 seconds" and "seconds" for address 0X00. This means that it will be the high nibble of the data in address 0X00 that stores the number of tens in the whole number of seconds, while the low nibble holds the unit's value. For example if the number of seconds was 54, then the 5 would be stored in the high nibble and the 4 would be stored in the low nibble. We will look at this when we look at the read action.

Just for completeness, we should discuss the CH bit, which is bit 7 of this memory location. This is used to stop the oscillator that the firmware is counting to keep track of time. If this CH bit is a logic '1', then the DS1307 will stop this oscillator. A logic '0' will start it. Note that as the number of tens in any variable will not exceed 5, then under normal circumstances this CH bit would not go to a logic '1'. Note that 5 in four-bit binary is 0101.

Now let's look at the write instructions in the program listing.

Line 131 setclock ();

This calls a subroutine to set up the clock, which sets the clock to our predefined time. Under normal circumstances, you would use some user inputs from switches to set the time. However, this would make the listing very long, and I am really only trying to show you how to use the DS1307. Perhaps you can make that modification to the program yourselves.

This subroutine is written between lines 99 and 113.

Line 101 MSSP2Cidle ();

The first thing we do is call the subroutine to check that the I²C lines are idle. This subroutine is between lines 32 and 35.

Line 102 MSSP2CStart ();

This calls the subroutine to create the start bit. This is between lines 41 and 45.

Line 103 MSSP2CWrite (0xD0);

This calls the subroutine to write to the slave. This is between lines 62 and 73. This calls the MSSP2Cidle () subroutine again and then loads the SSPBUF with the data that has been loaded into the local variable data. This variable will have been loaded with 0XD0, as this was sent to this MSSP2CWrite subroutine in the call instruction here. This is the address and control bit for writing to the DS1307 that must first be sent to the DS1307.

Line 67 while(SSPCON2bits.ACKSTAT)

This is inside the MSSP2CWrite subroutine. We know that after receiving this 0XD0 byte from the master, the DS1307 should send an acknowledgment signal back to the master. This is done by sending the SDA line low at this time. If the master did receive this acknowledgment bit, then the PIC would load a logic '0' into this ACKSTAT in the SSPCON2 register. Therefore, if this bit in the SSPCON2 register was still a logic '1', then it would mean that the master did not receive an acknowledgment bit from the slave. Therefore, this instruction is saying that while we did not receive the acknowledgment bit, we must carry out the instructions between lines 68 and 72. This is where the PIC sends a resend signal, and then waits for the I²C to settle down. Then the PIC goes to the label SEND, which is on line 63. Here the PIC tries sending the data 0XD0 again.

Line 104 MSSP2CWrite (0);

This repeats the preceding write procedure but this time with the value 0. This is 0X00, which is the first address in the DS1307 time register map (see Figure 12-3).

This means that the DS1307 knows we want to write to that address and that the data that follows must be written into that address. However, what about the acknowledgment bit that the slave must send to the master between receiving the address and control bit 0XD0 and this new address 0X00? Well, that is inside the MSSP2CWrite subroutine. As when the PIC now goes to that subroutine to send the address 0X00, the PIC will test to see if there had been a second acknowledgment bit with the instruction on line 67. In this way, the PIC will wait for the slave to send the acknowledgment bit between each write operation to the slave.

Line 105 MSSP2CWrite ((sec/10<<4)+(sec % 10));

In line 13, we loaded the value '10' into the variable 'sec'. However, this number is in the default radix of decimal and not in hexadecimal. This means we need to convert this decimal value into the correct nibbles that will load the tens and units part with the 1 and 0 as needed by the DS1307.

This instruction works in two parts to achieve this. The first part is **(sec/10<<4)**. This divides the value in 'sec' by 10, which will result in the value '1' (i.e., 0b00000001 in eight-bit binary), in this case. However, what the instruction now does is move the bits four places to the left. The result is now 0b00010000, which is what we want (i.e., 0b0001 in the high nibble).

Now the PIC will carry out the second part of the instruction, which is **+(sec % 10)** it adds to the 0b00010000, the result of the first part, the result of the instruction **sec % 10**. The '%' symbol means the remainder, and here we are talking about the remainder of the contents of the variable 'sec' after it has been divided by 10. The number written after the '%' sign is what the variable is divided by. Therefore, as the variable 'sec' currently has the number 10 in decimal in it, then this second part will be the remainder of 10/10 (i.e., remainder 0). This will be added to the result of the first part of the instruction. Therefore, the result of the complete instruction will be 0b00010000 in eight-bit binary. This is the data that will be written to the DS1307.

Let's look at another example. Consider the decimal number 52. The first part of the instruction will divide the 52 by 10, producing a result of 5 which is 0b00000101 in eight-bit binary. Now, that will be shifted four places to the left, giving the result 0b01010000. Now the second part of the instruction will produce the remainder of the calculation of dividing the 52 by 10. This will produce the result of 2 which is 0b00000010 in eight-bit binary. This result is now added to the first result as follows: 0b01010000 + 0b00000010, giving the final result of 0b01010010. This means the high nibble, which will be stored in the high nibble at address 0x00, will be 0101 (i.e., 5 for the 5 tens in 52). The low nibble will have 0010, which is 2. This procedure is representing a decimal number, such as 52 in binary-coded decimal (BCD). This is a useful process and is used a lot in programming microcontrollers.

I have to admit I find it fascinating how these instructions actually achieve what we want. I hope you do too or at least are beginning to understand why it is important that you do know how your instructions work.

Line 106 MSSP2CWrite (min);

This will write to the next location in the DS1307 memory the data that is stored in the variable 'min'. Note that it will be written into the next address in the DS1307 memory (i.e., address 0x01) because the DS1307 automatically incremented the contents of its pointer after it had received the data for sec in the previous instruction. You will see that we are not manipulating the data in the variable 'min' this time. This is because the data is written as 0x59 (see line 13). This is 0b01011001 in eight-bit binary. This converts to 1(64) + 1(16) + 1(8) + 1(1) = 89 in decimal, not the 59 minutes I want it to represent. However, the high nibble is 0b0101 (i.e., 5 as in 5 tens making 50). The low nibble would be 0b1001 (i.e., 9 as in 9 units).

What I have done is written the 59 in BCD myself when I declared the variable 'min' on line 13. This gets the number ready for the DS1307. It's not the correct thing to do but it works and saves memory.

Lines 107 to 111 do the same for the rest of the time memory locations in the DS1307 we want to set up.

Line 112 MSSP2CStop();

Calls the subroutine to send the stop signal to the slave. This then completes the first write session, which sets the DS1307 to the time and date I want it to start from.

We now have to write to the DS1307 to tell it the address that we want to start reading from to get the current time and date information from the DS1307.

Line 132 MSSP2Cidle ();

This checks that the I^2C is idle.

Line 133 MSSP2CStart ();

This sends another start signal.

Line 134 MSSP2CWrite (0xD0);

This sends the address for the DS1307 with the control bit still at a logic '0', as we are still writing to the DS1307.

Line 135 MSSP2CWrite (0);

This sends the address we want to start reading from (i.e., address 0x00).

Line 136 MSSP2CStop();

This sends the stop signal, as we have told the DS1307 the address of where we want to start reading from.

Line 139 writeString ("Time");

We are now inside the forever loop. The first thing we do is send the phrase "Time" to the LCD. Note that there is an empty space after the word "Time".

Lines 140 and 141 create the normal check that the I^2C is idle and then send the start signal.

Line 142 MSSP2CWrite (0xD1);

This writes the correct address of the DS1307, but now the control bit is a logic '1,' as we are going to read from the DS1307 from the location the pointer is currently pointing to. This will be the 0X00 address that was previously sent to the DS1307 in line 135.

Line 143 sec = MSSP2Cread();

This loads the variable 'sec' with the data that the PIC will read from the DS1307 with this instruction. Note that the DS1307 will also increment the contents of its pointer so that it is ready to send the next data in the next read request.

We must remember that the master is now in receiver mode and so it must generate an acknowledgment bit to tell the slave it has received the data. To see how this happens, we need to look at the instructions of the MSSP2Cread subroutine. These are written between lines 75 and 86.

Line 77 MSSP2Cidle();

The first thing we do is check that the I^2C is idle.

Line 78 SSPCON2bits.RCEN=1;

This sets the RCEN bit, which enables the MSSP to receive data using I^2C.

Line 79 while(!BF);

This gets the PIC to wait until the SSPBUF is filled with data from the DS1307.

Line 80 MSSP2Cidle();

This checks its idle again.

Line 81 ACKDT = (1)?0:1;

This checks to see if the ACKDT bit, which is the NACK, is a logic '1.' If it is, then the PIC resets it back to a logic '0,' as we don't want to send a NACK now.

Line 82 ACKEN = 1;

This sets this bit to a logic '1' to start the process of sending this acknowledgment bit to the DS1307. This bit is automatically cleared by hardware.

Line 83 MSSP2Cidle();

Checks if the I²C is idle.

Line 84 SSPCON2bits.RCEN=0;

This disables the read function of the MSSP, as we have read the data.

Line 86 return SSPBUF;

This exits the subroutine and gets the data in the SSPBUF ready to be loaded into the variable specified in the call instruction.

This subroutine will read the data sent by the slave, which is the DS1307 in this case, and send the acknowledgment bit as well.

Lines 144 and 148 carry out the same read instructions for the other time data.

Line 149 year = MSSP2CreadNAck();

This is the last read that the PIC will perform in this sequence, and so it must make sure that the PIC creates the NACK bit. We will look at the subroutine this instruction calls. This is between lines 87 and 98.

The important instructions are as follows:

Line 93 SSPCON2bits.ACKDT=1;

This just sets the ACKDT bit to a logic '1', which is the correct logic for the NACK signal. Note that in line 81, we weren't sending the NACK, so we had to check that the ACKDT bit was not set to a logic '1'. In this line, we set the ACKDT bit to a logic '1', as we want to send the NACK signal.

Line 94 SSPCON2bits.ACKEN=1;

This starts the process of sending this NACK signal to the DS1307.

Line 150 MSSP2CStop();

This sends the stop bit to the DS1307.

Lines 151 to 155 repeat the process of writing the address 0X00 to the DS1307. This is loaded into the pointer of the DS1307 to ensure the pointer is pointing to the address for the sec data (i.e., address 0X00). The DS1307 is now ready for the time and date to be read again by the PIC.

The program is now ready to display the time and date on the LCD.

The display will show the hours, minutes, and seconds in tens and units for the time on the first line of the LCD. It will then display the date, month and year in tens and units on the second line. To begin with, the LCD display will already be displaying the word "Time" (see line 139).

Line 156 lcdData = ((hour>>4)+0x30);

This loads the variable lcdData with the result of the instruction ((hour>>4)+0x30). This will move the data in the variable 'hour' four bits to the right. Assuming this is the first attempt to display the time, after the program had set the time, then the variable 'hour' should have 0b00100011 in eight-bit binary (i.e., 23 for 23hrs). After this first part of the instruction, it should now have the data 0b00000010 in eight-bit binary (i.e., all bits have been shifted four bits to the right). Note that with the shift operation, the bits that pass bit 0 or bit 7 are simply dropped off the variable and lost. The final part of this instruction adds 0x30 to it, which is 0b00110000. This means the final result will be 0b00110010 in eight-bit binary or 0X32. This is the ASCII for the number 2 that we want to display in the hour tens column. This is what is loaded into the variable lcdData. Note that the contents of the variable 'hour' will not have changed.

Line 157 lcdOut ();

This just calls the subroutine lcdOut and sends the data 0X32 to the LCD.

Line 158 lcdData = ((hour & 0x0F)+0x30);

This is again a two-stage operation. The first part of the instruction (hour & 0X0F) performs a logical bit AND with the contents of the variable 'hour' and the value 0X0F. This operation is shown in Table 12-6.

Table 12-6. *The Bit AND Operation*

	Bit 7	Bit 6	Bit 5	Bit 4	Bit 3	Bit 2	Bit 1	Bit 0
Hour	0	0	1	0	0	0	1	1
0X0F	0	0	0	0	1	1	1	1
Result	**0**	**0**	**0**	**0**	**0**	**0**	**1**	**1**

It's not too clear here what has happened, but what this instruction does is that the high byte in the result will always be a logical '0'. This is because if we AND a logic '0' or a logic '1' with a logic '0', the result will always be '0'. So really this instruction simply ignores the high nibble in the variable 'hour'.

The second part simply adds 0X30 to the result. In this case then, the value that is loaded into the variable lcdData is 0X33, the ASCII for the number 3. This is what we want, as the units for the hour is 3 as the hour value should be 23hrs.

Line 159 just sends this to the LCD.

Line 160 lcdData = 0x3A;

This loads the variable lcdData with the ASCII for the colon symbol ':'. This is used to separate the different parts of the display.

Line 161 sends this character to the LCD.

Lines 162 to 189 send the remaining characters to display the time and date.

Line 190 sendcursorhome ();

This calls the subroutine to send the cursor back to the beginning of the first line on the LCD.

The PIC then goes to line 137, where it starts the whole cycle again.

I hope this analysis has given you enough understanding of how we can program the PIC to use the DS1307. I hope you then feel able to extend this program to use the many functions of the DS1307. Of course, you could extend the first program to do everything you need without using the DS1307. The clock in the first program is very accurate. However, the DS1307 does have temperature compensation that will automatically adjust the crystal oscillator for the effects of temperature changes on the crystal. The idea is that my books give you a good starting point and a reference to help you on your way. Good luck.

Figure 12-4 shows the program working.

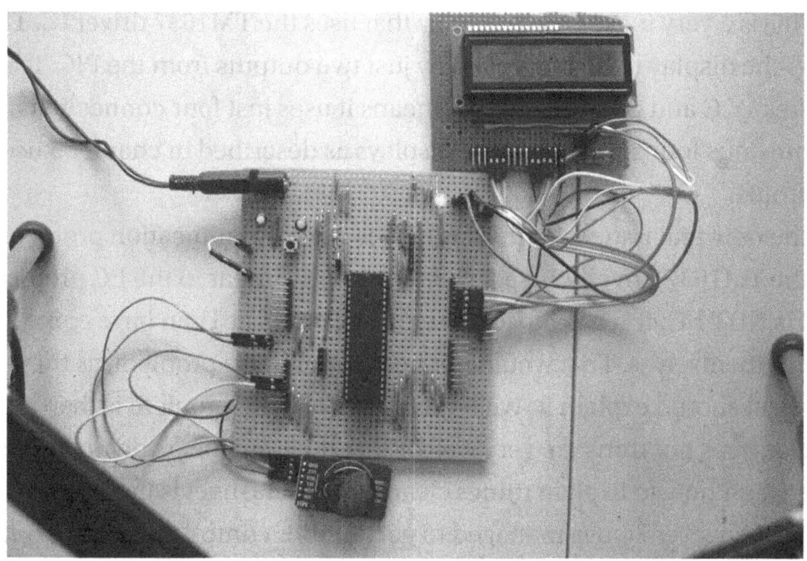

Figure 12-4. *The DS1307 working on the homemade board*

TM1637 and the Four Seven-Segment Display

The actual device we will use in this project is shown in Figure 12-5.

Figure 12-5. *The four seven-segment display*

This is a very inexpensive display that uses the TM1637 driver IC. This allows the display to be controlled by just two outputs from the PIC. It also requires VCC and ground, but that means it uses just four connections. The previous four seven-segment displays as described in chapter 3 used 12 outputs.

The only real issue with this module is the communication protocol that the TM1637 driver IC uses. The protocol is similar to the I^2C protocol but it is **NOT** I^2C. It is a protocol that the engineers at Titan have come up with themselves. That would not be too much of a problem, as the datasheet should explain it. Well, I don't know if the problem is that Chinese does not translate very well or that their engineers do not quite understand how to explain things clearly. The datasheet is not very helpful. However, I have managed to get it under control and I will explain how we can communicate with the TM1637 to control four seven-segment displays.

The TM1367 Driver IC

This is a 20-pin device that can control up to six seven-segment displays. It can also take inputs from a digital keypad. We will use it to control four seven-segment displays. To control the TM1637, we must send a series of command bytes followed by a series of data bytes that will turn the LEDs on and off in the seven-segment displays.

There are basically only four commands, which are listed in Table 12-7.

Table 12-7. *The Table for the Commands for the TM1367*

Bit 7	Bit 6	Bit 5	Bit 4	Bit 3	Bit 2	Bit 1	Bit 0	Usage
0	1	0	0	0	0	0	0	Write data to display registers Normal mode Automatically increase address pointer
0	1	0	0	0	0	1	0	Read keys scan data
0	1	0	0	0	1	0	0	Fixed address
0	1	0	0	1	0	0	0	Test mode

The only mode we will be using is the normal mode, which allows us to write data to the display registers. The address pointer will start with the address that we set it to. After that, it will automatically increase the address after we have written data to the current display register.

There are six data registers, and their addresses are listed in Table 12-8.

Table 12-8. *The Address of the Data Registers for the Seven-Segment Displays*

Bit 7	Bit 6	Bit 5	Bit 4	Bit 3	Bit 2	Bit 1	Bit 0	Usage
1	1	0	0	0	0	0	0	CH0 Display 0
1	1	0	0	0	0	0	1	CH1 Display 1
1	1	0	0	0	0	1	0	CH2 Display 2
1	1	0	0	0	0	1	1	CH3 Display 3
1	1	0	0	0	1	0	0	CH4 Display 4
1	1	0	0	0	1	0	1	CH5 Display 5

We can set the brightness of the display by using the appropriate command byte. Table 12-9 lists the various brightness commands. This brightness variation is achieved by varying the voltage across the LEDs with a pulse width modulated signal. We will set the LEDs to maximum brightness. Note that if bit 3 of the command was set to a logic '0', then the display would be switched off.

***Table 12-9.** The Command Bytes to Set the Brightness of the Display*

Bit 7	Bit 6	Bit 5	Bit 4	Bit 3	Bit 2	Bit 1	Bit 0	Usage
1	0	0	0	1	0	0	0	1/16 PWM set to 1/16
1	0	0	0	1	0	0	1	2/16 PWM set to 2/16
1	0	0	0	1	0	1	0	4/16 PWM set to 4/16
1	0	0	0	1	0	1	1	10/16 PWM set to 10/16
1	0	0	0	1	1	0	0	11/16 PWM set to 11/16
1	0	0	0	1	1	0	1	12/16 PWM set to 12/16
1	0	0	0	1	1	1	0	13/16 PWM set to 13/16
1	0	0	0	1	1	1	1	14/16 PWM set to 14/16

As we are only using four displays, we will use the first four addresses. I will refer to these addresses as follows:

1. first 0b11000000
2. second 0b11000001
3. third 0b11000010
4. fourth 0b11000011

To communicate correctly with the TM1637, we have to follow the correct procedure. This is their homemade protocol.

The procedure is as follows:

There are two communications wires, which are

- clk, which is a pseudo clock signal we must create. This has to change at a frequency of less than 250kHz.
- dio, which is the line that carries the information to the TM1637. The data on this line can only change when the clock signal is high.

Both these wires are outputs from the PIC, and we can use any outputs that are available.

We must create a start signal, which is created as follows:

- Starting with the clock line low, we send it to a logic '1.'
- At the same time, we drive the dio line from low to high.
- We then create a 2ms delay.
- After that, we drive the dio line back low.

It is this transition from high to low on the dio line while the clock is high that is interpreted as the start signal by the TM1367.

We must now send the command 0b01000000 or 0X40, which puts the TM1637 into normal mode; see Table 12-7.

The TM1637 will send back an acknowledgment signal to inform us that it has received the command. This acknowledgment signal is the TM1637 driving the dio line low starting at the negative or falling edge of the 8th clock signal as the 8th bit of information has been sent.

We must now send a stop signal to the TM1637 to give it time to set itself into this normal mode of operation. The stop signal is achieved by sending the dio line from low to high while the clock line is high.

We must now send another start signal.

We must now send the address of the first register we want to write to. This would be the address of CH0 the first of the four seven-segment displays we want to write to. The binary value we would send is 0b11000000 or 0XC0 (see Table 12-8). The TM1637 would open this register ready for us to send the data to it. When we have sent the data, the TM1637 would then automatically open the next address register.

After we have sent the first address, the TM1637 would respond with an acknowledgment signal.

We now send the data to turn on or off the LEDs on the first seven-segment display.

The TM1637 would respond with an acknowledgment signal.

We now send the data for the second, third, and fourth seven-segment displays, with the TM1637 sending an acknowledgment signal between them.

After we have received the last acknowledgment signal, we send a stop signal.

Now we send a final start signal, which we follow with a command to set the brightness of the display.

After this final command, we should get a final acknowledgment from the TM1637 and we should then send a stop signal to end all communication.

This process may look similar to the I²C protocol, but the start and stop signals are not the same. There is also one other major difference, which is that the information is sent out serially sending the LSB first. The I^2C sends the MSB first.

This is basically how we will set the TM1637 up ready for use. We will discuss how the instructions achieve this as we analyze the program.

The program will be in three parts, which are

- First allow the user to set the time of the clock. This will involve the use of three switches, which are
    - Increment on bit 0 of PORTA
    - Decrement on bit 1 of PORTA
    - Set on bit 2 of PORTA
- Then for 1 second display the actual time on the display.
- Then for the next 1 second we will display the temperature in °C on the display. This will involve the program using the TC74 to determine the temperature.

The two outputs for the clock and dio lines are

- clk on bit 0 of PORTB
- dio on bit 1 of PORTB

Listing 12-3 provides the complete code to so this.

Listing 12-3. TM1367 and the Four Seven-Segment Displays

```
/*
* File:   the 4 7seg display
Author: Mr H. H. Ward
displays the time and then the temperature
using the PIC18f4525
Created 11/06/2021
*/
```

```
#include <xc.h>
#include <conFigInternalOscNoWDTNoLVP.h>
#include <i2cProtocol.h>
#define clk PORTBbits.RB0
#define dio PORTBbits.RB1
#define zero    0b00111111
#define one     0b00000110
#define two     0b01011011
#define three   0b01001111
#define four    0b01100110
#define five    0b01101101
#define six     0b01111100
#define seven   0b00000111
#define eight   0b01111111
#define nine    0b01100111
#define SO      0b01100011
#define C       0b00111001
#define incButton PORTAbits.RA0
#define decButton PORTAbits.RA1
#define setButton PORTAbits.RA2
// declare any variables
unsigned char n, m, thigh;
unsigned char secUnits, minUnits = 0, minTens = 3,
hourUnits = 0, hourTens = 0, first = zero, second =
one,third = two, fourth = one;
float sysTemperature;
//some arrays
unsigned char displaynumber [10] =
{
zero,
one,
```

```
two,
three,
four,
five,
six,
seven,
eight,
nine,
};
//some subroutines
void delay (unsigned char t)
{
for (n = 0; n < t; n++)
{
TMR0 = 0;
while (TMR0 < 255);
}
}
void delayus (unsigned char t)
{
TMR3 = 0;
while (TMR3 < t);
}
void debounce ()
{
TMR0 = 0;
while (TMR0 < 105);
}
void tmStart ()
{
clk = 1;
```

```
dio = 1;
delayus (2);
dio = 0;
}
void tmAck ()
{
clk = 0;
delayus (5);
while (dio);
clk = 1;
delayus (2);
clk = 0;
}
void tmStop ()
{
clk = 0;
delayus (2);
dio = 0;
delayus (2);
clk = 1;
delayus (2);
dio = 1;
}
void tmByteWrite (unsigned char tmByte)
{
for (m = 0; m <8; m++)
{
clk = 0;
if (tmByte & 0x01) dio = 1;
else dio = 0;
delayus (3);
```

```
tmByte = tmByte >> 1;
clk = 1;
delayus (3);
}
}
void displaySet()
{
tmStart();
tmByteWrite(0x40);
tmAck();
tmStop();
tmStart();
tmByteWrite(0xc0);
tmAck();
tmByteWrite(first);
tmAck();
tmByteWrite(second);
tmAck();
tmByteWrite(third);
tmAck();
tmByteWrite(fourth);
tmAck();
tmStop();
tmStart();
tmByteWrite(0x8f);
tmAck();
tmStop();
}
void displayMsg()
{
second = second ^(0b10000000);
```

```
tmStart();
tmByteWrite(0x40);
tmAck();
tmStop();
tmStart();
tmByteWrite(0xc0);
tmAck();
tmByteWrite(first);
tmAck();
tmByteWrite(second);
tmAck();
tmByteWrite(third);
tmAck();
tmByteWrite(fourth);
tmAck();
tmStop();
tmStart();
tmByteWrite(0x8f);
tmAck();
tmStop();
}
void setTime ()
{
//set minutes
while (setButton)
{
displaySet();
fourth = displaynumber [minUnits];
if (!incButton)debounce ();
if (!incButton)
```

```
{
if (minUnits < 9)minUnits ++;
else minUnits = 9;
fourth = displaynumber [minUnits];
while (!incButton);
}
if (!decButton )debounce ();
if (!decButton)
{
if (minUnits > 0) minUnits --;
else minUnits = 0;
fourth = displaynumber [minUnits];
while (!decButton);
}
}
debounce ();
while (!setButton);
//*************************************************
while (setButton)
{
displaySet();
third = displaynumber [minTens];
if (!incButton)debounce ();
if (!incButton)
{
if (minTens < 5)minTens ++;
else minTens = 5;
third = displaynumber [minTens];
while (!incButton);
}
if (!decButton)debounce ();
```

```
if (!decButton)
{
if (minTens > 0)minTens --;
else minTens = 0;
third = displaynumber [minTens];
while (!decButton);
}
}
debounce ();
while (!setButton);
//sethours
while (setButton)
{
displaySet();
second = displaynumber [hourUnits];
if (!incButton)debounce ();
if (!incButton)
{
if (hourUnits < 9)hourUnits ++;
else hourUnits = 9;
second = displaynumber [hourUnits];
while (!incButton);
}
if (!decButton)debounce ();
if (!decButton)
{
if (hourUnits > 0)hourUnits --;
else hourUnits = 0;
second = displaynumber [hourUnits];
while (!decButton);
}
}
```

```
//*********************************************
debounce ();
while (!setButton);
while (setButton)
{
displaySet();
first = displaynumber [hourTens];
if (!incButton)debounce ();
if (!incButton)
{
if (hourTens < 2)hourTens ++;
else hourTens = 2;
first = displaynumber [hourTens];
while (!incButton);
}
if (!decButton)debounce ();
if (!decButton)
{
if (hourTens > 0)hourTens --;
else hourTens = 0;
first = displaynumber [hourTens];
while (!decButton);
}
}
debounce ();
while (!setButton);
return;
}
void interrupt isr1 ()
{
secUnits ++;
```

```
PIR1bits.TMR1IF = 0;
displayMsg();
TMR1H = 0b10000000;
}
void main()
{
PORTA = 0;
PORTB = 0;
PORTC = 0;
PORTD = 0;
TRISA = 0XFF;
TRISB = 0;
TRISC = 0;
TRISD = 0b00000000;
ADCON0 = 0;
ADCON1 = 0X0F;
OSCCON = 0X74;
T0CON = 0XC7;
T1CON = 0b00001111;
T3CON = 0b10010001;
INTCON = 0b11000000;
PIE1bits.TMR1IE = 0;
setTime ();
MSSP2CInit();
PIE1bits.TMR1IE = 1;
while (1)
{
MSSP2Cidle ();
MSSP2CStart ();
MSSP2CWrite (0x9A);
MSSP2CWrite (0x00);
```

```
MSSP2CRestart();
MSSP2CWrite(0x9B);
thigh = MSSP2CreadNAck ();
MSSP2CStop();
if (secUnits == 60)
{
minUnits ++;
secUnits = 0;
if (minUnits == 10)
{
minUnits = 0;
minTens ++;
if (minTens == 6)
{
minTens = 0;
hourUnits ++;
if (hourTens < 2)
{
if (hourUnits == 10)
{
hourUnits = 0;
hourTens ++;
}
}
else if (hourTens == 2)
{
if (hourUnits == 4)
{
hourUnits = 0;
hourTens =0;
}
```

```
316.    }
317.    }
318.    }
319.    if (minUnits & (0b00000001))
320.    {
321.    fourth = displaynumber [minUnits];
322.    third = displaynumber [minTens];
323.    second = displaynumber [hourUnits];
324.    first = displaynumber [hourTens];
325.    }
326.    else
327.    {
328.    fourth = C;
329.    third = SO;
330.    second = displaynumber [thigh % 10];
331.    first = displaynumber [thigh/10];
332.    }
333.    }
334.    }
335.    }
```

Analysis of Listing 12-3

There are really no new instructions, but there are some important issues to look at.

Lines 1 to 7 are the usual comments.

Lines 8 and 9 are the normal includes.

Line 10 include <i2cProtocol.h>

This includes a header file called i2cProtocol. I have created this header file that includes all the subroutines associated with using the I^2C protocol. It is made up of all the subroutines from lines 23 to 98 of Listing 12-2.

Lines 11 and 12 allocate the clk and dio outputs to bit 0 and bit 1 of PORTB. These are the two outputs that allow the PIC to communicate with the TM1637.

Lines 13 to 22 define the binary values for the labels 0 to 9. This is the data that needs to be sent to the TM1637 to light up the seven segments with the numbers 0 to 9.

Line 23 #define SO 0b01100011

We will display the temperature on the display in degrees centigrade. An example of what we would like to see on the display is shown in Figure 12-6.

Figure 12-6. *The display showing 23:°C*

I have referred to the superscript part of the display as SO. Line 23 defines the binary data required to display this on the seven-segment display.

Line 24 #define C 0b00111001

This defines the binary value to display the capital ‘C’ on the display.

Using this concept of turning on and off the LEDs in the seven-segment display you can define the binary values to display a whole range of characters on the display. You need to know that the seven-segment displays are all common cathode type. This means a logic ‘1’ will turn the particular LED on and a logic ‘0’ will turn it off.

Lines 25 to 27 allocate the input switches to bits 0, 1, and 2 of PORTA.

Lines 29, 30, and 31 create the variables that we will use in the program.

Lines 33 to 45 create an array of 10 memory locations in which we will store the binary values for the labels 0 to 9. These were defined previously in lines 13 to 22.

Lines 47 to 54 create our normal variable delay based on 32ms delay.

Lines 55 to 59 create our variable delay based on a 1µs delay. It uses timer3 which on line 273 is set as a 16-bit timer that counts in microseconds.

Lines 60 to 64 create our "debounce" delay, which is used to create a 13ms delay to allow the voltage on our switches to settle down to a logic '1' or a logic '0'. This is our software solution to the bouncing action of a switch.

Lines 65 to 71 create a subroutine to create the start signal for the TM1637.

Line 67 clk = 1;

This sets the output for the clock signal to a logic '1'. This output is on bit 0 of PORTB as defined in line 11. We need the clock line to be at a high so that the TM1637 would respond to a change on the dio line. If a change on the dio line happens when the clock line is low, the TM1637 would ignore it.

Line 68 dio = 1;

This sets the dio line to a logic '1'. We need this line to go high so that we can send it low while the clock is high. The TM1637 would then recognize this action as the start signal.

Line 69 delayus (2);

This calls the microsecond delay and sends the number 2 to it. This value of 2 would be loaded into the subroutine's local variable 't'. This then creates a 2µs delay. This keeps the clock signal high for 2µs, which is half of the periodic time for a 250kHz frequency.

Line 70 dio = 0;

This drives the dio line low. It is this transition from high to low that represents the start signal to the TM1637.

Lines 72 to 80 create the subroutine that gets the PIC to wait for the acknowledgment signal from the TM1637.

Line 74 clk = 0;

This sends the clock line low. This is the clock line creating the negative or falling edge of the 8th clock line. This is when the TM1637 should drive the dio line low.

Line 75 delayus (5);

This creates a 5μs delay. This should be enough time for the TM1637 to drive the dio line low.

Line 76 while (dio);

This test to see if the logic on the dio line is high or logic '1'. If it is, the test is true and the PIC does nothing. This makes the PIC wait for the TM1637 to drive the dio line low. This would be the acknowledgment signal from the TM1637.

Line 77 clk = 1;

This sends the clock line back high.

Line 78 delayus (2);

This creates a 2μs delay (half of the periodic time of the 250kHz frequency).

Line 79 clk = 0;

This drives the clock line low.

Lines 81 to 90 creates the stop signal subroutine.

Line 83 clk = 0;

This sends the clock line low. This is getting the clk line ready to high.

Line 84 delayus (2);

This creates a 2μs delay.

Line 85 dio = 0;

This drives the dio line low. This is getting the dio line ready to high, as the stop signal is the dio line going from low to high while the clock is high.

Line 86 delayus (2);

The 2μs delay.

Line 87 clk = 1;

Now send the clock high so that the TM1637 can respond to a change in the dio line.

Line 88 delayus (2);

The 2μs delay.

Line 89 dio = 1;

Now send the dio line high. This transitions from low to high while the clock line is high is interpreted by the TM1637 as the stop signal.

Lines 91 to 103 create a subroutine to write eight bits of information, be they an instruction or data, to the TM1637. Note that the TM1637 is expecting the LSB (least significant bit), which is bit 0 of the eight bits, to be sent first. This subroutine expects a byte of information to be sent up to it. This byte will be loaded into the local variable tmByte to be used in this subroutine.

Line 93 for (m = 0; m <8; m++)

This sets up a for do loop that the PIC will carry out eight times, once for each bit being sent.

Line 95 clk = 0;

This sends the clock line low.

Line 96 if (tmByte & 0x01) dio = 1;

This sets up a test that tests to see if the result of a logical bit AND operation with the eight bits in the variable tmByte and the binary value 0b00000001 is true or not. The result will only be true if bit 0 of the eight bits in tmByte was a logic '1.'

If the result of the test were true, then we would set the dio line high (i.e., to a logic '1').

Line 97 else dio = 0;

This is what the PIC will do if the test on line 96 was untrue. This would set the dio line low (i.e., to a logic '0').

Line 98 delayus (3);

This creates a delay of 3µs keeping the clk and the dio line at their current state for 3µs.

Line 99 tmByte = tmByte >> 1;

This shifts the bits in the variable tmByte one bit to the right. The current LSB (i.e., bit 0) is lost and what was bit 1 is moved to bit 0. At the other end, the MSB, bit 7, is moved to bit 6 and a logic '0' is shifted into bit 7. To help understand the process, we can look at Table 12-10.

***Table 12-10.** Shifting the Bits One Place to the Right*

	Bit 7	Bit 6	Bit 5	Bit 4	Bit 3	Bit 2	Bit 1	Bit 0
Before Shift	1	0	1	0	1	1	0	1
After Shift	0	1	0	1	0	1	1	0

Line 100 clk = 1;

This sends the clock back high.

Line 101 delayus (3);

This creates a 3µs delay.

This subroutine will make the logic on the dio line mimic what is in the variable tmByte one bit at a time. In this way, we have sent the contents of the tmByte out to the TM1637 serially one bit at a time (note, sending the LSB first). The contents of tmByte will be the eight bits that we want to send to the TM1637.

Lines 104 to 126 create a subroutine that allows us to write to the TM1637 and set the time of the clock. The subroutine does the following in order:

1. Calls the tmStart subroutine to send the start signal to the TM1637

2. Calls the tmByteWrite(0x40) subroutine and sends the eight bits 0b01000000, which is the command to put the TM1637 into normal mode. See Table 12-7.
3. Calls the tmAck subroutine to get the PIC to wait for the acknowledgment signal from the TM1637.
4. Calls the tmStop subroutine to send the stop signal to the TM1637.
5. Calls the tmStart subroutine again.
6. Calls the tmByteWrite(0xC0) subroutine and sends the eight bits 0b11000000, which loads the TM1637 address pointer with the address of the register for CH0, the first of the four seven-segment displays.
7. Calls the tmAck subroutine again.
8. Calls the tmByteWrite(first) subroutine, but this time it will send the eight bits that are required to light up the first seven-segment display with the value we want it to display. The eight bits that will be loaded into the variable first are set within lines 229 to 248.
9. Calls the tmAck subroutine.
10. The following six lines will send the eight bits for the second, third, and fourth seven-segment displays, followed by the tmAck subroutine.

Line 121 calls the tmStop subroutine.

Line 122 calls the tmStart subroutine again.

Line 123 tmByteWrite(0x8f);

This calls the tmByteWrite subroutine and sends the value 0b10001111 to be used in the subroutine. This is the command to set the brightness of the displays to the maximum brightness.

Lines 124 and 125 call the tmAck and tmStop subroutines.

In this way, this subroutine will set the clock display to what we want to start the clock at.

Lines 127 to 150 create a second subroutine that allows us to write to the TM1637. There is only one line that is different from the previous subroutine. However, because there is this one line that is different, we do need to create this second subroutine. There could be a more efficient way of doing this, but you have more time than me to think of it.

Line 129 second = second ^(0b10000000);

This is the line that is different. What it does is perform a logical EXOR with just bit 7 of the variable "second". The purpose in doing this can be explained as follows:

- Bit 7 of this variable does not have any effect on the number to be displayed on the second seven-segment display.
- However, what it does control is when the colon, or two dots, between the second and third displays are lit or not lit.
- A logic '1' in this bit 7 of the variable "second" means they will be lit.
- A logic '0' means they won't be lit.

The idea of how I want to use these two dots is that they should come on for 1 second and turn off for 1 second. Therefore, if we send this variable "second" to the TM1637 once a second, we can decide to turn these two dots on or off. This instruction will set bit 7 to a logic '1' if it was currently at a logic '0'. However, if it was already at a logic '1', then this instruction will load this bit with a logic '0'. Therefore, if we send this variable to the TM1637 once a second, this instruction will turn on and off the two dots between the second and third displays.

The rest of the instructions in this subroutine work in the same way as the previous subroutine.

Lines 151 to 250 allow the user to use the three buttons, increment, decrement, and set, to control the starting time of the clock. I will explain how the instructions set what number is displayed in the first seven-segment display.

Line 154 while (setButton)

This sets up a while loop that the PIC will carry out while the logic on the input allocated to the setButton is a logic '1'. Note that pressing the setButton will momentarily send the logic to a logic '0'.

Line 156 displaySet ();

This calls the subroutine displaySet to display the numbers on the seven-segment displays as we change the values to set the clock to the correct time.

Line 157 fourth = displaynumber [minUnits];

This loads the variable fourth with the number stored in the array displaynumber from the location indicated by the current contents in the variable minUnits. For example if the current contents of minUnits were zero (i.e., '0'), then the contents of the first memory location in the array displaynumber would be loaded into the variable fourth. The variable fourth will hold the value to control the fourth seven-segment display on the display module. This fourth seven-segment display will show the units number of the minutes for the clock display.

As we change the value in the variable minUnits, we can change the setting of the units for the minutes displayed on the clock.

Line 158 if (!incButton)debounce ();

This test to see if the logic on the input for the increment button has gone to a logic '0'. This would happen if someone pressed the increment button to increase the value in the current variable. If the test is true (i.e., someone has pressed the button), then the PIC would call the debounce subroutine. This subroutine is used to make the PIC wait the 13ms to allow the bouncing action of the switch to die down.

Line 159 if (!incButton)

Here we are testing to see if the increment button had really been pressed, as the logic would still be at a logic '0'. If the result of the test is true, the PIC will carry out the instructions between lines 160 and 165.

Line 161 if (minUnits < 9)minUnits ++;

If the increment button had been pressed, then the PIC should try to increase the number in the variable minUnits, as this is the current variable we are setting in this part of the program. However, we should appreciate that the value in the units of the minutes setting for the time could never go above the number 9. Therefore, this instruction is testing to see if the current value in the variable minUnits is less than 9. If the test is true, and the number in minUnits is less than 9, then we can carry out the one-line instruction, which increments the value in minUnits by one.

Line 162 else minUnits = 9;

This instruction is what the PIC will carry out if the test on line 161 was untrue. We simply set the value in minUnits to 9, as trying to increment the value further would be in error. Note that, in this subroutine, we are setting the time on the clock.

Line 163 fourth = displaynumber [minUnits];

Now we simply reload the variable fourth with the contents of the array displaynumber as indicated by the value in the variable minUnits.

Line 164 while (!incButton);

This is simply making the PIC wait until the logic on this input has gone back to a logic '1'. This would mean that the user had stopped pressing the increment button. There may be some occasions when you would have to call the debounce subroutine for this release of the switch action could cause the switch to bounce. In this instance, that approach is not needed. However, you should bear in mind that it might be needed.

Lines 166 to 172 do the same actions but now for the decrement button. In this case, we are seeing if the user wants to decrement the current value in the variable minUnits.

Line 169 if (minUnits > 0) minUnits --;

This is testing to see if the current value in minUnits is greater than '0'. If it is, we can go ahead and decrement the current value in minUnits. If the value is not greater than '0', then we simply load '0' into the variable minUnits.

The PIC will remain in this loop, allowing the user to increment or decrement the value in the current variable minUnits until the user presses the set button. This action of pressing the set button means the user wants to set the value in the units part of the minutes display to the current value in the variable minUnits.

Line 173 debounce ();

This calls the debounce subroutine as the user has just pressed the set button.

Line 174 while (!setButton);

This makes the PIC wait until the logic on the input for the set button has gone back to a logic '1'. If you didn't have this instruction in, then there is the possibility that the PIC would not enter into the next while loop. Comment this instruction out and see what happens.

Lines 178 to 200 perform the same actions but now for the variable minTens, which is used to set the number for the tens of minutes on the clock display.

Lines 202 to 225 perform the same actions but now for the variable hourUnits, which is used to set the number for the units of the hours on the clock display.

Lines 226 to 248 perform the same actions but now for the variable hourTens, which is used to set the number for the tens of the hours on the clock display.

Line 248 while (!setButton);

This makes the PIC wait for the logic on the set button to go back to a logic '1' after the final pressing of the set button.

Line 249 return;

This is to make sure the PIC returns back to the main program now that this subroutine has been completed.

Lines 251 to 257 create the ISR for when the PIC is interrupted and forced to go to this ISR. In this program, there is only one action that can cause this interrupt. That will be when timer1 rolls over. This will happen once every second, as timer1 will count from 32768 to 65536 at a rate of 32.768khz.

This ISR has been analyzed in Listing 12-1. However, there are extra instructions.

Line 253 secUnits ++;

This simply increments the contents of the variable secUnits. This will happen once every second. The contents of this variable are used to decide when to increment the contents of the variable minUnits when the PIC is used to keep track of the real time.

Line 255 displayMsg();

This calls the subroutine displayMsg to display the current value of the time on the clock. This means that the time display will update once every second.

Line 258 to 271 are the normal instructions to set up the PIC.

Line 272 T1CON = 0b00001111;

This turns timer1 on and sets it up as two eight-bit registers. This is so that we can load the TMR1H register with 0b10000000 or 0X80 in line 256. It configures the external oscillator as the source for the timer. This is the accurate crystal oscillator running at a frequency of 32.768kHz that is used for the RTC.

Line 273 T3CON = 0b10010001;

This sets timer3 as a 16-bit register. We set the divide rate to 2, and the source is the internal 8Mhz crystal. This means that timer3 will be counting at a frequency of 1Mhz (i.e., 8/4 = 2 and 2/2 = 1).

Line 274 INTCON = 0b11000000;

This enables both the global and peripheral interrupts.

Line 275 PIE1bits.TMR1IE = 0;

This controls the timer1 peripheral interrupt. We would normally set this bit to a logic '1' here. However, we don't want to use this interrupt until after we have set the correct time for the clock. Therefore, we will enable this interrupt later on line 278 after we have set the time.

Line 276 setTime ();

This calls the subroutine setTime to set the time for the clock.

Line 277 MSSP2CInit();

This calls the subroutine to initiate the MSSP (master synchronous serial port) to use the I²C protocol. This subroutine is with the header file I²C protocol. The only issue with this header file as it stands is that it is set to use the 9600 baud rate, and no other.

Line 278 PIE1bits.TMR1IE = 1;

This enables the timer1 peripheral interrupt now that we have set the correct time for the clock.

Line 279 while (1)

This sets up the forever loop so that the PIC does not carry out any of the previous instructions again.

Lines 281 to 288 are the instructions that get the PIC to obtain the temperature reading from the TC74 and store it in the variable thigh. We have analyzed these instructions before in chapter 10. This is why we have set up the PIC to use the I²C protocol.

Line 289 if (secUnits == 60)

This checks to see if the secUnits has been incremented to 60. If it has, then the PIC must carry out the instructions between lines 289 and 333. If the secUnits has not reached 60, then the PIC basically does nothing except respond to the interrupt.

Line 291 minUnits ++;

If we have reached 60 in the variable secUnits, then we will try to increment the minUnits as 1 minute has passed.

Line 292 secUnits = 0;

We must reset the value in secUnits back to 0.

Line 293 if (minUnits == 10)

Now we must test to see if the minUnits increment on line 291 has resulted in the value in minUnits becoming equal to 10. This cannot be allowed, as the units can only go from 0 to 9. If the test is true, then the PIC must carry out the instructions between lines 294 and 318.

Line 295 minUnits = 0;

We must reset the minUnits back to 0.

Line 296 minTens ++;

We must now add one to the minTens, as that is what a value of 10 (i.e., 0 in the units column and 1 in the tens column) should look like on the display.

Line 297 if (minTens == 6)

Now we must test to see if the increment in the minTens on line 296 has resulted in the minTens becoming equal to 6. This cannot be allowed, as the maximum value in the minTens column is 5. If the test is true, then the PIC must carry out the instructions between lines 298 and 317.

Line 299 minTens = 0;

Reset the minTens back to 0.

Line 300 hourUnits ++;

We must now try to increment the hourUnits.

Line 301 if (hourTens < 2)

Now we test to see if the hourTens variable is less than 2. If it is, then the PIC must carry out the instructions between lines 302 and 308.

Line 303 if (hourUnits == 10)

Now we test to see if the hourUnits value has become equal to 10. If it has, then the PIC must carry out the instructions between lines 304 and 307.

Line 305 hourUnits = 0;

We must reset the hourUnits back to 0.

Line 306 hourTens ++;

We must now try to increment the hourTens variable.

Line 309 else if (hourTens == 2)

This is the else statement that the PIC must carry out if the if test on line 301 was untrue. The PIC must carry out the if test on this line to see if the hourTens variable has been incremented to become equal to 2. The increment was carried out on line 306. If the test is true, the PIC must carry out the instructions between lines 310 and 316.

Line 311 if (hourUnits == 4)

This test to see if the hourUnits has become equal to 4. This could happen as a result of the instruction on line 300. If the test is true, then the PIC must carry out the instructions between lines 312 and 315.

Line 313 hourUnits = 0;

This simply resets the hourUnits back to 0.

Line 314 hourTens = 0;

This resets the hourTens back to 0.

In this way, the instructions between lines 289 and 318 allow the display to keep track of the current time and display the time using a 24hr display.

Line 319 if (minUnits & (0b00000001))

This is a test to see if the bit AND operation between the data in the minUnits variable and the binary value 0b00000001 is true (i.e., results in a logic '1'). Really, what this is testing is whether bit 0 of the variable minUnits has gone to a logic '1'. Bit 0 of this variable, and indeed any variable, is the LSB. As this variable minUnits holds the units column for the minutes, then this bit will alternate between a logic '1' and a logic '0' every minute. This means that this test will be true for one minute and untrue for the next minute.

The reason why I am doing this is so that we can decide when to display the time on the seven-segment display and when to display the temperature.

If the result of this test is true, then the PIC will carry out the instructions between lines 320 and 325. It will then ignore the instructions between lines 326 and 332.

Line 321 fourth = displaynumber [minUnits];

This will load the variable fourth with the contents of the array displaynumber indicated by the value in the variable minUnits.

Lines 322 to 324 do the same for the variable third, second, and first but with their respective numbers expressed by their respective variables.

Line 326 else

This is what the PIC must do if the test on line 319 was untrue.

Line 328 fourth = C;

This simply loads the variable fourth with the binary number for the character 'C.' This was defined on line 24.

Line 329 third = SO;

This loads the variable third with the binary number to display the superscript O. This was defined on line 23.

Line 330 second = displaynumber [thigh % 10];

This loads the variable second with the contents of the location in the array displaynumber indicated as the remainder of the calculation of the variable thigh after it has been divided by 10. The following example should help explain what this is doing.

If the variable thigh had the value 23, which is a temperature of 23°C, then we would want the units column of the temperature display to show 3. Well, if we divide 23 by 10 we will get the remainder 3. This is what we want to display in the second seven-segment display and that is what this instruction would achieve.

Line 331 first = displaynumber [thigh/10];

This would load the variable first with the contents of the array displaynumber indicated by dividing the variable thigh by 10. If thigh was 23 as before, then dividing the variable by 10 would result in the number 2. This is what we want.

You should appreciate that in the array displaynumber, the actual reference numbers of the locations in that array are the same as the binary values in those locations to display the same number on the seven-segment displays. For example, the third memory location in the array contains the binary number 0b01001111. This is the data needed to display the number 3 on the seven-segment display. Therefore, if we loaded a variable with the displaynumber [3], this would load the variable with 0b0101111 the binary to display the number 3 on the seven-segment display.

I hope this analysis has helped you to understand how the TM1637 can be controlled by creating this pseudo I^2C protocol. I believe that Titan has done this to avoid paying a license fee to Phillips for using the proper I^2C protocol. The idea is OK, but they really need to improve their data sheet and explain their protocol better.

I hope you have been able to follow my explanation of how we use the multiple if test to ensure the display increments the units and tens of the minutes and hours of the display.

Finally, I hope you can appreciate how we have used the bit testing to make some important decisions about flashing the two dots on the display and changing the display between the time and the temperature every second.

I hope you have fun using this very inexpensive display and breaking away from just using a library for the Arduino that doesn't explain what it does. I firmly believe you should fully understand how your programs work. Only then can you really say they are your programs.

Summary

In this chapter, we have learned how to use timer1 and its interrupt to create an RTC using just an external crystal oscillator. We then went on to learn how to use the DS1307 RTC module. Finally, we have learned how to use the TM1637 driver IC to control a very useful and inexpensive module with four seven-segment displays.

I hope you have found all three programs informative and you now feel more than ready to try your own projects.

In the next chapter, we will be extending our understanding of the LCD to be able to create our own characters to display on the LCD. We will also look at using the compare and capture features of the CCP module. In doing so, we will look at how we can implement low- and high-priority interrupts.

CHAPTER 13

Working with LCDs

In this chapter, we are going to learn how to create our own characters to be displayed on the LCD. We will also look at the compare and capture aspect of the CCP module. Finally, we will study how to use low- and high-priority interrupts.

After reading this chapter, you will be able to display characters of your own design on the LCD. You will be able to create a square wave at any frequency with a 50/50 duty cycle. You will also be able to perform some very accurate time measurement and use high-priority interrupts on the PIC18f4525.

Creating Your Own Characters on an LCD

In chapter 4, we studied how we can use the LCD to display ASCII characters. We learned how the LCD stored the pixel maps for the associated ASCII characters in its memory locations. We learned how we could access those memory locations to get the LCD to display the characters we wanted. As well as the memory locations that are used to store the pixel maps for those ASCII characters, there are 16 empty memory locations known as the CGRAM. The normal memory locations are known as the DDRAM. The addresses of the CGRAM are

0b00000000 to 0b00001111

The addresses of the DDRAM are

0b00100000 to 0b11111111

H. H. Ward, *Programming Arduino Projects with the PIC Microcontroller*,
https://doi.org/10.1007/978-1-4842-7230-5_13

The addresses of the DDRAM correspond to the ASCII values for the normal character set. This is so that we can access the correct memory location in the DDRAM by simply sending the desired ASCII for the character we want to display to the LCD. However, when accessing the CGRAM, we need to send the appropriate binary address value. This is because we don't know what character the pixel maps in those locations represent. This is because we need to design the maps ourselves.

The Pixel Maps

The size of the pixel grid depends on the resolution of the LCD display. The resolution of the LCD in this exercise is set to an eight-by-five grid. The empty grid is shown in Figure 13-1.

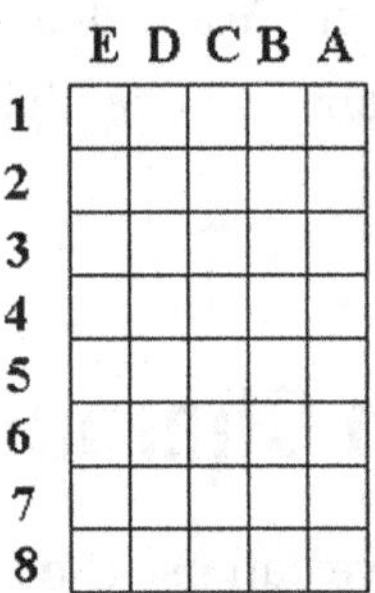

***Figure 13-1.** The eight-row-by-five-column grid of a pixel map*

To create a character, we have to turn on or off the particular cells in the grid. A logic '1' in the cell reference turns it on, and a logic '0' turns it off. Therefore, if we said that in row 1 columns A, B, D, and E were logic '1' and the rest were logic '0', then the pixel map would be as shown in Figure 13-2.

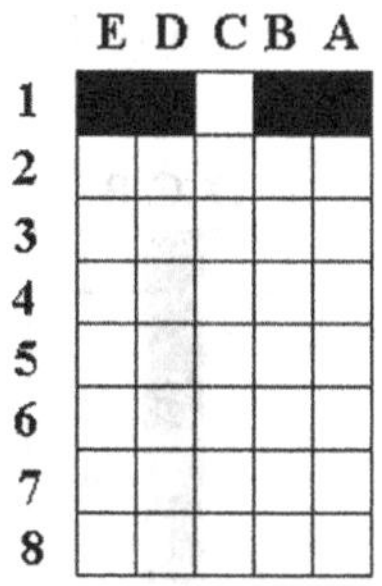

Figure 13-2. *The pixel map with row 1*

The process by which we create the pixel map in code is to write eight bytes, one for each row, to control the cells accordingly for all the rows in the map. However, it will only be bits 0 to 4 of each byte that control the pixel map. As an example to display a single line down the middle of the map, the eight bytes would be as follows:

- Row 1 0b00000100
- Row 2 0b00000100
- Row 3 0b00000100
- Row 4 0b00000100
- Row 5 0b00000100
- Row 6 0b00000100
- Row 7 0b00000100
- Row 8 0b00000100

The map would be as shown in Figure 13-3.

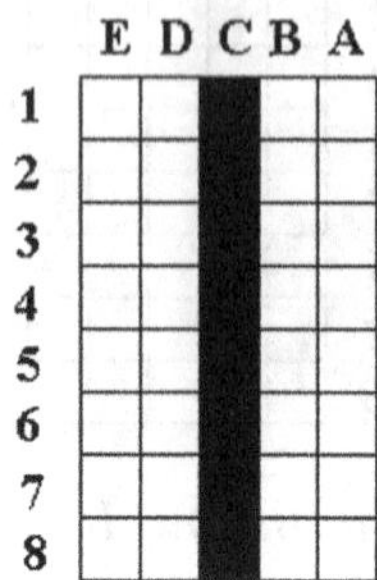

Figure 13-3. *The full pixel map for example 1*

I hope the process of how to create the pixel map is quite straightforward. What we need to know is how to write a program that will store our pixel maps in the 16 locations of the CGRAM. We know we can write instructions to the LCD as well as data to be displayed. We also know we use the logic on the RS pin to let the LCD know we want to write an instruction (i.e., the RS pin goes to a logic '0') or write data to be displayed (i.e., the RS pin goes to a logic '1'). So basically that is what we have to do. We set the RS pin to a logic '0' to let the LCD know that what follows next is an instruction. Then send the instruction 0b01000000, or 0X40, to tell the LCD we want to start writing to the CGRAM. The LCD will then go to the first address in the CGRAM and wait for the data, for the pixel map, to be sent to it. The program will then send the eight bytes that represent the pixel map we want to store. The LCD will then automatically go to the next CGRAM address and wait for the next eight bytes for the next pixel map to be sent to the LCD. When you have finished sending the eight bytes for each pixel map that you want to use, you must send the following instruction: 0b10000000 or 0X80. This tells the firmware on the LCD you have finished writing to the CGRAM. Note that you will have to put the LCD into the correct mode when you are writing the instruction 0X40 and 0X80 (i.e., instruction mode). However, when you are writing the data for the pixel maps, the LCD should be put into data mode. The whole process is best explained by writing a program to do this.

The program will write the data to display the four characters shown in Figure 13-4 to the CGRAM. Then, after displaying a simple message on line 1 of the LCD, the program will display the four characters from the CGRAM.

A Simple Exercise

As an exercise, can you work out the data for the four sets of eight bytes for the pixel maps of the four characters shown in Figure 13-4. Try this before you look at the program listing for this task. Also, to try and see how you are developing as a programmer, can you come up with a process by which we can save the series of eight bytes for each of the four characters. You should know that you will have to access these bytes from within your program. Don't worry too much about this task, but when you think you have completed the task, have a look at my program listing. I will not say that my approach is the only method, or indeed the best. The teacher's work is done when the student can improve on what the teacher does.

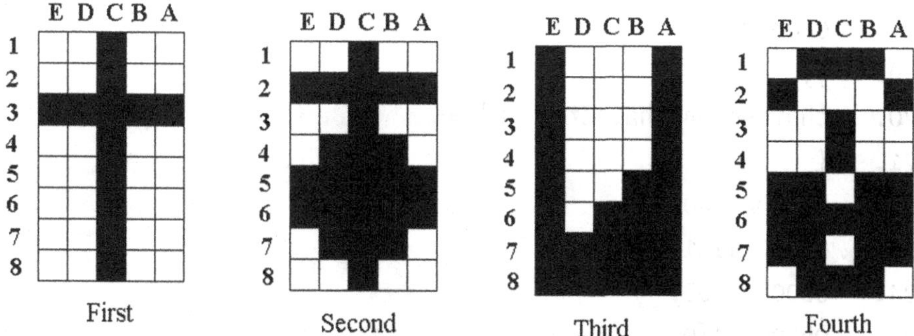

***Figure 13-4.** The pixel maps for the four characters*

Ok, now let's look at my approach in Listing 13-1.

Listing 13-1. CGRAM Task

```
/*This is a basic program to control the LCD using the PIC 18F4525
Written by H H Ward dated 22/05/21.
It writes to the CGRAM in the LCD
The display the four characters we have saved in the CGRAM*/
//some includes
#include <xc.h>
#include <conFigInternalOscNoWDTNoLVP.h>
#include <4bitLCDPortb.h>
char firstCharacter [8] =
 {
 0b00000100,
 0b00000100,
 0b00011111,
 0b00000100,
 0b00000100,
 0b00000100,
 0b00000100,
 0b00000100,
 };
 char secondCharacter [8] =
 {
 0b00000100,
 0b00011111,
 0b00000100,
 0b00001110,
 0b00011111,
 0b00011111,
```

```
0b00001110,
0b00000100,
};
char thirdCharacter [8] =
{
0b00010001,
0b00010001,
0b00010001,
0b00010001,
0b00010011,
0b00010111,
0b00011111,
0b00011111,
};
char fourthCharacter [8] =
{
0b00001110,
0b00010001,
0b00000100,
0b00000100,
0b00011011,
0b00011111,
0b00011011,
0b00001110,
};
void writeToCGram ()
{
rsLine = 0x00;
lcdData = 0x40;
lcdOut ();
rsLine = 0x10;
n = 0;
```

```
while (n < 8)
{
lcdData = firstCharacter [n];
lcdOut ();
n ++;
}
n = 0;
while (n < 8)
{
lcdData = secondCharacter [n];
lcdOut ();
n ++;
}
n = 0;
while (n < 8)
{
lcdData = thirdCharacter [n];
lcdOut ();
n ++;
}
n = 0;
while (n < 8)
{
lcdData = fourthCharacter [n];
lcdOut ();
n ++;
}
rsLine = 0x00;
lcdData = 0x80;
lcdOut ();
rsLine = 0x10;
}
```

```
void main ()
{
PORTA = 0;
PORTB = 0;
PORTC = 0;
PORTD = 0;
TRISA = 0Xff;
TRISB = 0x00;
TRISC = 0x00;
TRISD = 0x00;
ADCON0 = 0x00;
ADCON1 = 0x0F;
OSCTUNE = 0b10000000;
OSCCON = 0b01110100;
T0CON = 0b11000111;
TMR0 = 0;
while (TMR0 < 255);
setUpTheLCD ();
clearTheScreen ();
writeToCGram ();
while (1)
{
writeString ("Using the CGRAM");
line2 ();
lcdData = 0x00;
lcdOut ();
lcdData = 0x20;
lcdOut ();
lcdData = 0x01;
lcdOut ();
lcdData = 0x20;
lcdOut ();
```

```
lcdData = 0x02;
lcdOut ();
lcdData = 0x20;
lcdOut ();
lcdData = 0x03;
lcdOut ();
lcdData = 0x20;
lcdOut ();
lcdData = 0x48;
lcdOut ();
lcdData = 0x2E;
lcdOut ();
lcdData = 0x57;
lcdOut ();
lcdData = 0x2E;
lcdOut ();
lcdData = 0x31;
lcdOut ();
lcdData = 0x32;
lcdOut ();
lcdData = 0x33;
lcdOut ();
rsLine = 0x00;
lcdData = returnHome;
lcdOut ();
rsLine = 0x10;
}
}
```

Ok, so you should see that I have used four arrays to store the series of eight bytes for the four special characters. The first array is on line 9. We are also loading the arrays with the eight bytes when we declare them here. Did you set out the data for the eight bytes for each character correctly? Also, have you used arrays to store the data or something else? If it works, then it can't be wrong. Anyhow, I hope you did OK with that task if you tried it.

Analysis of Listing 13-1

I don't think there are any new instructions to analyze here. However, I will look at some of the more interesting sections of the program.

Line 53 void writeToCGRAM ()

This sets up a subroutine that is used for writing data to the CGRAM. Really, as the program only does this once and it doesn't allow you vary the data you are writing to the CGRAM, although that could be done by changing the eight bytes in the four arrays, then using a subroutine like this is not the best approach, as calling the subroutine uses up processor time. I will explain this aspect when we look at the interrupts in the last program in this chapter. However, let's see how this subroutine works.

You should remember, from my brief description earlier in this chapter, that we have to write the instruction to tell the LCD we want to write to the CGRAM. This instruction is 0X40.

Line 55 rsline = 0X00;

This loads the variable "rsline" with 0. This is to make sure that bit4 is a logic '0'. If you remember how the LCD works, you should know that we have to send a logic '0' to the RS pin, which is connected to bit 4 of PORTB, to tell the LCD we are sending an instruction. This instruction makes sure this happens.

Line 56 lcdData 0X40;

This loads the variable lcdData with the instruction 0X40.

Line 57 lcdOut ();

This calls the subroutine to send the data to the LCD. Therefore lines 55, 56, and 57 send the instruction to tell the LCD we are going to write to the CGRAM.

You should now appreciate that we are going to write to the first location in the CGRAM. This is at address 0x00. However, how does the LCD know we want to write to that address? We haven't told it that we want to write to that address. Well, the LCD has a pointer, just like the DS1307 we used in chapter 12. Indeed, as we will see later, all micros have a pointer of this type. This pointer is used to point to the address in the LCD's memory we want to go to, in this case write to or read from. When we used the instruction 0X40, the LCD loaded this pointer with the value 0x00, which is the address of the first memory location in the CGRAM. Now the LCD will open that address ready for us to send the data we want to write into it.

We have now finished sending instructions to the LCD. The next byte of information is not an instruction; it's data to be stored in the first CGRAM address. So what does that mean? Well I hope you know it means we have to send a logic '1' on to the RS pin. That's what we do next:

Line 58 rsline = 0x10;

This sets bit 4 of the variable rsline to a logic '1'. This means that the next time we send information to the LCD, we will be putting a logic '1' on the RS pin at the same time.

Ok, that means we are ready to send the first block of eight bytes to the CGRAM. This can be done in a "for do loop". However, as an alternative I have used a "while loop" that uses the variable 'n'. However, before we use the "while do loop", we must set the variable 'n' to zero.

Line 59 n = 0;

This loads the variable n with 0 ready for the "while loop".

Line 60 while (n < 8)

This sets up the “while loop”. The loop will run eight times, once for each byte we want to send to the CGRAM. I hope you can see why we need line 59.

Line 62 lcdData = firstCharacter[n];

This loads lcdData with the first byte, as n = 0, from the array “firstCharacter”. This array is where we stored the eight bytes for the pixel map of the first character.

Line 63 lcdOut ();

This sends the firstCharacter to the LCD.

Line 64 n++;

This increments the variable ‘n’, ready for the next run through the loop.

This first “while loop” sends all eight bytes for the pixel map of the first character to the area ‘1’ in the CGRAM.

Now we want to send the second pixel map. What happens now, in the LCD, is that the firmware automatically loads the pointer in the LCD with the address of the second area in the CGRAM (i.e., area ‘2’). This means that the LCD is waiting for us to send the next batch of eight bytes to be loaded into the area ‘2’ of the CGRAM.

Lines 66 to 72 do that for the second pixel map.

Lines 73 to 86 do that for the third and fourth pixel maps.

Now we need to tell the LCD we have finished writing to the CGRAM and we want to start using the pixel maps in the LCD. The instruction 0x80 tells the LCD that is what we are doing. Lines 87 to 89 do that. However, before we send the instruction, we have to make sure the RS pin will be sent to a logic ‘0’, as this is an instruction.

Line 90 rsline = 0x10;

This instruction ensures the RS pin will go to a logic ‘0’. The process by which this happens has been described in chapter 4.

Lines 92 to 110 are the normal instructions we have looked at before.

Line 111 writeToCGram ();

This calls the subroutine to write the pixel maps to the CGRAM.

Line 114 sends a simple message to the LCD, and line 115 sends the cursor to the start of the second line.

Line 116 lcdData = 0X00;

This loads the variable lcdData with 0X00. With previous analysis, I have said this is data we want to display on the LCD screen. We will see this in line 118. However, in reality it is not quite true. I have stated that it is really an address where the LCD will find the pixel map for the character we want it to display. It just so happens that most of the addresses have the same binary number as the ASCII for that character we want to display. However, with this address, which is 0x00, that is not the case. If this number were ASCII, it would be the "null" character. This number is simply the address of area '1' in the CGRAM. That is the area where we have stored our pixel map for the first character we designed. Therefore, in this way lines 116 and 117 will display the first of our special characters on the LCD.

Line 118 lcdData = 0X20;

This will now open up the area in the DDRAM at address 0x20. There, the LCD will find the pixel map to display an empty space on the LCD. Note, also, that as a planned coincidence, 0x20 is the ASCII for the space character. I know this description is quite wordy but I hope it shows how the memory areas in the LCD are organized to store the relevant pixel maps we will use.

Lines 116 to 131 will display the four special characters we have created on the LCD with a space between each character.

Lines 132 to 145 will display some more ASCII characters.

Lines 146 to 149 are used to show you how to change to instruction mode, for the instruction "returnHome" and back to data to be displayed mode.

Figure 13-5 shows the program working. I hope you have found this program interesting. The images you can create are not as detailed as with the matrix display in chapter 7, but the program can have its uses.

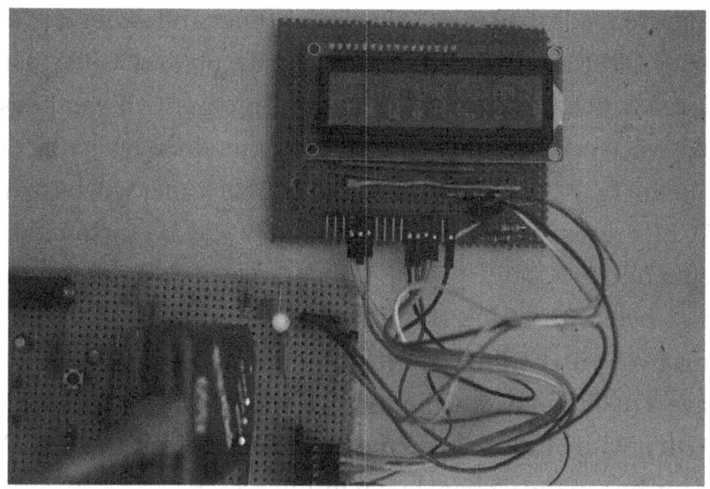

Figure 13-5. *The CGRAM program*

The CCP Module

In chapter 5, we used the PWM (pulse width modulation) aspect of the CCP module to vary the speed of a DC motor. In this chapter, we will look at the other two aspects of this module, namely the capture and the compare aspects.

The capture mode can be used for accurate timing of an event over a short period of time. What is captured is the current value in either timer1 or timer3, and it will be loaded into one of the CCPRX registers. The capture will happen when one of four specific actions occur on one of the CCP pins. The four actions are

- Every time the input goes from high to low; termed a falling edge.
- Every time the input goes from low to high; termed a rising edge.
- Every 4th rising edge.
- Every 16th rising edge.

The capture reads the 16-bit value in the timer and stores it in the register pair CCPRXH and CCPRXL, which make up the CCPRX. The 'X' is replaced with either a '1' or a '2', as there are two CCP modules in the PIC. We will work with the CCP2 module; therefore, when the event happens on the CCP2 pin, the current value in the timer will be loaded into the CCPR2 register. We can split the CCPR2 register up into two bytes, which would be

The high byte with CCPR2H storing bit 15 down to bit 8.

The low byte with CCPR2L storing bit 7 down to bit 0.

We have to tell the PIC which timer will be used as the capture source, and we do that with bits 6 and 3 of the timer3 control register, T3CON. This is done according to the values shown in Table 13-1.

Table 13-1. *The Selection of the Timer*

Bit 6 T3CCP2	Bit 3 TCCP1	Setting
0	0	Timer1 is the capture/compare source for both CCP1 and CCP2
0	1	Timer3 is the capture/compare source for CCP2 Timer1 is the capture/compare source for CCP1
1	0	Timer3 is the capture/compare source for both CCP1 and CCP2
1	1	

We will also have to tell the PIC which of the four events we want to use to trigger the capture. This is controlled with the setting of bits 3, 2, 1, and 0 of the CCP control register CCPXCON. This setting is shown in Table 13-2.

Table 13-2. The Capture Event Selection

Bit 3	Bit 2	Bit 1	Bit 0	Setting
0	1	0	0	Every falling edge
0	1	0	1	Every rising edge
0	1	1	0	Every 4th rising edge
0	1	1	1	Every 16th rising edge

Algorithm for the Bike Speed Program

We will use timer3 as the capture source for this program. We will use this capture process to determine the speed of a bicycle. There will be a sensor on the wheel that will pulse high then low once per revolution of the wheel. The principle behind the program is that we will zero timer3. Then on the next event we will capture the timer3 value and call this count1. Then on the next event we capture the timer3 value again and call this count2. We will then calculate a period by subtracting count2 from count1. The process will start again with zeroing the timer3 and the two count values.

The Speed of a Bicycle

If we start off by assuming the radius of a man's bike wheel is 14″. Then the circumference can be calculated as follows;

$C = 2\pi r = 2*3.14286*14 = 88''$

If we now assume an average speed is 15mph, then we can work out the possible value we would count up to for each revolution of the wheel.

One mile is 1760 yards or 63,360 inches. This means at 15mph the wheel will have covered 950,400 inches in one hour. If we now divide that by 3600, we get

Number of inches per second = 950400/3600 = 264.

We can now divide this by 88, the circumference of the wheel to convert this to revs per second.

Revs/sec = 264/88= 3 revs/sec.

This means the time taken to turn through 1 revolution = 1/3 = 333.333ms.

Knowing this value, we can now calculate the frequency at which timer3 must count. Note that the maximum value that timer3 can count up to is 65535, as we are setting timer3 to a 16-bit timer.

If we use our normal settings of using the internal oscillator set to 8MHz, then the system clock will run at 8MHz/4 = 2MHz. If we use the maximum divide rate of 8 for timer3, then timer3 will count at a frequency of 2MHz/8 = 250kHz. This means one count takes 4μs. If we use this time period for the counter to reach a value of 333.333ms, then the count would reach

333.333ms/4μs = 83333.25.

This is greater than the maximum value of 65535, so we can't use a frequency of 250kHz for timer3. It must be lower. Really, we should use the minimum speed to determine the setting of the oscillator and timer3 frequencies. Let the minimum speed be 1mph. Using the same value as before, we can see that at this speed the wheel will turn through 0.2rev/sec. This means it will take 5 seconds for the wheel to turn through one revolution. If we are to reach that time with a maximum count of 65535, then each count must take 5/65536 = 76.294μs. This means the frequency at which timer3 must count at is 1/76.294μs = 13.1072kHz. If we multiply this by 8, we get 104.857kHz for the frequency of the system clock. If we now multiply this by 4, we get 419.430kHz for the oscillator frequency. The internal oscillator can be set to 500kHz or 250kHz, which out of the eight settings, are the closest to the 419.439kHz we need. We must choose 250kHz.

At this setting, for the internal oscillator frequency, the system clock runs at 62.5kHz. With the maximum divide rate of 8, timer3 counts at a frequency of 7.8125kHz, which means one tick = 128μs. This means that to count to 5 seconds timer3 would reach a value of 39062.5 (i.e., 5/128μs), well within the range of 65525.

If we had chosen a value of 500kHz for the oscillator, then to count to 5 seconds timer3 would have to count up to 78125 which is outside the maximum range of 65535.

This means we must set the internal oscillator to a frequency of 250kHz. This is done by setting bits 6, 5, and 4 of the OSCCON register to 010.

To achieve a maximum divide rate of 8 for timer3, we must set bits 5 and 4 to 11. With these settings as our starting point, we can write the program listing.

To test the program we will use timer1 to create a 6Hz square wave that should produce a speed of 30mph. To create this 6Hz square wave, we will use the compare aspect of the CCP module. This will compare the value that timer1 has reached with a value stored in the CCPR1 register. When they become the same, then one of three actions can be set to happen;

- The CCPX can be driven high
- The CCPX can be driven low
- The CCPX can be driven high if it is currently low or be driven low if it is currently high.

Timer1 will count at the same rate as timer3, which means when timer1 reaches a value of 651 it will have reached a time of 651 × 126ms = 83.333ms, which is half the periodic time for a 6Hz square wave. So using this concept, we should be able to create a 6Hz square wave with a 50/50 duty cycle.

There will be two events in our program that will cause the PIC to perform some specific actions. The two events are

- The value in timer1 is equal to the value stored in CCPR1 (the "compare" function of the CCP module).
- This will cause the logic on the CCP1 pin to toggle from high to low or from low to high.

- The level of the CCP2 pin has gone from high to low (the "capture" function of the CCP module).
- This will get the PIC to load either count1 or count2 with the current value in timer3.

To ensure that these two events are not missed, we will use the interrupt facilities of the CCP modules. We will also make one a higher priority than the other to show you how the interrupts can have different priorities.

We will now look at Listing 13-2 to see how this works.

Listing 13-2. The Bike Speed Program

```
/*
* File:   bikeSpeedProg.c
Author: Hubert Ward
*written for the PIC18f4525
using both low and high priority interrupts
Created on 21 April 2020, 12:06
*/
#include <xc.h>
#include <conFigInternalOscNoWDTNoLVP.h>
#include <4bitLCDPortb.h>
#include <stdio.h>
//some definitions
#define slow PORTAbits.RA0
#define fast PORTAbits.RA1
#define slowest PORTAbits.RA2
#define LED0 PORTDbits.RD0
#define LED1 PORTDbits.RD1
//some variables
unsigned count1, count2;
```

```
float speed, period;
//some subroutines
void displaySpeed(float dp)
{
sprintf(str, "%.2f", dp);
writeString(str);
writeString(" mph");
}
void interrupt HP_int ()
{
PIR2bits.CCP2IF = 0;
LED0 = 1;
if (count1 == 0) count1 = CCPR2;
else
{
count2 = CCPR2;
period = (count2 - count1)*0.000128;
count1 = 0;
count2 = 0;
TMR3 = 0;
}
}
void interrupt low_priority LP_int ()
{
PIR1bits.CCP1IF = 0;
LED1 = 1;
if (TMR1 >= CCPR1) TMR1 = 0;
}
void main ()
{
PORTA = 0;
```

```
PORTB = 0;
PORTC = 0;
PORTD = 0;
TRISA = 0b00010111;
TRISB = 0x00;
TRISC = 0b00000010;
TRISD = 0;
ADCON0 = 0x00;
ADCON1 = 0x0F;
OSCCON = 0b00100100;
OSCTUNE = 0b10000000;
T0CON = 0b10000010;
T1CON = 0b10110001;
T3CON = 0b10111001;
INTCON = 0b11000000;
INTCON2 = 0;
INTCON3 = 0;
PIE1 = 0b00000100;
PIE2 = 0b00000001;
RCON = 0b10000000;
IPR1 = 0;
IPR2 = 0b00000001;
CCP1CON = 0b00000010;
CCP2CON = 0b00000100;
CCPR1 = 1953;
setUpTheLCD ();
writeString ("The Speed is");
while (1)
{
line2 ();
if (!slow) CCPR1 = 1302;
if (!fast) CCPR1 = 651;
```

```
83.    if (!slowest) CCPR1 = 1953;
84.    speed = 5/period;
85.    displaySpeed(speed);
86.    }
87.    }
```

Analysis of Listing 13-2

Most of the instructions have been looked at before. I will restrict the analysis to the more interesting instructions.

Lines 22 to 27 is a subroutine that uses the “sprintf” function to display the value of the float ‘speed’ to show the speed of the bike. It will also display the message mph for miles per hour.

Note that the “sprintf” function is in the stdio.h header files. That is why we need to include this header file as in line 11.

Line 28 void interrupt HP_int ()

This is one of the special subroutines termed ISR (interrupt service routine), which is used by the interrupts. This is for the “capture” function, which I have decided should have higher priority than the “compare” function. This means that if the PIC is actually carrying out the instructions of the compare function ISR and the capture function creates its interrupt request, then the PIC will have to leave that ISR and go through this higher-priority ISR. When it has completed this higher-priority ISR, the PIC will return to the lower-priority ISR to complete that routine. We will look at how this jumping from one ISR to the other works later in this chapter.

Line 30 PIR2bits.CCP2IF = 0;

There is only one high-priority ISR, so we don’t need to check which peripheral has created the interrupt. However, the first thing we should do is turn off the interrupt flag (IF) that caused the interrupt. This prevents it from causing another interrupt automatically. It also enables the PIC to see when it does cause the next interrupt. Note that the IFs of each peripheral do not return to logic ‘0’ automatically; this it must be done in software.

Line 31 LED0 = 1;

This is not part of the program. This is really a technique I use to test to see if the PIC is actually going into a subroutine. Really it is a debugging aid. If the LED does come on, then I know the PIC must have gone into the subroutine. I have left this instruction in to just show you one way of checking to see if an action does occur.

Line 32 if (count1 == 0) count1 = CCPR2;

This is a one-line test to see if the value in count1 is still zero. If it is, then the PIC must load count1 with the current value in the CCPR2 16-bit register.

This test will be true if this is the first event of the CCP2 pin. If this event is true, the PIC will skip the instructions on lines 33 to 40.

Line 33 else

This sets up the instructions that the PIC must carry out if the test on line 32 was untrue. There is more than one instruction that the PIC must do, so they are enclosed in a set of curly brackets.

Line 35 count2 = CCPR2;

This loads the variable count2 with the current value in the CCPR2 register. This will be after the second event on the CCP2 pin.

Line 36 period = (count2 - count1)*0.000128;

This will load the variable period with the difference between count2 and count1 after it has been multiplied by 128µ. This converts the number into a time period.

Line 37 count1 = 0;

This resets this variable back to 0.

Line 38 count2 = 0;

This resets this variable back to 0.

Line 39 TMR3 = 0;

This resets timer 3 back to 0 so that we start counting from 0 again.

Lines 32 to 40 load the variable 'period' with the time taken for the bike wheel to turn through one revolution.

Line 42 void interrupt low_priority LP_int ()

This sets up the second ISR. This ISR is for the "compare" function, and it will have a lower priority than the "capture" function.

Again, there is only one peripheral that could cause the low-priority interrupt, which means we don't need to test which peripheral caused the interrupt. If there was more than one peripheral that could cause the interrupt, we would have to test which one caused it by using a series of "if this then do that" type instructions. For example;

if (PIR1bits.CCP1IF == 1) then do this.

else if (PIR2bits.CCP2IF == 1) then do this.

You would replace the reference to the IF with the ones you want to test.

However, we don't need to do that here.

Line 44 PIR1bits.CCP1IF = 0;

We must turn the IF off.

Line 45 LED1 = 1;

This is the same debugging method as with the high-priority ISR.

Line 46 if (TMR1 >= CCPR1) TMR1 = 0;

This is testing to see if the value in timer1 is equal to or greater than the value stored in the CCPR1 register. We can't use just equal to, as by the time the PIC has gotten to this instruction, the value in TMR1 would have increased beyond the value in the CCPR1 register. TMR1 would only be equal to CCPR1 for one clock cycle.

Really, we don't need to ask this question here because the PIC would not be in this ISR if this test were not true. We could replace this instruction with just TMR1 = 0; the program would work just as well, if not better. I have included this full instruction so that I could explain why we need to use the >= with this type of test.

Now we will look at the interesting instructions of the main program.

Line 62 T0CON = 0b10000010;

This first new thing we have done here is make bit 6 a logic '0'. This sets timer0 to be a 16-bit timer so that it can count up to 65535. We don't really need to do this, but I wanted to show you what this bit 6 can do.

The next thing that is new is that bits 2, 1, and 0 are set to 010. This sets the divide rate of timer0 down to 8. This is because we are using a slower oscillator set to 250kHz. We still need timer0 to count at a rate of 7812.5Hz. Therefore, we need only divide the system clock by 8. System clock runs at a quarter of the oscillator rate, therefore 250k/4 = 62.5k. Then 62.5k/8 = 7182.5Hz.

Line 63 T1CON = 0b10110001;

This does the same but for timer1.

Line 64 T3CON = 0b10111001;

This does the same but for timer3.

Line 65 INTCON = 0b11000000;

This enables both the global and peripheral interrupts. Bits 7 and 6 are set to logic '1'.

Lines 66 and 67 set the INTCON2 and INTCON3 to 0, as we are not using any of their interrupt sources.

Line 68 PIE1 = 0b00000100;

This sets bit 2 to a logic '1' to enable the CCP1 peripheral interrupt.

Line 69 PIE2 = 0b00000001;

This sets bit 0 to a logic '1' to enable the CCP2 peripheral interrupt.

Line 70 RCON = 0b10000000;

This sets bit 7 to a logic '1' to enable the priority function of the interrupts.

Line 71 IPR1 = 0;

This sets bit 2 to a logic '0' to set the CCP1 peripheral a low-priority interrupt.

Line 72 IPR2 = 0b00000001;

This sets bit 0 to a logic '1' to make the CCP1 peripheral a high-priority interrupt.

Line 73 CCP1CON = 0b00000010;

This puts the CCP1 into the compare function.

Line 74 CCP2CON = 0b00000100;

This puts the CCP2 into the capture function.

Line 75 CCPR1 = 1953;

This loads the variable CCPR1 with the value 1953. This should create a time period of 1953x128m = 0.249984. This should create a square wave of 2Hz with a 50/50 duty cycle. This is because the periodic time would be 2 × 0.249984 = 0.499968. The frequency = 1/0.49968 = 2.000128Hz. This should produce a speed display of 10mph. The actual display is 9.94 mph (see Figure 13-6).

Lines 76 to 80 are some normal instructions.

Lines 81 to 83 are there so that we can change the value stored in the CCPR1 register and so change the speed of the bike. Note that changing the value stored in the CCPR1 register will change the frequency of the square wave. The duty cycle will still be 50/50, as the CCPR1 register simply controls the time for half of the periodic time of the square wave.

Line 84 speed = 5/period;

The period is loaded in line 36 as (count2 - count1) × 0.000128. The value of '5' is created as follows:

$$\frac{60 \times 60 \times 88}{63360} = 5$$

The 60×60 changes the seconds into hours.

The 88 converts the hours to a distance by multiplying by 88, the circumference of the bike wheel. We are dividing by 63360, as that is the number of inches in a mile.

Therefore, the number 5 changes the frequency of 1/period into miles per hour.

I hope this analysis does explain how these instructions work. I hope you can see how the logic '1's and '0's in these control registers do control how the PIC works.

One thing I should mention is that we are using the square wave output on the CCP1 pin, which is on bit 2 of PORTC, as the signal from the bicycle sensor on the wheel . This would then be inputted to the PIC on the CCP2 pin, which is bit 1 of PORTC.

Finding the Program Instructions

The following section looks at how the PIC finds its way around the memory locations to find the correct instructions.

Program Counter and the Stack

All the instructions and data for a program are stored somewhere inside the PIC's program and data memory area. The question we should be asking is how the PIC knows where to go to find these instructions. The answer is the program counter (PC). This is a register inside the PIC. In the PIC18f4525, the PC is a 21-bit register that is spread across three bytes:

- The PCL, PC Low Byte, which contains bits 0 to 7
- The PCH, PC High Byte, which contains bits 8 to 15
- The PCU, PC Upper Byte, which contains bits 16 to 20

It is easiest to just refer to the PC as one register and not the individual bytes. The purpose of the PC is to hold the address, in the PIC's memory, that the PIC must go to get the NEXT instruction, or part of instruction, in the program's listing. Note that the PC is always pointing to the NEXT location. This means that when MPLABX loads the program down to the PIC, it will load the address of the first instruction, in the main loop, into the PC. In the "fetch-and-execute cycle", the micro will look at the contents of the PC to find out where in the PIC's memory it must go to get this first instruction. Then, after getting this first instruction, the very first thing the micro does, before it even looks at the instruction, is increment the contents of the PC. This is so that the PC is already pointing to the NEXT location in memory.

The Stack

Well, that's all well and good as long as the micro simply goes on from one location to the next. However, what happens when the micro has to break out of this sequential operation to carry out the instructions in a subroutine or an ISR? It's quite easy for the call instruction to a subroutine to simply overwrite the contents of the PC with the location of the first instruction in the subroutine, and that is what happens. However, how does the micro know where to go back to in the main program from where it was called? This is where the "stack" comes in. This is an area of the micro's memory that is reserved as a temporary store of important addresses and sometimes data (with some micros). You should appreciate that before the micro actually carries out the call instruction, the PC will have already been incremented. This means it will contain the address of the NEXT instruction, after this call instruction. What the micro must do is store the current contents of the PC onto the stack. Now the micro can load the address of the subroutine into the PC. This means that, after carrying out the call instruction, when the micro now looks at the PC to find out where it must go, the PC will point it to the first instruction in the subroutine. After the micro has carried out the last instruction in the subroutine, it carries out a return or ret instruction from the subroutine. This return instruction does not have to be written into the subroutine by the programmer but it will have been added by the compiler. There is always a return instruction in the subroutine. There are occasions when you do add this return instruction, which is when you want to send some data back to the main program at the end of the subroutine. This return instruction gets the micro to retrieve the address that it had stored on the stack when it carried out the call instruction to go to the subroutine, and load it onto the PC. In this way, the micro can return back to the program at the instruction one after the call instruction.

Figure 13-6 may help explain the process.

Address	Instruction
0001	
0002	
0003	call
0004	

main program

Program Counter	
0004	before call
0100	call
0004	return

Stack
0004

Address	Instruction
0100	
0101	
0102	
0103	return

Subroutine

***Figure 13-6.** The call and return sequence*

The call instruction is at location 0X0003 in the main program. Before the PIC carries out this call instruction, the PC has the address 0X0004 as shown. In carrying out the call instruction, the PIC puts the address 0X0004, from the PC, onto the top of the stack. It then overwrites the contents of the PC with the address 0X0100. This is the address of the first instruction in the subroutine. The PIC then carries out the instructions of the subroutine. When the PIC carries out the return instruction, it overwrites the contents of the PC, which would have been 0X0104, with the address taken from the top of the stack, which is address 0X0004. This is how the PIC copes with jumping out of the main program, or another subroutine, to run a subroutine and returns back to the main program.

The Vector Table and the ISR

The ISRs operate in a similar fashion to the normal subroutine, but there is one difference. There is no call instruction in the main program that allows the PIC to overwrite the PC with the address of the ISR. This is because the PIC is forced to go to the ISR when, during the fetch-and-execute cycle, it detects that the interrupt bit has been set by whatever interrupt source caused the interrupt. What happens now is that the PIC will save the current contents of the PC onto the stack. Then it will go to one of two preset locations:

- The High-Priority Interrupt Vector at address 0X0008
- The Low-Priority Interrupt Vector at address 0X0018.

That is because the housekeeping firmware of the PIC will store the actual address of the ISRs that the PIC must go to find the first instruction of the ISRs in these two vector addresses. When an interrupt is detected, the PIC will store the current contents of the PC onto the stack, just as it did with the normal subroutine. This is so that it can find its way back to the instruction it was going to carry out before it was interrupted. The PIC will then go to the relevant vector to retrieve the address it must copy into the PC so that the PIC can go to the relevant ISR. When the PIC gets to the return instruction of the ISR, it will retrieve the correct address from the stack and load it into the PC. The PIC can then go back to the main program at the correct instruction.

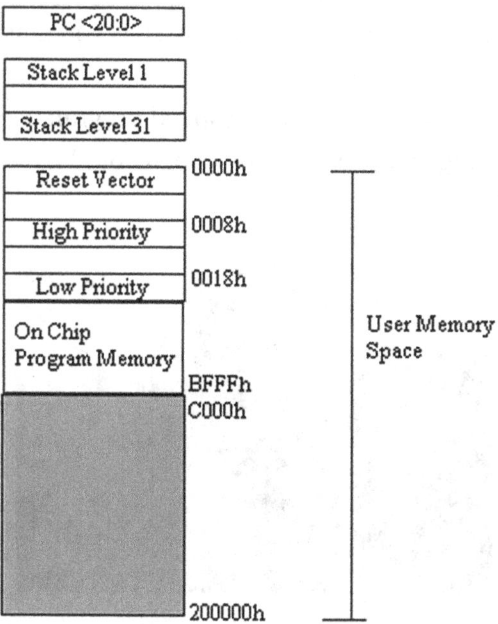

***Figure 13-7.** The memory map of the PIC*

Figure 13-7 shows some of the different areas of the PIC's memory. The stack is shown as a 31 level of memory so that it can store multiple return addresses for multiple calls. If you try to put too many return addresses onto the stack, you could get the error message of "stack overflow".

The reset vector is shown as address 0X0000. The PIC's firmware will store the address of the first instruction in the program listing in this vector address. This is so that if you reset the PIC, it will go to this vector and load the PC with the address stored there. The PIC will then be able to go to the first instruction in the program.

The actual instructions of the program will be placed in the remaining locations in the PIC 48kbytes of memory.

It's not essential that you understand how the PIC uses the PC and the stack. This explanation is really only a simplified look at the process. However, the more you understand the workings of the PIC, I believe, the better programmer you will become. I hope you can appreciate that there is a limit to the number of nested subroutine calls you make before you run out of space on the stack.

Figures 13-8 and 13-9 show the bike speed program working. I have not built it into something you could fix onto a bike, but I am sure you could do that if you so desired.

Figure 13-8. *The bike speed program displaying 9.94mph*

Figure 13-9. *The bike speed program displaying 29.50mph*

Summary

In this chapter, we have learned how to create our own characters to be displayed on the LCD. We have also looked at using low- and high-priority interrupts. Finally, we looked at using the compare and capture features of the CCP module and learned how to create a digital speedometer for our push bike.

In the final chapter, we will look at some more obscure instructions in C. We will also look at some of the logic instructions and at using the debugging ability of the MPLABX IDE to study how these instructions actually work.

CHAPTER 14

Analyzing Obscure Instructions and Logic Operators in C

This chapter is designed to take away some of the mystery of C programming. We will look at some obscure instructions and analyze how they work and we will use the debugging mode of MPLABX to confirm our analysis. We will then look at some of the more common logic operators in C and see how they work. To that end, I have come up with a series of programs that I can use to explain these strange instructions. So let's get to it.

Obscure C Instructions

Listing 14-1 includes some of the more obscure instructions, such as uint8_t, enum, strstr, strlen, memmove, and strncmp, and in my analysis I hope to explain what the instructions are doing.

Listing 14-1. Obscure C Instructions

```
/*
* File:   enumEtcTestProg.c
a program to test how some instructions in C work.
Author: Mr Hubert Ward
```


H. H. Ward, *Programming Arduino Projects with the PIC Microcontroller*,
https://doi.org/10.1007/978-1-4842-7230-5_14

```
Created on 03 September 2020, 22:10
*/
//some includes
#include <xc.h>
#include <conFigInternalOscNoWDTNoLVP.h>
#include <stdint.h>
#include <string.h>
#include <4bitLCDPortb.h>
//some definitions
#define testButton PORTAbits.RA1
//some variables
unsigned char n;
int result;
uint8_t tester;
char item[20] = "Hubert ward";
const char item1[6] = "Ward";
const char item2[10] = "ert";
char *itempoint;
enum value
{
zero,
one,
two,
three,
four,
five,
six,
seven,
eight,
nine
};
enum phase
```

```
{
first = 10,
second,
third,
fourth
};
void delay (unsigned char t)
{
for (n = 0; n < t; n ++)
{
TMR0 = 0;
while (TMR0 < 255);
}
}
void main()
{
PORTA = 0;
PORTB = 0;
PORTC = 0;
PORTD = 0;
TRISA = 0b00000010;
TRISB = 0x00;
TRISC = 0b00000000;
TRISD = 0x00;
ADCON0 = 0x00;
ADCON1 = 0x0F;
OSCTUNE = 0b10000000;
OSCCON = 0b01110000;
T0CON = 0b11000111;
setUpTheLCD ();
while (1)
```

```
{
PORTC = one;
delay (30);
PORTC = two;
delay (30);
PORTC = three;
delay (30);
PORTC = third;
delay (30);
PORTC = fourth;
delay (30);
while (!testButton);
tester = eight;
PORTC = tester;
delay (30);
while (!testButton);
if ( itempoint = strstr(item, item2))
writeString( itempoint);
else writeString( "None Found");
tester = strlen ("Hubert");
PORTC = tester;
delay (30);
while (!testButton);
tester = strlen ("Hubert Ward");
PORTC = tester;
delay (30);
while (!testButton);
memmove (item,item1,4);
itempoint = item;
line2 ();
while (!testButton);
```

```
99.  writeString (itempoint);
100. result = strncmp(item, item2, 1);
101. PORTC = result;
102. while (1);
103. }
104. }
```

Analysis of Listing 14-1

This first program uses a lot of arrays and displays on the LCD. Therefore, we will run this program using a practical board to show what happens with the instructions. I hope you will be able to run the programs yourselves and so see that the results do confirm my analysis. I have done so and they worked as expected.

Line 10 #include <stdint.h>

This ensures the compiler also includes the header file stdint.h. This is because on line 18 we are declaring a variable "tester". This is of the type unit8_t, which is from this header file. The term stdint possibly stands for standard integers, but I am not sure. It allows programmers to set up signed or unsigned integers that have a specific number of bits. The convention for declaring these variables is

- intN_t for signed integers.
- unintN_t for unsigned integers.

The 'N' is replaced by the number of bits you want to assign to the variable. The only advantage I can see over int and unsigned int is that you are not restricted to 16 bits. You could have 12 bits or 9 bits or 18 bits and so on.

Line 11 #include <string.h>

This header file is required for use of the "strstr" string type instruction on line 77.

Line 14 #define testButton PORTAbits.RA1

This defines the phrase testButton to represent the input on bit 1 of PORTA. I am using this to control when we move on from aspect of the program to the next. This is so that we can see that what happens is what we predicted.

Line 18 uint8_t tester;

This declares a variable called "tester". The term uint8_t is actually a label that has been defined in the header file stdint.h. It means that the variable "tester" will be eight bits in length. It is really the same as using the type "unsigned char". The only difference I can find is that in some compilers unsigned char can be treated differently. For example, one compiler may give the variable eight bits as it should, but another may give it 16 bits. However, if you used the uint8_t for the variable, then all compilers would give the variable two eight bits. Not much use really. I would prefer to just use unsigned char as I know the xc8 compilers will give it the eight bits I want.

To try and show that, this program simply creates an eight-bit variable called "tester" with this instruction. Then, on line 80 it loads the variable "tester" with the value stored in the variable "eight" and then displays it on PORTC in line 81.

Line 19 char item[20] = "Hubert Ward";

This creates an array that saves 20 locations in memory one after the other. The first 11 memory locations have the ASCII for each of the characters to spell out the phrase Hubert Ward. If I had only reserved eight memory locations as with the instruction char item[8] = "Hubert Ward", then the compiler would throw up an error, as there are too many characters to be stored in the eight memory locations.

The next two arrays have the phrase "cont" inserted before the term "char". If we had used the phrase "cont" here, then the complier would throw up an error. This is because on line 95 we are trying to move four items from the array item1 to this array. If we had used the phrase "cont" here, then we would be making the contents of the array constant. This would mean they could not be changed and so when the compiler came to the instruction on line 95 it would throw up an error. To test this change, this instruction to read as **const char item[20] = "Hubert Ward";**. You should see that the compiler now throws up an error. Change the instruction back to what it should be.

Line 20 const char item1[6] = "Ward";

This sets up a second array, and the first four locations store the ASCII to spell out Ward. These characters cannot be changed.

Line 21 const char item1[10] = "ard";

This sets up a third array and the first three locations store the ASCII to spell out ard. Again, these characters cannot be changed.

It will become clear what I am doing here when we get to line 95.

Line 22 char *itempoint;

This declares a pointer that we can use to point to locations within the arrays we have set up.

Line 23 enum value

This creates something that may be considered an array. What is does is define a list of labels that can be used to represent numerical values. The list is declared in the lines that are enclosed between the opening and closing curly brackets that follow. In this first enum array, the first label, "zero", is given the numerical value of '0.' The next label, "one", is given the numerical value of '1.' This is because we have not assigned a value to the first label in the array. The compiler will give the first label in the array the value '0' and then simply increment the value when assigned to all the other labels in the array.

Line 24 {

This is the opening curly bracket of this list of labels.

Line 35 };

This is the closing curly bracket of the list. Note that each item in the list ends with the comma ','. Also the final curly bracket ends with the semicolon ';' as this is the end of the instruction.

Line 36 enum phase

This creates a second array of type enum, but in this array the first label "first" is given the numerical value 10. This means that the values in the array start from 10 not 0. Therefore, the label "second" has the numerical value of 11, "third" has 12, and "fourth" has 13.

This action is similar to using the #define, but if you are going to give numerical values to a list of labels that simply increment from a given starting point, then this is a more efficient way of setting them out.

To show that all the given labels have the numerical values we expect, the program in lines 69 to 78 simply displays the label values on PORTC with a 1-second delay between displays.

I hope this helps explain some of the instructions in Listing 14-1.

Line 79 while (!testButton);

This stops the program at this point until we press the input A1 to make the input go to a logic '1'. This is just so that we can confirm the program is working as expected.

Line 80 tester = eight;

This loads the variable "tester" with the value 8.

Line 81 PORTC = tester;

This displays the contents of the variable tester on PORTC.

Line 82 delay (30);

This calls a 1-second delay.

Line 83 just waits for you to press the testButton.

Line 84 if (itempoint = strstr(item, item2))

This is the next new instruction. It sets out a test that will be true if the pointer "itempoint" can find the same characters that are listed in the array "item2", existing in the array "item".

If the test is true, then the PIC will carry out the instruction on line 85; note that it will not then carry out the instruction on line 86.

If the test is untrue, then the PIC will skip the instruction on line 85 and carry out the instruction on line 86.

To try to help understand what this instruction is doing, we will look at Figure 14-1.

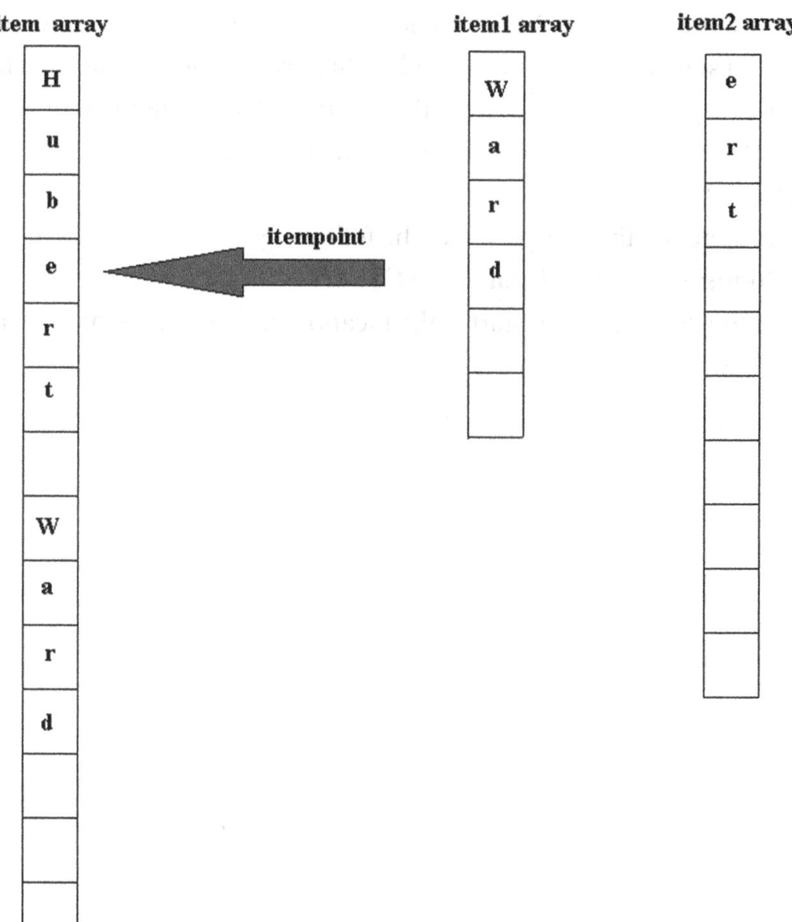

Figure 14-1. *The three arrays*

This shows the pointer "itempoint" is now pointing to the location with the character "e" in. This is because "e" is the first letter in the array "item2". The PIC has now found this letter in the array item. As the PIC has successfully found the character in the array "item", when we carry out the instruction on line 85 the PIC sends the characters that the pointer is pointing to the LCD. The PIC will send all the characters in the array "item" to the LCD starting at the letter 'e' and ending when it gets a null, which it doesn't display on the LCD, from the location in array "item" after the letter 'd'. In this way, the LCD will display the following;

ert Ward

If we changed the instruction to the following:

if (itempoint = strstr(item, item1))

then the pointer would start at the location in array "item" as shown in Figure 14-2.

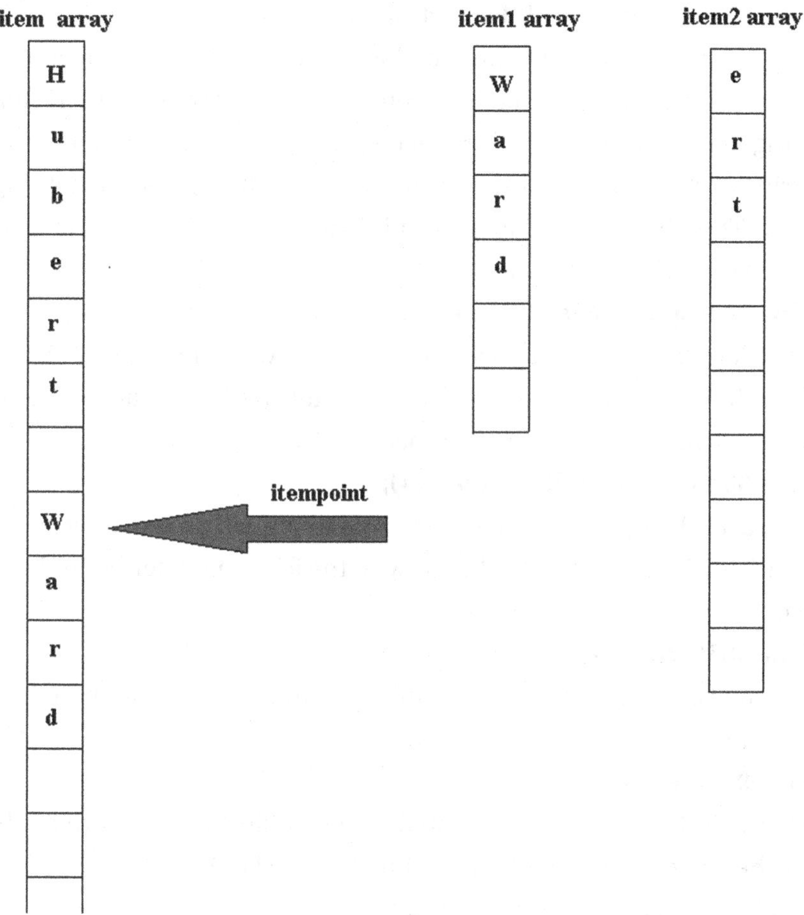

Figure 14-2. *The Three Arrays*

This would mean that the LCD would display the following:

Ward.

So this "strStr" instruction allows the PIC to search arrays for items that are in another array. Still quite a strange instruction but quite a powerful one. I hope this explanation does help you understand it better.

Line 87 tester = strlen ("Hubert");

This instruction uses the function "strlen" to count the characters that are in the string contained between the two quotation marks. It stops counting when it finds the null character that is always added to the end of a string of characters. In this case, there are six characters in the string "Hubert". Therefore, the variable tester is loaded with six and this is then displayed on PORTC in line 88.

Line 91 tester = strlen ("Hubert Ward");

This does the same, but now tester is loaded with the value of 11. This is just to show you that the space in not the null character that denotes the end of the string. The ASCII for the space is 0X20.

Line 95 memmove (item,item1,4);

This uses the function "memmove". What this will do is overwrite the first four locations in the array "item" with the four characters stored in the array item1.

Line 96 itempoint = item;

This makes the pointer "itempoint" point to the first location in the array "item".

Line 97 line2 ();

This calls the subroutine line2 in the header file 4bitLCDPortb.h. This moves the cursor to the beginning of line2 on the LCD.

Line 99 writeString (itempointer);

This sends to the LCD all the characters of the array that the pointer "itempoint" is pointing to.

Line 100 result = = strncmp(item, item2, 1);

This introduces the new instruction "strncmp". This will compare the ASCII totals of a number of characters in two arrays. The number of characters to be compared is declared using the final number in the brackets. In this case, we are only comparing the ASCII of the first character. What this will do is subtract the value of the ASCII in the second array from the ASCII of the first array. In this instruction, the second array is "item2" and the first array is "item". At this point in the program, the first character in the array "item2" is 'e'. The ASCII for this character is 101. The first character in the array "item" is now 'W'. The ASCII for this is 87. Therefore, subtracting item2 form item is 87 - 101 = -14. This is the value that is stored in the variable "result".

When this value is displayed on PORTC, you will see that the binary value is 0b11110010.

If you perform a 2's complement on this binary number, you will end up with 0b00001110, which is 14. This shows that 0b11110010 represents -14.

Try changing this instruction to

result = = strncmp(item2, item, 1);

You will see that the display on PORTC goes to 0b00001110, which is binary for 14. This is because we have swapped the arrays around, and the calculation is now 101 - 87 = 14.

I hope this analysis has shown you how some new and obscure instructions actually work. I have yet to find a use for these instructions, but I do think you will come across them, as I have.

Some Logic Operators

There are a range of logic operators in the C programming language. Some of the more common ones, and their symbols are as follows:

- The AND function, which has '&' and '&&'.
- The OR function, which has '|' and '||'.
- The EXOR function, which has '^'.

The following text will attempt to explain what these operators do. Also, we will use the MPLABX simulator to run the programs. This will allow us to single step through the instructions and use some watch windows to see what is happening with the program.

Also, as we will be using the same setup, as with the internal oscillator, timer0, and the ADC, we will be using a header file I have created previously to save time in writing the program listings. The header file is called PICSetup.h and is shown in Listing 14-2.

Listing 14-2. PICSetup.h

```
void initialise ()
{
PORTA = 0;
PORTB = 0;
PORTC = 0;
PORTD = 0;
PORTE = 0;
TRISA = 0XFF;
TRISB = 0;
TRISC = 0;
TRISD = 0b11111111;
TRISE = 0;
ADCON0 = 0;
ADCON1 = 0b00001111;
OSCTUNE = 0;
OSCCON = 0b01110100;
T0CON = 0b11000111;
}
```

You can see that it is really a subroutine called initialize. That is how we get the PIC to run the instructions in the header file. We simply call the subroutine from within the main program. Of course, we will have to include the header file in the listings we want to use it in. Also, we need to create this as a global header file. We went through how to create a global header file in chapter 1.

& Symbol

This is the bit AND in that individual bits are ANDED. The truth table for a two-bit logical AND function is shown in Table 14-1.

Table 14-1. *The 'AND' Truth Table*

B	A	F
0	0	0
0	1	0
1	0	0
1	1	1

You should appreciate that the result 'F' is only a logic '1' when both 'A' and 'B' are a logic '1'; hence the name of the function (Listing 14-3).

Listing 14-3. Testing the Bit AND '&' Operator

```
/*
* File:   logicsimulationProg.c
Author: H H Ward
*
Created on 21 November 2020, 15:56
*/
#include <xc.h>
#include <conFigInternalOscNoWDTNoLVP.h>
#include <PICSetUp.h>
//some variable
unsigned char a,b,c,d,e,f;
void main()
```

```
{
a = 0;
b = 0;
c = 0;
d = 0;
a = 2;
b = 5;
c = 13;
while (1)
{
d =(a & b);
}
}
```

Testing the Programs in MPLABX

All these short programs (Listings 14-2 and 14-3) can be tested in MPLABX. In the following example, we will test the '&' operator. To enable us to test these programs in MPLABX when we create the projects, we should choose the simulator as the tool in the select tool window as shown in Figure 14-3.

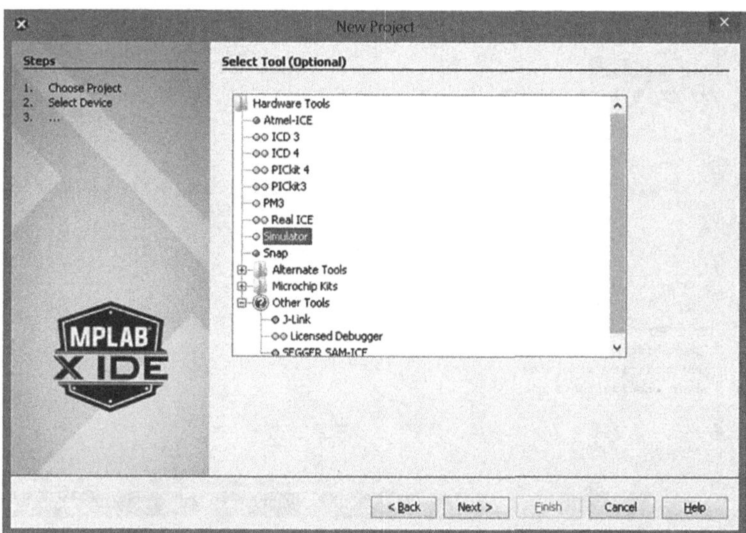

***Figure 14-3.** Selecting the simulator in the select tool window*

When you now come to build the program, you need to select the debug option from the main menu bar as shown in Figure 14-4.

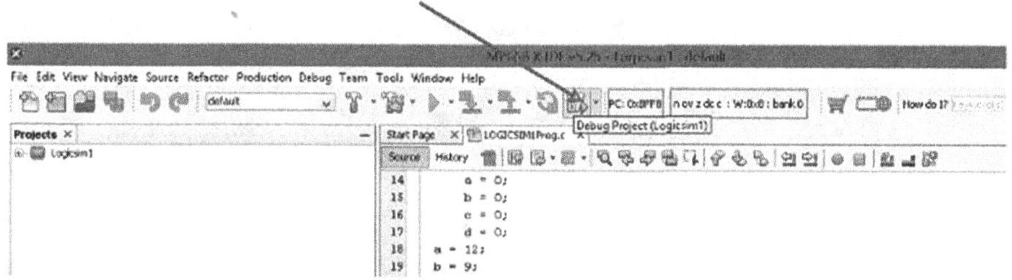

***Figure 14-4.** Selecting the debug tool*

Now when you compile the program, it should open up the following windows on your screen. They may need moving around a little, and I have already opened up a watch window and selected some items I wanted to watch. These are shown in Figure 14-5.

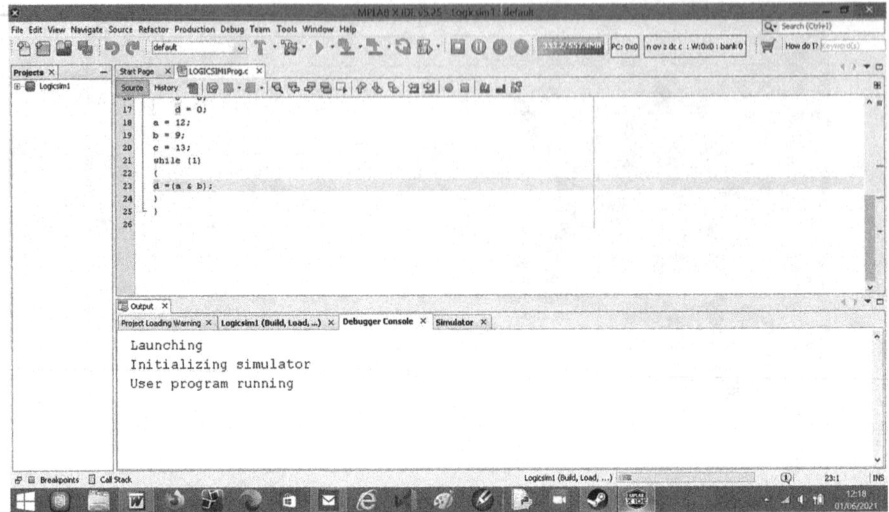

Figure 14-5. The simulated program running

To declare a watch window, you could choose the "windows" option from the main menu bar. Then select the Debugging tab and then the Watches tab from the fly-out menus as shown in Figure 14-6.

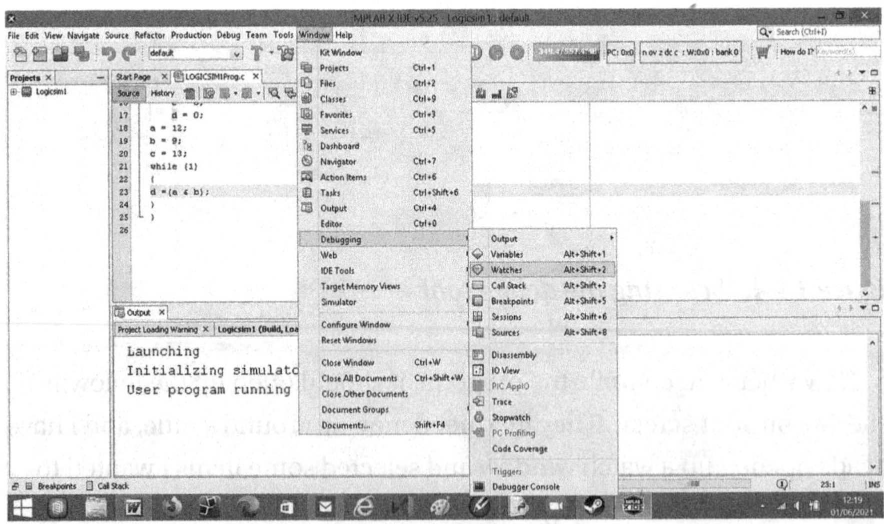

Figure 14-6. Selecting the Watches tab

Once you have the window opened, you can add a new watch by selecting Debug from the main menu bar and then New Watch from the fly-out window that appears, as shown in Figure 14-7.

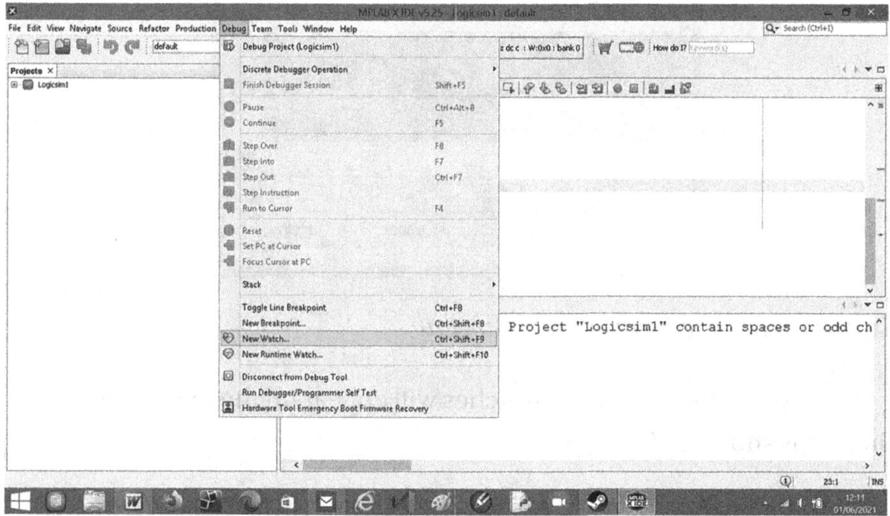

Figure 14-7. *Selecting New Watch*

The New Watch window should appear. You can select global symbols you want to watch as shown in Figure 14-8.

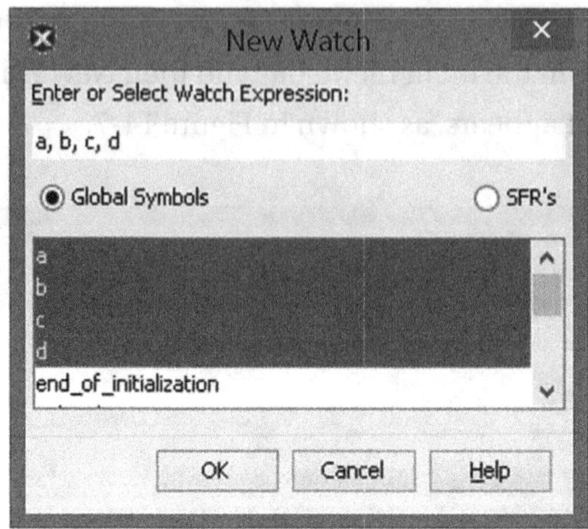

Figure 14-8. *The New Watch window*

Once you select OK, these watches will appear on the main editing window as shown in Figure 14-9.

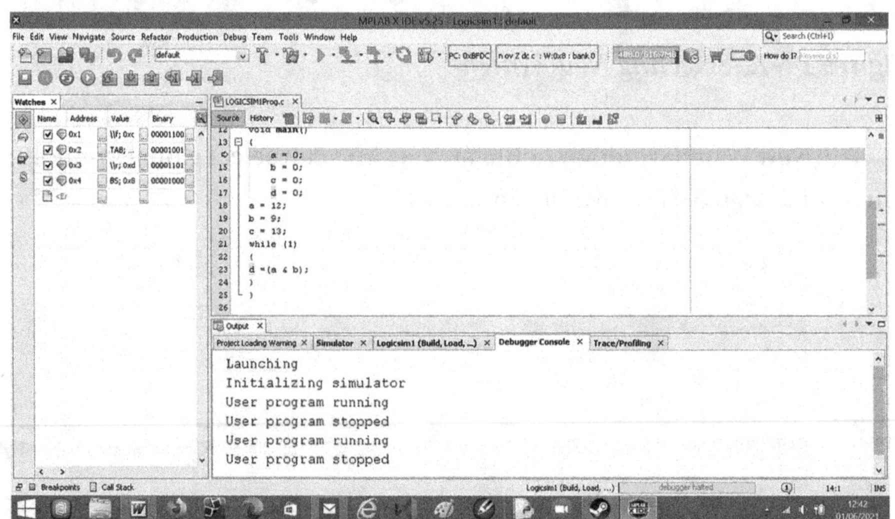

Figure 14-9. *The new watches added to the window*

I have removed the project tree window, as we don't really need it and I wanted to make the display a bit bigger. You may have to move your windows around a bit to get the best display for you. I have also moved the simulation tool bar to beneath the main menu bar.

The buttons for the simulation process are shown in Figure 14-10. Their uses are listed in Table 14-2.

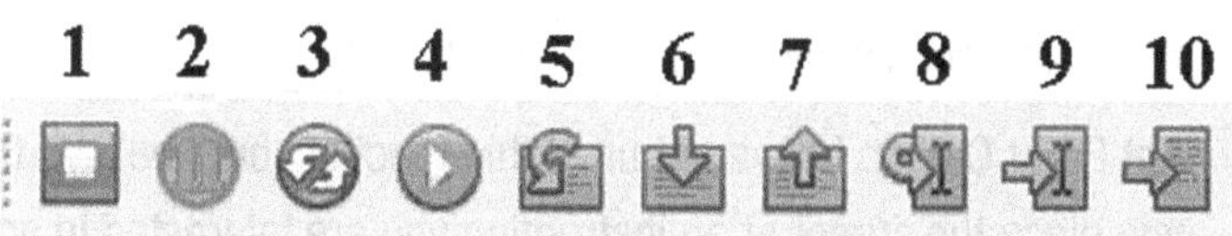

Figure 14-10. *The simulation buttons in MPLABX*

Table 14-2. *The Button Usage for Figure 14-10*

Number	Usage
1	Finishes the debugging session.
2	Pauses: Only available when the simulation is running.
3	Reset: This resets the simulation and sends the highlighted cursor to the start of the program.
4	Run: This gets the PIC to run the program.
5	Step Over: Used to get the PIC to miss out instructions. Used when single stepping through the program and you don't want the PIC to get stuck in a subroutine. I use this to miss out delay subroutines.
6	Step Into: Used to single step through the instructions of a program.
7	Step Out Of: Used to get the PIC to step out of a series of instructions. I have had difficulty in getting this to work.

(*continued*)

Table 14-2. *(continued)*

Number	Usage
8	Run to Cursor: This is a useful debug tool. If your program is long and you know the early parts work fine, you can place the cursor at an instruction that you want to start looking at. Then get the PIC to run the program by clicking key 4. The PIC will then halt the program at the instructions where you have inserted the cursor.
9	Set PC at Cursor: I have not used this function, but I believe that if you place the cursor at an instruction you are interested in and then click this button, the contents of the PC will be changed to point to that instruction. Then, clicking key 4 will make the PIC run the program starting from this instruction.
10	Focus cursor at PC: Again, I have not used this, but I believe that if you click this button the cursor will go to the instruction in the program that is at the point where the PC is currently pointing to.

In Figure 14-9, I have reset the program by pressing button 3, the reset button. The green highlighted line, which is the cursor position, is now at the start of the program. This is the first instruction of the main loop. The PC, shown on the main menu bar, is displaying the value 0XBFDC. If we now single step the program through its instructions, by pressing button 6 as in Figure 14-10, the PIC will carry out this first instruction a = 0; you should see the value for the variable 'a' change in the watch window from 12 to 0. The cursor will then move onto the next line, line 15 in the listing, ready to carry out the next instruction. You should see that the content of the PC has also changed to 0XBFE0.

Again, if you now single step through this and two more instructions, you will see that all four variables have changed to show 0 in their contents. I have set all four variables to 0 so that you can see how the instructions of the program change their values, especially the instruction on line 23.

You should see that lines 18, 19, and 20 change the values in the variables a, b, and c as expected. You should see that after line 20, the cursor jumps to line 23 directly. This is the first '&' instruction that is of interest. If my analysis of this instruction is correct, then the value in the variable 'd' should change to 0b00001000 as shown in Table 14-3. This is because in the two variables 'a' and 'b', only bit 4 is a logic '1' in both variables. When you now click the single step button, you should see the cursor has moved back to line 21 and the variable 'd' has changed as we expected. Single stepping the program now will just keep the PIC going through the while (1) loop. This is what we expect to happen.

I will now simply explain what the following logic instructions do, but I do hope you can single step through the programs as shown here and confirm that they do work as I have described.

Analysis of Listing 14-3

The instruction that tests the operation of this symbol is on line 23 d = (a & b). This will perform a logical AND between all the individual bits in both variables 'a' and 'b'. Only where the individual bits of both variables, a AND b, are at a logic '1' will the corresponding bit in the variable 'd' be set to a logic '1'. Therefore, we need to look at the individual bits in the variables. This is shown in Table 14-3.

Table 14-3. *The Action of the '&' Operator: Example 1*

Variable	Bit 7	Bit 6	Bit 5	Bit 4	Bit 3	Bit 2	Bit 1	Bit 0
a	0	0	0	0	1	1	0	0
b	0	0	0	0	1	0	0	1
Result d	0	0	0	0	**1**	**0**	**0**	**0**

Note that only with bit 3 are the bits a logic ‘1’ in both ‘a’ and ‘b’. This means that only bit 3 in the variable ‘d’ will be set to a logic ‘1’. This means the result in ‘d’ will be 0b00001000 in binary or 0X08 in hexadecimal and ‘8’ in decimal.

In another example, the variable ‘a’ is loaded with 14 and ‘b’ is loaded with 15. Table 14-4 shows what should happen.

Table 14-4. *The Action of the ‘&’ Operator: Example 2*

Variable	Bit 7	Bit 6	Bit 5	Bit 4	Bit 3	Bit 2	Bit 1	Bit 0
a	1	1	0	0	1	1	1	0
b	0	0	0	0	1	1	1	1
Result d	0	0	0	0	**1**	**1**	**1**	**0**

In the second example, shown in Table 14-4, we can see that the variable ‘d’ is simply a copy of the low nibble of the variable ‘a’. Note that a nibble is just four bits, and we can split a byte, which is eight bits, into a high nibble, bits 7, 6, 5, and 4, and a low nibble, bits 3, 2, 1, and 0.

This ‘&’ operator can be used for “bit masking”, where we can ensure that only a selected number of bits from one variable are copied into another variable. We can also use this to test if a particular bit in a variable is true. Consider Listing 14-4.

Listing 14-4. Bit Masking

```
/*
* File:   logicsimulationProg.c
Author: H. H. Ward
*
Created on 21 November 2020, 15:56
*/
#include <xc.h>
```

```
8.   #include <conFigInternalOscNoWDTNoLVP.h>
9.   #include <PICSetUp.h>
10.  //some variable
11.  unsigned char a,b,c,d,e,f;
12.  void main()
13.  {
14.  a = 0;
15.  b = 0;
16.  c = 0;
17.  d = 0;
18.  a = 12;
19.  b = 1;
20.  c = 0;
21.  if (a & 4) d = 1;
22.  else d = 0;
23.  }
```

This can be used to test if bit 2 of the variable ‘a’ is a logic 1. If it is, then ‘d’ will be loaded with 1. If it’s not, ‘d’ will be loaded with 0. Note that the variable ‘a’ does not have to equal 4, as any number that makes bit 2 of the variable ‘a’ a logic ‘1’ will result in this test being true. The test is just looking at bit 2 of the variable ‘a.’ You should appreciate that 4 in eight-bit binary is 0b00000100 (i.e., it sets bit 2 to a logic ‘1’). Also, 12 in eight-bit binary is 0b00001100. This also sets bit 2 to a logic ‘1.’

With lines 14 to 17, we load each variable with the value 0. This is again so that we can see the variables change as we single step through the programs. In line 19, we loaded the variable ‘a’ with 12, which puts a logic ‘1’ in bits 4 and 3.

Now, we get to line 21, which performs a bit AND with ‘a’ and 4. If the result is true, which in this case it will be, then you load the variable ‘d’ with the value 1 and you should see the change happen.

If you now run the program but change the value in the variable 'a' to 3, then the result of the 'if test' on line 21 will be untrue, and you load the variable 'd' with the value of zero.

Another very good application of the '&' operator is to split an eight-bit value into its two nibbles, or indeed any byte, word, or double word, into its separate nibbles. The following instruction will load the variable 'd' with the low nibble of what's in the variable 'b'.

d = (b & 0b00001111);

Consider the data in the variables shown in Table 14-5.

***Table 14-5.** Copying the Low Nibble*

Variable	Bit 7	Bit 6	Bit 5	Bit 4	Bit 3	Bit 2	Bit 1	Bit 0
Initial Value in 'd'	1	1	0	0	1	1	1	0
b	0	1	1	0	1	1	1	0
& with	0	0	0	0	1	1	1	1
Result d	0	0	0	0	**1**	**1**	**1**	**0**

Only the low nibble is copied into 'd'.

The next instruction will load the variable 'd' with just the high nibble of what's in the variable 'b';

d = (b & 0b11110000);

The && Operator

This is quite a different operation. Indeed, it will simply test to see if both variables have any of their bits set to a logic '1'. If they have, then the result is true. If any of the variables are at zero (i.e., have no bits set to a logic '1'), then the result of the test will be not true. Consider the instructions in Listing 14-5.

Listing 14-5. The && Operator

```
/*
* File:   logicsimulationProg.c
Author: H. H. Ward
*
Created on 21 November 2020, 15:56
*/

#include <xc.h>
#include <conFigInternalOscNoWDTNoLVP.h>
#include <PICSetUp.h>

//some variable
unsigned char a,b,c,d,e,f;
void main()
{
a = 0;
b = 0;
c = 0;
d = 0;
a = 5;
b = 1;
c = 3;
while (1)
{
if( a &&  b && c ) d= 1;
else d = 0;
   }
   }
```

All three variables will have one or more of their bits set to a logic '1'. This means that the result of the test would be true and so the variable 'd' would be loaded with a value of 1. The simulation is shown in Figure 14-11.

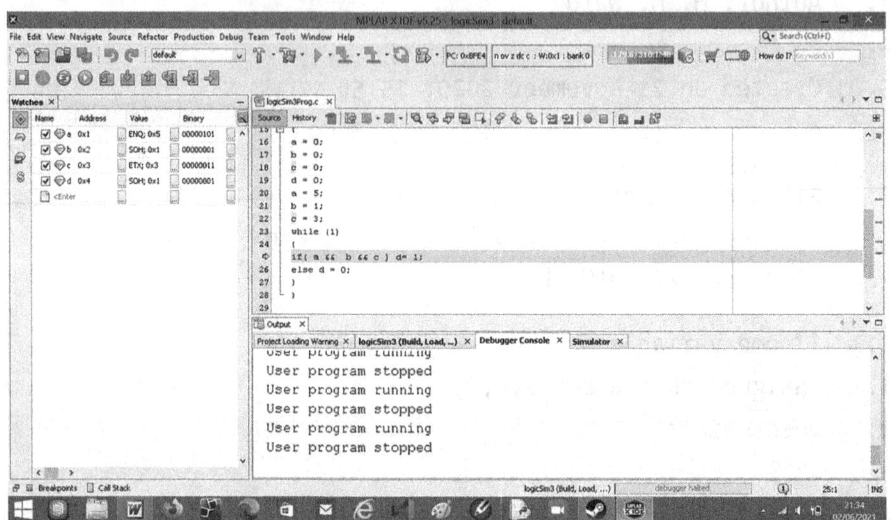

***Figure 14-11.** The simulated result with no variable set to zero*

If we now load the variable 'c' with a value of zero (i.e., set all bits in c to logic '0'), then the test will be untrue and d will be loaded with zero. Try it and see.

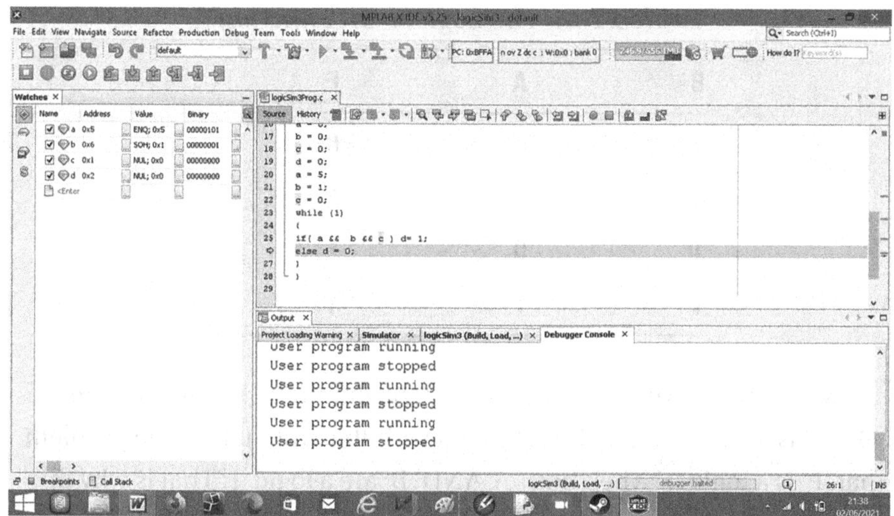

***Figure 14-12.** The simulated result with the variable C set to zero*

You can see in Figure 14-12 that the variable d has now gone to zero. Note that the PIC will be forced to carry out the 'else' instruction because this time the 'if test' result is untrue. When the value in C was 3 and the result of the 'if test' was true, the PIC simply ignored this 'else' instruction and went back to line 23.

The '|' Operator

This is a logical bit OR function which performs a logical OR function on each bit of the variables. The truth table for the two bit OR is shown in Table 14-6.

Table 14-6. *The Logical OR Function*

B	A	F
0	0	0
0	1	1
1	0	1
1	1	1

If we are being true to the concept of the output 'F' being a '1' when 'A' OR 'B' is a '1', then there is a problem with this truth table. The problem is that 'F' is a logic '1' when both 'A' AND 'B' are a logic '1'. That is why this function is sometimes referred to as "The Inclusive OR", as it includes the AND function. However, that is the function that we call the logical OR. The output 'F' is a logic '1' when 'A' OR 'B' is a logic '1' and also when they are both at a logic '1' (Listing 14-6).

Listing 14-6. The Bit OR | Operator

```
/*
* File:   logicsimulationProg.c
Author: H. H. Ward
*
Created on 21 November 2020, 15:56
*/
#include <xc.h>
#include <conFigInternalOscNoWDTNoLVP.h>
#include <PICSetUp.h>
//some variable
unsigned char a,b,c,d,e,f;
void main()
{
```

```
a = 0;
b = 0;
c = 0;
d = 0;
a = 5;
b = 9;
c = 0;
while (1)
{
d = (a | b);
}
}
```

We need to look at the bits in each of the variables. This is shown in Table 14-7.

Table 14-7. *The Logical OR Example*

Variable	Bit 7	Bit 6	Bit 5	Bit 4	Bit 3	Bit 2	Bit 1	Bit 0
a	0	0	0	0	0	1	0	1
b	0	0	0	0	1	0	0	1
Result d	0	0	0	0	**1**	**1**	**0**	**1**

With bit 3, the variable 'a' has a logic '0' but 'b' has a logic '1'; therefore, bit 3 in the variable 'd' goes to a logic '1'.

With bit 2, the variable 'a' has a logic '1' but 'b' has a logic '0'; therefore, bit 2 in the variable 'd' also goes to a logic '1'.

With bit 0, the variable 'a' has a logic '1' and 'b' has a logic '1'; therefore, bit 0 in the variable 'd' also goes to a logic '1'.

Note that with all the other bits, both 'a' and 'b' are logic '0', so the corresponding bit in the variable 'd' goes to a logic '0'.

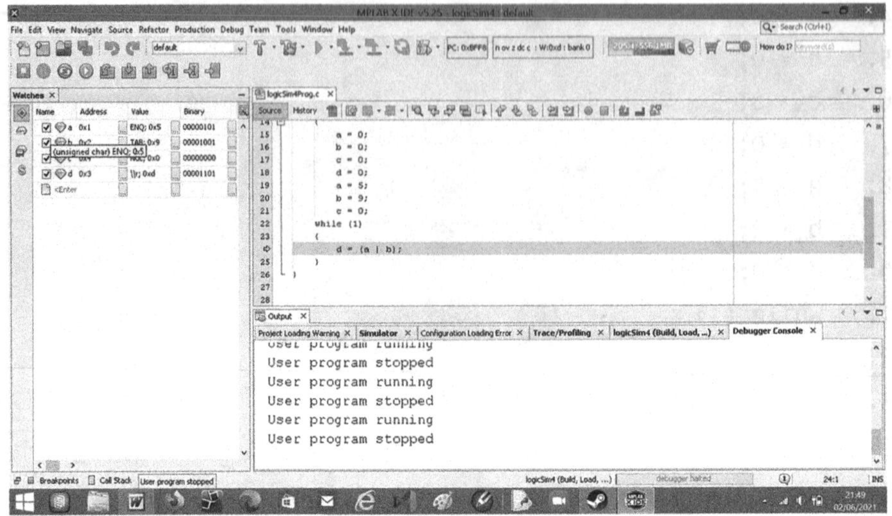

Figure 14-13. *The simulated logical OR function*

Figure 14-13 shows that the program works as expected.

The 'll' Operator

This is the logical OR operator, and it works in a similar way to the previous operator except that it does not need all the variables to have any of their bits set to a logic '1'. It looks at the whole eight bits as a byte. It then performs the logical OR test on the three bytes. This means if byte 'a' or byte 'b' OR byte 'c' OR byte 'a' AND 'b' AND 'c' has any bit set to a logic '1', then the result will be true. See Listing 14-7.

Listing 14-7. The OR || Operator

```
/*
* File:   logicsimulationProg.c
Author: H. H. Ward
*
```

```
Created on 21 November 2020, 15:56
*/

#include <xc.h>
#include <conFigInternalOscNoWDTNoLVP.h>
#include <PICSetUp.h>
//some variable
unsigned char a,b,c,d,e,f;
void main()
{
a = 0;
b = 0;
c = 0;
d = 0;
a = 5;
b = 9;
c = 13;
while (1)
{
if( a || b || c ) d= 1;
   else d = 0;
   }
   }
```

As all three variables will have some of their bits set to a logic '1', then the result will be true and 'd' will be loaded with a value of 1. This action is shown in Figure 14-14.

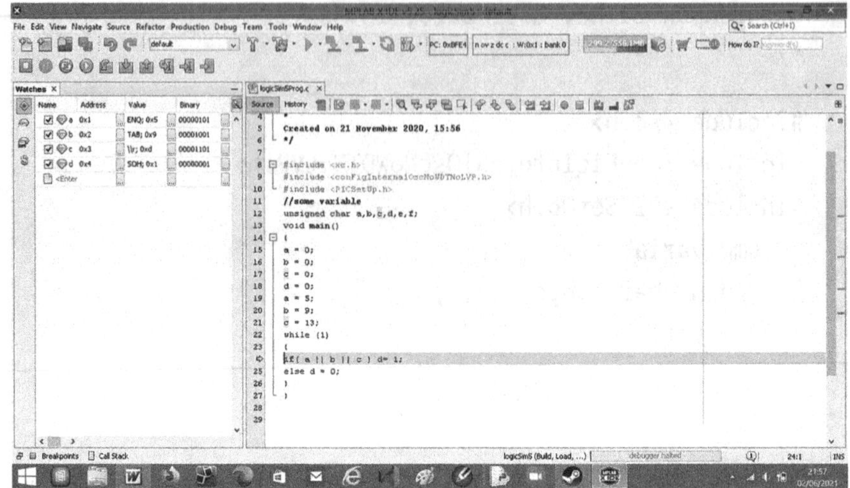

Figure 14-14. *The || instruction*

This concept can best be tested by setting the variable 'b' and 'c' to zero. This means that only the variable 'a' will have some of its bits set to a logic '1.' If you make the change and run the program again, you will see the results are the same as before.

However, only if all the variables are set to zero (i.e., all their bits are a logic '0') will the result of the test be untrue and 'd' will be loaded with a value of 0.

We can use this logic function to test if any bit in a variable has been set to a logic '1.' See Listing 14-8.

Listing 14-8. Another OR || Operator

```
/*
* File:   logicsimulationProg.c
Author: H. H. Ward
*
Created on 21 November 2020, 15:56
*/
```

```
#include <xc.h>
#include <conFigInternalOscNoWDTNoLVP.h>
#include <PICSetUp.h>
//some variable
unsigned char a,b,c,d,e,f;
void main()
{
a = 0;
b = 0;
c = 0;
d = 0;
a = 5;
b = 0;
c = 13;
while (1)
{
if( a || 0 ) d= 1;
else d = 0;
}
}
```

The instruction of interest is

if (a || 0) d= 1;

This is simply testing to see if any of the bits in the variable ‘a’ are set to a logic ‘1.’ If they are, then the result is true and ‘d’ will be loaded with the value 1. However, if we changed the value loaded into ‘a’ to 0, then the test will be untrue and ‘d’ will be loaded with the value 0. Try it and see what happens.

The ^ EXOR or Exclusive OR

I think of this as the true OR function, as the result will produce a logic '1' if only one of the two bits are at a logic '1' not both. It does not matter which variable has the logic '1' in the corresponding bit. The truth table for the EXOR is shown in Table 14-8.

Table 14-8. *The EXOR Truth Table*

B	A	F
0	0	0
0	1	1
1	0	1
1	1	0

You should see that the output 'F' is a logic '1' only when 'A' OR 'B' is a logic '1', not when both are a logic '1'. See Listing 14-9.

Listing 14-9. The EXOR ^ Operator

```
/*
* File:   logicsimulationProg.c
Author: H. H. Ward
*
Created on 21 November 2020, 15:56
*/
#include <xc.h>
#include <conFigInternalOscNoWDTNoLVP.h>
#include <PICSetUp.h>
//some variable
unsigned char a,b,c,d,e,f;
```

```
void main()
{
a = 0;
b = 0;
c = 0;
d = 7;
a = 0b00000101;
b = 0b11110100;
c = 13;
while (1)
{
d = ( a ^ b );
}
}
```

This will load the variable 'd' with the following data:

0b11110001.

Almost the same, except that this time bit 2 in the variable 'd' is a logic '0'. Note that bit 2 in both variable 'a' and 'b' are at logic '1' and so the true OR results in a logic '0'.

The EXOR can be used to toggle the logic in a bit.

Consider the following instructions:

```
while (1)
{
PORTBbits.RB0 ^= 1;
delay (30);
}
```

If we assume that bit 0 of PORTB is initially at a logic '0', then we first carry out the instruction PORTBbits.RB0 ^= 1;. This will perform an EXOR operation with bit 0 and a logic '1', and then the result will be that bit 0 of PORTB will go to a logic '1'.

The PIC then waits 1 second and attempts to carry out the instruction again. However, this time the logic on bit 0 will now be a logic '1', and so this time the result of the EXOR will be that the logic on bit 0 goes to a logic '0'.

Therefore, these two simple instructions will make an LED connected to bit 0 of PORTB turn on for 1 second and then turn off for 1 second continuously: a succinct bit of programming that is now hopefully easy to understand.

Now we will combine some of these logic functions with some other operators. We will test to see what happens.

The &= Function

With this function, the contents of the first variable, on the left, is bit ANDED with the contents of the second variable, on the right, and each bit in the first variable goes to a logic '1' if the bit AND is true and to a logic '0' if the bit and is untrue. See Listing 14-10.

Listing 14-10. The &= Operator

```
/*
* File:   logicsimulationProg.c
Author: H. H. Ward
*
Created on 21 November 2020, 15:56
*/
#include <xc.h>
#include <conFigInternalOscNoWDTNoLVP.h>
#include <PICSetUp.h>
//some variable
unsigned char a,b,c,d,e,f;
void main()
{
a = 0;
```

```
b = 0;
c = 0;
d = 0;
a = 0b00000101;
b = 0b11110100;
c = 13;
while (1)
{
d &= b;
}
}
```

To help explain how this works, we must look at the bits in the two variables. This is shown in Table 14-9.

Table 14-9. *The &= Operator*

Variable	Bit 7	Bit 6	Bit 5	Bit 4	Bit 3	Bit 2	Bit 1	Bit 0
Initial setting of 'd'	0	0	0	0	0	1	1	1
b	1	1	1	1	0	1	0	0
Result d	**0**	**0**	**0**	**0**	**0**	**1**	**0**	**0**

You can see that only with bit 2 in the initial setting for the variable 'd' and the variable 'b' are both set to a logic '1'. This means that only bit 2 of the result for the variable 'd' will be set to a logic '1', as only bit 2 has a logic '1' in both the initial setting for d and the variable b. All the rest don't have matching logic '1's.

The |= Function

This will do a similar operation to the last one, except that instead of doing a bit AND with all the bits, it will do a logical OR operation.

To help explain how this works, we must look at the bits in the two variables. This is shown in Table 14-10.

Table 14-10. *The |= Operator*

Variable	Bit 7	Bit 6	Bit 5	Bit 4	Bit 3	Bit 2	Bit 1	Bit 0
Initial setting of 'd'	0	0	0	0	0	1	1	1
b	1	1	1	1	0	1	0	0
Result d	**1**	**1**	**1**	**1**	**0**	**1**	**1**	**1**

In this way, if any of the individual bits in 'b' OR in 'd' are a logic '1', then the corresponding bit in 'd' will be set to a logic '1'. Note that the corresponding bit in d will go to a logic '1' if the bits in both variables are at a logic '1'. Remember this is really the inclusive OR. See Listing 14-11.

Listing 14-11. The |= Operator

```
/*
* File:   logicsimulationProg.c
Author: H. H. Ward
*
Created on 21 November 2020, 15:56
*/
#include <xc.h>
#include <conFigInternalOscNoWDTNoLVP.h>
#include <PICSetUp.h>
//some variable
unsigned char a,b,c,d,e,f;
```

```
void main()
{
a = 0;
b = 0;
c = 0;
d = 7;
a = 0b00000101;
b = 0b11110100;
c = 13;
while (1)
{
d |= b;
}
}
```

If we used the EXOR function as with the following line:

```
d ^= b;
```

Then with the same initial data as that shown in Table 14-10, we would get a similar result except that the only difference would be that bit 2 of the result in 'd' would now be a logic '0', as the EXOR would exclude the AND part where the initial value of bit 2 in 'd' and bit 2 in 'b' were both at a logic '1'.

The '%' or Modulus or Remainder Operator

This is used in conjunction with the division '/' operator. This is because some divisions can result in a remainder. Consider the division 8/3. This will result in 2 with a remainder 2. See Listing 14-12.

Listing 14-12. The Modulus % Operator

```
/*
* File:   logicsimulationProg.c
Author: H. H. Ward
*
Created on 21 November 2020, 15:56
*/
#include <xc.h>
#include <conFigInternalOscNoWDTNoLVP.h>
#include <PICSetUp.h>
//some variable
unsigned char a,b,c,d,e,f;
void main()
{
a = 0;
b = 0;
c = 0;
d = 0;
a = 0b00001000;
b = 0b00000011;
while (1)
{
c = a/b;
d  = a % b;
}
}
```

The variable 'a' is loaded with the value 8 and 'b' is loaded with the value 3.

On line 22, we state that the variable 'c' will be loaded with the integer part of 8/3 (i.e., 2). Then on line 23, we will load the variable 'd' with the remainder of the division, which in this case is also 2. The simulated result is shown in Figure 14-15.

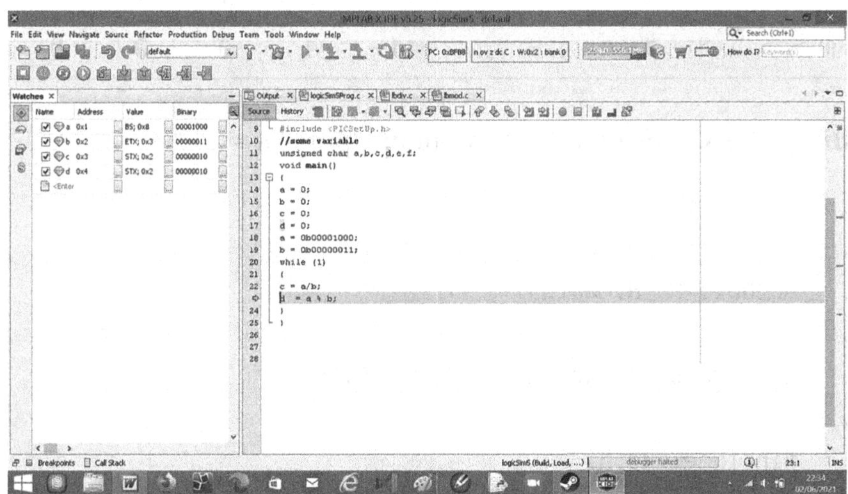

Figure 14-15. *The simulation of the Modulus % Operator*

Try the program with different values and you will see that the results follow the same pattern. Note that when you get to the instructions on lines 22 and 23, you should use the "step over" button, button 5. This avoids going into the math.h header file to run those functions.

The '~' Or 1's Complement

This operator simply flips the individual bits in a variable, which means all logic '0's become logic '1's and all logic '1's become logic '0's. See Listing 14-13.

To help explain how this works, we must look at the bits in the two variables. This is shown in Table 14-11.

Table 14-11. *The One's Complement*

Variable	Bit 7	Bit 6	Bit 5	Bit 4	Bit 3	Bit 2	Bit 1	Bit 0
Initial setting of 'd'	0	0	0	0	0	1	1	1
b	0	0	0	0	0	1	1	1
Result d	**1**	**1**	**1**	**1**	**1**	**0**	**0**	**0**

Listing 14-13. The Ones Compliment Operator ~

```
/*
* File:   logicsimulationProg.c
Author: H. H. Ward
*
Created on 21 November 2020, 15:56
*/
#include <xc.h>
#include <conFigInternalOscNoWDTNoLVP.h>
#include <PICSetUp.h>
//some variable
unsigned char a,b,c,d,e,f;
void main()
{
a = 0;
b = 0;
c = 0;
d = 7;
b = 0b00000111;
while (1)
{
d = ~b;
}
}
```

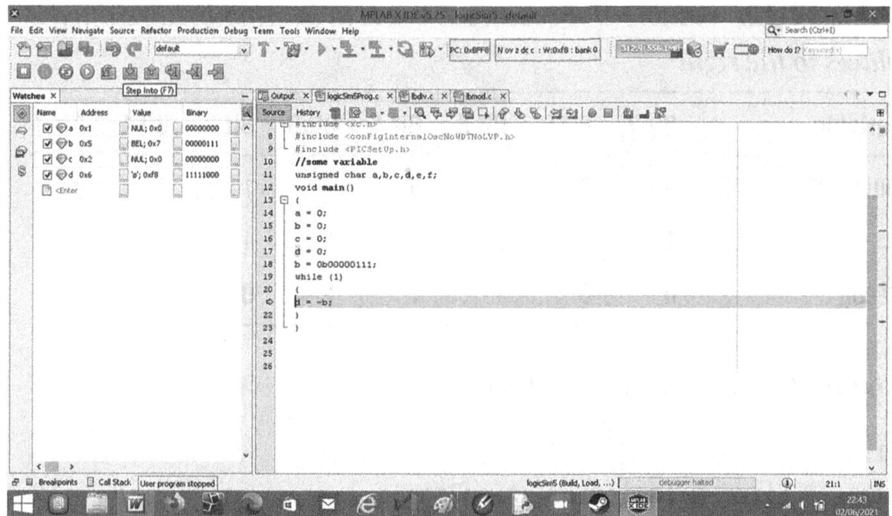

***Figure 14-16.** The simulated result of the ~ Ones Compliment*

Figure 14-16 shows that the program runs as expected.

The '<<n' or '>>n' Operator

These two operators simply shift the bits either left, as with '<<n', or right, as with '>>n'; the number of bits shifted is indicated by the value 'n' in the instruction. This shifting operation can be operated on the one variable (i.e., shift the bits in the one variable to the same variable). However, to save the contents of the first variable, the bits can be shifted and loaded into a second variable. In this later version, the bits in the first variable are left unchanged. See Listing 14-14.

To help explain how this works, we must look at the bits in the two variables. This is shown in Table 14-12.

Table 14-12. *Vaiable 'd' Becomes What is in 'b' after being shifted 2 places to the right*

Variable	Bit 7	Bit 6	Bit 5	Bit 4	Bit 3	Bit 2	Bit 1	Bit 0
Initial setting of 'd'	0	0	0	0	0	1	1	1
b	1	1	0	0	1	1	1	0
Result d	**0**	**0**	**1**	**1**	**1**	**0**	**0**	**0**

Listing 14-14. The Shifting Instruction

```
/*
* File:   logicsimulationProg.c
Author: H. H. Ward
*
Created on 21 November 2020, 15:56
*/
#include <xc.h>
#include <conFigInternalOscNoWDTNoLVP.h>
#include <PICSetUp.h>
//some variable
unsigned char a,b,c,d,e;
void main()
{
a = 0;
b = 0;
c = 0;
d = 7;
e = 0;
a = 8;
b = 0b11001110;
```

```
21.   while (1)
22.   {
23.   c = b >> 4;
24.   d = b << 2;
25.   e = (b << 4 | b >>4);
26.   }
27.   }
```

In line 23, we are shifting the bits 0b11001110 four bits to the right. This means that the current value in bits 3, 2, 1, and 0 are lost as they fall away when they are shifted. This instruction will result in the c = 0b00001100.

You should appreciate that the two logic '1's in bits 7 and 6 of the variable 'b' are lost when shifted and loaded into the variable 'd' in line 24. This instruction will result in the d = 0b00111000.

Line 24 will swap the two nibbles around, in that what was the low nibble in b will become the high nibble in e. Also, the high nibble from b becomes the low nibble is e. Therefore, after this instruction e = 0b11101100.

Note that the contents of 'b' will be unchanged. These results are shown in Figure 14-17.

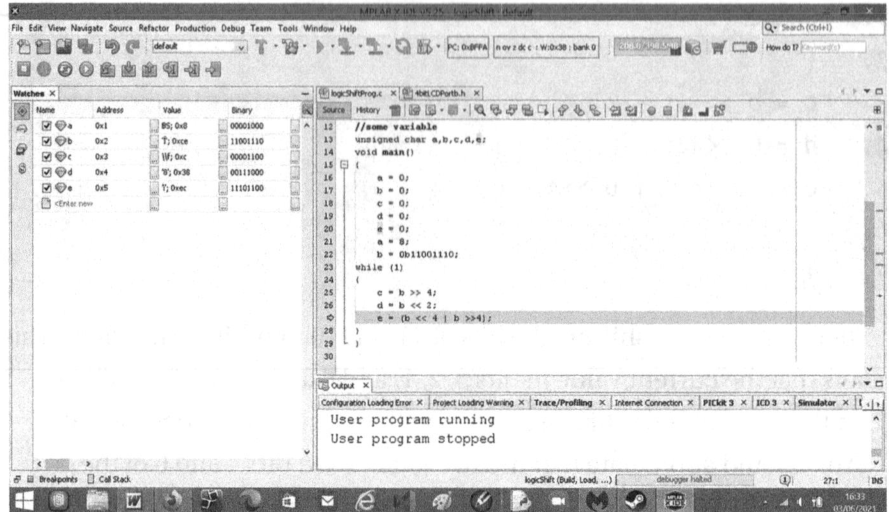

Figure 14-17. *The Shifting Simulated Results*

Summary

In this chapter, we have looked at some unusual instructions in C. I hope you have found this chapter and the entire book useful and informative. This is now the end of this, my third, book on the PIC18f4525. I hope you have found my books useful.

APPENDIX

Additional Insights

In this appendix, I will analyze some of the more common aspects of C programming and how they apply to PIC microcontrollers. I will also cover some useful concepts that will help in the understanding how microcontrollers work, such as operators, number systems, and keywords.

Data Types and Memory

To help understand the different data types used in C, it would be helpful to appreciate their relationship to the micro's memory. PIC micros have three areas of memory:

- Program Memory Area
- Data RAM
- Data EEPROM

The Program Memory Area

This is where all the instructions of your programs are stored. With the PIC18f4525, the program memory area has 48kbytes of memory, even though it uses a 21-bit address bus which can address up to 2Mbytes. This means it has 4096 memory locations that can store eight bits of data,

H. H. Ward, *Programming Arduino Projects with the PIC Microcontroller*,
https://doi.org/10.1007/978-1-4842-7230-5

which will be either logic '1' or logic '0'. Therefore, we can say each memory locations stores eight binary bits termed a byte. These 48kbytes of memory mean that the PIC18f4525 can store 24,576 single-word instructions.

This memory is nonvolatile, which means that when the power is removed, the information in the memory is not lost.

The Data RAM

This is where the program can store any temporary information. Therefore, any variables that you declare in your program use this area of memory. The PIC18f4525 has 4096 memory locations, each capable of storing eight bits of data (i.e., one byte of data).

This memory is volatile memory, which means when the power is removed, all the information is lost.

The Data EEPROM

This is used for storing any information that the program does not want to lose if the power to the PIC is removed. This means it is nonvolatile memory.

Variables

When we create a variable in the program listing, we are actually getting the compiler to reserve one or more memory locations in the PIC's data memory area. The number of memory locations required by the label depends upon the number of bits required by what you want to store using the variable. In this way, the term "variable" is linked with the different data types used in C programming. You should appreciate that all data, no matter what it represents, is just a collection of binary bits. As such, they are simply binary numbers. We simply give these binary numbers some meaningful names which all go under the heading "variables".

This then gives rise to the term "data types", as the variables will have different number of binary bits, such as the following:

8 bits (termed a byte).

16 bits (termed a word).

32 bits (termed a double word).

The more common data types are listed in Appendix A.

Appendix A: Data Types

Type	Size	Minimum Value	Maximum Value
char	8 bits	–128	127s
unsigned char	8 bits	0	255
int	16 bits	–32,768	32,767
unsigned int	16 bits	0	65,535
short	16 bits	–32,768	32,767
unsigned short	16 bits	0	65,535
short long	24 bits	–8,388,608	8,388,607
unsigned short long	24 bits	0	16,777,215
long	32 bits	–2,147,483,648	2,147,483,647
unsigned long	32 bits	0	4,294,967,295
float	32 bits		

Floating Point Numbers

Type	Size	Min Exponent	Max Exponent	Min Normalized	Max Normalized
float	32	–126	128	2^{-126}	2^{128}
double	32	–126	128	2^{-126}	2^{128}

All C programs use operators that perform logical operations on data within programs. The more common operators are listed in Appendix B.

Appendix B: Some Useful Definitions

Bit Operators:

Operator	Description
&	AND each bit
|	OR each bit (inclusive OR)
^	EXOR each bit (exclusive OR)
<<n	Shift left n places
>>n	Shift right n places
~	One's complement (invert each bit)

Example: If x = 1111 1111 then:

Operation	Result
x & 0X0F	0000 1111
x | 0X0F	1111 1111
x^0X0F	1111 0000
x = x<<2	1111 1100
x = x>>4	0000 1111
x = ~x	0000 0000

Appendix C: Mathematical and Logic Operators

Operator	Description
+	Leaves the variable as it was
-	Creates the negative of the variable
++	Increments the variable by 1
--	Decrements the variable by 1
*	Multiplies the two variables y = a × b
/	Divides y= a/b
%	Used to get the remainder of a division of two variable m = a%b
<	Less than: If (y < a) means y is less than a
<=	Less than or equal to: If (y < =a) means y is less than or equal to a
>	Greater than: If (y > a) means y is greater than a
>=	Greater than or equal to: If (y > =a) means y is greater than or equal to a
=	Makes the variable equal to: y = 3 After this, y takes on the value of 3
!	Not if: (!PORTBbits.RB0) if not bit 0 of portb, which means if bit 0 of portb is logic ‘0’
&&	Whole register AND
||	Whole register OR
?	Test operator: y = (a>0) ? a : –1; This test to see if ‘a’ is greater than 0. If it is, then y becomes equal to ‘a’, if it’s not then y = –1

Appendix D: Keywords

Keyword	Function
typedef	Allows the programmer to define any phrase to represent an existing type
#ifndef	Checks to see if a label you want to use has not been defined in any include files you want to use. If it has, it does not allow you to define it now. If it hasn't, you are allowed to define it now
#define	You can define what your label means here
#endif	Denotes the end of your definition after the #ifndef code
sizeof	Returns the size in number of bytes of a variable

Global variables are variables that once declared can be read from or written to anywhere from within the program.

Appendix E: Numbering Systems Within Microprocessor-Based Systems

Introduction

As will become evident in the study to come, microprocessor-based systems use the binary number system. This is because the binary number system can only have one of two digits, either a '0' or a '1'. These states have been called logic '0' or logic '1', as in electronic devices. Note also that all the logic operations, such as AND, OR, NAND, NOR, NOT, and EXOR, work using binary format. The binary format can be used to mimic the logic states of "TRUE" or "FALSE" precisely; and best of all, they can be represented by voltage (i.e., 0V for logic '0' and +5V for logic '1').

Therefore, it is essential that the modern engineer gains a full understanding of the binary number system. This appendix is aimed at teaching the reader all they need to know about binary numbers.

Binary Numbers

These are a series of '0's and '1's that represent numbers. With respect to microprocessor-based systems, the numbers they are representing are themselves representing codes for instructions and data, used within microprocessor-based programs. We, as humans, cannot easily interpret binary numbers, as we use the decimal number system. The decimal number system uses the base number 10, which means that all the columns we put our digits in to form numbers are based on powers of 10. For example, the thousands column is based on 10^3, and the hundreds column is based on 10^2. The tens is on 10^1 and the units is 10^0. Try putting 10^0 in on your calculator using the x^y button and you will find it equals 1; in fact any number raised to the power 0 will equal 1.

Converting Decimal to Binary

Probably the first step to understanding binary numbers is creating them (i.e., converting decimal to binary). There are numerous ways of doing this, but I feel the most straightforward is to repeatedly divide the decimal number by 2, the base number of binary. This is shown in the following:

Example 1

Convert 66 to binary.

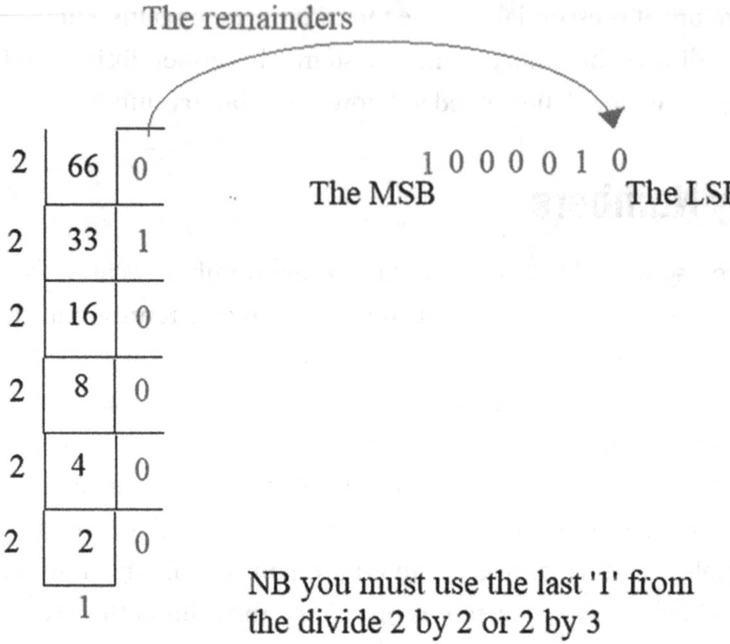

Simply keep on dividing the number by 2, putting the answer underneath as shown, with the remainder to the side. You should note that all the remainders are either **0** or **1**. These digits actually make up the binary number. Note also that the last division always results in an answer '**1**'; we stop there, with no more dividing.

To create the binary number, we take the top of the remainders, as shown, and put it into the least significant bit, or column, for the binary number. The other remainder digits follow on, thus making up the complete seven-digit number.

Converting from Binary to Decimal

It would be useful to determine if the binary number shown does actually relate to 66 in decimal. This is done by converting back into decimal the binary number 1 0 0 0 0 1 0. To do this, we must realize that numbers are displayed in columns. The columns are based on the base number of the system used. With binary numbers, the base number is 2; therefore, the columns are based on powers of 2. This is shown in the following table:

Base No	2^7	2^6	2^5	2^4	2^3	2^2	2^1	2^0
Decimal equivalent	128	64	32	16	8	4	2	1
Binary number		1	0	0	0	0	1	0

To complete the conversion, we simply sum all the decimal equivalents where there is a 1 in the binary column.

In this case the sum is: 64 + 2 = 66.

Example 2

Convert 127 to binary and check the result.

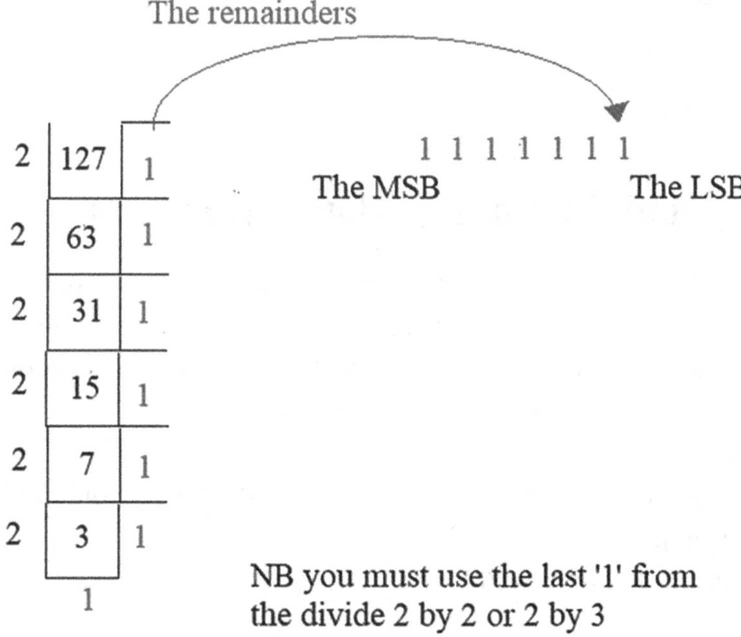

Base No	2^7	2^6	2^5	2^4	2^3	2^2	2^1	2^0
Decimal Equivalent	128	64	32	16	8	4	2	1
Binary Number	0	1	1	1	1	1	1	1

To complete the conversion, we simply sum all the decimal equivalents where there is a 1 in the binary column.

In this case the sum is 64 + 32 + 16 + 8 + 4 + 2 + 1 = 127

Exercise 1

Covert the following numbers to binary and check your results by converting back to decimal. **Show All Workings Out.**

99

255

137

Adding and Subtracting Binary Numbers

Adding and subtracting numbers are perhaps the most basic operations we can carry out on numbers. Binary numbers follow the same rules as decimal, but there are only two allowable digits. Also, computers don't actually subtract numbers, as the following will show.

Exercise 2

Add the following decimal numbers in eight-bit binary notation (check your answers):

23 + 21, 35 + 123, 125 + 75

Worked example

Remember binary numbers have only two digits: '0' or '1'

Add 23 to 21 in eight-bit binary.

Method:

Convert to eight-bit binary and add. Remember the following four rules:

0 + 0 = 0

0 + 1 = 1

1 + 0 = 1

1 + 1 = 0 with 1 to carry

23 in eight-bit binary is

0 0 0 1 0 1 1 1 **note we must state all eight bits, as it is eight-bit binary.**

By the same process, 21 in binary is 0 0 0 1 0 1 0 1

Therefore, the sum is 0 0 0 1 0 1 1 1

+ 0 0 0 1 0 1 0 1

---

0 0 1 0 1 1 0 0

To check your answer, put the result into the look-up table then add the decimal Equivalent.

Power	2^7	2^6	2^5	2^4	2^3	2^2	2^1	2^0
Decimal Equivalent	128	64	32	16	8	4	2	1
Binary Number	0	0	1	0	1	1	0	0

Sum is 32 + 8 + 4 = 44

Subtracting Binary Numbers

Exercise 3

Microprocessor-based systems actually subtract numbers using a method which is addition. This involves using the 2's complement of a number; it is best explained by example, as follows:

Subtract the following decimal numbers using eight-bit binary 2's complement (check your answers):

128 - 28, 79 - 78, 55 - 5, 251 - 151

Worked example

Convert the two numbers to binary using the method shown previously.

128 in eight-bit binary is 10000000 **NOTE we MUST use ALL eight bits.**

28 in eight-bit binary is 00011100

Take the 2's complement of 00011100, as this is the number that we are subtracting from 128.

Only create the 2's complement of the subtrahend, the number we are subtracting with.

Note that we must use a full eight-bit number, putting extra 0 in where needed.

To take the 2's complement, first take the complement and then add binary 1 to the complement. The complement of the binary number is found by simply flipping all the bits (i.e., a '0' becomes a '1' and a '1' becomes a '0').

Complement of 00011100 is 1 1 1 0 0 0 1 1

add binary 1 + 0 0 0 0 0 0 0 1

---

1 1 1 0 0 1 0 0

Now add the 2's complement to the first binary number as shown:

1 0 0 0 0 0 0 0
+1 1 1 0 0 1 0 0

---

result is 0 1 1 0 0 1 0 0

Note The last carry into the ninth digit is discarded, as there can only be the specified number of digits, eight digits in this case. Don't forget we added 1, so we should give it back.

The binary result converts to 100 in decimal. This is the correct result. Check your answers in the usual way.

Note that computers subtract by this method, because we can only create an adder circuit in logic.

The Hexadecimal Number System

Microprocessor-based systems can only recognize data that is in binary format. In its most basic form, this means that all data inputted at the keyboard should be in binary format. This is quite a formidable concept. Just think: every letter of every word must be inputted as a binary number. It takes at least four binary digits to represent a letter, and so typing words into a computer would be very difficult indeed. Thankfully, word processing programs take ASCII characters to represent the letters you press at the keyboard.

With the type of programs we will be writing into microcomputers, we will actually be typing in two characters to represent the codes for the instructions or data of the programs we will write. If we were to type these in as binary numbers, it would take eight binary bits to make each code.

This would be very time consuming and difficult to get right. To make things easier, we will use the hexadecimal numbering system. This system has 16 unique digits, the first 9 of which are

0 1 2 3 4 5 6 7 8 9

After this, we cannot use 10, as this uses two digits: a 1 and a 0. Therefore, we must use six more unique digits. To do this, we use the first six letters of the alphabet. Therefore, the full 16 digits are

0 1 2 3 4 5 6 7 8 9 A B C D E F

Remember that we are going to use the hexadecimal number to represent binary digits, and this revolves around the idea that one hexadecimal digits represent four binary digits, as the four binary bits in decimal go from 0 to 15 (i.e., 16 numbers). Therefore, every eight-bit binary number can be represented by two hexadecimal digits. This makes typing in the code for programs much quicker and more secure than using the full binary numbers that computers use. Note that to accommodate the user typing inputs as hexadecimal digits, there is a program in the micro's ROM to convert the hexadecimal to binary for us. However, we will look at converting binary to hexadecimal.

Exercise 4

Convert the following eight-bit binary numbers to hexadecimal:

10011110, 10101010, 11111111, 11110000, 00001111 & 11001101

Worked example

Method: Split the eight bits into two four-bit numbers. Convert each four-bit number into the decimal equivalent and then look up the hexadecimal for the decimal equivalent in the look-up table. **NOTE: Treat each set of four binary bits as a separate binary number.**

Convert 1 0 0 1 | 1 1 1 0

Dec 9 | 14

Hex 9 | E

Answer 10011110 in Hex is 9E

In this way, eight-bit binary numbers can be converted into two hexadecimal digits.

Appendix F: Building Circuit Boards

Within this book, I have used a prototype board that I have built myself, as well as small circuit boards. This approach is useful in that it can save money and facilitate access to the different circuit boards you may want to use. However, you should use this approach only if you are confident in building circuit boards on a vero board. The following section may be helpful if you decide to build your own boards. I must add that I am not perfect with my circuit boards, but if you take it steady, as I do, and check your work carefully, then you can achieve some rewarding work.

Preparation

As with most things, preparation is one of the most important aspects of any work. You need to produce a good circuit diagram that you are confident works as you want it to. To that end, a good ECAD (electronic computer-aided design) software package would be very useful. I have used the following;

The Circuit Diagram

- Proteus. This is a software from Labcentre. It can be used to simulate electronic circuits and confirm that they work correctly. If you also buy the add-on for microcontrollers; then, you can simulate a lot of your PIC programs. I have used this in the past while working as a college lecturer. However, Proteus is not free.
- Tina. This is from Designsoft. It works in the same way as Proteus and you can buy the student version for around £50.00.

The Vero Board Plan

Once you have confirmed that your circuit works, you should then produce a plan of how you are going to lay out your circuit on the vero board. A good plan is essential, as it can save space and show you where to place your links across the strips of copper and, most important of all, where to cut the copper tracks to isolate parts of your circuit from each other.

Preparing to Solder

You must have the correct tools. The following is a list of those I feel are essential.

You should have a soldering station with a variable temperature setting and small clips that can be used to hold the components. The one I use is shown in Figure F-1.

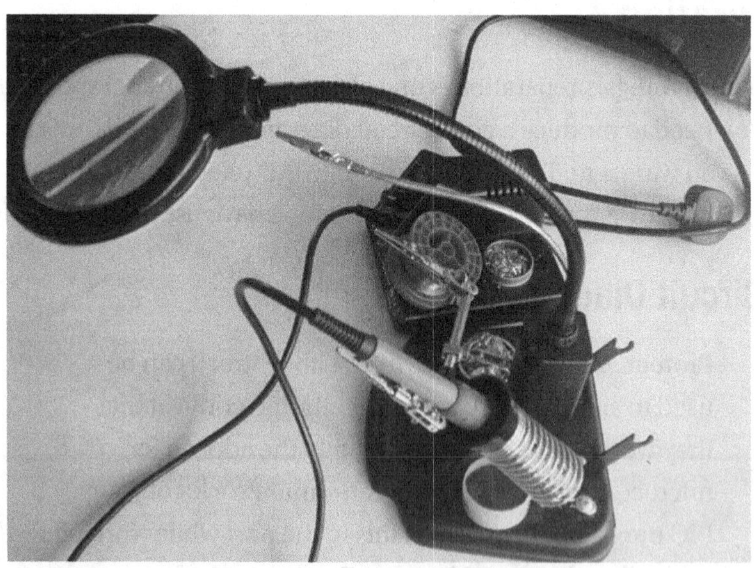

Figure F-1. *A typical soldering station*

I normally set the temperature to around 400°C.

Before you solder anything, you should make sure the tip of your soldering iron is clean. I have a ball of wire wool to clean the loose solder off, and then I use a damp sponge to clean the tip.

I always try to do my soldering outside, as the fumes are not pleasant. If that's not possible, you should make sure there is plenty of ventilation to take the solder fumes away from you.

I don't normally use flux, but sometimes this can make it easier to solder.

You will need a multimeter to test your circuit for continuity and correct voltage at the various points around the circuit. A typical multimeter is shown in Figure F-2.

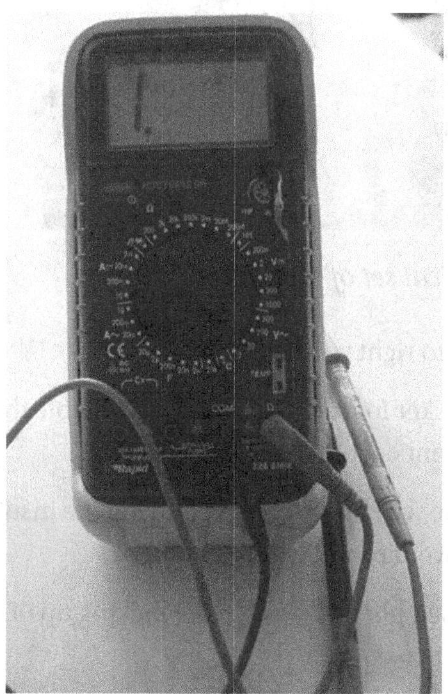

Figure F-2. *A typical multimeter*

You will also need some other quality tools. A typical set of tool is shown in Figure F-3.

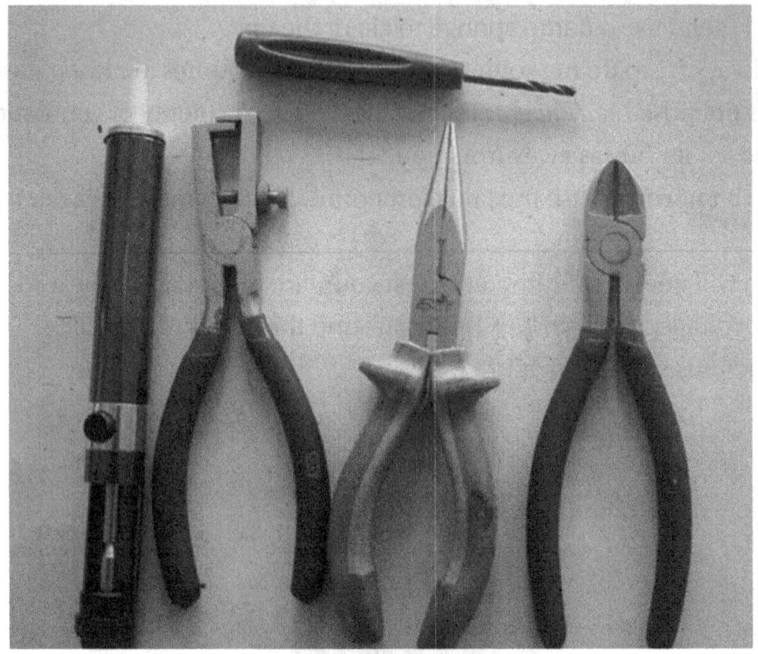

Figure F-3. *A typical set of tools*

Going from left to right we have

- Solder sucker for removing solder to enable the replacement of components.
- Adjustable wire stripper for removing the insulating plastic cover around wire.
- Snub-nosed pliers to enable the picking up of small components.
- Wire cutter for cutting your wire to length.

The top tool is a track cutter to cut the copper track on a vero board to isolate the parts of the circuit from each other.

Naturally, you will need some vero board, which can be bought in different sizes. However, to enable the easy application of solder, you must clean the tarnish off the board. You could use wire wool or emery cloth, but I prefer to use a hardened rubber made for the job. Figure F-4 shows the one I use on some vero boards.

Figure F-4. *Vero board with the tarnish remover*

Figure F-5 shows the track cutter I use.

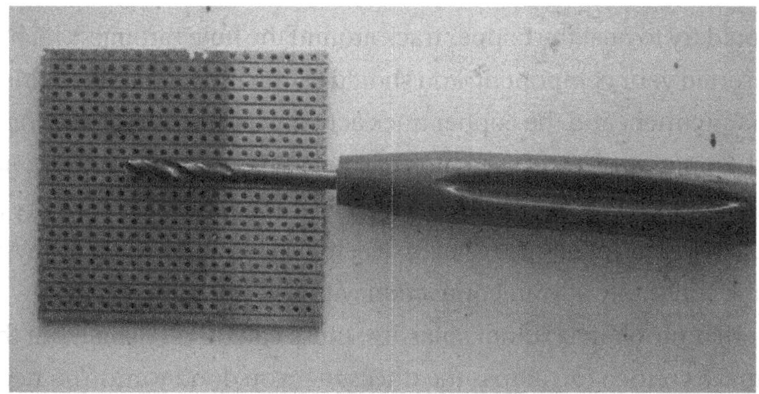

Figure F-5. *A typical track cutter*

This track cutter is simply a small drill bit built into a handle. One thing I should say is that when you use it, make sure that all copper has been removed, even those small loose bits. Even the smallest bit of copper could still bridge across the hole you have just drilled.

You could be spending quite a bit to set yourself up with the tools you need, around £80 to £100, but it should be worth it if you can build your own circuit boards.

Tinning the Components

Now you have got your tools and you have cleaned everything you are going to use, you are ready to solder. I always "tin" my components, even my small link wires, before I solder them into the board. This is applying a layer of solder to the wire part of the components. You should heat the wire from underneath, and then when the wire is hot enough, apply the solder on the top and it allow it to run down the wire part. You are really trying to make the wire part and solder for a mixed new material ready to be soldered onto the board. You should take care not to melt the insulation of the wire or the components.

Soldering the Components

You should try to heat the copper track around the hole through which you have inserted your component. You should try and make sure the solder on the component and the copper track actually mix together as the heat is applied. Sometimes, if you get a blob of solder on the component or track, you might think it has soldered but it hasn't. This is when you get a dry joint, in which there is a lot of solder but no electrical connection. It is always good to test the continuity of your connection with your multimeter.

Another problem is solder splashes: these can be very small but they could make connection across the tracks that you don't want. You need a good magnifying glass to look for these. My soldering station has a magnifying glass with a light around it; very useful.

Patience and Practice

I cannot guarantee that even if you follow all the advice I have previously listed, you will be successful with your builds. Everyone makes mistakes when they try something new. The best advice I can give is use patience. Don't rush your work. Check that your circuit diagram is good and the vero plan is right. That includes mine in this book. I do check everything I put into my books but sometimes a small error can slip through.

Practice what you do on small bits first: you can never get too much practice. The more you practice, the better you get at anything.

Once again, I must state that I cannot guarantee that if you build your circuit using my plans it will work correctly. There are so many mistakes that anyone can make when building circuit boards. You must check your circuit over carefully and correctly. My wife will tell you I check everything at least three times before I turn it on. The most important check you must make before you turn your circuit on is to check that there is no short-circuit between the positive supply and ground, as this could cause the power supply to overheat.

Appendix G: The LCD Header File for Eight-Bit Mode

We have used the LCD in four-bit mode for all the programs in this book. However, if you have the spare I/O, then using the LCD in eight-bit mode is a bit easier. As promised, I am inserting the header file I have written to use the LCD in eight-bit mode. Note that the LCD is connected to PORTB; if you want to use a different board, you should change the definition references.

```
/* A header file to use the LCD in 8 bit Mode
Written By Mr H. H. Ward dated 31/10/15.*/
//some definitions
#define firstbyte      0b00110011
#define secondbyte     0b00110011
#define lines2bits8     0b00111100
#define eightBitOp     0b00111000
#define twoLines       0b00101100
#define incPosition    0b00000110
       #define cursorNoBlink  0b00001100
       #define clearScreen     0b00000001
       #define returnHome      0b00000010
       #define lineTwo         0b11000000
       #define doBlink         0b00001111
       #define shiftLeft       0b00010000
       #define shiftRight      0b00010100
       #define lcdPort         PORTB
       #define eBit            PORTAbits.RA0
       #define RSpin           PORTAbits.RA1
       //some variables
       unsigned char lcdData, lcdTempData, rsLine;
       unsigned char n;
       //the subroutines
       char lcdInitialis [7] =
       {
       firstbyte,
       secondbyte,
       lines2bits8,
       incPosition,
       doBlink,
       clearScreen,
```

```
returnHome,
};
void sendData ()
{
lcdPort = lcdData;
eBit = 1;
eBit = 0;
TMR0 = 0; while (TMR0 < 15);
}
void lcdOut ()
{
lcdTempData = lcdData;
sendData ();
}
void setUpTheLCD ()
{
RSpin = 0;
n = 0;
while (n < 7)
{
lcdData = lcdInitialis [n];
lcdOut ();
n ++;
}
RSpin = 1;
}
void line2 ()
{
RSpin = 0;
lcdData = lineTwo;
lcdOut ();
```

```
RSpin = 1;
}
void writeString (const char *words)
{
while (*words)
{
lcdData = *words;
lcdOut ();
*words ++;
}
}
void clearTheScreen ()
{
RSpin = 0;
lcdData = clearScreen;
lcdOut ();
lcdData = returnHome;
lcdOut ();
RSpin = 1;
}
```

Note that this uses two bits on PORTA for the 'eBit' and 'RSpin'.

The following is the configuration header file for the 18F4525 used in the programs in this book.

1. /*This is a header file to set the configuration words for my projects
2. It is written by myself, Mr. H. H. Ward, for the PIC18F4525
3. It was created on the date 02/01/2019*/
4. // PIC18F4525 configuration bit settings

```
// 'C' source line config statements
// CONFIG1H
#pragma config OSC = INTIO67    // oscillator selection bits (internal oscillator block, port function on RA6 and RA7)
#pragma config FCMEN = OFF    // fail-safe clock monitor enable bit (fail-safe clock monitor disabled)
#pragma config IESO = OFF    // Internal/external oscillator switchover bit (oscillator switchover mode disabled)
// CONFIG2L
#pragma config PWRT = OFF    // Power-up timer enable bit (PWRT disabled)
#pragma config BOREN = SBORDIS    // Brown-out reset enable bits (Brown-out reset enabled in hardware only (SBOREN is disabled))
#pragma config BORV = 3    // Brown-out reset voltage bits (minimum setting)
// CONFIG2H
#pragma config WDT = OFF    // Watchdog timer enable bit (WDT disabled (control is placed on the SWDTEN bit))
#pragma config WDTPS = 32768    // Watchdog timer postscale select bits (1:32768)
// CONFIG3H
#pragma config CCP2MX = PORTC    // CCP2 MUX bit (CCP2 input/output is multiplexed with RC1)
```

19. #pragma config PBADEN = ON // PORTB A/D enable bit (PORTB<4:0> pins are configured as analog input channels on reset)
20. #pragma config LPT1OSC = OFF // Low-power timer1 oscillator enable bit (timer1 configured for higher-power operation)
21. #pragma config MCLRE = ON // MCLR pin enable bit (MCLR pin enabled; RE3 input pin disabled)
22. // CONFIG4L
23. #pragma config STVREN = ON // Stack full/underflow reset enable bit (stack full/underflow will cause reset)
24. #pragma config LVP = OFF // Single-supply ICSP enable bit (single-supply ICSP disabled)
25. #pragma config XINST = OFF // Extended instruction set enable bit (instruction set extension and indexed addressing mode disabled (legacy mode))
26. // CONFIG5L
27. #pragma config CP0 = OFF // Code protection bit (Block 0 (000800-003FFFh) not code-protected)
28. #pragma config CP1 = OFF // Code protection bit (Block 1 (004000-007FFFh) not code-protected)
29. #pragma config CP2 = OFF // Code protection bit (Block 2 (008000-00BFFFh) not code-protected)
30. // CONFIG5H

```
#pragma config CPB = OFF    // Boot block code protection bit (Boot block (000000-0007FFh) not code-protected)
#pragma config CPD = OFF    // Data EEPROM code protection bit (Data EEPROM not code-protected)
// CONFIG6L
#pragma config WRT0 = OFF    // Write protection bit (Block 0 (000800-003FFFh) not write-protected)
#pragma config WRT1 = OFF    // Write protection bit (Block 1 (004000-007FFFh) not write-protected)
#pragma config WRT2 = OFF    // Write protection bit (Block 2 (008000-00BFFFh) not write-protected)
// CONFIG6H
#pragma config WRTC = OFF    // Configuration register write protection bit (Configuration registers (300000-3000FFh) not write-protected)
#pragma config WRTB = OFF    // Boot block write protection bit (Boot block (000000-0007FFh) not write-protected)
#pragma config WRTD = OFF    // Data EEPROM write protection bit (Data EEPROM not write-protected)
// CONFIG7L
#pragma config EBTR0 = OFF    // Table read protection bit (Block 0 (000800-003FFFh) not protected from table reads executed in other blocks)
#pragma config EBTR1 = OFF    // Table read protection bit (Block 1 (004000-007FFFh) not protected from table reads executed in other blocks)
```

44. #pragma config EBTR2 = OFF // Table read protection bit (Block 2 (008000-00BFFFh) not protected from table reads executed in other blocks)
45. // CONFIG7H
46. #pragma config EBTRB = OFF // Boot block table read protection bit (Boot block (000000-0007FFh) not protected from table reads executed in other blocks)
47. // #pragma config statements should precede project file includes
48. // Use project enums instead of #define for ON and OFF

Appendix H: The ASCII Character Set

This is just an extract of the ASCII character set, but it does show the main ones we use.

High Nibble	0000	0010	0011	0100	0101	0110	0111
Low Nibble	CG.Ram Location						
xxxx 0000	1		0	@	P	\	P
xxxx 0001	2	!	1	A	Q	a	Q
xxxx 0010	3	“	2	B	R	b	r
xxxx 0011	4	#	3	C	S	c	s

(*continued*)

High Nibble	0000	0010	0011	0100	0101	0110	0111
Low Nibble	**CG.Ram Location**						
xxxx 0100	5	$	4	D	T	d	t
xxxx 0101	6	%	5	E	U	e	u
xxxx 0110	7	&	6	F	V	f	v
xxxx 0111	8	’	7	G	W	g	w
xxxx 1000	1	<	8	H	X	h	x
xxxx 1001	2	>	9	I	Y	i	y
xxxx 1010	3	*	:	J	Z	j	z
xxxx 1011	4	+	;	K	[	k	{
xxxx 1100	5	‘	<	L		l	l
xxxx 1101	6	-	=	M	]	m	}
xxxx 1110	7	.	>	N	^	n	
xxxx 1111	8	/	?	O	_	o	

Appendix I: The LCD Instruction Set

Function	B7	B6	B5	B4	B3	B2	B1	B0	Execution time
Clear screen	0	0	0	0	0	0	0	1	1.53ms
Description	Clear all display data. It also sends the cursor back to the start of the display. Sets the DDRAM address to 0								
Return home	0	0	0	0	0	0	1	x	1.53ms
Description	This sends the cursor back to the start of the display. Sets the DDRAM address to 0. The 'x' means it does not care what logic is in that bit								
Entry mode	0	0	0	0	0	1	I/D	SH	39µs
Description	This sets the cursor movement after entry (I/D); logic '0' in this bit means cursor is decremented, logic '1' means cursor is incremented. In the SH bit, logic '0' means don't shift the cursor; logic '1' means shift the cursor								39µs
Display control	0	0	0	0	1	D	C	B	39µs
Description	D bit logic '0' display is off; logic '1' display is on. C bit logic '0' cursor is off Logic '1' cursor is on B bit logic '0' cursor blink is off Logic '1' cursor blink is on								
Cursor/display shift	0	0	0	1	S/C	R/L	X	x	39µs

(*continued*)

Function	B7	B6	B5	B4	B3	B2	B1	B0	Execution time
Description	S/C bit logic '0' means the cursor is shifted. Logic '1' means the display is shifted. R/L bit logic '0' means shift left; logic '1' means shift right								
Function set	0	0	0	1	1	0	X	x	39μs
Description	Configuration data to set up the LCD (Send First)								
Set CGRAM address	0	1	A5	A4	A3	A2	A1	A0	
Set DDRAM address	1	A6	A5	A4	A3	A2	A1	A0	
Write data CGRAM or DDRAM RS pin is a logic '1'	D7	D6	D5	D4	D3	D2	D1	D0	43μs

Index

H. H. Ward, *Programming Arduino Projects with the PIC Microcontroller*,
https://doi.org/10.1007/978-1-4842-7230-5

D

E

F, G

H

I

J

K

L

M

N

O

P, Q

R

S

T

U

V

W, X, Y, Z

Printed in the United States
by Baker & Taylor Publisher Services